Spirit of Nobility
Sermons on the Weekly Torah Portion

Genesis and Exodus

Michael Scharf
Publication Trust
Yeshiva University Press
RIETS

MAGGID

Rabbi Aaron Levine

SPIRIT OF NOBILITY
SERMONS ON THE WEEKLY TORAH PORTION
GENESIS AND EXODUS

The RIETS Hashkafah Series
Rabbi Daniel Z. Feldman, Series Editor

The Michael Scharf Publication Trust of
Yeshiva University Press

Maggid Books

Spirit of Nobility
Sermons on the Weekly Torah Portion
Genesis and Exodus

First Edition, 2020

Maggid Books
An imprint of Koren Publishers Jerusalem Ltd.

POB 8531, New Milford, CT 06776-8531, USA
& POB 4044, Jerusalem 9104001, Israel
www.maggidbooks.com

© The Estate of Rabbi Dr. Aaron Levine *zt"l*, 2020

Papercut Cover Photo © David Fisher Art

The publication of this book was made possible through the generous support of *The Jewish Book Trust*.

All rights reserved. No part of this publication may be reproduced, stored in a retrieval system or transmitted in any form or by any means, electronic, mechanical, photocopying, or otherwise, without the prior permission of the publisher, except in the case of brief quotations embedded in critical articles or reviews.

ISBN 978-1-59264-559-6, *hardcover*

A CIP catalogue record for this title is available from the British Library

Printed and bound in the United States

*In loving memory of
Sarah Levine*

Contents

Foreword xi
Preface xiii

GENESIS

BERESHIT
Let Us Make Man 5
The Sign Given to Cain 9
For Me the World Was Created 13
The Wallenberg Affair 17
Bar Mitzvah 22
The First Contract 24
The Repentance of Cain 27

NOAḤ
The Fear and Dread of You Shall Be upon
Every Beast of the Earth 33
The Sharing of Haftarot 36
The Rollercoaster Personality 40
The Triumph and Disappointment of Noah 44

LEKH LEKHA
Jewish Identity   49
The Man of Caution Displays Boldness   53
Terrorism   56
The Mitzvah to Settle the Land of Israel   60
The Struggle for Religious Freedom   64
The First Marital Dispute   69
Saving a Jew from Peril; Its Limits   73

VA-YERA
Among My People I Dwell   79
Salt: The Paradoxical Symbol   84
The Burst of Laughter That Lasted Forever   88

ḤAYYEI SARAH
The Ideal Marriage   95
When Jewish Sovereignty Is Threatened   99
Kindness and Truth in Matchmaking   103
Silence in the Institution of Marriage   108

TOLEDOT
Ma'aseh Avot Siman le-Banim   113
Mirmah and Armah: The Man Derush Made into a Hero   117
Abimelech   122
Blending Keshet with Ḥerev   126
Stealing the Blessings – Revisited   130

VA-YETZE
The House of Joseph a Flame   137
The Mispronounced Name   141

Thanksgiving   145
Rachel Weeps for Her Children   149
The Exchange between Rachel and Leah   152

VA-YISHLAḤ

Let's Set the Record Straight   159
Preemptive War   163
The Jewish Cold War Ethic   167
The Jewish Attitude toward the Protectors of Terrorism   171
The Reproof of the Wicked and the Reproof of the Righteous   175
I Will Not Let You Go Unless You Have Blessed Me   177
The Kibbud Av of Esau   179

VA-YESHEV

And Hashem Was Preparing the Light of the Messiah   187
Compassion and Divine Justice   192

MI-KETZ

When Is a Security Measure Self-Restraint?   197

VA-YIGGASH

For It Was to Be a Provider That God Sent Me Ahead of You   203
Three Black Days   208
When the Idealist Bends to the Pragmatist   214
Reunions   218
How to Produce an Emotional Impact   222
The Balance between Freedom and Restraint   225

VA-YEḤI

From There He Shepherded the Stone of Israel   231

By You Shall Israel Bless   234
The Limits of Loyalty   239
Peace: At What Price?   242
Two Contrasting Views of the Host Country   247
I Will Separate Them within Jacob   250
The Issachar and Zebulun Partnership   254

EXODUS

SHEMOT

What Is Justice?   261
Welcoming the Sabbath   265
The Defeat of Deep Thought   269
The Dual Morality   273
Hakkarat Ha-Tov   276
Mosheh Rabbeinu's Ten Other Names   279

VA-ERA

Defense Mechanisms   285
How to Negotiate with a Tyrant   289
The World Community's Spectacular Dai   293
I Shall Bring You to the Land   297

BO

The Son Who Got Squeezed Out   303
Bottling Up Emunah   308
The Public and Private Sign   312

BE-SHALLAḤ

The Sea Saw and Fled   319

Justice and Mercy   324
The Song of Deborah   328
The PLO and Amalek   332
The Day the Pardes Resonated   336
The Public Woman and Tzeniut   341
They Will Leave with Great Wealth   344

YITRO

Re-Creating the Revelation Experience in Our Time   349
Profundity in Simplicity   352

MISHPATIM

For the Children of Israel Are Servants to Me   359
Distance Yourself from a False Word   364
Balancing the Rights of the Victim and the Rights of the Accused   369

TERUMAH

Holy of Holies   375
The Crown of Torah   380
Whoever Adds, Detracts   384
The Minimax Mitzvah of Talmud Torah   389

TITZAVVEH

Wiping Out the Federal Deficit   395

KI TISSA

A Spectrum of Views of the Klal   403
The End Game of the Persian Gulf War   406
The Irrational Defense   410

VA-YAK'HEL–PEKUDEI

You Will Find Favor and Goodly Wisdom in the Eyes of God and Man 417

Donations versus Total Commitment 422

The Generosity of Giving 427

Discovering the Gap 431

Glossary 435
Bibliography 450
Name Index 464
Subject Index 477

Foreword

Rabbi Dr. Aaron Levine was a quintessential gentleman and scholar, embodying the values of Torah virtue and ethical behavior that he taught in his classes and writings. He was a world-renowned economist who served as the Samson and Halina Bitensky Professor of Economics at Yeshiva University, and as the editor of *The Oxford Handbook of Judaism and Economics*. His published works, including *Free Enterprise and Jewish Law*, and *Case Studies in Jewish Business Ethics,* are considered classics in the domain of Jewish business ethics and law.

In addition, Rabbi Levine served as the Rabbi of a synagogue in Brooklyn for many years, during which time he inspired his congregation with homilies on the Torah portion of the week and on the Festivals, providing timely commentary on the topics of our times. As the grandson and namesake of the Reisher Rav, a preeminent Polish scholar who was the author of *Ha-Derash ve-ha-Iyyun*, a masterful collection of insights into the Torah, Rabbi Levine adroitly continued his family tradition of extracting penetrating ideas and lessons from the weekly Torah portions.

This book, edited with love by his family, is a compilation of Rabbi Levine's sermons on the weekly Torah portion that he delivered in his synagogue. Each essay is a self-standing gem, offering timeless wisdom in both scholarly and succinct fashion. Rabbi Levine's penchant for academic precision, combined with his reverence for the word of God, enabled him to convey an authentic Torah Weltanschauung for the complex political and socioeconomic challenges of the modern age. We are now all able to be beneficiaries of these pithy pearls of perspicacity.

Foreword

The Talmud (*Ḥagigah* 15b) teaches us: אם דומה הרב למלאך ה' צבקות יבקשו תורה מפיהו ואם לאו אל יבקשו תורה מפיהו, "if the Rabbi resembles an angel of God, then learn Torah from his lips, but otherwise do not learn Torah from his lips." One only had to gaze at Rabbi Levine's countenance to recognize the face and demeanor of an angel. Those of us who were privileged to be his students can attest that he was a man who occupied a special plane of holiness. This book, endowed with the beauty of the words that once emerged from Rabbi Levine's lips, is similarly blessed with the sanctity of his spirit.

It is thus with great pleasure that we present this important volume in homiletics as the latest installment in the RIETS Press series. We are of course indebted to our indefatigable executive editor, Rabbi Daniel Feldman, as well as to the past and present visionaries and architects of the RIETS Press, former Presidents Rabbi Dr. Norman Lamm and Richard M. Joel, President Rabbi Dr. Ari Berman, Rabbi Zevulun Charlop, and RIETS Dean Rabbi Menachem Penner. It is through their herculean efforts on behalf of the Yeshiva that we continue to imbibe the fruits of YU and RIETS scholarship.

Rabbi Yona Reiss
Director, RIETS Press

Preface

With deep gratitude to Hashem, we present this volume of sermons of our dear father, Rabbi Dr. Aaron Levine, *zt"l*.

A renowned authority on Jewish business ethics, Rabbi Dr. Levine was the Samson and Halina Professor of Economics at Yeshiva University. A paragon of *Torah u-madda*, he published widely on the interface between economics and Jewish law, particularly as it relates to public policy and modern business practices.

Rabbi Dr. Levine was also a distinguished pulpit rabbi, toiling tirelessly in the rabbinate for nearly thirty years. In his sermons, he would urge his congregants to seize nobility, to leap toward greater achievement in religious observance and refinement of character. In his personal conduct, he was the very embodiment of those ideals.

This volume is a selection of Rabbi Dr. Levine's sermons on the weekly Torah portion, transcribed from his manuscripts dating from 1982 to 2011.

We extend our heartfelt gratitude to Rabbi Yona Reiss for including this volume in the works published under the auspices of the Rabbi Isaac Elchanan Theological Seminary of Yeshiva University, and for his eloquent and meaningful Foreword. To Rabbi Daniel Z. Feldman, we express our sincere appreciation for his enthusiasm toward this work and his steadfast devotion in shepherding it though the publication process.

To Matthew Miller, Rabbi Reuven Ziegler, Ashirah Firszt, Tomi Mager, Ita Olesker, Shira Finson, and Caryn Meltz of Maggid Books, we

Preface

extend a special note of thanks for their thoughtfulness, dedication, and professionalism in bringing this book to publication.

Rabbi Dr. Levine was born on the second day of Passover and passed away on the first day of Passover. On Passover, we observe the mitzvah of *haggadah*, the telling of the story of the Exodus, so that we can feel as if we ourselves had gone out of Egypt. As Rabbi Dr. Levine noted, "We are bidden to somehow leap the generations and touch the lives of our ancestors, to make the biblical figures come alive and vicariously feel their pain and triumph, to feel the birth pangs of a nation of Hashem."

May the recounting of these sermons strengthen our Jewish identity and commitment to the Torah, connecting us not only with our father, the author of this work, but with the previous generations, back to Abraham, Isaac, and Jacob.

Family of Rabbi Dr. Aaron Levine, *zt"l*

Genesis

Bereshit

Let Us Make Man

October 20, 1984

Human arrogance and pride are sometimes so intense that we crave recognition for even imaginary achievements. Yes, in a moment of generosity, man will acknowledge the contribution of others to his work and perhaps even allow others to take credit from some minor achievement of his. But when it comes to his magnum opus, his crowning achievement, his work of unparalleled genius, man will yearn for nothing less than universal recognition. He will fight with a ferocious tenacity any attempt to detract from his achievement.

Such is human affairs. But when the Master of the Universe created the world, His name was attached to all His creations except His crowning creation, man. With respect to man, Hashem said, *"na'aseh adam,"* "Let us make man" (Genesis 1:26). This phrase is quite dangerous. It could lead to an error that, God forbid, there was more than one Creator. When Moses recorded the Torah, he objected to the phrase.[1] When the seventy-two scholars were summoned by Ptolemy II Philadelphus

---

1. Genesis Rabbah 8:8.

Bereshit

to translate the Torah into Greek, each independently recognized the prudence of changing the phrase to "I shall make man."[2]

Why did the Torah record the creation of man in this manner? Our Sages tell us it was to teach us that just as Hashem consulted with the Heavenly Hosts, so, too, it is proper for an eminent person to consult with those of a lower status.[3]

What was the result of this consultation? *Ḥesed* said, "Let him be created because he will perform acts of kindness." *Emet* said, "Let him not be created because he is full of falsehood." *Tzedek* said, "Let him be created because he will perform righteous deeds." *Shalom* said, "Let him not be created because he is full of strife." To break the deadlock, Hashem took truth and cast it to the ground, as it is written, "He hurled truth down to the earth" (Daniel 8:12). Then the ministering angels protested, "Hashem, how can You treat Your seal[4] in such a manner?" Hashem responded, "Let truth rise from the earth," as it is written, "Truth springs up from the earth" (Psalms 85:12).[5]

What the Midrash is telling us, in our view, is that Hashem proclaimed that man could achieve his divine potential not by trying to arrive at truth or peace directly, but rather by utilizing his capabilities, i.e., righteousness and kindness. With those capabilities, truth will sprout from the earth. Why? Because truth and peace are diametrically opposed to each other. One who relentlessly pursues truth will harbor an intolerance for those with views that differ from his. He will also have an impatience and contempt for those who do not share his fervor and enthusiasm. Before we know it, the battle lines of ideology are clearly drawn.

On the other hand, the champion of peace has a completely accommodating nature. He tolerates any evil, big or small, for the sake of peace. He has the divine wisdom to arrive at the magic blend of truth and peace. Moreover, both truth and peace are really empty concepts, mere

---

2. *Megillah* 9a.
3. R. Solomon b. Isaac (*Rashi*, France, 1040–1105), *Rashi* to Genesis 1:26, s.v. "*na'aseh adam*"; Genesis Rabbah 8:8.
4. The seal of Hashem is truth. *Shabbat* 55a.
5. Genesis Rabbah 8:5.

platitudes. Only one who understands righteousness and kindness has a concept of truth and peace, and can synthesize these elements. While truth and peace detract from each other, righteousness and kindness reinforce one another. The man who is committed to a society where everyone respects the rules and abides by them, and in the microcosm of his own world, fulfills all his commitments, will never give up on a system of justice, even when he is the victim of injustice.

The individual must sacrifice himself for the interests of society. Hence, from the legalistic man is born the sacrificing, compassionate man. The man who has a profound sense of kindness will be satisfied only with a profound justice, a justice that takes into account all external costs and benefits, and all long-term and short-term effects of one's actions.

Why did Hashem choose to allow the creation of man to be so open to error and misunderstanding? It was to teach man the lesson that it is precisely at those moments of *na'aseh adam*, when man feels the deep anguish of being denied credit for his achievement, when man is not the cynosure or the center of attention, that he makes his greatest contribution of *imitatio Dei*. For the building blocks of creative progress are not the grand insights into truth and moments of peace that man achieves, but rather it is the sparks of righteousness and kindness throughout time that coalesce and produce the powerful moral climate that brings about advances in truth and lasting peace. It was not any profound insight that the Jewish State should exist and that Israel belongs to the Jews, or the uneasy peace that the superpowers achieve through a balance of power, that brought about the creation of the State of Israel, but rather the sparks of suffering, death, and even evil that took place, the great Holocaust that decimated the flower of Jewry.

And why did the Jewish State have to be formed from the blood and tears of Jews? Why could it not have been formed in a much easier way? If we ask such a question, we have no concept of eternity and permanence.

Now, if Hashem gave credit to the Heavenly Hosts for partial truth and even for opposing views because those views crystallized man's divine potential, then so must we. And we must realize that every achievement is not an isolated event, but rather builds on the shoulders of giants. We are dwarfs resting on the shoulders of giants.

"God saw all that He had made, and, behold, it was very good" (Genesis 1:31). As R. Samson Raphael Hirsch states, every creation by itself is good, but when everything harmoniously blends together and works as a unit, it is "very good."[6]

---

6. R. Samson Raphael Hirsch (Germany, 1808–1888), Genesis 1:31.

The Sign Given to Cain

October 17, 1987

In the waning months of the Reagan Presidency, the Administration is desperately trying to secure for itself a place of honor in history. Toward this objective, the Administration is touting the emerging treaty between the United States and Russia banning intermediate-range ballistic missiles as a landmark in U.S.–Soviet relations and the beginning of a new epoch of world stability and peace.[1]

---

1. The Treaty between the United States of America and the Union of Soviet Socialist Republics on the Elimination of their Intermediate-Range and Shorter-Range Missiles was signed in Washington, DC, by President Ronald Reagan and General Secretary Mikhail S. Gorbachev on December 8, 1987. The treaty was ratified by the U.S. Senate on May 27, 1988, and went into effect on June 1, 1988. See *International Legal Materials* 27 (January 1988): 90–97; John Walcott and Gerald F. Seib, "Reagan and Gorbachev Sign Ban on Intermediate-Range Missiles; They Promise to Seek Cuts in Long-Range Arsenal as 3-Day Summit Starts," *Wall Street Journal*, December 9, 1987, 1; Adam Pertman, "INF Treaty Ratified in Time for Summit," *Boston Globe*, May 28, 1998, 1; Don Oberdorfer, "Summit Brings Better Ties but No Arms Breakthrough; INF Pact Activated; Delay Is Seen for Treaty on Long-Range Missiles," *Washington Post*, June 2, 1988, A1.

Far from characterizing the emerging accord as an exemplary cooperative effort between the superpowers, critics view it as a product of a combination of Russian desperation and American bungling.[2]

Russia's economy has been aptly described as a perfect equilibrium – no industry and no agriculture. Half the country has no telephone service and the other half is waiting for a dial tone. Soviet leaders are well aware that it will take nothing short of a drastic reduction in military spending to improve the standard of living of the restless population. Hence the Russian-initiated push for a limited ban on intermediate-range missiles.[3]

Given our deep-seated distrust of the Russians, we countered that their proposal would be acceptable only if they agreed to a provision for stringent on-site inspection. In the United States, the military–industrial complex, which has a vested interest in the continuation of the arms race, went along with the call for on-site inspections because they never in their wildest dreams expected the Russians to accept it.

But, to our surprise, the Soviets did agree to a total ban on intermediate-range ballistic missiles. The forum of a treaty makes the issue of verification less important. And because we completely distrust the Russians and do not want to expose our secrets to them, we took a 180-degree turn and dropped our insistence on rigid on-site inspections, reasoning that spy satellites would detect gross cheating.[4]

Since the agreement is not borne out of cooperation, there is a real fear that it will engender competition in other areas, especially monstrous chemical warfare. Here, verification is all-important but impossible to achieve. No agreement will be made, and there may also be an escalation of conventional build-up, especially in the Soviet–West German border where the Soviets enjoy a 3:1 tank advantage.[5]

---

2. See Anthony Lewis, "Reagan and the Russians," Abroad at Home, *New York Times*, October 4, 1987, A23.
3. Philip Taubman, "The World: Gorbachev's Groundwork for Summit No. 3," *New York Times*, October 11, 1987, A2.
4. David Aaron, "Verification: Will It Work?," *New York Times*, October 11, 1987, A37.
5. Gary Putka, "NATO Quandary: As Missile Pact Looms, the West Is Groping for a Defense Strategy – Old Policy Verges on Success, and That Seems to Raise More Fears than Cheers; 'We Have No Time to Lose,'" *Wall Street Journal*, June 11, 1987, 1;

The Sign Given to Cain

In their analysis of the cause of the first world war, the murder of Abel at the hands of Cain, our Sages found the underlying cause of the bloodshed to be man's essentially competitive nature, his inability to demonstrate even an iota of flexibility and cooperation.

What circumstances precipitated the murder? Cain and Abel divided the world between them. Cain took the immovable property and Abel the moveable property. Then Cain complained that Abel was standing on his land, and Abel complained that Cain was wearing his clothes.[6] Before long, the dispute turned into a murder. This episode reveals that man lacks even a modicum of flexibility and cooperation.

Ever since the first murder of man by his fellow man, humankind has occasionally given serious attention to how to prevent future occurrences of murder and war. Every approach that man has devised has already been anticipated in the interpretation our Sages have offered of the sign that Hashem gave Cain to prevent wild creatures from taking revenge on him for the murder of Abel.

One view in the Midrash is that Hashem showed that He favored Cain by making the sun set after its usual time.[7] Because people saw that Hashem favored Cain, they were afraid to attack him.[8] In this fashion, ever since the inauguration of the nuclear age, utopians have pointed out that if only the scientific communities of the world would demonstrate the peaceful, i.e., God-like, uses of atomic energy, nobility would literally shame monstrous use of the atom into oblivion.[9]

But, as R. Isaac b. Moses Arama notes, a sophisticated sign is often lost on man.[10] We find ourselves vacillating between two other approaches developed by man. One is the *keren* approach, based on

---

Christopher Hanson, "Missile Accord Has Risks: Moscow Still Leads in Conventional Arms," *Sun Sentinel*, September 19, 1987, 10A.
6. Genesis Rabbah 22:7.
7. Genesis Rabbah 22:12 (opinion of R. Judah).
8. *Rashi* to Genesis Rabbah 22:12, s.v. "*hizriah lo galgal hamah.*"
9. See Paul Boyer, *By the Bomb's Early Light: American Thought and Culture at the Dawn of the Atomic Age* (New York: Pantheon, 1985), 109–121; David O. Woodbury, "Here Is the Utopian Promise of the Peacetime Atom," *Look*, August 9, 1955, 26–31.
10. See R. Isaac b. Moses Arama (*Akedat Yitzhak*, Spain, ca. 1420–1494), *Akedat Yitzhak, Bereshit, sha'ar* 11.

the view that Hashem caused a horn to grow on Cain's head to provide him with a weapon against potential attackers.[11] The other is the *kelev* approach, based on the view that Hashem provided Cain with a dog to protect him.[12]

The approach that dominates thinking today is the *keren* approach. We are always obsessed with the need to devise more efficient means of killing our fellow man. We adopt the MAD strategy.[13]

With that strategy, sometimes we withdraw and think that the best way to ensure one's survival is to retreat and suffice ourselves with inferior weapons. We are completely satisfied to merely defend ourselves. This is the *kelev* approach.

But I would submit that no significant progress will be made until we follow R. Nehemiah's approach, that the sign given to Cain was leprosy.[14] The powers must demonstrate convincingly that warring parties must be isolated and quarantined, that war is anathema, monstrous, and ugly, having no place in human society. A joint U.S.–Russian resolution for an arms embargo against Iran and Iraq would do more to promote mutual trust and world peace than a hundred summit conferences. Until we adopt the leprosy approach, we will continue to straddle between the *keren* and *kelev* approaches.

---

11. Genesis Rabbah 22:12 (opinion of Abba Jose b. Kesari).
12. Ibid. (opinion of Rav).
13. "MAD" is an acronym for "Mutual Assured Destruction," a doctrine of military strategy and national security policy in which a full-scale use of weapons of mass destruction by two opposing sides would effectively result in the complete annihilation of both sides. See Joseph Grieco, G. John Ikenberry, and Michael Mastanduno, *Introduction to International Relations: Enduring Questions & Contemporary Perspectives* (London: Palgrave, 2015), 213–222; Robert Jervis, "Mutual Assured Destruction," *Foreign Policy* 133 (November–December 2002): 40–42.
14. Genesis Rabbah 22:12 (opinion of R. Nehemiah).

For Me the World Was Created

October 8, 1988

On the heels of the Festival of Simḥat Torah, whereupon we celebrate the singularity of Hashem's gift of the Torah to us, we read today the story of creation, where we celebrate the singularity of man.

Man, we all know, was created on the sixth day.[1] Why? It is analogous to inviting a guest to a banquet only after everything is completely ready.[2] It is in order for man to pronounce *bishvili nivra ha-olam*, "for me the world was created."[3]

R. Saadiah Gaon amplifies and extends this concept by positing that what is most prized is always placed in the center. Man, the supreme creature by dint of his intelligence and moral freedom, inhabits the earth.

---

1. Genesis 1:26–31.
2. *Sanhedrin* 38a.
3. See Mishnah, *Sanhedrin* 4:5; *Sanhedrin* 37a.

The earth is the center of the universe. Everything in the universe, not only the earth, was created for man's sake.[4]

Well, it appears that modern science is bent on knocking man off his pedestal. For more than seventy years, science has been teaching that the universe consists of at least 100 billion galaxies, and the Milky Way Galaxy, in which we live, is but one. Moreover, the Milky Way Galaxy has at least 100 billion stars, of which our sun is but one. Each star may have many planets revolving around it. It is estimated that there are at least 600 million worlds in the universe that are quite similar to Earth.[5] And we have a bad cosmic address to boot. We are at least thirty thousand light years off the center of the Milky Way Galaxy.[6]

These scientific claims assault our cherished beliefs. But every *yeshivah* student has experienced the delight that a *Rambam* can explain away many difficulties. Maimonides disagrees with R. Saadiah Gaon and posits that man is supreme only in the sublunar world. Everything that Hashem created has an independent purpose, not necessarily just to serve man. Furthermore, man is not the crown of creation; sentient creatures that are superior to us may exist in the universe.[7]

While Maimonides rescues us from the crude threat that scientific theories pose to our religious teachings, there is a more subtle threat here, which is much more ominous.

In *Kedushah*, we describe Hashem as *kadosh, kadosh, kadosh*, which denotes God's Transcendence. He is aloof from mankind, separate, the same before and after He created man. Unfathomable! But also

---

4. R. Saadiah Gaon (Baghdad, 882 or 892–942), *Ha-Emunot ve-ha-De'ot, Ma'amar* 4, Introduction.
5. See Stephen B. Dole, *Habitable Planets for Man* (New York: Blaisdell, 1964), 103.
6. Harlow Shapley, "A Determination of the Distance to the Galactic Center," *Proceedings of the National Academy of Sciences of the United States of America* 25, no. 3 (March 15, 1939): 113–118. Recent research indicates that the Earth is approximately 26,000 light years from the center of the galaxy. See Daniel J. Majaess, "Concerning the Distance to the Center of the Milky Way and Its Structure," *Acta Astronomica* 60, no. 1 (March 2010): 55–74.
7. Maimonides (*Rambam*, Egypt, 1135–1204), Guide of the Perplexed 3:12–13. For a discussion of the views of R. Saadiah Gaon and Maimonides regarding man's position in the universe, see R. Norman Lamm, *Faith and Doubt: Studies in Traditional Jewish Thought* (New York: Ktav, 1971), ch. 4.

melo khol ha-aretz kevodo, "all the earth is filled with His Glory." This is the Immanence of God. He is intimately involved in our destiny and yearns for our love. With every leap forward in Transcendence, having a glimpse in the twentieth century that there are indeed 100 billion galaxies, we gain an expanded concept of God's Transcendence. But at the same time, we may begin to think that we are insignificant, that Hashem does not have time to bother with us.

Every leap in an expanded concept of Transcendence must be accompanied by a similar leap in our concept of God's Immanence. How should we interpret our bad cosmic address and the possibility of extraterrestrial life? We should regard it as an endearing gesture of Hashem to ensure our success. "Jealousy, lust, and glory remove a person from the world."[8]

We can also infer that, in a manner of speaking, Hashem is not a social snob. He will frequent the cosmic slums and alleys. In the true fashion of *ve-halakhta bi-derakhav* (lit., "you shall walk in His ways") (Deuteronomy 28:9), we should not be social snobs. There is a personal and humbling lesson that can be derived from our bad cosmic address and our insignificance in the context of the universe.

But we must redouble our efforts to leap in the area of Immanence, *kavod*, when we are already expanding our concept of *kedushah*. In a recent article in *Tradition,* Dr. George Shlessinger points out that the latest advance in the science of cosmology is the discovery of rare coincidences that are vital to the existence of a stable universe. One example is that each star contains a marvelously delicate balance between the forces of gravity and electromagnetism. If the strength of these forces would vary by only a tiny amount, by just $1/10^{40}$, it would spell catastrophe for the whole universe.[9]

What we have here is that Hashem speaks to gravity and electromagnetic forces within the context of an infinite universe and says to them, "I have set the boundaries for your operation. You have no freedom to change your course at all, not even by a tiny amount."

---

8. Mishnah, *Avot* 4:21.
9. George N. Schlesinger, "The Anthropic Principle," *Tradition: A Journal of Orthodox Thought* 23, no. 3 (Spring 1988): 1 (citing Paul Davies, *Superforce* [New York: Simon & Schuster, 1985]).

In contrast, man has moral freedom.[10] He can defy Hashem because he has free will. Then his virtue is magnified. We deserve great reward for virtue, and failure is tragic. Because we can choose good, evil must be punished. This gives us tremendous self-worth. *Bishvili nivra ha-olam* has to be understood not in terms of superiority and domination, but rather responsibility and a sense of mission.

We should identify with today's *haftarah*, which charges us with the cosmic mission of being "a light unto the nations" (Isaiah 42:6). On Simḥat Torah, we leap in the area of *kevod ha-Torah*. With abandon, we personalize the Torah. We dance with it. We kiss it. We show our outpouring of affection. So, too, every time we read anew the story of creation, we must review the scientific discourse and realize our expanded concept of *kadosh, kadosh, kadosh*, that we are being given a glimpse into the 100 billion galaxies. "How abundant are Your works, Hashem; with wisdom You made them all" (Psalms 104:24). But at the same time, we must also leap in our understanding of "all the earth is filled with His Glory."

---

10. R. Saadiah Gaon, *Ha-Emuot ve-ha-De'ot, ma'amar* 4; Maimonides, *Mishneh Torah, Teshuvah* 5:1.

The Wallenberg Affair

October 28, 1989

The relationship between David and Jonathan is cited by our Sages as the ideal of noble friendship. For his part, Jonathan, the heir to the throne of his father Saul, demonstrated a profound bond of love and intense loyalty to his father's rival, David. Jonathan was David's confidant, and he defended David to the hilt.

The extreme price that Jonathan paid for his love and loyalty to David is depicted in today's *haftarah*. David is missing at the Rosh Ḥodesh feast. Saul inquires why. When Jonathan begins to defend David, Saul launches into a tirade and says that Jonathan's loyalty to David is a perversity of the highest order! "You demonstrate that you love him more than yourself and are not concerned that people will say that you are not really my son. You were really born of a different father!" cries Saul. Then Saul, in anger, casts his spear at Jonathan.[1]

How did David reciprocate? I would suggest that it was by going beyond the covenant of friendship between him and Jonathan, as

---

1. I Samuel 20:27–33.

Bereshit

expressed by Jonathan, "God shall be a [witness] between me and you, and between my offspring and your offspring" (I Samuel 20:42). David views Jonathan as immortal and shows a deep friendship and reaching out to his son Mephibosheth.[2] In contrast to the practice of kings of destroying every last scion of the deposed king to eliminate any threat to them, this was not the case with David.

David's goal was to dredge up every last survivor of Jonathan to show him kindness, and he finds Mephibosheth. David gives him an estate and makes him a member of his household. By doing so, David passes the test of jealousy because Mephibosheth shames him in Halakhah[3] and then David saves him.[4] It was jealousy that drove Saul to persecute David. When David returned from battle, the women from all the towns of Israel came out to sing with timbrels to greet King Saul. The rejoicing women said, "Saul has slain his thousands, and David his tens of thousands" (I Samuel 18:7). Saul grew very angry, and the matter was disturbing in his eyes.[5]

But David passes the test and then saves Mephibosheth from execution in the episode of the Gibeonites. Three years of famine occur and David inquires of the *Urim ve-Thummim* the cause of the dearth.[6] David learns that it is the descendants of the Gibeonites at Nob, the city of Priests, who gave refuge to David.[7] In the time of Joshua, the leaders of the Children of Israel had sworn not to harm them,[8] but Saul tried to strike them down when the City of Nob gave refuge to David.[9]

Now the Gibeonites demand a measure of extraordinary cruelty against the descendants of Saul, that they should be hanged.[10] This is

---

2. II Samuel 9:7.
3. *Berakhot* 4a.
4. II Samuel 21:7.
5. II Samuel 18:7.
6. II Samuel 21:1.
7. Ibid.
8. Joshua 9:15. The Gibeonites had deceived Joshua to make peace with them when Joshua conquered the Land of Israel by claiming that they were from a distant land. Joshua 9:3–13. When their deception was discovered, the Gibeonites were spared but were relegated to the position of woodchoppers and water drawers. Joshua 9:21.
9. I Samuel 22:19.
10. II Samuel 21:6.

all a *hora'at sha'ah*.[11] But David must ensure that Mephibosheth is not taken, so he turns the tables on them and says, "I will do the soliciting."[12] He is not afraid that he will be accused of high-handedness, something that will destabilize his monarchy.

The gap between the David–Jonathan ideal and reality has recently catapulted into Jewish consciousness with the revelation that Raoul Wallenberg might still be alive.[13] The Swedish diplomat is credited with saving the lives of perhaps 100,000 Hungarian Jews in 1944 to counteract the very incarnation of evil, Adolph Eichmann. Eichmann's evil, organized genius and obsession to decimate Hungarian Jewry could be countered only by an equal force of goodness, the goodness of Raoul Wallenberg, who was imbued with a singular mission, indefatigable energy, and creative selflessness.

Historians admire Wallenberg's brilliant ingenuity in crafting Swedish passports to save Jews. The Swiss and Vatican passports were almost worthless because the Germans were so attentive to detail. But Wallenberg's passport was a work of genius. It featured stamps, seals, signatures, and countersignatures, embellished with the triple crown of the Swedish government. It inspired respect and told the Jewish people that they were not abandoned outcasts; someone cared for them.[14]

Wallenberg also got his government to commit to what amounted to unlimited resources to ensure the survival of Hungarian Jews. He set up a pervasive intelligence network, anticipating Nazi raids on safe houses and deportation plans. Once getting wind of a raid on a safe house, Wallenberg faced down a Nazi commander: "This is Swedish territory. You have no right to be on the premises. By agreement between the Royal Swedish government and the Royal Hungarian government,

---

11. R. Moses Alshekh (*Alshekh*, Safed, 1508–1593), *Marot ha-Tzove'ot*, II Samuel 21:1. The Alshekh explains that it was permissible for David to hand over the descendants of Saul to be killed to prevent a desecration of Hashem's name under the circumstances.
12. II Samuel 21:6.
13. Helen Davis, "New Optimism on Fate of Wallenberg," *Jewish Week*, October 20, 1989, 19; Carey Goldberg, "Family Search for Wallenberg Turns to Soviet Prison Records," *Jewish Week*, October 27, 1989, 21.
14. John Bierman, *Righteous Gentile: The Story of Raoul Wallenberg, Missing Hero of the Holocaust* (Harmondsworth: Penguin Books, 1982), 50–52.

these men are specifically exempt from labor service." This apparently made no dent in the Nazi commander's mind. Then Wallenberg interposed himself between the Nazi police and the Jews and declared, "You'll have to shoot me first."[15]

He knew how to speak to evil. He spoke to the Nazis' self-interest. In protesting a transport of Jews, he said, "My neutral country protects Germany's interests all over the world. Think of the repercussions if my country learns of this incident, refusing to recognize that these people are protected by the Swedish crown."[16]

Then there was the story of how he intercepted a train to Auschwitz, climbing up to the roof and distributing his passports amidst shooting by the Germans.[17]

Well, Wallenberg disappears in 1944 in Hungary.[18] The last sign of him was when he was in Russian protective custody. The saga of his life and captivity since then, a captivity that astonishingly may be continuing to this very day, forty-four years after his initial capture, is the story of two failures of the David–Jonathan ideal. The Russians, while first denying Wallenberg's capture, thought he was a spy. Why? Because it was utterly insulting to the Russians to believe that Wallenberg was wandering around Hungary to save and protect Jews. What nonsense. Selfless humanitarianism was alien to the Russian mentality, especially when directed at Jews.[19] And then there was the failure of Sweden to act decisively in seeking his release, rebuffing the United States' offer to help.[20]

Every time the region of the Soviet Union changed hands, there was another threat to investigate the whereabouts of Wallenberg and press for his release. But, alas, the United States and, until 1967, Israel, did not participate.[21] World Jewry could have done more!

---

15. Ibid., 92.
16. See ibid., 91–92.
17. Ibid., 91. An eyewitness, Sándor Andrai, believes that the German officers deliberately shot above Wallenberg's head to avoid hitting him because they were so impressed by his courage. Ibid.
18. Ibid., 119.
19. Ibid., 209.
20. Ibid., 124–125.
21. Ibid., 190–199, 205–208.

The Wallenberg Affair

In 1948, a grateful Hungarian Jew sponsored the sculpture of an eighteen-foot statue of Wallenberg. The statue, which depicted Wallenberg struggling with a snake with a swastika on its head, bore the inscription: "Our eternal gratitude to a man who stood for humanity amidst inhumanity." The statue was erected in a square in central Budapest and a dedication ceremony was to be held. Well, the ceremony never took place because the Russians removed the statue.[22] But one thing can never be removed, the heroic personality of Wallenberg. It must be projected onto all humankind. He must be immortalized by Jewish education, secular education, and indeed the world educational system. He must be inscribed in the book of righteous gentiles.

---

22. Ibid., 203.

Bar Mitzvah

October 21, 1995

According to our Sages, the Good Inclination first arrives with the attainment of the status of *bar mitzvah*, but the Evil Inclination is with us since birth.[1]

This is a mystifying statement because if the Good Inclination does not arrive until the age of *bar mitzvah*, every child should be mischievous, totally out of control, and a disciplinary nightmare. Also, the arrival of the Good Inclination should catapult the quality of life to greater heights and be an event of some sort, an emotional charge, an intellectual insight, or maybe even a culinary delight.

The answer is "God saw all that He had made, and, behold, it was very good" (Genesis 1:31). "Very good" refers to the Evil Inclination.[2] The dark side of the work of the Evil Inclination is to urge us to do all kinds of terrible things, even monstrous things. But this is only a small part of the portfolio of the Evil Inclination. His major work is to cultivate in us

---

1. Ecclesiastes Rabbah 4:15.
2. Genesis Rabbah 9:7.

a healthy appreciation for all types of good that are inferior or spurious. One of his favorite tactics is to make us love good for a reward, and to love mediocrity. Good then is the product of pressure from parents, the community, or peers. He also tries to dim our visions, lower our ambition, and love good intentions that do not culminate in action, making us content to do the begrudging charitable act.

The Evil Inclination's first triumph is that when the Good Inclination arrives, it is a non-event. Why? Because the Good Inclination is difficult to distinguish from the Evil Inclination. The Evil Inclination resembles the Good Inclination by complementing us on all these inferior forms of good and telling us "very good."

What is the real McCoy, the authentic good? It is good pursued for its own sake, and it is the good that is the fuel that heightens our ambition to a higher one, an ever-increasing standard.

The First Contract

October 31, 2001

The first contract in human history took place between two brothers, Cain and Abel. In terms of a deal, it eclipsed the wildest imagination of Donald Trump. The scope entailed the division of the assets of the world. Cain took the real estate, and Abel all the moveable property.[1]

In short shrift, the brothers revisited the deal and it fell apart. Cain told Abel, "I own all the land. Your sheep has no grazing rights on my land, and you have no right to stand on my land." Then Abel said, "All moveable property belongs to me, including the clothes on your back." Well, one thing leads to another, and before you know it, Cain kills Abel.[2]

Were the brothers so obtuse that they did not anticipate the problem of grazing and clothing rights? No. In the context of the megadeal that the brothers crafted, grazing rights and clothing rights were truly trivial and it would be a matter of unimaginable mean-spiritedness for each to deny the other his right.

---

1. Genesis Rabbah 22:7.
2. Ibid.

So what happened? The attitude that they brought with them to the original negotiation changed radically with the traumatic event of their offerings to Hashem. "Hashem turned to Abel and his offering, but to Cain and his offering, He did not turn" (Genesis 4:4–5). Cain had failed as a firstborn. Hashem tells him, "Surely, if you improve yourself, you will be forgiven. But if you do not improve yourself, sin rests at the door" (Genesis 4:7).

One thing is for sure. Cain went away from Hashem's reproof with a different understanding of the birthright. What would prevail? His sense of responsibility, the cultivation of virtue? Or would he become a slave to his baser emotions of envy and jealousy?

Unfortunately, Cain revisited the original agreement with envy and jealousy and not with a new sense of responsibility. Cain then felt cheated by the original agreement.

The same message that Hashem gave Cain, He imparts to each and every one of us. We all make promises, oral and written commitments. Our attitude toward these commitments is not static or stable. It is constantly in a state of flux. We are constantly revisiting these promises. If we are involved in a lifelong endeavor of improving ourselves, refining our sense of responsibility and cultivating virtue, we are constantly asking ourselves: Are we doing enough to meet our commitments and fulfill our end of the deals? In all the deals we make, if we are not working to improve ourselves, we are moving down the slippery slope of "sin rests at the door." The more we are filled with envy and jealousy when we revisit our commitments, the more we will feel cheated.

Social scientists see progress in human development when we move from a chaotic state to a civilized one.[3] The law of the jungle ends and the rule of reason begins. It is when we arrange human relations with contracts and the government enforces those contracts. A society with a corrupt legal system that does not enforce contracts suffers from poor infrastructure and has a low per capita income compared to countries

---

3. See John Scott and Gordon Marshall, eds., *A Dictionary of Sociology*, 3rd ed. (New York: Oxford University Press, 2009), 601–602, s.v. "Progress."

such as the United States that enforce contracts.[4] So we pride ourselves on being far superior to Indonesia and Russia. But in the United States, we are the most litigious society on the face of the earth. Economists see this only in terms of lost output. But a society that is challenging and revisiting contracts reflects the state of morality of the society too.

---

4. Douglass C. North, *Institutions, Institutional Change and Economic Performance* (Cambridge: Cambridge University Press, 1990), 54; Michael Trebilcock and Jing Leng, "The Role of Formal Contract Law in Economic Development," *Virginia Law Review* 92, no. 7 (2006): 1520–1536; Paulo Mauro, "Corruption and Growth," *Quarterly Journal of Economics* 110, no. 3 (1995): 681–712.

The Repentance of Cain

October 25, 2003

The first murderer to appear on the world scene, Cain, was also a pioneer in *teshuvah*. Cain moved from "Am I my brother's keeper?" (Genesis 4:9) to "Is my iniquity too great to be borne?" (Genesis 4:13).

But Cain's *teshuvah* appears to be quite meager. Arguably, it could even be characterized as pathetic.

The most basic element of repentance is *hakkarat ha-ḥet*, "acknowledgment of sin." Where is the *hakkarat ha-ḥet*? Murder brings misery to the victim's family. It is a tragedy to the victim, an unfulfilled potential. It is ugly and obnoxious. It defaces the *tzelem Elokim* in man. "The voice of your brother's blood cries out to Me from the ground" (Genesis 4:10).

But Cain makes his pronouncement "Is my iniquity too great to be borne?" only after Hashem issues His decree of condemnation and Cain wants a divine form of mitigation. Cain's pronouncement is motivated by fear of death.

Moreover, *Rashi* tells us that "Is my iniquity too great to be borne?" is not a declaration but rather a petition: Master of the Universe, You have the heaven and earth on Your shoulder. Can You not tolerate my sin? And then "Cain left the presence of Hashem" (Genesis 4:16). As the Midrash explains, Cain left the Divine Presence with meekness, like one who steals the *de'ah elyonah* (lit., "the Supreme Knowledge"), i.e., as if he were fooling Hashem.[1]

Permit me to suggest that what we have here really is the manifestation of Hashem's mercy. Hashem says, "I see here a spark of *teshuvah*. Let's see if you can build on it." This episode is an application of "open for Me an opening the size of the eye of a needle and I will open for you an opening the size of a banquet hall."[2] Hashem says, "I'll give you seven generations to complete the *teshuvah*."

It is in this vein that we should understand the dispute among our Sages with respect to the nature of the sign that Hashem gave Cain. Some say it was a dog to warn Cain of danger.[3] Some say it was a horn to protect him.[4] Some say it was leprosy.[5] And others say it was a letter of Hashem's name etched on Cain's forehead.[6]

I submit that there is no dispute here. Hashem essentially tells Cain: You have seven generations to elevate your *teshuvah*. What will happen to you and the moral climate in these seven generations? Will you just survive? The sign will then be only the dog and the horn. Or will you really engage in penitence so that you will appear as a leper, acknowledging that murder is abhorrent and ugly? If you achieve this, then you can attain even the sign of Hashem on your forehead. You can bring everyone to see the *tzelem Elokim* in you, the former murderer. You can lift up society.

The measure of Cain's success after seven generations is how he was found when revenge finally caught up with him – dead with a horn.[7]

---

1. *Rashi* to Genesis 4:13; Genesis Rabbah 22:13.
2. See Song of Songs Rabbah 5:3; *Midrash Tanhuma, Toledot* 18; *Pesikta de-Rav Kahana* 15:6.
3. Genesis Rabbah 22:12 (opinion of Rav).
4. Ibid. (opinion of R. Abba Jose b. Kesari).
5. Ibid. (opinion of R. Nehemiah).
6. *Targum Yonatan*, Genesis 4:15; *Midrash Aggadah*, Genesis 4:15.
7. *Midrash Tanhuma, Bereshit* 11.

Perhaps a better measure is the attitude of the serial murderer Lemekh. His wives separated from him, fearful that Hashem would take revenge on their husband. Lemekh calms them down and says, "Don't worry. This is just an accident." "If Cain suffered vengeance at seven generations, then Lemekh at seventy-seven generations" (Genesis 4:24). My family will return after seventy-seven generations.

I ask you: Did not Lemekh return to "Am I my brother's keeper?" He was blind yet he went hunting and shot his deadly arrow at the command of his son Tuval-Cain. He ended up killing Cain. And when he clapped his hands in despair, he killed Tuval-Cain as well.[8]

Are these two other deaths caused by the blind hunter or an accident? I, for one, would say it was gross negligence. Lemekh says, "Have I slain a man by my wound and a child by my bruise?" (Genesis 4:23). I did not tear Cain up with my own hands, as Cain did to Abel. It is just my arrow that killed him. It is no surprise that with this type of rationalization, the Flood was not far off from coming, destroying the entire world.

I see in Lemekh the Palestinian Authority ten years ago at Oslo.[9] We believed in their promises to repudiate terror and seek peaceful coexistence. But terror was never seen by the Palestinian Authority as a leper. Instead, we hear from them echoes of Lemekh, that regardless of any acts of terror, they were only blind hunters. They did not cause the wound. They were never responsible for the incitement, the corruption, the diversion of humanitarian aid for the financing of terror, or the smuggling of arms. And then if ninety-six lives were blown up and hundreds

---

8. Ibid.; *Yalkut Shimoni, Bereshit* 28; *Rashi* to Genesis 4:23.
9. The Declaration of Principles on Interim Self-Government Arrangements, commonly referred to as the "Oslo I Accord," was concluded secretly between the Government of Israel and the Palestine Liberation Organization in Oslo, Norway, on August 20, 1993. The accord was subsequently signed at a public ceremony in Washington, DC, on September 13, 1993. In addition to the accord, the parties signed Letters of Mutual Recognition, dated September 9, 1993, in which the PLO recognized the right of the State of Israel to exist and renounced terrorism and other acts of violence against the State. See Clyde Haberman, "Mideast Accord: The Secret Peace/A Special Report; How Oslo Helped Mold the Mideast Pact," *New York Times*, September 5, 1993, A1; "Mideast Accord; Statements by Leaders at the Signing of the Middle East Pact," *New York Times*, September 14, 1993, A12 (transcript of statements on September 13, 1993).

of Israelis became victims of terror,[10] "it is not my bruise." The child is crushed because of Occupation, not from my bruise.

As long as the Palestinian Authority sees no leper, we must deal with them with the dog approach, by erecting a security wall,[11] and with the horn approach, by engaging in a preemptive strike to root out terror.

---

10. Steve Chapman, "Overlooking Brutality; A Torturous Dilemma for Israel," *Chicago Tribune*, September 9, 1999, 21 (reporting that between January 1, 1996, and May 1, 1998, ninety-six Israelis were killed and 707 Israelis were injured in terrorist attacks).
11. See Melissa Radler, "US Vetoes Condemnation of Security Fence at UN," *Jerusalem Post*, October 16, 2003, 3.

Noaḥ

The Fear and Dread of You Shall Be upon Every Beast of the Earth

November 8, 1986

According to Tradition, the Generation of the Flood was guilty of the most vile corruption in the form of idolatry and sexual immorality, yet its fate of annihilation was not sealed until the transgression of *ḥamas* became prevalent.[1]

What is *ḥamas*? It is theft of less than a penny's worth.[2] Compared to the sin of murder, this is a minor offense.

Why was *ḥamas* the reason for the annihilation? Perhaps the question itself is the answer. As long as sin is accompanied by guilt, social outrage, and at least some tension, even the most egregious sin can be

---

1. *Sanhedrin* 108a.
2. *Genesis Rabbah* 31:5.

reversed. But when man becomes comfortable with sin, a point of no return has been reached.

What is *ḥamas*? It is a sin for which no legal recourse is available. Suppose a competitor wants to ruin his rival. He sends several friends to sample his rival's merchandise, posing as big buyers. They then decide that they do not like the quality of the merchandise and do not buy. When people hide their evil under the cloak of respectability, claiming that they are living within the confines of the law, social outrage is muted. Maybe someone will even admire the man who is able to beat the system through his shrewdness. We are then only a small step away from devising ideologies and philosophies that will justify any form of evil. *Zadnu* – We have justified sin.[3]

Well, if a sense of dread and guilt is necessary to prevent man from being entirely swallowed up by his own evil, it is equally important in allowing the man of *kodesh* to make increasing penetration into and sanctification of the world of *ḥol*. Hence, when Hashem blessed Noah after he emerged from the Ark, He gave him more or less the same blessing that He gave Adam, the blessing of "be fruitful and multiply," but with the peculiar phrase "the fear of you and the dread of you shall be upon every beast of the earth" (Genesis 9:2).

What does this mean? When man conquers his external environment, how do we know that he has made a conquest? It is because the vanquished display an element of dread and submission. This applies equally to man's inner world.

Noah represented the perfect harmony of Shem, Ham, and Japheth. Noah was the insular man. To suffuse Shem and Japheth with holiness, a feeling of dread was necessary. If this feeling is absent, holiness is overwhelmed and converted into the mundane.

Today, there is a schism in the Jewish community. Perhaps a fruitful improvement would occur if there would be a redistribution of fear. There are those who are *kodesh kadashim*, who are petrified that their *kedushah* and singular mission will be tainted. But there must be some movement to *ḥol*, to sanctify it. Energy must be directed toward

---

3. See R. Hayyim Joseph David Azulai (Ḥida, Jerusalem, 1724–1806), *Kaf Aḥat, siman* 19 (*Vidui*), s.v. "*zadnu.*"

identifying all the moral dilemmas faced by people in the professions, towards *Eretz Yisrael*, and the practical problems of the Jewish people.

At the same time, those who feel very comfortable with *ḥol* should have some fear. Those who are involved in synthesis perhaps show an equal fascination with *kodesh* and *ḥol*. People feel very comfortable about the professions. They worry only about the Sabbath and *kashrut*, but not about the underlying values of the professions. Fear must emerge. There must be a sense of crisis or at least tension.

Noah blessed Japheth, "May God extend Japheth, but he will dwell in the tents of Shem" (Genesis 9:27). Let us continue with "Hashem blessed Abraham with everything" (Genesis 24:1).

The Sharing of *Haftarot*

November 4, 1989

An apparent oddity in the selection of the *haftarah* reading is the sharing of today's *haftarah*, *Rani Akarah*, with *Parashat Ki Tetze*.[1]

One possible approach to explaining why the *haftarah* of *Rani Akarah* is shared by *Noaḥ* and *Ki Tetze* can be built on the *Malbim*'s comment on the key verse, "For like the waters of Noah this shall be to Me: Just as I swore that the waters of Noah would never again pass on earth, so I have sworn not to be wrathful with you or to rebuke you" (Isaiah 54:9). This represents the Master of the Universe's proclamation of endearment to us, His chosen people. Just as he swore that he would not subject the entire creation once again to a flood, so, too, we, His people, are equivalent to the

---

1. The verses constituting the *haftarah* of *Rani Akarah*, lit., "sing out, O barren one," are at Isaiah 54:1–10. The *haftarah* for *Parashat Noaḥ*, according to Ashkenazi custom, is at Isaiah 54:1–55:5, and according to Sephardic custom, is at Isaiah 51:1–10. The *haftarah* for *Parashat Ki Tetze* is at Isaiah 54:1–10.

entire creation, and once *galut Edom* is over, Hashem will never bring us into exile again.[2]

But perhaps an element of reproof and challenge is presented by the sharing of *haftarot*. We note that the *parashah* of *Noaḥ* records none of the 613 commandments, while *Ki Tetze* contains more commandments than any other *parashah* in the Torah.[3] A contrast of a primitive, brutal society on the one hand and an enlightened and advanced society on the other hand hence emerges.

Our Sages inform us that while the Generation of the Flood committed many egregious sins, their fate was not sealed other than because of theft, and particularly *ḥamas*.[4] Illustrative of *ḥamas* is a peddler besieged by many thieves, each taking away a tiny fruit of less than a penny's worth.[5] The peddler becomes impoverished, but all the perpetrators escape legal liability. It was this transgression that triggered the Flood.

Now, I ask you: Does this transgression not pale in significance compared to wholesale immorality and theft, which the Generation of the Flood in all its perversity was guilty of? But regarding the sin of *ḥamas*, Hashem proclaims, "I have created a Good Inclination and an Evil Inclination and given man the mission of subduing the Evil Inclination, but man has failed. And not only has he failed, but the Good Inclination has become the servant of the Evil Inclination."

The decent element in man insists that society have a legal framework. A state of law and order is of course the product of the Good Inclination. But it is possible for the Good Inclination to degenerate to the legal environment in that it merely serves to pacify, to bribe, the Evil Inclination. Instead of inspiring respect for one's fellow man, the

---

2. R. Meir Loeb b. Jehiel Michel Weisser (*Malbim*, Poland, Romania, and Russia, 1809–1879), *Malbim* to Isaiah 54:9.
3. According to *Sefer ha-Ḥinnukh*, *Parashat Ki Tetze* contains seventy-four commandments, consisting of twenty-seven positive commandments and forty-seven negative commandments. R. Aaron b. Joseph ha-Levi (*Ra'ah*, Spain, ca. 1235–1300), *Sefer ha-Ḥinnukh*, eds. R. Yitzhak Yeshayah Weiss, R. David Zicherman, and R. Yitzhak Weinstein (Jerusalem: Makhon Yerushalayim, 1992), mitzvot nos. 532–605.
4. *Sanhedrin* 108a.
5. *Genesis Rabbah* 31:5.

legal environment is then viewed with mockery, as a challenge to evade by finding all the loopholes and avoiding the violation of technicalities. Then the legal environment becomes the work of the Evil Inclination.

Lest we think that this can happen only in a primitive and brutal society but not in advanced civilization, we read beyond *Rani Akarah* today and step into the world of *Parashat Re'eh* with the *haftarah* of *Aniyyah So'arah*, lit., "afflicted, storm-tossed one."[6] The key phrase here is "Establish yourself through righteousness, distance yourself from oppression" (Isaiah 54:14). Now, we could think that if a society expands its legal systems in both scope and depth, becoming the society of the 613 mitzvot, we would not fall into the trap of *ḥamas*. No, instead we become perhaps even more vulnerable. In the business world, man creates the corporation, which allows him to limit his liability and mask responsibility for evil. In criminal law, man's compassion and sophistication create categories of offenses in accordance with severity, but evil men use this system to create plea bargaining.

Now, how do we detect early on if the Evil Inclination is invading the legal system and beginning to make the Good Inclination work as his tool and not let it reflect the work of the Good Inclination? I would submit that the answer is that we must ask the question: Does sin or crime produce outrage?

Perhaps the greatest challenge that we face today in our legal system, which is working to mute or even silence outrage, is the treatment of juvenile offenses. One year ago, we were shocked when a youthful offender burned down a local synagogue.[7] Today, we are shocked by the defacement of our synagogue and sukkah!

The Torah, too, believes in mitigating the sins of minors, but not in wringing out the accompanying shame and guilt that should be felt from juvenile crime. "If a daughter of a Priest will be desecrated through adultery, she desecrates her father" (Leviticus 21:9).[8] In a similar vein,

---

6. Isaiah 54:11–55:5. The *haftarah* for *Parashat Noaḥ*, according to Ashkenazi custom, is at Isaiah 54:1–55:5, and thus includes the verses constituting the *haftarah* for *Parashat Re'eh*.
7. Leonard Buder, "15-Year-Old Boy Is Indicted as Adult in Synagogue Fire," *New York Times*, October 4, 1988, B3.
8. *Sanhedrin* 52a; Rashi to Leviticus 21:9, s.v. "*et aviha hi meḥallelet.*"

Noah responds to Ham's crime with vehemence by punishing Ham's fourth child, Canaan.[9] Why? Because unless the first post-diluvian sin is reacted to with vehemence and outrage, the Flood syndrome begins once again. The more outrage we feel when a crime is committed, the more we are keeping the Evil Inclination out of the legal system.

---

9. Genesis 9:25.

The Rollercoaster Personality

November 1, 2003

In the personality of Noah, the Torah gives us a dizzying shift in human potential. We are introduced to Noah as an *ish tzaddik*, a "righteous man," and perfectly righteous for his generation.[1] Noah gives Hashem the finest moment in all of human history to that point of 1656 years. When he emerges from the Ark, he offers sacrifices. It is not the offering of Cain and Abel. It is not the sentiment of sharing, but rather the *olah*, that everything is for Hashem. There was no prior day in human history when more sacrifices were brought with a more pure sentiment than when Noah emerged from the Ark.

But in a short while, Noah becomes the *ish ha-adamah*, a "man of the earth." When the earth has not a shred of vegetation, Noah has misplaced priorities. Instead of planting a vital crop such as wheat, he

---

1. Genesis 6:9.

The Rollercoaster Personality

plants a vine and produces grapes. He then becomes drunk and naked, inviting the immorality of his son Ham.[2]

What happened to Noah? How did the righteous man descend so low to become the naked drunkard?

Permit me to theorize that when Noah emerged from the Ark, he thought that with the extermination of all the wickedness, the post-diluvian world would be just like the pre-diluvian world. Before the Flood, the curse "by the sweat of your brow shall you eat bread" (Genesis 3:19) was fulfilled in only the most minimal way. Man planted once in forty years, moderate and constant temperatures prevailed, continents and seasons did not exist, and fruit never rotted.[3] Man's mobility was greater than the Concord. Sure, there would be challenges after the Flood. The human population was tiny while the population of ferocious animals was huge, but Noah felt that he could persevere.

He was so mistaken. The world would never be the same. The key phrase, "Continuously, all the days of the earth, seedtime and harvest, cold and heat, summer and winter, day and night, shall not cease" (Genesis 8:22), would be fulfilled to its fullest. Ceaseless work under torturous climatic changes and limited mobility would be the order of the day. With such a huge population of ferocious animals, what chance did the tiny human population have to survive? Imagine the tension and stress. Ham castrated Noah. How dare Noah bring more people into the world? Great conflict would surely emerge.

The problem is that when Hashem pronounces the new world order, He does it with the phrase "Hashem said in His heart" (Genesis 8:21). According to Nahmanides, "day and night, shall not cease" was a secret that Hashem did not reveal to all.[4]

Well, when Noah planted the vine, he knew enough to realize that the world would not be the same. Then, all the challenges that he faced seemed impossible to meet. An overwhelming sense of vulnerability overtook him, which bred anxiety and then denial. He must have thought that for the first crop, let's try something safe, the vine from the Garden

---

2. Genesis 9:20–22.
3. *Midrash Aggadah*, Genesis 8:22.
4. Nahmanides (*Ramban*, Spain, 1194–1270) to Genesis 8:21.

Noah

of Eden. It will work just as the antediluvian system worked. And it did, growing into a grape and becoming wine in no time![5]

How does the *ish ha-adamah* return to being the *ish tzaddik*? Noah must concentrate on Hashem's consolation, "Be fruitful and multiply and fill the land. The fear and dread of you shall be upon every beast of the earth and upon every bird of the heavens, in everything that moves on earth and in all the fish of the sea" (Genesis 9:1–2).

The *Malbim* points out that there is no reference to *kivshuha*, to "subdue the earth," as is found in the blessing that Hashem gave to Abraham.[6] You will achieve dominion by means of man's superiority and the dignity of human life. "For in the image of God He made man" (Genesis 9:6).

I ask you: Was there ever a time in human history when we had more self-doubt or felt more anxiety about our physical and spiritual survival than when we experienced the Holocaust? If Noah needed assurances after the Flood, we also needed assurance as a people at that time that we are the *am segullah* and *nahalat Hashem*. Where was our sign?

Permit me to propose that Hashem gave us a sign. He outdid the sign that he gave Noah. Hashem created for us a State. We rose from the ashes of the crematorium to Statehood and then to "the fear and dread of you shall be upon every beast of the earth and upon every bird of the heavens," reaching a peak in the 1967 War. And "be fruitful and multiply and fill the land… in everything that moves on earth and in all the fish of the sea; in your hand they are given" (Genesis 9:1–2) was also fulfilled after the Holocaust. The President of Malaysia has said that the Jews rule the world.[7] This is so. In every profession and endeavor, whether it is business, academia, or government, the Jew rises to the top and accounts for a far disproportionate share of the stellar achievements.

But the blessings regarding "fear and dread" and "be fruitful and multiply" were both marred and not at full potential. We are a

---

5. *Pirkei de-Rabbi Eliezer* 23; *Yalkut Shimoni, Noah* 61.
6. See Genesis 1:28.
7. See Editorial, "Islamic Anti-Semitism," *New York Times*, October 18, 2003, A12 (commenting on speech by Prime Minister Mahathir Mohamad of Malaysia to the Tenth Islamic Summit Conference, Putrajaya, Malaysia, October 16, 2003).

superpower but we face daily terror. We have made great contributions to civilization, disproportionate to our numbers, but we get only hatred and jealousy for it, not appreciation and recognition. How do we achieve these blessings? It is by greater striving for unity and affection among us to recognize the divine image in man.

Let us merit to witness "the kingdom will be Hashem's" (Obadiah 1:21). "Hashem will be King over all the land; on that day Hashem will be One and His Name will be One" (Zechariah 14:9).

The Triumph and Disappointment of Noah

October 16, 2004

In the medium of prayer, Noah achieves a great success, but also a great disappointment.

Our Sages draw a contrast between Noah and Moses. When Hashem tells Moses that we sinned with the Golden Calf and "now, desist from me… I shall annihilate them and I shall make you a great nation" (Exodus 32:10), Moses would hear nothing of starting all over, that he should survive and everyone else should be destroyed. It triggered the greatest prayer in the history of the world. "Moses pleaded before Hashem, his God" (Exodus 32:11). But when Hashem told Noah that he would survive "for it is you that I have seen to be righteous before Me in this generation" (Genesis 7:1), but everyone else would be destroyed, Noah was not moved to pray to save the world.[1]

---

1. *Zohar* 1:67b, 1:106a, 3:15a. The Flood is referred to as "the waters of Noah" (Isaiah 54:9) as a result of Noah's failure to pray for his generation. *Zohar* 1:67b. The *Or ha-Ḥayyim* explains that Noah did not pray because Hashem revealed to him that

The Triumph and Disappointment of Noah

But there is also a triumph in prayer for Noah. "Hashem smelled the pleasing aroma, and Hashem said in His heart, 'I will not continue to curse again the ground because of man'" (Genesis 8:21). What transformed Noah? It must be that in the years between entering and emerging from the Ark, Noah captured some of the sparkle of "Moses pleaded before Hashem."

Moses expressed the worthiness of the Jewish people for survival. "Remember for the sake of Abraham, Isaac, and Israel, Your servants" (Exodus 32:13). This says, according to R. Samson Raphael Hirsch, that the achievement of the Patriarchs was so magnificent that some of the glitter had to have been transmitted to their children.[2] When you look at the child, you see the parent. "I have not seen a righteous man forsaken or his children begging for bread" (Psalms 37:25). If you know the father, a *tzaddik*, how could you not take pity on his son? And the stubbornness of the nation, the very reason for our destruction, is the reason for our survival.[3]

Noah starts out not believing that the Generation of the Flood deserved to be saved, so he does not pray. But the year that he spent in the Ark was a year of overwhelming work, taking care of all the creatures. Each had a different dietary need and a different schedule. The lion kicked him because he was once late in feeding him.[4]

R. Dessler says that love is a product of giving.[5] When we give, we develop the notion that the recipient deserves what we give him or her. If one seeks mercy by praying for his friend, and he himself needs the same thing for which is he praying, the one who prays is answered first.[6] It is not a game of who is answered first, but a condition of prayer itself. When we do not see "I shall make you a great nation" in our prayer, we are on the way to splitting the very heavens.

---

the fate of his generation had been sealed, and Hashem therefore did not give him an opening to pray. By contrast, Hashem gave Abraham the opportunity to pray for Sodom. See *Or ha-Ḥayyim* to Genesis 6:13.
2. R. Samson Raphael Hirsch, Exodus 32:13.
3. Ibid., Exodus 32:11.
4. *Midrash Tanḥuma, Noaḥ* 9.
5. R. Eliyahu Eliezer Dessler (Lithuania, England, and Benei Berak, 1892–1953), *Mikhtav me-Eliyahu*, 5th ed., vol. 1 (Benei Berak, 1965), *Kuntrus ha-Ḥesed*, ch. 4, pp. 35–27.
6. Bava Kamma 92a; Rashi to Genesis 21:1, s.v. "*ve-Hashem pakad et Sarah.*"

Lekh Lekha

Jewish Identity

October 15, 1983

For a man whose essence is goodness, kindness, and magnanimity, being called upon by Hashem to act contrary to his nature represents a trial and tribulation. Such a man was Abraham. Most of the Ten Trials that Abraham faced required him to act in a cruel, alienating, and distancing manner, contrary to his nature.[1] His remark to Lot, "Please separate from me" (Genesis 13:9), however, was not one of the Ten Trials.[2]

---

1. See R. Elijah b. Solomon Zalman (Vilna Gaon or *Gra*, Vilna, 1720–1797), *Kol Eliyahu, Va-Yera*; R. Yaakov Kamenetsky (New York, 1891–1986), *Emet le-Yaakov: Sefer Iyyunim ba-Mikra al ha-Torah*, 3rd ed. (New York, 2007), *Toledot*, 153.
2. The Mishnah at *Avot* 5:3 states that Abraham was tested with ten trials and withstood them all. The commentators differ in their enumeration of the Ten Trials. According to *Rashi*, the Ten Trials were: (1) the persecution of Abraham by Nimrod, which forced Abraham to hide underground for thirteen years (*Pirkei de-Rabbi Eliezer* 26); (2) the casting of Abraham into a burning furnace at Ur-Kasdim (*Rashi* to Genesis 11:28); (3) the commandment to leave his homeland (Genesis 12:1); (4) the famine in the land of Canaan, which required him to leave the land (Genesis 12:10); (5) the kidnapping of Sarah by Pharaoh (Genesis 12:14–15); (6) the capture of Lot by the Four Kings, which required Abraham to wage war to rescue him (Genesis 14:12–16);

Lekh Lekha

Did Abraham not misjudge Lot? After living in Sodom, Lot continues as an exemplar of kindness even though it is a capital offense in Sodom to behave in this manner. When three angels visit Lot, Lot makes a feast for them and bakes *matzot*.[3] Lot himself does the work, with no help from his wife and daughters. He is even prepared to offer his daughters for immorality, all for his guests!

Lot was saved from Sodom because "Hashem remembered Abraham, so He sent Lot from amidst the upheaval" (Genesis 19:29). As the *Maharal* puts it, Hashem saw the Abraham in Lot.[4] Lot showed that he had no bond with the decadent society and was the guardian of Abraham's secret that Sarah was his wife. Even a furtive glance would have given away the secret. What people would not do out of greed!

Why then did Abraham distance himself from Lot? The nature of their dispute explains this. Lot heard the divine pronouncement "to your offspring I will give this land" (Genesis 12:7). He ascribed maximum magnanimity to the promise as it also pertained to himself.[5] He reasoned, the land belongs to Abraham, but since Abraham has no children, it now belongs to me, his nephew. Just as Lot was the exemplar of magnanimity in matters between man and his fellow man, so, too, he expected nothing less from a divine promise. He expected consistency in behavior between man and God, and between man and his fellow man.

---

(7) being informed at the Covenant between the Parts that his offspring would suffer under four monarchies (Genesis 15:7–21); (8) the commandment to circumcise himself and his son (Genesis 17:9–14); (9) the commandment to drive away his son Ishamael and Hagar (Genesis 21:9–13); and (10) the commandment to sacrifice his son Isaac (Genesis 22:1–2). *Rashi* to Mishnah, *Avot* 5:3.

Maimonides, by contrast, restricts the list of the Ten Trials to those that are explicitly mentioned in the Torah rather than recorded in the Midrash. He thus omits the persecution by Nimrod and the casting of Abraham into the fiery furnace from his enumeration of the Ten Trials. He also omits the Covenant between the Parts as a trial. Instead, Maimonides includes Abraham's taking Hagar as a wife and the kidnapping of Sarah by Abimelech as two trials, and he counts the alienation of Hagar and the alienation of Ishmael as two separate trials. Maimonides to Mishnah ad loc. For another alternative listing of the Ten Trials, see R. Jonah b. Abraham Gerondi (*Rabbeinu Yonah*, Spain, ca. 1200–1263) to the Mishnah *ad locum*.

3. Genesis 19:3.
4. R. Judah Loew b. Bezalel (*Maharal*, Prague, ca. 1525–1609), *Gur Aryeh*, vol. 1, *Va-Yera*.
5. See *Rashi* to Genesis 13:7.

Jewish Identity

What a contrast between him and the Patriarchs. The Patriarchs ascribed the most niggardly interpretation to Hashem's promise as it pertained to themselves. The *Keli Yakar* comments that for each of the Patriarchs, Hashem used the phrase "to you and your offspring" in connection with the promise to give them the Land of Israel.[6] In fact, Abraham was tantalized by "Arise, walk about the land through its length and breadth, for to you will I give it" (Genesis 13:17). So was Jacob tantalized by "the ground upon which you are lying, to you will I give it and to your descendants" (Genesis 28:13). Yet the phrase "to you" was fulfilled only with respect to a burial plot.[7] Abraham got it only after shrewd negotiation.[8] Isaac, who was concerned only with the wells that Abraham's servants had dug during Abraham's lifetime, was fearful that he would not get even those.[9] Indeed, Jacob was almost not buried in the Land of Israel if not for the vow of Joseph.[10]

Could Abraham form an ideological marriage with Lot, ascribing magnanimity to the divine word, or instead approach it with a sense of awe and reverence, picturing only what was to be if spiritual perfection were maintained, always obsessed with the fear *shema yigrom ha-ḥet*?[11]

If an article of faith is approached with *ḥesed* but without an element of awe and reverence, could the Jewish people have survived the Servitude in Egypt, the destruction of the First and Second Temples, the Crusades, the Spanish Inquisition, the Russian pogroms, and the great Holocaust?

Today, our holy institutions are perhaps plagued with an imbalance between *ḥesed*, on the one hand, and awe and reverence on the other. The synagogue is a place where Jews unite, a place of joy, a place of enormous acts of kindness, and a focal point for the most idyllic relationship in Jewish life – the Rabbi and his congregants! What is missing

---

6. See R. Ephraim Solomon b. Aaron Luntshits (*Keli Yakar*, Leczyca, 1550–1619), *Keli Yakar* to Exodus 6:3.
7. Ibid.
8. Genesis 23:3–20.
9. Genesis 26:15–18.
10. Genesis 50:5.
11. See Nahmanides to Genesis 15:2, 15:7. Abraham was concerned that perhaps sin would prevent the divine promise from being fulfilled.

Lekh Lekha

is the element of awe and reverence. "How awesome is this place! This is none other than the abode of God and this is the gate of the heavens" (Genesis 28:17).[12]

Talmud Torah is also appreciated as Hashem's gift to us of intellectual stimulation, a genuine religious experience of joy, completely unrelated to frivolity and debauchery. But when the accompanying feeling of awe and reverence is missing, the study of Torah becomes at best subservient, just another competing intellectual activity. It lacks a singularity and uniqueness. Would we ever think of substituting sleep for food?

Let us remember that though Abraham alienated Lot, he also risked his life to save him. Lot would be the progenitor of Ruth, the great-grandmother of David. "I have found David, my servant" (Psalms 89:21).[13] Lot was saved to preserve what was beautiful, the exemplar of *ḥesed*, but to build upon it a dash of reverence and awe. This will produce the Messiah.

---

12. This is the proclamation of Jacob upon awakening from his dream in which he saw angels ascending and descending a ladder to heaven. Genesis 28:10–15.
13. See Genesis Rabbah 41:5 (explaining the phrase "I have found David" to refer to finding Ruth as a future descendant of Lot).

The Man of Caution Displays Boldness

November 3, 1984

If we would analyze our Forefather Abraham's conduct as he was subjected to the Ten Trials, we would find that he generally avoided exposing himself to danger and used his resourcefulness to avoid danger and unnecessary risk, but with two notable exceptions.

First, he intervened in the war of the Four Kings against the Five Kings. The decadent elements of society were waging war against each other. Well, initially Abraham must have thought about it and just wished each side *hatzlahah rabbah* against its opponent. He does not think of intervening until he hears that Lot has been taken captive.[1] Then he acts with boldness bordering on recklessness. He has a band of a mere 318 people and no weapons, only the ordinary earth that was turned into spears.[2] He and the band divide up and pursue the enemy

---
1. Genesis 14:14.
2. Genesis Rabbah 43:3.

into the night, not being overconfident that the murkiness of the night would be enough to reverse the trend of battle.[3]

Why the self-sacrifice for a nephew who had fallen out with him and did not deserve to live together with him? The *Me-am Lo'ez* answers that Abraham did this to preserve his spiritual accomplishments, for the countenance of Lot resembled that of Abraham.[4] Nimrod was the head of the consortium of the Four Kings[5] and was claiming that Abraham had finally seen the light, that he, Nimrod, was a deity, and had repudiated his monotheistic views. Abraham had to expose this fraud! His whole spiritual edifice would collapse if he did not do so!

A second episode when Abraham displayed boldness bordering on recklessness was in connection with *berit milah*. Hashem commanded Abraham to perform the mitzvah, but Abraham did not receive instructions regarding the specific requirements of the obligation. Should he perform it secretly or publicly? He received conflicting advice. Aner said not to perform it openly because Abraham would become vulnerable; his enemies would try to kill him.[6] So what did Abraham do? He performed the circumcision openly, by day, "on the very day that Hashem commanded him to do so" (Genesis 17:23). This was another instance of boldness for the purpose of asserting his distinctiveness, his identity.

If we look about in our physical and natural world, we observe man's utter obsession with preserving his material and financial assets. There is life insurance, health insurance, homeowner's insurance, car insurance, forced pensions. Any event that is subject to the laws of probability will be insured by Llyods of London. The financial manager is a means of hedging against risk. He buys a portfolio of stock and buys put options on that stock. But this is not perfection. There is grand hedging where you can buy and sell the whole market through stock index

---

3. Genesis 14:15.
4. R. Jacob Culi (Constantinople, ca. 1685–1732), *Me-Am Lo'ez*, Genesis 14:24, trans. R. Shemuel Yerushalmi, *Yalkut Me-Am Lo'ez: Sefer Bereshit* (Jerusalem: Mossad Yad Ezra, 1968), 310.
5. In the biblical account of the war of the Four Kings against the Five Kings, Nimrod is referred to as Amraphel. See *Eruvin* 53a; *Midrash Tanḥuma, Lekh Lekha* 6; Rashi to Genesis 14:1, s.v. "*Amraphel*."
6. *Midrash Tanḥuma, Va-Yera* 3.

futures. This is still not perfection, so there are options on stock index futures. And the Pentagon is always involved in war games.

Now, I ask: Do we have the same concern for our spiritual treasures? Do we simply let these treasures slip away? And in the area of Jewish identity, the Jew must assert his essence, his moral character, showing the world that he is more honest, more efficient, more proficient, more dependable, and more reliable. This will compensate for leaving early Friday, for absence from work on *yom tov*, and for his special dietary laws, for the five-o'clock shadow of the Jew.

It was no coincidence that Abraham chose to display his boldness on two occasions. Those instances are really two sides of the same coin! Why is it worth it to display boldness in fighting to preserve our spiritual treasures? It is because this constitutes the very essence of our identity, not merely an advantage that we have over someone else.

And now to preserve what we have in the way of spiritual treasures, we have to be more than passive. To preserve what we have, we must assert our identity in the positive sense.

Assertion of our identity and self-preservation of our spiritual treasures tend to reinforce each other and create the Jew of upward flight. "The birds, however, he did not cut up" (Genesis 15:10).

Terrorism

October 26, 1985

We have all been horrified and our sense of elemental justice has been severely assaulted by the recent escalation of acts of terrorism in the form of hostage taking. Our feeling of helplessness in dealing with this plague in human society was given temporary relief by the daring action of our government in the Achille Lauro affair.[1] Our government

---

1. On October 7, 1985, four militants representing the Palestine Liberation Front hijacked the Italian *Achille Lauro* liner off the coast of Egypt on its route from Alexandria to Ashdod, Israel. The hijackers directed the vessel to sail to Tartus, Syria, and demanded the release of fifty Palestinians then in Israeli prisons. After the Syrian government refused to grant permission to dock at Tartus, the hijackers murdered one of their hostages, Leon Klinghoffer, a sixty-nine-year-old Jewish American man in a wheelchair. The *Achille Lauro* then headed back towards Port Said. After two days of negotiations, the hijackers agreed to abandon the liner in exchange for safe conduct. They were flown towards Tunisia aboard an Egyptian commercial airliner. On the orders of President Ronald Reagan, the plane carrying the hijackers was intercepted by F-14 Tomcats and directed to land at a NATO base in Sicily, where the hijackers were arrested by the Italians. See Judith Miller, "Hijackers Yield Ship in Egypt; Passenger Slain, 400 Are Safe; U.S. Assails Deal with Captors," *New York Times*,

demonstrated the conviction to take decisive action against terrorism even at the cost of straining important international relationships.[2]

Hostage taking is, of course, not a new phenomenon. The first recorded incident of hostage taking occurred in today's portion. Our Forefather Abraham hears that his kinsman Lot was seized as a hostage in the war of the Four Kings against the Five Kings.[3]

How does Abraham react? He inducts his entire *yeshivah* of 318 students and pursues the four superpowers. Why Abraham took all his students in the battle of the superpowers is incomprehensible. We would imagine that he would stand back and just wish both sets of combatants *hatzlaḥah rabbah*. Intervening to save his nephew cannot itself explain his *mesirut nefesh*.

The *Me-am Lo'ez* tells us that Lot's countenance resembled that of Abraham.[4] Nimrod imagined that he had now finally won his life-long struggle for supremacy by capturing Lot. Abraham had previously forced Nimrod to sign a document acknowledging that he was not a deity. Now Nimrod would have Lot, who resembled Abraham, tell everyone that Nimrod had not in fact signed the document.[5] If Abraham would not intervene, everything that he had accomplished to elevate society from *tohu va-vohu* would be for naught.

What was at stake here was not just an ideological battle, but much more. Abraham lived in an era when power and intimidation were the dominant forces in interpersonal relations. Might not only made right, but the most powerful deified himself. If there is no God, then man is God, and the more powerful manipulate the less powerful. But if there is a God, acknowledgment of God must manifest itself at the very least in

---

October 10, 1985, A1; Bernard Gwertzman, "U.S. Intercepts Jet Carrying Hijackers; Fighters Divert It to NATO Base in Italy; Gunmen Face Trial in Slaying of Hostage," *New York Times*, October 11, 1985, A1.

2. Bernard Gwertzman, "Reverberations; The U.S. May Pay a High Price for Its Triumph," *New York Times*, October 20, 1985, A1.
3. Genesis 14:14.
4. R. Jacob Culi, *Me-Am Lo'ez*, Genesis 14:24.
5. R. Yisroel Yakkov Klapholtz, *Otzar Aggadot ha-Torah: Likkutei Aggadot she-Ne'esfu mi-Talmud Bavli vi-Yerushalmi Midrashim ve-Sifrei Rishonim* (Benei Berak: Pe'er ha-Sefer, 1981), 125.

Lekh Lekha

elemental justice and compassion. If Abraham was to preserve the kind of *ḥesed* that he had established to replace the *tohu va-vohu* of human relations, he had to intervene, even at the risk of laying down his own life.

Similarly, the State of Israel has already enunciated its policy of non-negotiation with terrorists.[6] Acceding to the demands of terrorists undermines the very foundation of security with respect to law and order, and serves only to encourage future acts of terrorism. R. Jacob Emden says that the Tribe of Benjamin had the right to wage war after the incident of the Concubine at Gibeah[7] to defend its right to try its own tribesmen accused of crimes and protect them from summary execution by the other Tribes.[8] Giving up its right to try accused criminals is tantamount to sanctioning chaos. Every Jew must be prepared to lay down his life to preserve the very foundations of human society, law and order, and respect for human rights.

Another important lesson is derived from Abraham's dealing with terrorists in his peculiar refusal to accept the booty of the war. He responds to the King of Sodom's proposal "give me the people and take the possessions for yourself" (Genesis 14:21) by passionately proclaiming, "Neither a thread nor a shoestrap, I will not take anything of yours, so you will not say 'It is I who made Abram wealthy'" (Genesis 14:23). But Abraham had no hesitation to accept prodigious gifts from Pharaoh under false pretenses that he was Sarah's brother – "He treated Abram well for her sake" (Genesis 12:16). So why the violent reaction to the offer to accept the spoils of war, which were rightfully his?

The answer, I submit, is that the champion of law and order desperately wants to be removed from even the remotest taint of ulterior motive. He is afraid that his motive will be misunderstood by his contemporaries and certainly posterity. So Abraham rejects the spoils

---

6. "Rabin: Peace Is Up to the Arabs," *New York Jewish Week* (Manhattan ed.), July 27, 1974, 16 (reporting that Prime Minister Yitzhak Rabin stated during an interview, "I don't believe that Israel can negotiate with terrorists who have declared that their purpose is the destruction of Israel."); "Mustn't Be Hesitant on Policy, Rabin Says," *Jerusalem Post*, December 10, 1975, 1.
7. Judges 19:1–21:25.
8. R. Jacob Emden (*Ya'avetz*, Altona, 1697–1776), *Haggahot ha-Ya'avetz, Sanhedrin* 16b, s.v. "*mitzvah ba-shevet la-dun et shivto.*"

and thereby torpedoes any possibility of lessening the impact that his heroism could have on the advancement of the cause of law and order.

One final lesson: Abraham pursues the terrorists *ad Ḥovah*, "as far as Hobah" (Genesis 14:15), which is to the north of Damascus. *Rabbeinu Beḥaye* understands this to mean that Abraham pursued the terrorists until they themselves acknowledged the corruptness of their ways.[9] As Judah proclaimed when Joseph's silver goblet was found in the sack of Benjamin, "God has uncovered the sins of your servants" (Genesis 44:16).

How timely are these two messages. Egypt also opposed terrorism but only because it received two billion dollars of American aid, not because it acknowledges the intrinsic evil of terrorism or holds Jewish blood of any value.[10] When there is no authentic commitment, its President can be caught in one lie after another. And when there is no conviction to fight terrorism *ad Ḥovah*, the media will always distract us with feature stories that explain the desperation of the terrorists, why they need a platform, and even victims will embrace their captors. Society's outrage is then mellowed.

---

9. R. Bahya b. Asher (*Rabbeinu Beḥaye*, Saragossa, 1255–1340), *Rabbeinu Beḥaye al ha-Torah*, Genesis 14:15. The Hebrew word "*ḥovah*" means guilt.
10. See Jonathan Broder, "Egypt Demands U.S. Apology; Mubarak Seeks to Calm Angry Mood of Nation," *Chicago Tribune*, October 15, 1985, 1 ("Ever since Egypt signed a peace treaty with Israel in 1979, its economic development has been dependent on massive infusions of U.S. aid, now topping $2 billion a year. The price of this aid continues to be peace with Israel.").

The Mitzvah to Settle the Land of Israel

October 31, 1987

The sweep of history often dwarfs an event that at its time seemed momentous. And so we may imagine that the covenant that Hashem strikes with Abraham at the time He commands him with *berit milah* would somehow become subsumed within the covenant at *Mattan Torah*. Not so, says Nahmanides. The Jewish people are part of two covenants: the covenant of Abraham and the covenant of Sinai. At Sinai, in return for Hashem's pronouncement that we should be an *am segullah*, we accepted the 613 mitzvot. What is the covenant of Abraham? It is Hashem's pronouncement "I shall be a God to them" (Genesis 17:8) in exchange for identifying with the promise of the inheritance of the Land of Israel.[1]

---

1. See Nahmanides to Genesis 15:18.

The Mitzvah to Settle the Land of Israel

The mitzvah of possession and settlement of the Land of Israel, as R. Joseph B. Soloveitchik posits, is an orphaned mitzvah.[2] The establishment of the State of Israel revitalized the mitzvah. This is not only because the State is a mechanism to develop the infrastructure of the Land, to create economic incentives to encourage settlement, but Jewish sovereignty adds a qualitative dimension to the mitzvah of settlement of the Land of Israel. Settlement of the Land under Jewish sovereignty is not the same as settlement of the Land under British auspices.

Now, there are alarmists in Israel, led by Kahane, who feel that the Jewish character of the State of Israel is being threatened. To make their case, they point to the enormous difference between the rate of growth of the Jewish population and that of the Arab population in Israel. Time is our enemy here. Passivity toward this problem will surely doom us![3]

We are all familiar with Kahane's solution, deportation of the Arabs. But in Jordan in 1977, he recanted, fully realizing that his plan could not be implemented without violence unless adequate incentives would be provided. Accordingly, he proposed that Arabs who were willing to leave would be compensated for property and given bonuses, occupational training, and preferences for visas. But he turned to world Jewry to finance these incentives.[4]

Now, I submit that the plan is a derailment from the covenant of Abraham that was alluded to for positive action for Jewish identity as represented in the *berit milah*. Kahane's approach is dragging us into the Covenant between the Parts, which gives us the panorama of the persecution of Jews throughout the millennia, from the severing of the ram, which signifies the deprivation of our superior status, making us second-class citizens, to the cutting of the heifer, which denotes servitude, to the cutting of the goat, which represents the stripping of our sense of independence.[5] We were made to feel that we were merely extensions of the personalities of our host country, having no right to even exist.

---

2. R. Joseph B. Soloveitchik (New York, 1903–1993), *Ḥamesh Derashot* (Jerusalem: Makhon Tal Orot, 1974), 88–89.
3. Meir Kahane, "Emigration Is the Only Solution," *Judaism* (Fall 1977): 394.
4. Ibid., 403.
5. R. Samson Raphael Hirsch, Genesis 15:9–21.

Lekh Lekha

The only item that was not cut in the Covenant between the Parts was the birds.[6] They have no claws. Their distinguishing characteristic is their feathers, the power of upward flight, the ability to soar the heavens.

Throughout the ages, we Jews, both secular and religious, were made to feel a special fate and lot by the terrible persecution of the centuries. And I ask: Are we to reverse roles and become the persecutors? If we want to emphasize the aspect of identifying with Abraham, we should become the defenders of the persecuted Jewish unborn children. Let us take to heart Dr. Glick's observation that twenty thousand legal abortions are performed in Israel each year, with another forty thousand illegal ones. The population grows by only seventy thousand each year. We are missing potentially two million citizens because of the shameless law! In a country that executes only one criminal in forty years, we do nothing for the unwanted child. We should at the very least inform the mother of the option of adoption and the risks of abortion. We should also dispel any false beliefs regarding the health of a child that they imagine is impaired.[7]

At the same time, we should note the *tamim* aspect of the covenant of Abraham, "I am *Kel Shakkai*; walk before Me and be *tamim*" (Genesis 17:1). *Tamim* corresponds to the divine attribute of *Shakkai*.[8] We can go to the boundary. In using simple technologies, such as population control of Arabs, we can go to the very boundary of *mirmah* with the Arabs.

But the most prominent feature to note is that the more the Israeli society resembles the pluralistic American society, the more it will be attractive to Arabs of rising expectations. But the more we intensify our

---

6. Genesis 15:10.
7. Shimon M. Glick, "A Humane Alternative to National Suicide," *Jerusalem Post International Edition*, October 24, 1987, 9.
8. R. Samson Raphael Hirsch, Genesis 17:1. The Name of Hashem of *Shakkai* is explained by the Sages as a compound of "*She-amar le-olam dai*," that Hashem said to the world "enough." *Ḥagigah* 12a; *Rashi* to Genesis 43:14. For additional commentary on the Name of *Shakkai*, see *Rashi* to Genesis 17:1 (interpreting *Shakkai* as a compound of *she-yesh dai*, that there is enough in Hashem's divinity for every creature) and *Rashi* to Genesis 28:3 (interpreting *Shakkai* as a compound of *she-dai be-virkhotav*, that Hashem's blessings are sufficient for those who are blessed by Him).

efforts to establish a State that welcomes Halakhah in every aspect of life, yea, the more we practice our Jewishness openly and proudly, the less attracted the Arabs will be to stay in Israel. They will leave of their own accord.

As an article of faith, when we will struggle to identify with Abraham the "*Ivri*,"[9] who stood on one side and the world on another side,[10] then we will succeed. The utopian approach will be blessed by Hashem, and the problem of losing the Jewish character of the State will become insignificant.

---

9. Genesis 14:13.
10. Genesis Rabbah 42:8 (opinion of R. Judah). R. Samuel Jaffe Ashkenazi (*Yefeh To'ar*, Constantinople, 1525–1595) interprets R. Judah's opinion to mean that if the entire world were placed on one side of a scale and Abraham on the other, Abraham would counter-balance the entire word. *Yefeh To'ar* ad loc.

The Struggle for
Religious Freedom

November 11, 1989

Various episodes in the life of Abraham are described in the Torah in minute detail. It is therefore a matter of puzzlement that Abraham's most daring adventure, his miraculous escape from the burning furnace, is not given explicit mention. Instead, only a veiled reference is found in the introduction to the Covenant between the Parts.[1]

Yeshuot Malko suggests that the recording of the feats of the Patriarchs in the Torah is only for the purpose of *ma'aseh avot siman le-banim*.[2] Now, if Abraham's confrontation with Nimrod was only the story of a

---

1. The reference to the burning furnace in the Covenant between the Parts is the phrase "I am Hashem Who brought you out of Ur-Kasdim" (Genesis 15:7). See *Rashi* to Genesis 11:28; Genesis Rabbah 38:13.
2. R. Israel Joshua Trunk of Kutno (*Yeshuot Malko*, Poland, 1820–1893), *Likkutei Torah, Pesaḥim* 118a, reprinted in R. Hayyim Elazar Wachs (Poland, 1822–1889), *Nefesh Ḥayah al ha-Torah: Bereshit; Derashot le-khol ha-Shanah* (Brooklyn, NY: Zinger, 2001), 249–250.

The Struggle for Religious Freedom

man desiring to practice his religious beliefs privately and quietly, and willing to put his life on the line if threatened and persecuted, it would be a model for us. But no! Abraham was a confrontationist, a gadfly, a preacher. It is the story of the *Ivri*. He stood on one side, and the world stood on another side.[3] He wanted nothing less than to convert the whole world. He confronted Nimrod, "If you are a deity, change the course of the sun. Make it rise in the west and set in the east. If you are a deity, read my mind."[4]

If we trace the struggle for religious freedom in America, it indeed begins with a small desire, of being free to practice one's religious beliefs privately without persecution. But religious practice inevitably comes into conflict with society's laws and value system.

In our own struggle for religious freedom, we had to convince the government that our parochial education met state educational standards.[5] And in the 1950s, when the institute of *sheḥitah* was threatened, we had to demonstrate that it was indeed humane.[6]

---

3. Genesis Rabbah 42:8 (opinion of R. Judah). R. Samuel Jaffe Ashkenazi interprets R. Judah's opinion to mean that if the entire world were placed on one side of a scale and Abraham on the other, Abraham would counter-balance the entire word. *Yefeh To'ar* ad loc.
4. *Midrash ha-Gadol*, Genesis 11:28.
5. See Alvin I. Schiff, *The Jewish Day School in America* (New York: Jewish Education Committee Press, 1966), 227–228; Doniel Z. Kramer, *The Day Schools and Torah Umesorah: The Seeding of Traditional Judaism in America* (New York: Yeshiva University Press, 1984), 122–123.
6. In 1958, the U.S. Congress passed the Humane Methods of Slaughter Act. Pub. L. No. 85–765, 72 Stat. 862, amended by Humane Methods of Slaughter Act of 1978, Pub. L. No. 95–455, § 5, 92 Stat. 1069, 1069 (codified at 7 U.S.C. §§ 1901–1906). In general, the law requires that livestock be rendered insensible to pain by mechanical, electrical, or chemical means before being shackled or hoisted for slaughter. 7 U.S.C. § 1902(a). According to Jewish law, however, the animal must be conscious at the time of *sheḥitah*. In response to testimony from representatives of American Jewry, including notably Rabbi Dr. Isaac Lewin, the law explicitly recognized *sheḥitah* as humane and exempted the handling or preparation of livestock for ritual slaughter from the terms of the law. Ibid., §§ 1902(b), 1906. For testimony in defense of *sheḥitah*, see "Humane Slaughtering of Livestock; Hearings before the Committee on Agriculture and Forestry," U.S. Senate, 85th Cong. 2d. Sess., on S. 1213, S. 1497 and H.R. 8308 (1958), 148–174, 337–343; "Humane Slaughtering of Livestock and

But the struggle advances to new levels. We say that *kashrut* is subject to objective standards and therefore the State should prosecute for consumer fraud.[7] We want the judicial system to enforce the request for a *get* in the case of the civil dissolution of marriage.[8] And then we want accommodation in the workplace for Sabbath observance. Finally, we challenge the military and demand that a soldier be allowed to wear a *kippah*, even though it might disrupt military discipline.[9]

It is therefore a matter of deep anguish to have learned that recently a professor of sociology at a major university announced that his midterm examination would be on Yom Kippur.[10] Allowing such a deed would set us back almost to square one. Such insensitivity! Such

---

Poultry; Hearings before a Subcommittee on Agriculture and Forestry," U.S. Senate, 84th Cong., 2d. Sess., on S. 1636 (1956), 138–146.

7. For a survey of kosher fraud statutes in the United States, see Mark A. Berman, "Kosher Fraud Statutes and the Establishment Clause: Are They Kosher?," *Columbia Journal of Law and Social Problems* 26, no. 1 (Autumn 1992): 13–19.

8. See Avitzur v. Avitzur, 58 N.Y.2d 108, 446 N.E.2d 136, 459 N.Y.S.2d 572 (1983) (enforcing provision in the *ketubbah* that a husband appear before a *beit din* to enable his wife to obtain a *get*), *cert. denied*, 464 U.S. 817 (1983); Minkin v. Minkin, 180 N.J. Super. 260, 434 A.2d 665 (Super. Ct. Ch. Div. 1981) (finding that a court order to force a husband to give his wife a *get* does not violate the Establishment Clause of the First Amendment to the U.S. Constitution). After *Avitzur* was decided, New York enacted a law that effectively prevents a husband from obtaining a civil divorce until he swears to the court that he has given his wife a *get*. N.Y. Dom. Rel. Law § 253 (McKinney Supp. 1983–1984).

9. In 1981, an Orthodox Jew, S. Simcha Goldman, sued the U.S. Secretary of Defense after being denied the right to wear a *kippah* while on military duty as an officer in the Air Force. Goldman v. Sec'y of Defense, 530 F. Supp. 12 (D.D.C. 1981). See also Bitterman v. Sec'y of Defense, 553 F. Supp. 719 (D.D.C. 1982) (similar case). Although the District Court ruled in favor of Goldman, the decision was reversed on appeal. Goldman v. Sec'y of Defense, 734 F.2d 1531 (D.C. Cir. 1984). The Supreme Court subsequently affirmed the appellate decision. Goldman v. Weinberger, 475 U.S. 503 (1986). In response to that litigation, Congress passed a law that generally allows a member of the armed services to wear an item of religious apparel while wearing the uniform of the member's armed force. National Defense Authorization Act for Fiscal Years 1988 and 1989, Pub. L. No. 100–180, § 508(a)(2), 101 Stat. 1019, 1086–1087 (1987) (codified at 10 U.S.C. § 774 (1988)). For a discussion of the *Goldman* case and the ensuing legislation, see Louis Fisher, "Nonjudicial Safeguards for Religious Liberty," *University of Cincinnati Law Review* 70 (2001): 72–78.

10. "Professor Criticized for Exam on Yom Kippur," *New York Times*, October 14, 1989, A26.

The Struggle for Religious Freedom

intolerance! But what was more disturbing, something that rips our heart, is that the Jewish students essentially caved in. Only thirteen opted for the research paper.[11] These students were, of course, secular Jews, but Yom Kippur is holy even for secular Jews.

I would suggest that the caving in is connected to another extraordinary event, which earned the headlines of the *Jewish Week*.[12] A group of Jewish scholars met with the Dalai Lama, just before he received his Nobel Peace Prize. The scholars went away from the meeting uttering statements that bordered on, or were outright, apostasy, while one of the organizers of the event said, "I consider myself a man with Jewish roots and Buddhist wings."[13]

Why are these events connected? Because when Abraham was presented with the proposal of the King of Sodom, "Give me the people and take the possessions for yourself" (Genesis 14:21), he vehemently refused and replied, "Neither a thread nor a shoestrap, I will not take anything of yours, so you will not say 'It is I who made Abram wealthy'" (Genesis 14:23). Because of this vehement reply, the Children of Israel merited the obligations of *tzitzit* and *tefillin*.[14]

What message is being imparted here? *Tzitzit* and *tefillin* are the most visible outward signs of Jewishness. But even these signs can be the mystique of the Jew or, God forbid, the cause of the gentile to mock and ridicule us. Which will it be? Well, if we fight with purity of motive and integrity for what we stand for, *tzitzit* and *tefillin* will be viewed by the gentile, even the Sodomitic gentile, who is already looking for the self-interest element, as our mystique. Abraham fought the battle for a principle, to rescue Lot, and on a deeper level to expose the fraud of Nimrod that he had captured Abraham.[15] Abraham did not want his

---

11. Tamar Kaufman, "Berkeley Prof, Known for Civil Rights, Penalizes Jewish Students on Yom Kippur," *Jewish Advocate*, October 26, 1989, 3.
12. Arthur J. Magida, "The Dalai Lama Listens for Jewish Secrets," *Jewish Week*, October 27, 1989, 28, 42; Tamar Kaufman, "Jewish Grant Piqued Interest of Dalai Lama," *Jewish Week*, October 27, 1989, 28.
13. Kaufman, "Jewish Grant Piqued Interest of Dalai Lama," 28.
14. *Sotah* 17a. Cf. Genesis Rabbah 43:9 (stating that the mitzvah of *yibbum* was given in reward for Abraham declaring that he would not take a "shoestrap").
15. R. Jacob Culi, *Me-Am Lo'ez*, Genesis 14:24, trans. R. Shemuel Yerushalmi, *Yalkut Me-Am Lo'ez: Sefer Bereshit* (Jerusalem: Mossad Yad Ezra, 1968), 310.

Lekh Lekha

motive, now or in the future, to be suspect; he did not want anyone to think that he fought for selfish gain.

When we fight for our religious principles without dilution, without adulteration, and without being sympathizers with other cultures and religions, if we regard our roots in Judaism and look to the *kanfei nesharim* for our wings, then we are fighting for religious freedom in the last frontier, preparatory for our cosmic mission of being "a light unto the nations."[16]

---

16. Isaiah 42:6, 49:6.

The First Marital Dispute

October 15, 1994

The first marital dispute in the Torah is recorded in today's portion. It is between Abraham and Sarah, and is expressed in all too familiar terms for contemporary society, echoing Sarah's words to Abraham, "*ḥamasi alekha*," the hurt inflicted upon me by others is all your fault![1]

The details: Sarah is childless. She gives her handmaid Hagar to Abraham, saying, "Perhaps I will be built up through her" (Genesis 16:2). Hagar conceives immediately. Then, Sarah's esteem was lowered in the eyes of Hagar.[2] Hagar tells visitors that Sarah is not a righteous woman, that she is not what she appears to be.[3]

This was no small dispute. Sarah expressed rancor in her statement "let Hashem judge between me and you" (Genesis 16:5), which

---

1. Genesis 16:5.
2. Genesis 16:4.
3. *Rashi* to Genesis 16:4.

cost her forty-eight years of her life.[4] And because Sarah oppressed Hagar, Nahmanides says that we suffer today at the hands of the Ishmaelim.[5]

We cannot but be tempted to speculate, what if? Could the dispute with all its disastrous consequences have been avoided? A marriage counselor steeped in the teachings of our Sages would, I submit, respond in the affirmative. *Rashi* reads into "*ḥamasi alekha*" a complaint regarding why Abraham did not importune Hashem that Sarah should have children when he prayed for himself that he should have children, saying, "What can You give me seeing that I go childless?" (Genesis 15:2).[6]

We tend to think that it is saintly to always be a *ne'elav*.[7] This might very well be true with respect to petty insults. We should just swallow them and not hold the perpetrator responsible. But if the insult really

---

4. R. Bahya b. Asher, *Midrash Rabbeinu Beḥaye al Ḥamishah Ḥumshei Torah*, Genesis 15:5; Genesis Rabbah 45:7 (Lvov ed. 1874). The Midrash explains that Sarah had been worthy to live as long as Abraham. According to the view that Sarah lost forty-eight years of her life, Sarah had been worthy to live the same number of years as Abraham had lived, i.e., 175 years, but she lived only 127 years. See R. Jehiel Michel b. Uzziel (Halberstadt, ca. 1680–1730), *Nezer ha-Kodesh*, Genesis Rabbah 45:7 and R. Samuel b. Joseph Strashun (*Rashash*, Lithuania, 1794–1872), *Ḥiddushei ha-Rashash* to Genesis Rabbah 45:5 (citing *Rabbeinu Beḥaye*'s version of the *Midrash Rabbah*). See also R. Ezekiel Feivel b. Zev Wolf (*Maharif*, Vilna, 1755–1833), *Be'ur Maharif* to Genesis Rabbah 45:5 (Wagshal ed.).

    Other versions of the Midrash record that Sarah lost thirty-eight years of her life. See, e.g., Genesis Rabbah 45:8 (Warsaw ed. 1897). Explaining that alternative calculation, commentators state that Sarah was supposed to live until Abraham died, so that Abraham would not suffer as a result of Sarah's passing. Sarah was ten years younger than Abraham. See Genesis 17:17. Consequently, if Sarah would have lived until Abraham died, she would have lived 165 years, i.e., thirty-eight years more than 127 years. See R. Samuel Jaffe Ashkenazi, *Yefeh To'ar* to Genesis Rabbah 45:7; R. Enoch Zundel b. Joseph (Białystock, d. 1867), *Etz Yosef* to Genesis Rabbah 45:5; R. Zev Wolf Einhorn (*Maharzu*, Vilna, d. 1862), *Perush Maharzu*, ad loc. (citing *Yefeh To'ar*).

5. Nahmanides to Genesis 16:6.
6. *Rashi* to Genesis 16:5.
7. See *Gittin* 36b ("Those who suffer insults (*ha-ne'elavin*) but do not inflict them, who hear themselves reviled and do not answer back, who perform [religious precepts] out of love and rejoice in chastisement, of such the Scripture states, 'those who love Him are like the sun when it goes forth in its might' [Judges 5:31].").

The First Marital Dispute

hurts, "You shall not hate your brother in your heart; you shall reprove your fellow and do not bear a sin because of him" (Leviticus 19:17).

Or ha-Ḥayyim says that Sarah suppressed her heart.[8] But *Rashi* is a *parashan*, so why does he introduce a *midrash* that does not fit into the immediate incident? The answer is that *Rashi* felt that it was so out of character for Sarah to say "let Hashem judge between me and you," that it must be that the complaint against Abraham that he did not pray on her behalf colored her attitude toward Hagar. If Sarah would have confronted Abraham, perhaps he would have had an answer, i.e., that he cannot pray for a double miracle.[9]

We often get into trouble by avoiding confrontation. We convey impressions that we never meant to convey.

What did Sarah mean by "perhaps I will be built up through her"? Did she intend to use Hagar just to evoke divine compassion for herself to have her own child by bringing a rival into her household?[10] In that case, Sarah's pain was self-imposed. Or was she resigned that she would not have a child and derived some satisfaction from the fact that Abraham would have a child? If that were the case, the tension was not justified. Abraham should have intervened. And finally, what role does Abraham play in the changed attitude of Hagar toward Sarah? Hagar thought that Sarah had freed her. This emboldened Hagar.[11]

Abraham and Sarah were the ideal couple. They were educated and pious, and so sensitive to each other. *Va-tikkaḥ Sarai* (Genesis 16:3) – *lakaḥtah be-devarim*, she persuaded Hagar by praising Abraham.[12] And Abraham did not jump on the suggestion. He resisted Sarah's suggestion to give Hagar to him.[13] Yet, the dispute happened with all its disastrous consequences.

---

8. R. Ḥayyim b. Moses ibn Attar (*Or ha-Ḥayyim*, Morocco, 1696–1743), *Or ha-Ḥayyim* to Genesis 16:5–6.
9. See *Ta'anit* 8b; R. Joseph ha-Levi Ettinger (Moravia, d. 1782), *Edut bi-Yosef*, *Va-Yera* ¶ 33.
10. See *Rashi* to Genesis 16:2, s.v. "*ibbaneh mi-mennah*."
11. *Or ha-Ḥayyim* to Genesis 16:5–6.
12. *Rashi* to Genesis 16:3. Sarah told Hagar how fortunate Hagar would be to be the wife of such a holy man.
13. Nahmanides to Genesis 16:2.

Lekh Lekha

Ma'aseh avot siman le-banim.[14] That this happened is the building block of the world. When domestic harmony is disrupted, it is a *ḥurban*. But when domestic harmony is achieved, it can build worlds.

---

14. See Nahmanides to Genesis 12:6 (quoting *Midrash Tanḥuma, Lekh Lekha* 9).

Saving a Jew from Peril; Its Limits

November 8, 2003

The date: 1939. A cloud of peril overhung European Jewry. The gates of emigration, even to the United States, were effectively closed. The scene: Irving Bunim's office. Enter an anxious petitioner, Rabbi Yosef Farber. He was desperate to get his family to Palestine to escape Europe. Bunim says that the British White Paper requires potential immigrants to Palestine to have a cash reserve of at least $5,000, an enormous sum in those days. Bunim gives him this. He then tells Rabbi Farber that a bank account with $5,060 will be opened in his name. The extra $60 is intended to make the British think that the new bank account had already earned interest. He also instructs the Rabbi to tell the immigration office that he does business with Bunim.[1]

---

1. Amos Bunim, *A Fire in His Soul* (Jerusalem: Feldheim, 1989), 79–83.

Lekh Lekha

We are a people that abides by ethical rules, not only the rules of the Torah, but also *dina de-malkhuta*.[2] But when the issue is the saving of innocent life, if no other means are available, all the prohibitions of the Torah, except the three cardinal sins of idolatry, murder, and adultery, are set aside.[3]

The source for this approach is the episode of Abraham and Sarah in Egypt. It is one of the Ten Trials of Abraham.[4] So how Abraham conducted himself is certainly a model for emulation. In this respect, Abraham sets up a preemptive lie. It is a lie for Sarah to say even before anyone initiates a conversation with them. "Please say that you are my sister, that it may go well with me for your sake, and that I may live on account of you" (Genesis 12:13). I'll be able to fend off marriage proposals by saying that the gifts are not sufficient.[5] So Abraham lied to preserve his life.

Everything seemed to end well, but a troubling question remains. If Abraham accepted the gifts under false pretenses, shouldn't he have returned them?

My question is outlandish. On the surface, Pharaoh is protesting, "What is this you have done to me?" (Genesis 12:18). But we are "believers, the children of believers."[6] So in truth, Pharaoh was a fiendish mendicant. Sarah was coerced to go to Pharaoh. It matters not whether the ones who come to get her are the Fedayeen or ambassadors clothed in royal raiment. Thugs are thugs. And we know that Sarah disclosed to Pharaoh that she was Abraham's wife and he just could not have cared less.[7] Through free will, he made up his mind to violate Sarah even though she was married. And this, of course, would necessitate the elimination of Abraham, as he was harboring the dark secret that she was really his wife.

---

2. *Gittin* 10b.
3. *Sanhedrin* 74a.
4. *Rashi* and Maimonides to Mishnah, *Avot* 5:3.
5. R. Obadiah b. Jacob Sforno (*Sforno*, Italy, ca. 1470–1550), *Sforno* to Genesis 12:13; R. Shelomoh al-Batzravi (d. 1930), *Devar Shelomoh: Perush le-Sefer Bereshit* (Tel Aviv, 1932), 36.
6. *Shabbat* 97a.
7. Genesis Rabbah 41:2.

It is only divine intervention in human affairs that prevented Pharaoh from violating Sarah. "Hashem afflicted Pharaoh along with his household with severe plagues" (Genesis 12:17). Also, according to Tradition, every time Pharaoh approached Sarah, an invisible angel beat the daylights out of him.[8]

Well, Pharaoh was guilty of a capital offense on multiple counts. There should have been a change of regime and Pharaoh should have been decapitated for his sins. I would say that he got a very light punishment. He got away with murder. He got away with his veneer of piety and innocence when he was, in fact, a miscreant. He should have been removed from the throne and been killed. It would have been absolutely brazen gall for Pharaoh to demand back the gifts. And for Abraham to offer to give them back would diminish the ugliness of Pharaoh's sin.

Ma'aseh avot siman le-banim. Today, fifty years after the Holocaust, Jews are aggressively making headway in claiming bank accounts, insurance policies, and compensation for assets confiscated by the Nazis.[9] What is the result? My outlandish question: "Why are Jews so aggressive? Why do they dig deeper and deeper to discover more names and more information?" Well, *halo devarim kal ve-ḥomer.* Abraham did not give back the gifts even though only Hashem, he, and Sarah knew the truth. In the eyes of the whole nation, by contrast, Pharaoh was duped; he was more like a victim than a villain. Certainly, when we have objective proof of our claims, we should not abandon them. Abandoning them would do nothing less than diminish the ugliness of the Nazi crimes.

I say that Abraham did not give back the gifts because he did not want to diminish the ugliness of Pharaoh's sins. How do I know? It was how he reacted to the proposal of the King of Sodom that Abraham give him the people and take the property. "Neither a thread nor a shoestrap, I will not take anything of yours, so you will not say 'It is I who made Abram wealthy'" (Genesis 14:23). He did not want anything to create a diversion from the focus of saving Lot and exposing Nimrod's fraud.

---

8. Ibid.; *Rashi* to Genesis 12:17, s.v. *"al devar Sarai."*
9. Michael J. Bazyler, *Holocaust Justice: The Battle for Restitution in America's Courts* (New York: New York University Press, 2003), 59–268.

Lekh Lekha

This explains his *mesirut nefesh* to save Lot, fighting with an army of only 318 men against the four world powers.

If we combine the personality of Abraham in how he dealt with Pharaoh with the personality of Abraham in how he dealt with the King of Sodom, everyone will have the feeling that the Jew hates scams and does everything to promote his values. We then move in the direction of "your offspring shall inherit the gate of its enemies" (Genesis 22:17). We become the "light unto the nations."[10]

---

10. Isaiah 42:6, 49:6.

Va-Yera

Among My People I Dwell

October 22, 1983

Our attitude toward holiness often vacillates between admiration from afar and subconscious fear that totally embracing it will bring in its wake discomfiture or worse. Such was the ambivalence of the Shunammite Woman, the central character of today's *haftarah*. She was a discerning individual, recognizing the holiness of Elisha. A fly would dare not approach his table.[1] His table was therefore akin to Hashem's altar. And she had ample evidence that Elisha never entertained impure thoughts.[2] Her recognition of holiness turned into admiration: "Let us now make a small, walled attic and place there for him a bed, a table, and a lamp, so that whenever he comes to us, he can turn in there" (II Kings 4:10).

But did her grand act reflect a grand heart that was longing for a closer connection to holiness, or did it represent merely a desire to

---

1. *Berakhot* 10b.
2. Ibid.

wall off its influence, so that when Elisha would come, he could "turn in there"? There he would have all his needs – a bed, a table, and a lamp.

Elisha was to soon find out. He tells his attendant Gehazi to ask her "What can be done for you? Can something be said on your behalf to the King or the commander of the army?" (II Kings 4:13). Do you desire to make closer associations with the King or the General? The King is the grand sentimentalist, reflecting the heart of the entire Israel,[3] and the General, who leads you in battle, represents the feeling of aloneness, fighting the whole society, that man's emotions are strained when he accepts *kedushah* fully and totally.

The Shunammite answers, "Among my people I dwell" (ibid.). I do not need excitement or adventure in my life. I want only to blend into society, not to leap higher to the King or the General.

Perhaps she was thinking of the brilliance of David, who said that the 613 mitzvot are really eleven mitzvot.[4] They represent the eleven virtues that the Torah demands, and great personalities are selected who personify these virtues.[5] As King David said, "Hashem, who may sojourn in Your Tent? Who may dwell on Your Holy Mountain? One who walks in perfect innocence" (Psalms 15:1–2). This refers to Abraham.[6] The man of "among my people I dwell" will accept faith, but only to the extent that society will recognize it as a virtue. Carrying faith to the degree that Abraham did results in society viewing him as a simpleton, with no independent intelligence, and manifesting a blend of cruelty and insanity, as in the *Akedah*.[7]

---

3. Maimonides, *Mishneh Torah, Melakhim* 3:6.
4. *Makkot* 24a. The eleven virtues are enumerated at Psalms 15. The psalm describes one who (1) walks in perfect innocence; (2) does what is right; (3) speaks the truth from his heart; (4) has no slander on his tongue; (5) has done his fellow no evil; (6) has not cast disgrace upon his close one; (7) considers a contemptible person repulsive; (8) honors those who fear Hashem; (9) swears to his detriment without retracting; (10) does not lend his money on interest; and (11) does not take a bribe against the innocent.
5. *Midrash Shoḥer Tov*, Psalms 15; *Makkot* 24a.
6. *Midrash Shoḥer Tov*, Psalms 15:2 (citing as a proof text Hashem's commandment to Abraham, "Walk before Me and be perfect" [Genesis 17:1]); *Makkot* 24a.
7. See *Rashi* to Genesis 22:4, s.v. "*ba-yom ha-shelishi*" (explaining that Hashem waited until the third day of Abraham's travels to reveal to him the location for the *Akedah* so

"One who has no slander on his tongue" (Psalms 15:3) refers to Jacob.[8] Not to malign a fellow man is regarded as a virtue, but not when one is fighting desperately to establish his identity, to build a nation, and prevent a blessing from falling upon the quintessence of evil and the most undeserving person, Esau. Society regards such a person as a coward, lacking manliness.

One who "has done his fellow no evil" means "*lo yarad le-ummanut ḥavero.*"[9] To be fair and responsible and decent in business means to compete fairly, not to use predatory tactics. But refraining from invading someone's livelihood is often perceived by society as ineptitude, passivity, and unimaginativeness rather than fairness and decency.

One who "speaks the truth from his heart" (Psalms 15:2) refers to R. Safra.[10] Practicing truthfulness to the extent of admitting truth that resides in one's heart, which no one can contradict, is regarded by a cynical society as foolishness.

But does being uncomfortable with *kedushah* as manifested by the Shunammite's remark "among my people I dwell" warrant the tantalization of being given a child, only that the child should die and require resurrection? Is this the reward for the Shunammite who made a grand gesture?

The torture process was necessary to educate the Shunammite that her outlook on life was totally misguided. When she is told "at this season next year, you will be embracing a son" (II Kings 4:16), she wants a guarantee that he will be a *ben kayyama*. She pleads with Elisha, "Do

---

that it should not be said that Hashem confused Abraham unexpectedly and caused him to act out of insanity).

8. *Makkot* 24a (citing as a proof text Jacob's statement "perhaps my father will feel me and I shall be as a mocker in his eyes" [Genesis 27:12]).
9. *Makkot* 24a.
10. Ibid. The story is recorded that once while R. Safra was reciting the *Shema*, a customer offered to buy his merchandise. Prohibited from interrupting his religious duty, R. Safra could not indicate his acceptance of the offer even through a facial expression. Interpreting R. Safra's apparent indifference as dissatisfaction with his bid, the prospective buyer increased his offer. Upon completing his religious duty, R. Safra confessed to the customer that he had heard the initial bid and resolved in his heart to accept it. R. Safra then could not accept the higher offer. *She'iltot de-Rav Aḥai Gaon, Va-Yeḥi*, no. 36.

Va-Yera

not disappoint your maidservant" (ibid.), requesting a guarantee that he will confer her only bliss and no pain at all.

But the request is so unreal. It denies her very humanity. There is no other human experience that is so filled with anguish and pain than raising children. And after raising a child, "therefore a man shall leave his father and his mother and cling to his wife, and they shall become one flesh" (Genesis 2:24). The death of the child and his resurrection are necessary to show her that her desire for a painless existence denies her humanity.

In the crisis, she rejects her husband. His view of *kedushah* consists entirely of respect and deference. When she tells him that she is going to the Prophet, he asks her, "Why are you going to him today? It is not a New Moon or a Sabbath" (II Kings 4:23). And she is willing to fall at the feet of the Prophet and speak to him directly without the intermediation of Gehazi. Her embrace of *kedushah* achieves for her for the first time the title "mother" – "The boy's mother said: '[I swear] as Hashem lives and as you live, I will not leave you'" (II Kings 4:30).

Her total embrace of *kedushah* earns a reciprocal response from Elisha. He placed his mouth upon the boy's mouth, his eyes upon his eyes, and his palms upon his palms.[11] His words, his vision, his actions, become completely fused with the child, signifying a total embrace of *kedushah*.

And this child was no ordinary child. His name was Habakkuk, meaning the man who was embraced twice, i.e., once by his mother and another time by the Prophet.[12] The man made a singular contribution to Jewish philosophy and *hashkafah*. While David condensed the Torah into eleven principles, Isaiah into six,[13] and Micah into three,[14] Habakkuk

---

11. II Kings 4:34.
12. *Zohar* 1:7b.
13. Isaiah 33:15 ("One who [1] walks with righteousness and [2] speaks with truthfulness, [3] who spurns extortionate profit and [4] shakes off his hands from holding a bribe, [5] who seals his ears from hearing of bloodshed, and [6] shuts his eyes from seeing evil").
14. Micah 6:8 ("He has told you, O man, what is good! What does Hashem require of you but to do justice, love kindness, and walk humbly with your God.").

said it is all one principle: "The righteous person shall live through his faith" (Habakkuk 2:4).[15]

No one can escape pain and unpleasantness in life. Only a fool would believe that he can. The *tzaddik* will totally embrace *kedushah* and feel that his entire lifeblood comes from it. The quality of his life is living the life of *kedushah*. He thrives on it and finds delight in it.

---

15. *Makkot* 24a.

Salt: The Paradoxical Symbol

November 7, 1987

I would submit that there is no other *parashah* in the Torah that presents such a stark contrast in human potential as today's reading. On the one hand, we are exposed to the most ignominious chapter of human selfishness and misanthropy, the episode of Sodom. The people of Sodom have no portion in the World to Come.[1] On the other hand, we read of the most glorious moment of human selflessness and devotion to Hashem, the triumph of the *Akedah*.

Verily, if we look at the two episodes more closely, both are represented for posterity in the exact same symbol, salt. Sodom is represented in the form of a pillar of salt that Irit, the wife of Lot, was turned into because she took a glance backward at the destruction of Sodom.[2] Yet we are bidden to always bring salt to our tables, as our tables are

---

1. Mishnah, *Sanhedrin* 10:3; *Sanhedrin* 109a.
2. Genesis 19:26.

Salt: The Paradoxical Symbol

in place of the Altar,[3] and all sacrifices on the Altar are required to be salted.[4] Now, which sacrifice in human history was the most sublime and lofty? Was it not the *Akedah*?

Yes, Abraham and Sodom were light years apart in their spiritual dimensions, but the essence of each could be captured in a tiny grain of salt.

Salt has contradictory physical properties. On the one hand, it is a preservative, and on the other, it is a decaying agent.[5] In short, it represents contradiction.

Now, Sodom ostensibly professed the philosophy of "what is mine is mine, and what is your is yours," according to a *Tanna* in *Avot*.[6] But in reality, they never found an instance where their fellow's benefit did not detract from their own welfare. It was a society obsessed with the need to prevent the emergence of a climate of indolence. This was reflected in their economic organization and economic incentive system. If one had one ox, he was obligated to pasture the animals of the whole town for one day. If one had no oxen, however, he was required to pasture all the oxen in the town for two days.[7]

It was a society very much concerned with the spillover effects of economic activity. The people of Sodom did not want strangers to benefit from the wealth of the community. The Sodomitic judge was charged with the responsibility of making sure that any stranger who entered the city would leave penniless.[8]

Insularity and communal avariciousness as opposed to individual selfishness turned often into more degenerate forms, making it a capital offense to assist the poor. The height of Sodom's decadence is perhaps represented in the last fateful moments of its existence. The woman who had borrowed salt from her neighbor as a way of letting on that

---

3. *Berakhot* 55a; *Ḥagigah* 27a.
4. Leviticus 2:13 ("on your every offering shall you offer salt").
5. A reference to salt as a decaying agent is found in the expression at Psalms 107:34 of "*eretz peri le-meleḥah*" ([He turns] a fruitful land into a salty waste).
6. Mishnah, *Avot* 5:10.
7. *Sanhedrin* 109a.
8. *Pirkei de-Rabbi Eliezer* 25.

Va-Yera

she and her husband harbored guests was fleeing town.[9] Instructed not to look back, she did.[10]

But the verse says that Lot's wife peered *me-ahorav,* "behind him" (Genesis 19:26). It should have said that she peered *me-ahoreha,* "from behind herself." The term *"me-ahorav"* signifies that this selfish woman was, at the moment of truth and the moment of divine retribution, thinking only of herself. She looked after him, beyond her husband's death, and said, "He is penniless. From where will I draw my support?"[11] The circle of concern for Sodom then became smaller and smaller, starting perhaps with an obsessive concern to preserve the wealth of the community, but ending in a degenerate concern to preserve the self.

Sodomites always found contradiction, even when it did not exist. They always found a conflict between their own interest and that of their fellow man. Symbolically, they always tasted salt in their food, even when it was not there. And when they saw the conflict between decency and self-preservation, they always leaped in favor of self-preservation.

Abraham lived with actual contradiction. He was smothered in salt, yet never tasted it. He prodigiously expended his resources on others, diminishing himself, choosing the self-decaying element of salt. But he understood that by choosing the self-diminishing path, he would be conserving himself, achieving immortality. And his greatest triumph was the willing submission to literal self-decay to adhere to the command of Hashem.

Was anyone ever confronted with Hashem's contradicting Himself to such a degree as when Hashem seemed to recant on His promise to Abraham "through Isaac will offspring be considered yours" (Genesis 21:12)? Now Hashem is asking him to sacrifice his own child. From

---

9. Genesis Rabbah 51:5; *Yalkut Shimoni, Va-Yera* 85. According to the Midrash, it was the custom of Lot's wife to serve guests only saltless food. Lot instructed her to add a little salt for these guests. She responded, "Do you wish to introduce this evil custom here?" Genesis Rabbah 50:4. She then left the house to borrow salt from the neighbors. As a result, the Sodomites learned that Lot had guests.
10. Genesis 19:26.
11. *Keli Yakar* to Genesis 19:17; R. Jacob Culi, *Me-Am Lo'ez,* Genesis 19:26, trans. R. Shemuel Yerushalmi, *Yalkut Me-Am Lo'ez: Sefer Bereshit* (Jerusalem: Mossad Yad Ezra, 1968), 380.

Salt: The Paradoxical Symbol

where would come the destiny of the Jewish people? From where would emerge the great nation "like the stars of the heavens and like the sand on the seashore" (Genesis 22:17)? It was all supposed to come from Isaac.

Abraham was able to make himself into dust and ashes, achieving a dimension of awe and self-abnegation that we simply do not know today at all. Abraham resolved the conflict by leaping for self-decency and self-denial.

Salt is also the symbol of the Priesthood[12] and Royalty,[13] representing the ability to unite opposite and diverse forces into an integrated whole.[14]

And there is another property of salt. If it is added to food in an appropriate amount, it gives seasoning to the food, but if it is added in excess, it spoils the food.[15] So, too, in leadership, salt represents that perfect balance between self-assertiveness and reticence.

Finally, we must remember, "Any meal offering that you offer to Hashem shall not be prepared leavened, for you shall not cause to go up in smoke from any leavening or fruit-honey as a fire-offering to Hashem" (Leviticus 2:11). No arrogance and no artificial sentiment.[16] The natural sweetness of Torah must emerge.

---

12. See Numbers 18:19 (referring to the Priesthood as "an eternal salt-like covenant before Hashem, for you and your offspring with you"); *Rashi* ad loc.
13. II Chronicles 13:5 ("Surely you should know that Hashem, God of Israel, gave kingship over Israel to David forever, to him and his children a salt-like covenant.").
14. Salt contains the opposite properties of water and fire, signifying the Attribute of Mercy and the Attribute of Justice. *Rabbeinu Beḥaye al ha-Torah*, Leviticus 2:13; *Keli Yakar* to Leviticus 2:11. See also R. Yaakov Tzvi Mecklenburg (Germany, 1785–1865), *Ha-Ketav ve-ha-Kabbalah*, Leviticus 2:13, Numbers 18:19.
15. See Nahmanides to Leviticus 2:13.
16. See R. Aaron b. Joseph ha-Levi, *Sefer ha-Ḥinnukh*, mitzvah no. 117; R. Hayyim Meir Hager (*Imrei Ḥayyim*, Benei Berak, 1887–1972), *Imrei Ḥayyim: Kuntrus ha-Likkutim al ha-Torah u-Moadim* (Tel Aviv: Makhon Zekher Hayyim, 1976), 75–76; R. Eliyahu Kitov (Israel, 1912–1976), *Sefer ha-Parshiyyot*, vol. 5 (Jerusalem, 1985), 55.

The Burst of Laughter That Lasted Forever

November 15, 2003

There probably was never a burst of laughter that got someone into more trouble with the *Ribbono shel Olam* than that of our Matriarch Sarah. Hashem complained to Abraham about her laughter of disbelief that she would bear a son in her old age. And when she denied the laughter, saying "I did not laugh" (Genesis 18:15), who rebuked her? Some say it was Hashem.[1]

Why all this harshness over the temporary lapse of probably the most righteous woman who ever walked the face of the earth? Moreover,

---

1. Jerusalem Talmud, *Sotah* 7:1; R. David b. Naphtali Hirsch Fraenkel (Berlin, 1707–1762), *Korban ha-Edah* to Jerusalem Talmud ad loc., s.v. "*ela im Sarah bilvad*"; R. Zev Wolf Einhorn, *Perush Maharzu* to Genesis Rabbah 48:20, s.v. "*kammah kirkukhim*." Some commentators say that the angels rebuked her. See, e.g., *Targum Yonatan*, Genesis 18:15; *Rabbeinu Behaye al ha-Torah*, Genesis 18:15. According to other commentators, Abraham rebuked her. See, e.g., Nahmanides to Genesis 18:15; *Sforno* to Genesis 18:15; *Or ha-Hayyim* to Genesis 18:15.

The Burst of Laughter That Lasted Forever

it was a laughter that was visible to no one but herself. It was a suppressed laughter – "Sarah laughed to herself" (Genesis 18:12).

Perhaps the key here is that the laughter was the product of absurdity, and absurdity is a vital factor in forging the Jewish nation and keeping the Jewish family on course today as well.

For Sarah, the greatest moment in her life was when Hashem spoke to her. But her greatest moment was also apparently her most shameful moment, as Hashem, in effect, said to her that she lied.

In the thinking of the *Sefat Emet*, the conversation that Hashem had with Sarah about her laughter was not a shameful moment for her.[2] Sarah undoubtedly did *teshuvah* with all her heart and soul for her temporary lapse in having total faith in Hashem. When one does total *teshuvah* for a sin, one is entitled to expect that the sin is wiped out, as if it never occurred. This is what the verse implies, "Sarah denied it, saying, 'I did not laugh,' for she was frightened" (Genesis 18:15). Because she was God-fearing, she felt that she could deny that she ever laughed.

Hashem accepts her *teshuvah* and says, "Better that you do not wipe out the laughter of absurdity. You need it as a tool to achieve full progress and blessing and avoid disaster." Hashem tells her, in essence, "Elevate the laughter of absurdity so that it will work as a merit for you."

Yes, when Isaac was born, the scorner had a field day that inflicted the pain of the laughter of absurdity on Abraham and Sarah. A child is born to old, frail parents. They would never survive. They would never raise him for greatness. There would never be continuity. This mockery would block out the absurdity.

But absurdity must be elevated. It becomes the measure of how far Abraham and Sarah must go in the *ḥinnukh* of Isaac. They must implant in him that he "keep the way of Hashem, doing charity and justice" (Genesis 18:19), until Isaac makes an absurdity out of the machinations of the Evil Inclination.

Isaac was a happy man. His *gevurah*, according to the *Sefat Emet*, produced joy.[3] Then came the evil son, Ishmael. He tried to imitate Isaac,

---

2. R. Yehudah Aryeh Leib Alter (*Sefat Emet*, Poland, 1847–1905), *Sefat Emet, ḥelek* 1, *Va-Yera*, s.v. *"be-pasuk va-tikhaḥesh Sarah."*
3. *Sefat Emet, ḥelek* 1, *Va-Yera*, s.v. *"be-inyan shemo shel Yitzḥak."*

Va-Yera

but he did so only superficially. He too assumed the outward appearance of a happy person. But between the happiness of Isaac and the happiness of Ishmael, Isaac reflected the joy of *gevurah*, while Ishmael reflected levity, and made an absurdity out of the severest prohibitions, the three cardinal sins.[4]

Sarah knew the difference and proclaimed, "Drive out this slave-woman with her son" (Genesis 21:10). Abraham did not perceive the incipient threat to Isaac. Hashem had to intervene and say, "Whatever Sarah tells you, heed her voice" (Genesis 21:12).

The laughter of absurdity works in a very insidious manner. It can even appear as a righteous sentiment in a decadent person.

The angels created a sensation in Sodom. They smote everyone with blindness.[5] So when Lot told his sons-in-law to escape, he was implying that it would be absurd to stay. But they regarded it lightly. "He seemed like a jester in the eyes of his sons-in-law" (Genesis 19:14). Why? They reasoned that Lot said that Hashem would destroy the city, and if Hashem destroys the city, it is absurd to flee. If you deserve punishment, you cannot possibly hide. And if you deserve to be saved, you will be saved even from a burning furnace.[6] So what is the point of fleeing from Hashem's punishment? Absurdity argues to flee and not to flee. We need to know when absurdity is the counsel of the Good Inclination and when it is the counsel of the Evil Inclination.

In modern times, Hashem tells us, "Why are you denying your laughter that comes from absurdity? Your enemies designed to make you think 'From the ashes of the crematorium, can we possibly rise to Statehood and become a mini-superpower in the Middle East? The rise from the ashes is an absurdity. It cannot happen.' But it did." Hashem showed us His hand in human history.

"Is anything beyond Hashem? At the appointed time (*la-mo'ed*), I will return to you at this time next year (*ka-et ḥayyah*), and Sarah will have a son" (Genesis 18:14). If we skip every fifth letter in this verse,

---

4. See *Rashi* to Genesis 21:9; Genesis Rabbah 53:11.
5. Genesis 19:11.
6. R. Jacob Culi, *Me-Am Lo'ez*, Genesis 19:14, trans. R. Shemuel Yerushalmi, *Yalkut Me-Am Lo'ez: Sefer Bereshit* (Jerusalem: Mossad Yad Ezra, 1968), 377.

starting with the *mem* of the word *la-mo'ed*, until the word "*ḥayyah*," we get the word "*Mashiaḥ*" (Messiah).[7]

When we hear the calumny that the world heaps upon us, we think that the coming of the Messiah is an absurdity. But this is precisely the setting in which the Messiah will come, *be-heseḥ ha-da'at* (lit., "removal of thought").[8] This is especially true when the calumny is absolutely false in terms of our accomplishments. "That they keep the way of Hashem, doing charity and justice" (Genesis 18:19).

Not only is the idea that the coming of the Messiah is an absurdity in light of the calumny, but the calumny is an absurdity because we aspire for greatness in keeping the way of Hashem. With this combination of absurdities, the footsteps of the Messiah are heard around the corner.

---

7. R. Michel Dov Weissmandl (Slovakia and New York, 1903–1957) (cited in *Sekhar ve-Onesh*, vol. 3 (2001), 293).
8. *Sanhedrin* 97a.

Ḥayyei Sarah

The Ideal Marriage

November 17, 1984

An ancient but beautiful wedding custom is recorded in the *Me-Am Lo'ez*.[1] The Sabbath before the wedding, two Torah scrolls are taken out of the ark, with the groom honored with taking out the second scroll. He holds the scroll until *maftir*, at which time he is called up for the portion of "Now Abraham was old, well on in years" (Genesis 24:1), which describes the wedding of Isaac and Rebecca. Hence, the wedding of Isaac and Rebecca is the prototype of the ideal Jewish wedding. Every ḥatan and kallah focuses his and her attention on this wedding. What follows naturally, therefore, is for the groom to identify with Isaac and the bride with Rebecca.

But what a shock we are in for. Rebecca is put to a character test. Eliezer says that if it should come to pass that after he asks the young

---

1. R. Jacob Culi, *Me-Am Lo'ez*, Genesis 24:2, trans. R. Shemuel Yerushalmi, *Yalkut Me-Am Lo'ez: Sefer Bereshit* (Jerusalem: Mossad Yad Ezra, 1968), 484.

lady to incline her pitcher to him, she says, "Drink, and I will even give your camels to drink," she will be the designated one for Isaac.[2]

What actually happens is that Eliezer is standing near the well and says, "Let me please sip a little water from your jug" (Genesis 24:17). An ordinary person would respond, "Gentleman, help yourself!" But Rebecca gives him water from her canteen and offers to give the camels to drink as well. A camel, according to Tradition, can drink so much water at one time that it can go without drinking for the next three days![3] Now, there were ten camels.[4] Can you imagine the poor girl? She is engaged in exhausting labor on behalf of a stranger who is in robust health, and he does not interrupt her and offer to do the hard work of giving his camels to drink!

Rebecca's conduct speaks well of her magnanimous nature, but what does it say of Eliezer, who is Isaac's proxy? Is this what the woman has to look forward to in the marriage, an instant readiness to succumb to any demand of her husband, however unreasonable?

I would submit that the answer to the dilemma can be found by focusing on another aspect of the episode, Eliezer's presentation of jewelry to Rebecca. He bedecked her with a golden nose ring that weighed a *beka* and two bracelets that weighed ten golden *shekalim*.[5] What is the meaning of the gifts? *Rashi* points out that the golden nose ring represents the *shekalim* donated by the Children of Israel to the Temple, and the two bracelets represent the Two Tablets, which contained the Ten Commandments.[6]

What we therefore face is the symbolic marriage of *tohu va-vohu* to Torah and communal offerings in the Temple, the Abrahamic tradition of refining the *ḥesed* personality to conform to the dictates of the Torah, which is the significance of the Ten Trials of Abraham. How would the tradition continue? With the building of the Jewish nation. The nation would be built only if the woman who would bear children to carry on

---

2. Genesis 24:14.
3. R. Samson Raphael Hirsch, Genesis 24:17–20.
4. Genesis 24:10.
5. Genesis 24:22.
6. *Rashi* to Genesis 24:22.

the Abrahamic tradition would completely surrender to the dictates of the Torah. An extraordinarily magnanimous nature, one that would accommodate even unreasonableness, would be the nature that would bend to the dictates of the Torah even if they would not be understood by the dictates of logic.

Hence the proper identification to be made is that both the *ḥatan* and the *kallah* are Rebecca, and Isaac is the symbol of the ideals of Torah and *avodah*. Both partners must enter into the marriage strongly committed to the ideals of Torah and be prepared to make even the ludicrous sacrifice for these ideals.

The man and the woman, as we all know, each bring into the marriage one of the letters of the divine name. The man brings the *yud* and the woman the *heh*. Together they form the Divine Name.[7] *Heh* is the easiest letter to pronounce. It requires neither the curving of the lips nor pressure from the tongue, only the exhalation of breath.[8] It may appear that the woman is taken for granted, just as the letter *heh*. But her role in forming the Name of Hashem is even greater than the man's. As R. Ahron Soloveichik has said, man's mission is to transmit the content of Sinai, but the woman's role is to transmit the fire of Sinai, the experience of Sinai.[9]

Today, sometimes the roles are reversed, with the wife doing the homework with the children, both religious and secular, and the husband conferring his "fire." Unfortunately it is not the fire of Sinai, but rather the fire of the tensions and pressure of his professional or business life!

---

7. *Sotah* 17a; Rashi ad loc., s.v. "*shekhinah beneihen*."
8. *Midrash Tanḥuma* (Buber), *Bereshit* 16; *Midrash Shoḥer Tov*, Psalms 62:1. Expounding on the verse "These are the generations of the heavens and earth *be-hibare'am* [when they were created]" (Genesis 2:4), the Midrash states, "Read not *be-hibare'am*, but rather *be-heh bare'am* [with the letter *heh*, He created them]," signifying that Hashem created the world as effortlessly as pronouncing the letter *heh*. This Midrash is alluded to in *Akdamus Millin* 12–13, where the Poet states "and with a letter, slight and lacking substance, He readied all His work." See also *Menaḥot* 29b.
9. R. Ahron Soloveichik (Chicago, 1917–2001), *Logic of the Heart, Logic of the Mind: Wisdom and Reflections on Topics of Our Times* (Jerusalem: Genesis Jerusalem Press, 1991), 16–19.

Note that the Name of Hashem that the man and woman form represents the Attribute of Mercy.[10] Indeed, with the practice of generosity, both to each other and to Hashem, a climate of *emunah* is created for the children. Abraham practiced generosity not only between man and his fellow man, but also between man and God.[11]

Which *parashah* is juxtaposed to the *parashah* of *shiddukhim*? It is the struggle of Abraham to secure a burial plot for Sarah.[12] The divine promise that the Land of Canaan would belong to his children was not taken by Abraham as a wedge or a weapon to demand a free plot from the inhabitants, which was indeed offered to him. Instead, he took pains to buy it, and to do so publicly.[13] He viewed the divine promise therefore as merely a glimpse into the ultimate reality.

When the bride and groom enter into their marriage with the willingness to be generous towards Hashem and towards each other, their children will acquire *emunah shelemah*. What demands this unstinting loyalty to the extent of absurdity is not the bride or groom, but rather *da'at Torah*. When each mate embodies *da'at Torah*, no sacrifice is too great for each to make for the other.

---

10. See *Rashi* to Genesis 1:1, s.v. "*bara Elokim*"; R. Shabbetai b. Joseph Bass (*Siftei Hakhamim*, Prague, 1641–1718), *Siftei Hakhamim* to *Rashi* ad loc., n. 40; *Rashi* to Exodus 34:6.
11. Mishnah, *Avot* 5:19; *Rabbeinu Yonah* ad loc. (noting that Abraham was a "*nediv lev*" (generous), as indicated by Genesis 18:7 ("he took a calf, tender and good" for his guests)); *Sukkah* 49b; *Rashi* ad loc., s.v. "*nediv*"; *Hagigah* 3a; *Rashi* ad loc., s.v. "*nediv*"; *Rashi* to Psalms 47:10, s.v. "*am Elokei Avraham*."
12. Genesis 23:2–20.
13. Genesis 23:17–18.

When Jewish Sovereignty Is Threatened

November 9, 1985

Today's portion presents an astonishing contrast between two great women in Jewish history. One, Rebecca, the mother of the Jewish nation, is portrayed as the quintessence of natural goodness and blind trust. "The man was astonished at her, reflecting silently to know whether Hashem had made his journey successful" (Genesis 24:21). Eliezer stands in wonderment of her. How far can he extend the test of magnanimity before she cracks? A robust servant and his entourage seated on camels do nothing to assist her. Rebecca alone is scurrying about to provide water for ten camels and she utters not a word of protest that she is being abused or taken advantage of in any manner. She also displays blind loyalty in leaving secure and familiar surroundings for the unknown.

In contrast, Bath-sheba, the mother of Jewish royalty and sovereignty, is depicted as a shrewd, resourceful person, full of intrigue. It does not take much to convince her that a seemingly innocuous event represents a threat of the most mortal kind to her. Bath-sheba was promised by David that her son Solomon would succeed to the throne.[1] Now she knows that another son of David, Adoniyahu, the son of Haggith, is positioning himself to be King. He assembles fifty men to run before him and boasts, "I shall reign" (I Kings 1:5). He makes a party, inviting some dignitaries, but none of whom represent the legitimate organs of the government.[2]

What was Bath-sheba to make of this? Was Solomon's throne threatened? The Rebecca in her said, "Be trusting of David's promise and in Nathan's prophecy. Nothing is in danger. Adoniyahu is merely engaged in wishful thinking, consistent with his spoiled nature from youth – 'All his days, his father never saddened him by saying, "Why have you done this?"' (I Kings 1:6)."

But Nathan warns her that Adoniyahu's action is the incipient plan of a rebellion, and her very life is at stake; it is a repeat of Absalom's rebellion. It also started with Absalom providing himself with fifty men to run before him and no reaction from David. And it progressed to Absalom beginning to breed discontent with David's administration of justice. Absalom proclaims, "If only someone will appoint me judge in the land" (II Samuel 15:4). No reaction. Then he goes to Jerusalem and inveigles two hundred of David's close associates to join him. No reaction. He sends spies throughout Israel and instructs them that when they hear the *shofar*, they should announce "Absalom has become King in Hebron" (II Samuel 15:10). No reaction. Ahitophel, the most brilliant man in Israel, is inducted into the camp of Absalom.[3] No reaction.

It is only when "the conspiracy was powerful" (II Samuel 15:12), and David hears that "the heart of every man of Israel has turned to Absalom" (II Samuel 15:13), that David finally reacts. But it is too late. Despondency and despair already prevail.

When did the revolution begin? For a Rebecca, all the early events are disregarded and are not considered to have anything to do

---

1. I Kings 1:13, 1:17, 1:30.
2. I Kings 1:7–8.
3. II Samuel 15:12.

with the revolution because all kinds of excuses can be made for the conduct. But Nathan sees the parallel, and it is striking. Absalom's rebellion began with fifty men running before him. He convinces Bath-sheba that Adoniyahu represents a mortal threat. He warns her that if Adoniyahu becomes King, to secure his position, he will undoubtedly insist that her relationship with David was a forbidden one and will have her and Solomon executed.[4] She must assume the worst scenario.

What we have here is a dichotomy. When it comes to interpersonal relationships, the model is Rebecca, the paragon of generosity and trust in the goodness of man. But when Jewish sovereignty is threatened, Bath-sheba is the model. We react with paranoia at the very first threat, with frantic vehemence that our honor and very being are at stake, and that we must validate the prophecy of our destiny.

If a lie is not challenged, it can become a policy. And if a policy is not challenged, it can be implemented. November 10, 1985, marks the tenth anniversary of the infamous U.N. resolution that equated Zionism with racism.[5] Some perhaps will laugh and say, "Well, of course. If the Arabs would sponsor a resolution that the Earth is flat, it would pass with the African and Soviet bloc coalition."[6] But if a lie is not challenged, it can become a policy.

And it is not coincidental that November 10 is the forty-eighth anniversary of Kristallnacht, the beginning of the systematic extermination of European Jewry.

---

4. I Kings 1:12; R. David Kimhi (*Radak*, Provence, ca. 1160–ca. 1235), *Radak* to I Kings 1:21.
5. G.A. Res. 3379, Elimination of All Forms of Racial Discrimination (Nov. 10, 1975) (adopted by a vote of 72 to 35, with 32 abstentions). The resolution was subsequently revoked by U.N. General Assembly Resolution 46/86, Elimination of Racism and Racial Discrimination, on December 16, 1991, by a vote of 111 to 25, with 13 abstentions.
6. See Dr. Josephine M. Brown, "The United Nations Today," *Women Lawyers Journal* 70, no. 3 (Spring 1984): 18 (noting that "in General Assemblies of 157 members, the 51 African states-members voting with the Arab bloc of 21 or more, and the Soviet bloc of 12 states, have a comfortable majority which can pass any resolution"); Ken Cummins, "Declining Influence: America's Failure to Act in the U.N.," *South Florida Sun-Sentinel*, November 10, 1985, 1.G (citing former U.N. official and long-time U.N. observer Matthew Gordon as saying "Count them up, the Arabs and Africans have the majority… The Soviet Union and the People's Republic of China are just going along with things they think these countries will like.").

Ḥayyei Sarah

How do we respond? It is with all our resourcefulness. Bathsheba's approach is to assume that David does not know of Adoniyahu's actions. She arouses his anger and jealousy with an exaggeration of the lavishness of the feast held in David's old age.[7] But Nathan adopts a different tack. He says to King David, "Can it be that this matter has come from my lord the King, and you have not informed your servant who will sit on the throne of my lord the King after him?" (I Kings 1:27). Have you not informed me that my prophecy was vitiated? Nathan evokes shame and guilt in David.[8]

David responds by countering every action of Adoniyahu. If Adoniyahu is coronated secretly, Solomon must be coronated publicly, amidst wild shouting.[9] If Adoniyahu is coronated at a rushing brook, Solomon must be coronated at a placid brook, symbolizing the peace that will prevail during his reign.[10] If Adoniyahu invited dignitaries, illegitimate symbols of authority, an evil General and a deposed High Priest,[11] David must counter with the highest symbols of legitimacy, the High Priest, Tzadok, and the head of the Sanhedrin.[12]

Now we feel that the illegitimate military – that is, the terrorist Arafat – is trying to implement the infamous U.N. resolution. We must counter with the legitimate military of each civilized nation. Our enemies are now also the organs of fake prophets, e.g., Farrakhan. We must counter with true prophets. We must not rest until the entire universe proclaims "*am Yisrael ḥai*."

---

7. I Kings 1:19 ("He has slaughtered ox, fattened bull, and sheep in abundance, and has invited all the King's sons, as well as Abiathar the Kohen and Joab, the commander of the army; but he has not invited your servant Solomon.").
8. See *Malbim* to I Kings 1:27.
9. I Kings 1:39-40.
10. Adoniyahu proclaimed himself King at the Zohelet Stone, near En-rogel. I Kings 1:9. According to *Metzudat Tziyyon*, the name Zohelet signifies that the location was near a rushing stream of water. R. Jehiel Hillel b. David Altschuler (Galicia, 18th cent.), *Metzudat Tziyyon* ad loc. Solomon, by contrast, was coronated at Gihon, near a placid body of water. I Kings 1:33; *Rashi* ad loc., s.v. "*el Giḥon*."
11. I Kings 1:7. Abiathar was a deposed High Priest. *Rashi* ad loc., s.v. "*ve-im Evyatar ha-Kohen*."
12. I Kings 1:32, 1:38. Benaiah b. Jehoiada was the head of the Sanhedrin. See *Berakhot* 4a; *Rashi* ad loc.

Kindness and Truth in Matchmaking

November 29, 1986

It is often said that there is no area in the human experience so capable of surprising us and even defying logic than the area of *shiddukhim*. And so it was with our Forefather Abraham. Head and shoulders above his contemporaries in stature, he sets out to find an appropriate bride for Isaac. All local candidates are rejected out of hand, and he dispatches his trusted emissary Eliezer to a distant land, a journey of seventeen days.[1] Only by the turn of extraordinary circumstances, divinely assisted, does the search turn up a wonderful girl, Rebecca, the true exemplar of kindness.

But along with the deal come the in-laws. To be charitable, they can be described only as decadent rogues.

---

1. *Pirkei de-Rabbi Eliezer* 16. According to the Midrash, Eliezer made the journey in three hours. Ibid.

Ḥayyei Sarah

Did not Abraham overlook the obvious! Could there have been a more suitable match for Isaac than the daughter of Abraham's trusted servant Eliezer? Eliezer is described as *"avddo,"* "his loyal servant," *"zekan beito,"* "one who is part of the household for many years," observing first-hand every nuance of kindness, and *"ha-moshel be-khol asher lo"* (lit., "one who controlled all that belonged to Abraham") (Genesis 24:2), someone who absorbed totally the essence of his master.[2] And he had a wonderful daughter. Eliezer was one of the greatest luminaries in Jewish history, meriting to enter the Garden of Eden alive.[3] Now, would not a match with Eliezer's daughter send a very clear message to the world that the exemplary student is worthy of becoming part of Abraham's family through marriage?

But when Eliezer has the impudence to suggest to Abraham that he also has an eligible daughter,[4] Abraham turns him away with a vengeance. No diplomacy, just "My son is blessed, and you are cursed, and one who is cursed cannot cleave to one who is blessed."[5]

The reason, I submit, is that our Forefather Abraham knew that he was very different from his son. Abraham, the extrovert, was imbued with visionary zeal. But Isaac was an introvert, straining and stretching

---

2. Genesis Rabbah 59:8; Yoma 28b; R. Samuel Eliezer b. Judah ha-Levi Edels (*Maharsha*, Poland, 1555–1631), *Ḥiddushei Aggadot, Yoma* 28b, s.v. *"ha-moshel"* and *"Damesek."* The Talmud at *Yoma* 28b interprets the phrase that Eliezer had control over his master's household to mean that Eliezer had dominion over the teachings of his master. The Talmud derives this interpretation from the reference to Eliezer at Genesis 15:2 as *"Damesek Eliezer,"* an acronym for *"doleh u-mashkeh,"* he draws and gives others to drink, signifying that Eliezer drew from the Torah of his master Abraham and taught others Torah.
3. *Derekh Eretz Zuta* 1.
4. *Rashi* to Genesis 24:39; Genesis Rabbah 59:9. Eliezer said to Abraham *"ulai* (perhaps) the woman will not want to follow me to this land" (Genesis 24:5) as a pretext for Abraham to tell him that Isaac could marry Eliezer's daughter if the woman whom Eliezer found refused to return with him. Eliezer's intention is alluded to at Genesis 24:39, when Eliezer recounts his conversation with Abraham to Rebecca's family, in that the word *"ulai"* is spelled without the letter *vav*. R. Zev Wolf Einhorn, *Perush Maharzu* to Genesis Rabbah 59:9, s.v. *"ulai lo soveh."*
5. *Rashi* to Genesis 24:39; Genesis Rabbah 59:9 (identifying Eliezer with a Canaanite, who was cursed by Noah).

every molecule of his being to produce the most sublime and pure sentiment toward Hashem.[6]

Isaac inaugurated *Minḥah*, the afternoon prayer.[7] He did not inaugurate *Shaḥarit*, which involves the dedication of one's first waking thoughts toward Hashem, or *Ma'ariv*, which involves directing one's thoughts to Hashem after one is finished with his daily toil, but *Minḥah*, which involves tearing oneself away from the middle of one's work. Isaac was the *olah temimah*.[8]

Now, if a woman who was raised in Abraham's household would be matched to Isaac, she would fully expect that Isaac would continue in the path of Abraham. The image that would stand in front of her would be the hero figure of Abraham, battling the whole world, the adventurous life. What a disappointment she would encounter in Isaac, who would be withdrawn, always working to perfect his communion with Hashem. He would never leave the Land of Israel.[9]

Now, because Abraham spread his wealth around, interacting with society, he evoked the sentiment of "a Prince of God is in our midst" (Genesis 23:6). But Isaac, who withdrew, engendered jealousy.[10]

Ma'aseh avot siman le-banim. It is the way that Isaac demonstrated how to handle adversity that taught the Jewish people how to survive adversity and rise above it. Would we have even retained the singular attitude toward *Eretz Yisrael* if it were not for Isaac, who never left the Land? And upon reflection, if Isaac would have married a woman who had been raised in Abraham's home, the entire personality and life experience of Jacob might have been different. How would such a woman have reacted to the crisis of a childless marriage? Would it have been in the same manner as Sarah had reacted, giving Isaac a

---

6. See *Zohar* 1:119b (associating Isaac with the attribute of *gevurah*).
7. *Berakhot* 26b (commenting on the verse "Isaac went out to converse in the fields towards evening" [Genesis 24:63]).
8. Genesis Rabbah 64:3; *Rashi* to Genesis 25:26, s.v. "*ben shishim shanah*"; *Rashi* to Genesis 26:2.
9. Isaac was an *olah temimah* and was therefore not permitted to leave the Land of Israel. Genesis Rabbah 64:3.
10. See Genesis 26:16 ("Abimelech said to Isaac, 'Go away from us, for you have become much mightier than we.'").

slavewoman – "Perhaps I will be built up through her" (Genesis 16:2)? But the consequence of this was that the child turned out to be a bad influence. Then there is no need to tread on eggshells: "Drive out this slavewoman with her son" (Genesis 21:10). This is the natural reaction of the Abrahamic type. Continuity means everything and therefore marriage to a slavewoman is a calculated risk.

But to Rebecca, this was unthinkable. The *olah temimah* cannot risk impure genetics![11] As a result, Esau is not a stepson, but a child. And a child, no matter how bad, is still a child. This necessitates a delicate balancing act between Jacob and Esau. Jacob can rise above Esau only through trickery and, as a result, Jacob becomes persecuted.

This is how we survived all the persecution of the generations because, again, *ma'aseh avot siman le-banim*. No gentle or luxurious existence was the life of Isaac or Jacob.

Now, this is perhaps the meaning of Abraham's statement to Eliezer "you are cursed." That is, at your best, you are a loyalist, par excellence. But the very quality that you are my slave stands potentially to be a curse in the marriage of my son. He must develop in a different world than I did and he needs a woman who will allow him to be an independent person and not expect a clone of me.

Besides the lesson for parents not to forget about the needs of their children in finding a match for them, there is a message for the broader collective. And that is if we ask ourselves what type of Jew evokes the sentiment of "a Prince of God is in our midst," the answer is someone in the mold of Abraham, someone who is perceived by the world community as a great benefactor of society by virtue of his achievements, such as Nobel Prize winners. But what of the saintly man, the giant of the spirit in Torah and *yir'at Shamayim*? He goes completely unnoticed, and even in our circles, he is often unappreciated!

But Eliezer regards the success of his master as a grand act of truth and kindness on the part of Hashem.[12] How can this be? I understand the kindness to the in-laws, but what is the kindness to Abraham? He is

---

11. See *Rashi* to Genesis 25:26, s.v. "*ben shishim shanah*."
12. See Genesis 24:49 ("And now, if you intend to do kindness and truth with my master, tell me; and if not, tell me, and I will turn to the left or to the right.").

the greatest personality of his time. The answer is that Eliezer realized that no matter how high the Prince of God is, if he does not stand on the foundation of the highest, most noble morality, his achievements can all go up in a puff of nuclear smoke! The continuation of *ḥesed* depends on the inner purity of fear of Heaven.

Silence in the Institution of Marriage

November 9, 1996

Our Sages extol the behavioral trait of silence. Recall R. Shimon's dictum, "All my days I have been raised among the Sages and I found nothing better for oneself than silence" (*Avot* 1:17).

R. Avigdor Miller applies this teaching to the institute of marriage. In his opinion, part of the "ten commandments" of a successful marriage is the operation of R. Yose's dictum, "Do not converse excessively with a woman" (*Avot* 1:5).[1]

His thesis requires elaboration and clarification. Silence has its place. Do not engage excessively in idle chatter, as *Midrash Shemuel*

---

1. R. Avigdor Miller (Brooklyn, 1908–2001), *Career of Happiness: True Joy in the Home* (Brooklyn, NY: Yeshiva Gedolah Bais Yisroel, 2000), 157–158; R. Avigdor Miller, "The Ten Commandments of Marriage 1," Thursday Night Audio Lecture No. 620, avail. at www.simchashachaim.com.

Silence in the Institution of Marriage

understands this.² Another aspect of excessive speech is speech that can get you in trouble! We are speaking to the person who performs acts of kindness in the most prodigious manner. "Let your house be open wide; treat the poor as members of your household" (*Avot* 1:5). Regarding this the *Tanna* says, "Do not speak too much to your wife." You will cause her to start thinking, my husband is so generous with his time and resources to total strangers. What does he do for me and our children? "*A fortiori* with regard to another man's wife [do not speak excessively]" (ibid.). Do not brag about your good deeds. Your friend's wife will think, if this is what he does for strangers, you can imagine what he does for his own family. And she starts to think about how her own husband measures up!

Another type of speech that should be avoided is speech that incites.

Our Sages offer a formula for marital bliss. In spiritual matters, the wife should defer to her husband. In mundane matters, the husband should defer to his wife.³ How then is it possible for a God-fearing couple to have any disputes? The answer is that they argue over which category a particular issue falls into.

The *Tanna* tells us, "Do not converse excessively with a woman." Do not engage in persuasive speech with your wife, trying to convince her that more and more issues fall into the category of spiritual matters. This is an abuse. *A fortiori*, if you make your pronouncements to your friend's wife, you will be wrecking someone else's marriage.

It is quite true that sometimes silence is golden, but sometimes silence is lethal and destructive. An example is in today's *sidrah*. "Rebecca raised her eyes and saw Isaac; she inclined while upon the camel" (Genesis 24:64). Commenting on this verse, the *Netziv* explains that ever since this first encounter with Isaac, Rebecca held Isaac in awe.⁴ She did not have the same relationship with Isaac as Sarah did with Abraham and thus did not challenge Isaac's impression of Esau and reveal

---

2. *Midrash Shemuel*, Avot 1:5.
3. *Bava Metzia* 59a.
4. R. Naphtali Tzvi Yehudah Berlin (*Netziv*, Russia, 1816–1893), *Ha'amek Davar*, Genesis 24:65, s.v. "*va-tikkaḥ ha-tza'if.*"

to Isaac that Esau was a *tzayid be-piv* (deceiver) (Genesis 25:28).[5] And as the *Or ha-Ḥayyim* says, commenting on the verse "you shall reprove your brother and do not bear a sin because of him" (Leviticus 19:17), one should not refrain from reproving his fellow, as his fellow might repent in response to the reproof.[6] And finally, there is the speech that bridges the generation gap and makes an eternal impact. It is when parents engage in animated Torah discussions at the Sabbath table to show their children that Torah and mitzvot are "our life and the length of our days."[7]

---

5. The phrase "*tzayid be-piv*" (lit., "trapping was in his mouth") is understood by the Midrash to refer to Esau's attempts to deceive Isaac through his speech into believing that he was righteous. For example, Esau would ask Isaac whether one is required to tithe salt or straw, creating the false impression that he was meticulous in the performance of mitzvot. *Midrash Tanḥuma, Toledot* 8.
6. *Or ha-Ḥayyim* to Leviticus 19:17.
7. Evening Prayer, Blessings of the *Shema*.

Toledot

Ma'aseh Avot Siman le-Banim

November 5, 1983

In most areas of human endeavor, pioneering effort provides the basis for steady upward advancement and progress. Not so in the spiritual realm. This was the harsh reality that Isaac faced.

The period of human history stretches over six thousand years, divided into three equal epochs: *tohu va-vohu* (nothingness); the period of Torah; and the Messianic era.[1] Abraham inaugurated the era of Torah.[2] As *Rashi* explains, the phrase "the souls that they made in Haran" (Genesis 12:5) refers to the converts that Abraham and Sarah made.[3] The elevation that was achieved in Abraham's lifetime, culminating in the recognition by the decadent society that "a Prince of God is in our

---

1. *Avodah Zarah* 9a; *Sanhedrin* 97a.
2. *Avodah Zarah* 9a.
3. *Rashi* to Genesis 12:5; *Rashi* to *Avodah Zarah* 9a, s.v. "*ella min ve-et ha-nefesh.*"

midst,"[4] was short-lived. Upon Abraham's death, all the wells that his servants had dug in his lifetime were stopped up and filled with earth by the Philistines.[5] Isaac did not inherit a plateau on which to build but rather witnessed an atavistic reversion to *tohu va-vohu*. Also, from Isaac's very birth, the world denied his link to Abraham. The scorners of the generation said that Sarah conceived through Abimelech.[6]

Then when he carried forth the banner of Abraham, disseminating Godliness in the world, Isaac met with envy and contention. He built wells. The first he called *Esek* because the herdsmen of Gerar quarreled and involved themselves with his herdsmen, saying "the water is ours" (Genesis 26:20). The second well, *Sitnah*, was even worse, generating even more enmity and harassment.[7] But then with no logic came *Reḥovot*.[8] Isaac understood that the atavistic reversion was merely eloquent testimony to the great *kedushah* of Abraham. Whenever *kedushah* departs, its opposite or mirror image fills the void, like *tumat ledah*.[9] Also, the repudiation that he faced from the decadent society was eloquent testimony to his exalted status, as "he who is greater than his fellow, his Evil Inclination is greater as well."[10]

Our Sages tell us that in the Messianic era, Hashem will slay the Evil Inclination in the presence of the righteous and the wicked. To the righteous, the Evil Inclination will appear as a towering hill. To the wicked, it will appear as a thread of hair. Both the righteous and the wicked will weep. The righteous will weep, saying, "How were we able to overcome such a towering hill?" The wicked will weep, saying, "How is it that we were unable to conquer this thread of hair?"[11]

---

4. Genesis 23:6 (declaration by the children of Heth to Abraham when Abraham negotiated the purchase of the Cave of Mahpelah).
5. Genesis 26:15.
6. *Rashi* to Genesis 25:19, s.v. "*Avraham holid et Yitzḥak*."
7. Genesis 26:21.
8. Genesis 26:22.
9. Leviticus 12:1–5; R. Shmuel Bornsztain (*Shem mi-Shemuel*, Poland, 1855–1926), *Shem mi-Shemuel: Al Seder Parshiyyot ha-Torah u-Mo'adei Kodesh*, 9th ed., vol. 3 (Jerusalem, 1992), *Tazria* (5675/April 1915), p. 223 (citing the *Kotzker Rebbe*).
10. *Sukkah* 52a.
11. Ibid.

Ma'aseh Avot Siman le-Banim

Isaac did not allow adversity to destroy him. It was rather regarded by him as evidence of his exalted status and spurred him on to great achievement. "The man became great and kept becoming greater until he was very great" (Genesis 26:13). He went full circle from "whoever hears will laugh for me" (Genesis 21:6) to "then our mouth will be filled with laughter" (Psalms 126:2).

Ma'aseh avot siman le-banim. The life experience of the Patriarchs is indicative of the further course of Jewish destiny. Isaac's life symbolizes *gerut*, continuous contention. Jacob's life represents the second part of the Egyptian bondage. "This is how I was: By day, scorching heat consumed me, and frost by night; my sleep drifted from my eyes" (Genesis 31:40).

But the Redemption will take place in the reverse order. "I will remember My covenant with Jacob, and also My covenant with Isaac, and also My covenant with Abraham will I remember, and I will remember the Land" (Leviticus 26:42).

Now, the legacy of the Redemption will be akin to servitude. The State of Israel was established out of pity and guilt that our world had for a pulverized, dehumanized slave. The allies of Israel expected nothing more than a vassal-state relationship, with servile obedience. At the same time, Israel's very existence was not taken seriously. "Whoever hears will laugh for me" (Genesis 21:6). It was met with incredulity. She could not survive amidst the twenty million Arabs.[12]

Then progress came and contention began, the arm-twisting and argumentation. And now, with suicidal attacks, it evokes *Sitnah*, more harassment.

---

12. Within hours of Israel's declaration of independence on May 14, 1948, Egypt, Syria, Trans-Jordan, Iraq, and Lebanon invaded Israel. Reginald Seigel, "Arab Nations Attack Israel," *UPI NewsTrack*, May 15, 1948. The combined population of those countries then was at least twenty million. See Department of Economic Affairs, Statistical Office of the United Nations, *Demographic Yearbook, 1949–1950* (New York, 1950), 71, 77 (estimating the population of Egypt, Syria, Jordan, and Lebanon in 1948 to be approximately 19.5 million, 3.1 million, 0.4 million, and 1.2 million, respectively; estimating the population of Iraq in 1947 to be 4.8 million).

Toledot

We are now awaiting the stage of the recognition that "a Prince of God is in our midst," a solid basis of "for from Zion will the Torah come forth, and the word of Hashem from Jerusalem" (Isaiah 2:3).

Mirmah and *Armah*: The Man *Derush* Made into a Hero

November 16, 1985

Deeply ingrained in our Tradition is the belief that Jacob, our Forefather, is the very personification of truth and integrity. "Grant truth to Jacob" (Micah 7:20). Yet, his conduct in a variety of episodes of his life seems to belie this description. His conduct often appears to border on duplicity.

Take one first glimpse into his personality, the episode of the sale of the birthright. We encounter Esau returning from a hunting expedition, famished and exhausted. He spots the pot of lentils of Jacob and craves desperately for it. The poor soul seems to be near death as he forgets all civil manners and asks Jacob to pour the contents of the pot down his throat.[1] Jacob agrees on the condition that Esau will sell his

---

1. Genesis 25:30.

Toledot

birthright to him.[2] Jacob apparently wrests something of great value from Esau, the birthright, at a bargain price!

Rather than understanding Jacob's conduct as involving even a scintilla of impropriety, our Sages staunchly defend him. Esau is the personification of the primordial snake and represents *armah*, insidious guile. Jacob, however, represents *mirmah*, the outward boundary of permissible shrewdness.[3]

Most basically, the birthright was of no value to Esau. "Esau spurned the birthright" (Genesis 25:34). He despised it even before he sold it to Jacob.[4] We can take our pick of commentaries. Ibn Ezra suggests that the birthright meant nothing to Esau because Isaac was not wealthy and the double portion of inheritance accorded to the first-born son would amount to no advantage.[5] Nahmanides objects to Ibn Ezra's pauperization of Isaac and says that before *Mattan Torah*, there was no law requiring the first-born son to receive a double portion.[6]

The *Gaon Beit ha-Levi* goes one step further. In his view, the birthright represented negative value to Esau. The tradition was that the servitude described in the Covenant between the Parts would not begin in Abraham's lifetime.[7] Now, Esau was fearful that as a descendant of

---

2. Genesis 25:31–33.
3. Expounding on the verse "your brother came with *mirmah* and took your blessing" (Genesis 27:35), *Targum Onkelos* and *Rashi* interpret "*mirmah*" to mean cleverness, indicating that Jacob acted appropriately in obtaining Isaac's blessing. In Maimonides' commentary to the Mishnah, by contrast, *armah* is understood as permissible deception and *mirmah* as impermissible deception. Maimonides, *Perush ha-Mishnayot, Temurah* 5:1. Tosafot Yom Tov explains that Maimonides' statement is limited to the use of the terms *armah* and *mirmah* by the Sages, and does not reflect the meaning of those terms as used in the Pentateuch. Thus, the term *mirmah* at Genesis 27:35 denotes permissible deception. *Tosafot Yom Tov* to Mishnah, *Temurah* 5:1.
4. *Da'at Zekenim* to Genesis 25:34.
5. Abraham b. Meir ibn Ezra (Ibn Ezra, Spain, 1089–1164), Ibn Ezra to Genesis 25:34.
6. Nahmanides to Genesis 25:34.
7. Genesis Rabbah 44:20. In the Covenant between the Parts, Abraham asked if he would be included in the Servitude. Hashem answered, "You shall come to your ancestors in peace" (Genesis 15:15), signifying that Abraham would not be included in the Servitude. See *Rashi* to Genesis 15:15, s.v. "*ve-attah tavo*" and *Siftei Ḥakhamim* to *Rashi* ad loc.

Mirmah and Armah: The Man Derush Made into a Hero

Abraham, he might be subject to servitude. He therefore had to disavow his status as a child, let alone a first-born son.[8]

What Jacob did was maneuver to pay as little as he could for something that Esau regarded as useless. But Esau could always fixate on the fact that the birthright was very valuable to Jacob. It would take shrewdness to catch him in a moment when he would not be thinking of this. The moment came when Esau was famished!

And the *Keli Yakar* posits that the stew of lentils had a special symbolic significance. It is the food of mourners. Jacob was in essence saying to Esau, "Every day, you put your life in danger when you go hunting. I might as well eat lentils now, sitting in mourning for you. Do you really think that you will outlive Isaac? Why do you need the birthright?"[9]

When we relate the sale of the birthright to modern society, we find much relevance. Collective bargaining seems to fit into the model. Labor tries to negotiate a settlement at a level above the minimum that it thinks its membership would accept. At the same time, management tries to impose a settlement on labor below the maximum that management would be willing to offer. Within the range of labor's requirements and management's maximum offer lies the permissibility of maneuvering in the form of shrewdness to strike the best bargain. The usual obligation of full disclosure that generally applies when the item of sale has an objective market value does not apply here.

But there is also the mitzvah element of *mirmah*. Jacob, as we know, was separated from his beloved son Joseph for twenty-two years. This separation, we are told, was measure for measure, as Jacob separated from his father for thirty-six years. During that time, Jacob did not fulfill the mitzvah of *kibbud av*. Now, he is not held at fault for the fourteen years that he studied in the *yeshivah* of Shem and Eber.[10]

But this is astonishing. Jacob's stay with Laban was at the insistence of both his parents. The answer is very simple. If he really valued his parents, he would not have come to the master deceiver with his

---

8. R. Yosef Dov Soloveitchik (*Beit ha-Levi*, Belarus, 1820–1892), *Beit ha-Levi al Derush u-Milei de-Aggadata, Toledot* (Jerusalem, 1985), 36–37.
9. *Keli Yakar* to Genesis 25:32.
10. *Rashi* to Genesis 37:34; *Megillah* 16b–17a.

Toledot

guard lowered. How could he strike such a deal of initiating an offer to work for seven years for Rachel and allow himself to be deceived? This is shockingly brought out by Rachel and Leah when they say "Are we not considered by him as strangers?" (Genesis 31:15). When a man marries off a daughter, he gives her a dowry, but our father sold us into marriage.

The mitzvah element of *mirmah* becomes apparent when we realize that we are living in a fateful period. Our President embarks on a summit meeting.[11] May Hashem give him a good measure of *mirmah*. And it is now time for both parties to the nuclear disarmament talks to dangle in front of each other a stew of lentils, as if to say that if we do not negotiate in good faith, we may, God forbid, both end up eating the food of mourners.

The Middle East peace process is now also entering a new stage, with Peres' initiative to Jordan.[12] May Hashem give him *mirmah* too.

But let us merit to witness the influence of Jacob in the fullest form, that is, the man of a "boundless heritage."[13] Let us see the elevation of insidious guile to the form of permissible shrewdness. And let the sparkle of justice shine as well.

There is also the sparkle of justice in the *mirmah*. How? According to Tradition, Jacob bought the birthright on the day that our Patriarch Abraham died.[14] The whole family was thrown into a depression.

---

11. Bernard Gwertzman, "Toward the Summit: Gauging the Outcome; On Road to the Summit: A Parallel to '55," *New York Times*, November 15, 1985, A12.
12. Elaine Sciolino, "Peres, at the U.N., Proposed to Visit Jordan for Talks," *New York Times*, October 22, 1985, A1.
13. See *Shabbat* 118a–b. The Talmud records that one who delights in the Sabbath is given an "unbounded heritage." This statement is based on Isaiah 58:13–14, "If you restrain your foot because it is the Sabbath; refrain from accomplishing your own needs on My holy day; if you proclaim the Sabbath 'a delight' and the holy [day] of Hashem 'honored,'… I will provide you with the heritage of your Forefather Jacob, for the mouth of Hashem has spoken." These verses do not refer to Abraham, whom Hashem told "Arise, walk about the land through its length and breadth" (Genesis 13:17), nor Isaac, to whom Hashem said "for to you and your offspring will I give all these lands" (Genesis 26:3), but rather Jacob, of whom it is written "You shall spread out powerfully westward, eastward, northward, and southward" (Genesis 28:14). *Shabbat* 118b.
14. *Rashi* to Genesis 25:30, s.v. *"min ha-adom ha-adom."*

Mirmah and Armah: The Man Derush Made into a Hero

But the wicked Esau goes to the field and returns exhausted. Exhausted from what? He committed five heinous crimes on that day. He killed a man, he violated a betrothed woman, he denied Hashem, he denied the Resurrection of the Dead, and he despised the birthright.[15] It was in this condition that Jacob observed him on that fateful day. Jacob chose that day to pursue the birthright because he rose up in righteous indignation. How could a wicked person be the spiritual leader of a family destined for spiritual greatness?

---

15. *Bava Batra* 16b; *Keli Yakar* to Genesis 25:34.

Abimelech

December 6, 1986

For the past several weeks, Ronald Reagan has been under furious attack for his conduct of foreign affairs. Revelations have emerged that huge secret arms shipments were sent to Iran and a portion of the proceeds was diverted to the Contras in Central America.[1] Many people began to detect shades of Richard Nixon in the President as he reacted by vigorously defending the apparent illegal arms sales to a terrorist State and at the same time claiming that he had no knowledge at all of the diversion of the funds to the Contras.[2]

Instead of shades of Richard Nixon, what we are seeing here, I would suggest, is the reincarnation of the ancient Head of State Abimelech, who had dealings with our Patriarchs. He too vacillated between protestation of innocence and righteous defense of his policies. When

---

1. Bernard Weinraub, "Iran Payment Found Diverted to Contras; Reagan Security Adviser and Aide Are Out," *New York Times*, November 26, 1986, A1.
2. Richard J. Meislin, "President Invites Inquiry Counsel; Poll Rating Dives; 46% Approve Reagan's Work, Down 21 Points," *New York Times*, December 2, 1986, A1.

Abraham confronts him with the matter of the stolen wells, he responds, "I do not know who did this thing; furthermore, you have never told me, and moreover, I myself have heard nothing of it except for today" (Genesis 21:26).

As the *Malbim* understands this, Abimelech was saying, "I did not order this act or hear the complaint from you. I just heard it now from you. And finally, I did not even hear this through a rumor."[3]

This same Abimelech who would claim complete ignorance of what was going on was also capable of rising up in righteous indignation to defend his actions. And hence, when he had designs on Sarah, he made what he thought were sufficient inquiries and determined from Abraham, Sarah, and even the camel driver that Sarah was Abraham's sister![4] "In the innocence of my heart and integrity of my hands have I done this" (Genesis 20:5).

Abimelech's investigative fervor was not, however, a function of state-of-the-art management science at the time. No. Information gathering was merely a manipulative tool that he used to confer a veneer of legitimacy on the policy that he was promoting at the time. The quality of the information he sought hence depended upon his secret agenda.

When Abimelech's objective was to take Sarah to his palace, he sufficed himself with a superficial inquiry. Why do I say superficial? Because, as our Sages point out, when a stranger enters town, what constitutes proper inquiry? It is to ask the stranger if he has lodging, if he is in need of food.[5] But the Philistines seemed to be obsessed with one, and only one, thing: What is the relationship of Sarah to Abraham? Everyone in the party was asked this. Quite an improper question! Does this question not invite a self-protective response, that Abraham should say that she is his sister? If Abimelech and his cohorts were really God-fearing people, they would have understood that the statement "she is my sister" was merely a defensive tactic and would have sought to correct the impropriety of their questions. They would have probed deeper to find

---

3. See *Malbim, Ha-Torah ve-ha-Mitzvah*, Genesis 20:5.
4. R. Jacob Culi, *Me-Am Lo'ez*, Genesis 20:5, trans. R. Shemuel Yerushalmi, *Yalkut Me-Am Lo'ez: Sefer Bereshit* (Jerusalem: Mossad Yad Ezra, 1968), 401.
5. *Bava Kamma* 92a.

Toledot

out if in fact Sarah was not also married to Abraham, and was his sister only in a *lomdishe* sense, as *Rashi* points out.[6]

Now, in Abimelech's encounter with Isaac, his objective was to eject him from his kingdom and humiliate him at the same time, to turn the tables on the righteous man and make him feel that his continued residence in the land constituted a threat to the moral climate of society. Abimelech is consumed with jealousy, so he desperately looks for a pretext. He marshals all the intelligence-gathering apparatus of the State. It rivals the KGB and the CIA combined. "Abimelech King of the Philistines gazed down through the window" (Genesis 26:8). He penetrates to the very core of Isaac's private existence. In modern parlance, he wires him and videotapes his every move. Abimelech wants to be sure that when he confronts Isaac, it will be devastating, and Isaac will be completely disarmed. Then, with righteous indignation, Abimelech says, "She is your wife! How could you say, 'She is my sister'?" (Genesis 26:9).

He also waits for a time after "his days there lengthened" (Genesis 26:8). Abimelech has a file on Abraham. He is very attentive to precedent. He knows that Abraham excused himself from the pretext that Sarah is his sister because Abraham told him that any time that he and his wife move to a particular area without explicit instruction from Hashem, he is afraid that he is in danger, so he says that Sarah is his sister.[7] So Abimelech waits until Isaac stays a long time in his land to embarrass him for his unnecessary ploy, as if to say, "You resided with us a long time. You know that the people here are God-fearing, so why did you use a pretext? You, Isaac, are a danger to the moral climate of society." It is necessary to promulgate the law "whoever touches this man or his wife shall surely be put to death" (Genesis 26:11). This was not intended for Isaac's benefit, but instead to harm him. It meant that

---

6. *Rashi* to Genesis 20:12. Abraham said that Sarah was his sister because she was the daughter of Abraham's father Terah. Genesis 20:12. In fact, Sarah was the daughter of Terah's son, Haran, and thus was Abraham's niece rather than Abraham's half-sister. *Sanhedrin* 58b; *Rashi* to Genesis 11:29 (noting that Iscah, the daughter of Haran, is Sarah). *Rashi* explains that the term "sister" could be used to refer to a niece because grandchildren are akin to children. See *Yevamot* 62b. Sarah was thus considered a daughter of Terah.
7. See *Rashi* to Genesis 20:13.

no one may do business with Isaac; perchance he would stumble in the sin of *eshet ish*.[8]

Abimelech thought that this would be sufficient to drive Isaac out of the land, but the devious plan failed. Isaac was in any event successful. The only avenue left for Abimelech was the crude, direct approach – "Go away from us because you have become much mightier than we" (Genesis 26:16).

Most often, significance is attached to a name. Abimelech is the Head of State, but he is not a King. He is only the father (*av*) of a king (*melekh*).[9] Abimelech was paternalistic. He identifies himself with the Kingdom. Whatever was good for him was good for the Kingdom. And what he found personally objectionable was no good for the Kingdom.

We are now seeing in the Reagan Presidency the excesses of the glorification of the self-interest motive. The excess is being transferred to the public sector. The President is bending and even violating the laws of the land to fit into his idealism and vision.

We need to replace Abimelech with *avrekh*, the title given to Joseph by Pharaoh.[10] According to R. Yose, *avrekh* is derived from the root word *birkayim*, "knees," signifying that everyone will bend their knees to him in submission to his authority.[11] Yes, the President should have ideals and vision. But he should be the first citizen of the land, always obedient to the laws of the land. He should also have something else that the spirit of Joseph gave us, that is, "he was the provider to all the people of the land" (Genesis 42:6), the great sentimentalist reflecting the heart of the nation. When this comes to the fore, we will indeed be replacing "there is but no fear of God in this place" (Genesis 20:11) with Joseph's proclamation, "I fear God" (Genesis 42:18).

---

8. R. Naphtali Tzvi Yehudah Berlin, *Ha'amek Davar*, Genesis 26:11.
9. Cf. *Rashi* to Genesis 41:43, s.v. "*avrekh*" (defining "*av*" as a patron of the king); *Rashbam* to Genesis 41:43, s.v. "*avrekh*" (defining "*av*" as an officer of a king).
10. Genesis 41:43.
11. *Rashi* to Genesis 41:43, s.v. "*avrekh*"; *Sifrei*, Deuteronomy 1.

Blending *Keshet* with *Ḥerev*

December 2, 1989

In today's portion, we encounter for the first time a joint prayer effort between a husband and a wife. "Isaac entreated Hashem opposite his wife" (Genesis 25:21). Our Sages understand this to mean that Isaac prayed on one side of the room and Rebecca on the other.[1] And Hashem listened to Isaac's prayer rather than to Rebecca's.[2]

This was not a competition of sorts, with Hashem preferring Isaac's prayer over Rebecca's. Rather, Rebecca's prayer was the one for self-fulfillment; she yearned for the opportunity for motherhood. But Isaac was confident that he would have children. There was, after all, a divine promise to Abraham that "through Isaac will offspring be considered yours" (Genesis 21:12). His prayer was mainly that Rebecca should be the mother of his children.[3]

---

1. *Rashi* to Genesis 25:21, s.v. "*le-nokhaḥ ishto.*"
2. Ibid., s.v. "*va-ye'etar lo.*"
3. *Sforno* to Genesis 25:21.

Blending Keshet with Ḥerev

What we have here is an instance of the principle that if one seeks mercy by praying for his friend, and he himself needs the same thing for which is he praying, the one who prays is answered first.[4] It is the manifestation of the *ḥesed* element in *tefillah*. One who is imbued with a *ḥesed* drive in *tefillah* desperately wants his prayer to be answered and therefore trembles from the statement of our Sages that "one's prayer is not accepted unless he takes his heart into his hands."[5] And so he is driven to attach himself to a *tzibbur* because "the Holy One, Blessed is He, does not despise the prayer of the congregation,"[6] even if wicked people are found in the congregation.

Today, women do heroic acts in *tefillah*, just as in biblical times. Specifically, many take the maximalist view of their obligation rather than a minimalist view. Nahmanides understands *tefillah* as a supplication for divine mercy, "*raḥamei*," that vitiates the whole concept of *mitzvat aseh she-ha-zeman gerama*, a "positive time-bound commandment," and that women are obligated in *tefillah* just as are men.[7] But Maimonides takes a minimalist view; they are obligated only on a biblical level.[8] On a biblical level, *tefillah* has no structure, no set time, and no *nusaḥ*. On a rabbinic level, it is however a *mitzvat aseh she-ha-zeman gerama*. The *Magen Avraham* says that women can fulfill their obligation with *modeh ani* and *taḥanunim*,[9] but *nashim tzidkaniyyot* reject this, and pray three times a day. So, too, the *pesak* of R. Yaakov is not relied upon and women with small children pray.[10]

But simultaneous today with this extraordinary conduct is the movement of woman prayer groups. Motivated by a desire for a meaningful prayer experience, these women are very meticulous not to violate Halakhah in their prayer group and fully know that they should not call it a *minyan*.

---

4. *Bava Kamma* 92a; *Rashi* to Genesis 21:1, s.v. "*ve-Hashem pakad et Sarah.*"
5. *Ta'anit* 8a.
6. *Berakhot* 8a.
7. Nahmanides, *Hasaggot* to Maimonides, *Sefer ha-Mitzvot, mitzvat aseh* no. 5.
8. Maimonides, *Mishneh Torah, Tefillah* 1:1–2.
9. See R. Abraham Abele b. Hayyim ha-Levi Gombiner (*Magen Avraham*, Poland, ca. 1637–1682), *Magen Avraham* to *Shulḥan Arukh, Oraḥ Ḥayyim* 106:2.
10. R. Yaakov Kamenetsky, *Emet le-Yaakov: Al Arba'at Ḥelkei ha-Tur ve-ha-Shulḥan Arukh*, commentary on *Shulḥan Arukh, Oraḥ Ḥayyim* 106:2, ed. R. Daniel Yehudah Neustadt (Cleveland: Makhon Emet le-Yaakov, 2000), 59n131.

Toledot

Much has been said with regard to the issue.[11] Permit me to suggest that the phenomenon should be analyzed in terms of whether it promotes or detracts from the element of *ḥesed* in *tefillah*. At once, it is *keshet* at the expense of *ḥerev*.[12] But it is also perhaps misdirected energy because women who are imbued with the inspiration to carry their prayer obligation beyond the position of the *Magen Avraham* should follow the lead of Hannah on the fateful day on *yom tov* when her prayer for a child was answered.[13]

What is so special about Hannah's prayer? R. Soloveitchik says that she must have prayed hundreds of times for a child. The answer is that when Elkanah asks her, "Why are you weeping?... Why are you morose? Am I not better to you than ten children?" (I Samuel 1:8), it is then when Hannah realizes how utterly alone she is and she enunciates *tefillah* in her heart.[14]

There is a paradox in communal prayer. On the one hand, it is a *ḥerev*. We become aware that we are part of a congregation and it is powerful – "The Holy One, Blessed is He, does not despise the prayer of the congregation." On the other hand, we realize that we are not in control. We cannot manipulate or maneuver. We are totally dependent

---

11. See, e.g., R. J. David Bleich, "Religious Experience? tefillah be-tzibbur?," *Sh'ma: A Journal of Jewish Responsibility* (October 18, 1985): 146–149. For additional sources published after the date of this sermon, see, e.g., R. Avraham Weiss, *Women at Prayer: A Halakhic Analysis of Women's Prayer Groups*, 3rd ed. (Hoboken, NJ: Ktav, 2001); R. Mayer Twersky, "Halakhic Values and Halakhic Decisions: Rav Soloveitchik's Pesak Regarding Women's Prayer Groups," *Tradition: A Journal of Orthodox Thought* 32, no. 3 (Spring 1998): 5–18; Aryeh A. Frimer and Dov I. Frimer, "Women's Prayer Services – Theory and Practice," *Tradition: A Journal of Orthodox Thought* 32, no. 2 (Winter 1998): 5–118.
12. Jacob told Joseph, "I have given you Shekhem, one portion more than your brothers, which I took from the hand of the Amorite with my sword (*ḥerev*) and with my bow (*keshet*)" (Genesis 48:22). The "sword" refers to *tefillah*, and the "bow" refers to supplication. *Bava Batra* 123a; *Midrash Tanḥuma, Be-Shallaḥ* 9. Cf. *Rashi* to Genesis 48:22, s.v. "*be-ḥarbbi u-ve-kashti*."
13. See I Samuel 1:12–18. Hannah's prayer was answered on Rosh Ha-Shanah. *Rosh ha-Shanah* 11a.
14. See R. Shalom Carmy, "Destiny, Freedom, and the Logic of Petition," *Tradition: A Journal of Orthodox Thought* 24, no. 2 (Winter 1989): 27 (discussing comment of R. Joseph B. Soloveitchik).

on Hashem. For Hashem to answer a prayer is a *ḥesed*. So the source of power must be purified with a sense of awe and trembling that we stand in front of Hashem. The sword must be brandished with the bow. And it is here where the influence of righteous women can make an enormous impact, improving the decorum and sense of awe in communal prayer amidst "he stood in one corner and prayed, and she stood in that corner and prayed." [15]

---

15. *Rashi* to Genesis 25:21, s.v. "*le-nokhaḥ ishto*."

Stealing the Blessings – Revisited

November 17, 1990

One of the most troubling passages in the entire Torah is the conspiracy of Rebecca and Jacob to secure Isaac's blessing for Jacob, depriving Esau of his due.[1] How do we reconcile the duplicity and deception with the high moral principles of the Torah? Moreover, for people of the spirit, such as Rebecca and Jacob, would not a morsel of material goods be sufficient support? Why then all the maneuvering to secure a material blessing?

The moral outrage is somewhat reduced in consideration that the driving force behind the deception, Rebecca, was merely acting upon the prophecy that she was given of "the elder shall serve the younger" (Genesis 25:23). Also, when Isaac realized that he was duped, far from regretting what he had done, he pronounces *"gam barukh yihiyeh"* (he [i.e., Jacob] shall remain blessed) (Genesis 27:33). Finally, Jacob carries

---

1. Genesis 27:5–17.

out every element of his mother's instructions. He brings the two kid goats, he wears the *bigdei ḥamudot*,[2] he wears the hair on his neck and his hands. But the obvious element to ensure that the masquerade would succeed, to disguise his voice, he did not do because it would go against his grain. "Perhaps my father will feel me" (Genesis 27:12). He secretly wanted to be discovered.[3]

It is in this context of mitigation that we should examine the *Malbim's* thesis regarding the difference of opinion between Isaac and Rebecca. Isaac knew very well that his two sons were very different. Esau is described as "one who knows hunting, a man of the field," and Jacob as an *"ish tam, yoshev ohalim,"* "a wholesome man, abiding in tents" (Genesis 25:27). Now, Isaac believed that material striving in itself is not meritorious. Only if it could be subordinated to a higher calling would it be worthy. Isaac loved his son Esau and wanted to confer merit upon him. By giving him a blessing of material wealth, he would enable Esau to support Jacob, and Jacob could devote himself to spiritual matters. It would be a partnership in the finest sense of Issachar and Zebulun.[4]

But Rebecca knew better. She was more perceptive than Isaac and knew the truth. Esau was a scoundrel and could not be trusted! She therefore set out to ensure that Jacob would have the material blessing so that he could support himself.

---

2. Rebecca clothed Jacob in Esau's *bigdei ḥamudot*. Genesis 27:15. Onkelos translates this phrase as "clean garments." *Targum Onkelos* ad loc. An alternative interpretation is that *"ḥamudot"* means "coveted," signifying that Esau coveted these garments and stole them from Nimrod. *Rashi* ad loc., s.v. *"ha-ḥamudot."* According to the Midrash, these garments had originally belonged to Adam. Genesis Rabbah 65:16.
3. *Makkot* 24a. In his commentary to *Makkot* 24a, R. Zevi Hirsch Chajes (*Maharatz Ḥayot*, Austria, 1805–1855) explains that the use of the word *"ulai"* (perhaps) instead of the word *"pen"* (lest) denotes that the speaker desires that the contingency will occur. For example, when Abraham sent his servant Eliezer to find a wife for Isaac, Eliezer said to Abraham *"ulai* (perhaps) the woman will not want to follow me to this land" (Genesis 24:5). Eliezer had a daughter of his own whom he wished Isaac would marry, so he used the term *"ulai."* Similarly, Jacob's use of the term *"ulai"* indicates that Jacob secretly desired that Isaac would discover the truth.
4. Malbim, *Ha-Torah ve-ha-Mitzvah*, Genesis 27:5.

Toledot

But we must realize, as the *Malbim* himself points out, that much more than material blessing was at stake.[5] Isaac's blessing included "be a lord to your kinsmen" (Genesis 27:29). This was the blessing of control and sovereignty over the material world. Yes, in a primitive society, the *yoshev ohalim* can very easily suffice himself with a morsel. To achieve this, he could pick berries and go hunting. If Esau would not begrudge him even this morsel, Jacob could act just as Isaac did when Abimelech became jealous and said, "Go away from us because you have become much mightier than we" (Genesis 26:16). Isaac just withdrew.

But what about the future, when the entire world would be inhabited and each country would establish a government? The government would set the rules for the legal environment for the entire society. Government at its worst will enslave and brutalize, dehumanize the masses to serve the ruling class. At best, government is a democracy. But here again, at least it is only *mirmah* because logrolling, pork barreling, and coalitions of minorities can always subvert the will of the majority. Take note of Arrow's Impossibility Theorem.[6] As far as a futuristic society is concerned, even if the *yoshev ohalim* is content with his morsel, willing to tolerate brutal discrimination to earn his livelihood, the bearer of the tradition of being "a light unto the nations"[7] cannot live in an immoral society. Government will devise policies on issues such as abortion, euthanasia, criminal justice, and tariffs. For each, Halakhah has a particular viewpoint! No, it would be nothing less than shirking a sacred responsibility to turn over the reins of government to Esau.

The elements needed for Jacob's success are spelled out. *Ma'aseh avot siman le-banim*. If you want to enter the political arena, first you

---

5. Ibid.
6. The theorem states that when voters have three or more distinct alternatives, no rank-order voting system can convert the ranked preferences of individuals into a community-wide ranking while also satisfying a specific set of criteria of fairness. The criteria are: (1) if every voter prefers alternative X over alternative Y, the community prefers X over Y; (2) if every voter's preference between X and Y remains the same, the community's preference between X and Y will also remain the same; and (3) no single voter possess the power to determine the community's preference, i.e., "non-dictatorship." See Kenneth J. Arrow, "A Difficulty in the Concept of Social Welfare," *Journal of Political Economy* 58, no. 4 (August 1950): 328–346.
7. Isaiah 42:6, 49:6.

Stealing the Blessings – Revisited

must come with an agenda for social wellbeing according to the Torah, not just as a pressure group for very selective programs of Jewish interest. It must be two goat-kids, one a *pesaḥ* and the other a *ḥagigah*. The *pesaḥ* symbolizes communal wellbeing, and the *ḥagigah* symbolizes enhancement of that wellbeing.[8]

Next, it is not enough to espouse higher moral principles. No, our proposals must have form and concreteness, symbolized in the *bigdei ḥamudot*. We must also display prudence with respect to the consequences and ramifications of what we *say* and what we *do* – Rebecca placed the skins of the goat-kids on Jacob's *neck* and *arms*.[9] But the program itself must be pure, unadulterated, uncompromising, in the form of "the voice is the voice of Jacob" (Genesis 27:22).

We all know that Jacob's experiences reflected the principle of *middah ke-neged middah*. Because he deceived Isaac, he was deceived by Laban[10] and by his own children.[11]

Permit me to suggest that this was not a punishment but rather the hard knocks of education. If you, Jacob, want to enter the political realm, if you want to take on the challenge of the reins of government, you must be rid of every trace of naïveté and innocence, every trace of *temimut*. The *tam* is overwhelmed in the political arena by *mirmah*. And therefore, as an educational device, to put you on guard for every moment that you may be betrayed, you must be made to feel acutely what it is like to be betrayed on a very personal and intimate level, on the level of a wife and child, so you can develop the character trait of being the guardian of Jewish values and programs.

And this type of training is indeed necessary because the ultimate role for the Jewish people, as the angel pronounced at the *Akedah*, is

---

8. See *Pesaḥim* 70a. The *korban ḥagigah* is eaten before the *korban pesaḥ* to enable the *korban pesaḥ* to be eaten *al ha-sova* (while satiated). Eating the *korban pesaḥ* while satiated is an enhancement of the basic mitzvah of eating the *korban pesaḥ*.
9. Genesis 27:16.
10. See Genesis Rabbah 70:19.
11. *Zohar* 1:185b; R. Jacob Culi, *Me-Am Lo'ez*, Genesis 37:34, trans. R. Shemuel Yerushalmi, *Yalkut Me-Am Lo'ez: Sefer Bereshit* (Jerusalem: Mossad Yad Ezra, 1968), 678; Louis Ginzberg, ed., *Ginzei Schechter*, vol. 1 (New York: Beit Midrash ha-Rabbanim ba-Amerika, 1928), 140; *Ba'al ha-Turim* to Genesis 27:35, s.v. "*be-mirmah*."

Toledot

"your offspring shall inherit the gate of its enemies" (Genesis 22:17). This does not mean military conquest. No! The "gate" is where the Elders sit.[12] It means that ultimately all the legal systems of the world will recognize the sovereignty of the Torah in shaping the legal environment.[13]

This same sentiment was expressed in a pure moment of faith by the decadent society itself. At that climactic moment when Laban agreed to Rebecca's match with Isaac, he blessed his sister that she should be the bearer of the children whose descendants will "inherit the gate of their enemies" (Genesis 24:60).

---

12. See Deuteronomy 22:15, 25:7; *Ibn Ezra* to Lamentations 5:14; *Rashi* to Job 29:7.
13. See R. Samson Raphael Hirsch, Genesis 22:17.

Va-Yetze

The House of Joseph a Flame

December 1, 1984

In our way of thinking, good counteracts evil. Our Patriarch Jacob had a grander concept. Greatness overwhelms mediocrity. As his family grew and the building blocks of the Jewish nation came into being, each child represented a different attribute of goodness. Yet Jacob did not have the confidence to face Esau until Joseph was born. Why? Because Joseph is the flame that would consume Esau. "The house of Jacob will be fire, the house of Joseph a flame, and the house of Esau for straw" (Obadiah 1:18).[1]

I would submit that if we analyze the contrast that our Sages draw between Joseph and Esau, we find that the intention of our Sages is not to point out Esau's deficiencies, but rather to tear into his virtue.[2] Though our Sages depict Esau as a miscreant, first-class, he is extolled

---

1. *Rashi* to Genesis 30:25; *Bava Batra* 123b.
2. See *Yalkut Shimoni*, Judges 5:51.

for his great virtue; he excelled in *kibbud av ve-em*. Moreover, he is regarded as a model to emulate with respect to this mitzvah.[3] But his preeminence in this respect, we submit, is significantly eroded when we consider two aspects of the comparison that our Sages make between Joseph and Esau.

First, whereas Esau strove to kill his brother in his mother's womb and as a result, Rebecca was injured and could not bear another child,[4] Joseph sought to protect his mother by stationing himself in front of her when Esau confronted Jacob.[5] In addition, whereas Esau was not forgiving to Jacob, Joseph was generous and forgiving to his brothers. We may very well ask, if someone really cares about his parents, does he not know that sibling strife simply tears them up?

Second, whereas Esau said, "May the days of mourning for my father draw near" (Genesis 27:41), Joseph said, "Is my father still alive?" (Genesis 45:3). If someone really cares for his parents, he does not regard attendance to them as a burden.

Why do our Sages negate Esau's *kibbud av ve-em*? Well, if someone is raised by two perfectly righteous parents, something must rub off on him. But why did Esau adopt the mitzvah of honoring one's parents as his mitzvah more than any other mitzvah, and excelling in it to the point of becoming a model for others? Could it possibly have been a mitzvah that he perceived fit into his grasping, avaricious nature? The answer is that the more he would give, the more he could demand of his sons. He could be an absolute tyrant in the name of religion.

Well, Esau was a fickle man.[6] From such an attitude toward honoring one's parents, only deterioration through the generations could be expected. This practice of honoring one's parents would, with the passage of time, produce a monstrous nation of Amalek, Aggag, Haman.

Joseph was the true *sitno shel Esav*, the true "antagonist of Esau,"[7] because Joseph was concerned with making investments to improve the

---

3. Deuteronomy Rabbah 1:15.
4. *Yalkut Shimoni*, Judges 5:51; *Midrash Aggadah*, Genesis 26.
5. *Rashi* to Genesis 33:7.
6. Ruth Rabbah, *pesiḥata* 3; *Yalkut Shimoni*, Proverbs 21:8 ¶ 959.
7. *Rashi* to Genesis 30:25; *Bava Batra* 123b.

quality of life. Joseph, as our Sages tell us, believed in the Resurrection of the Dead, whereas Esau did not.[8] Esau was concerned only with the here and now, how to give in order to take. But Joseph was concerned with the future, with improving the quality of life for the future.

On the surface, Joseph may appear to have been deficient in fulfilling the obligation of honoring one's parents as he did not send a message to his father when he had a chance to do so,[9] and he treated his brothers very harshly.[10] But, as R. Samson Raphael Hirsch points out, he did this because what would he accomplish by revealing himself as a potentate?[11] This is not the relationship that he wanted, that of a potentate and his subjects. He wanted to re-enter the inner family circle, to re-establish the intimate relationship of old, with all its tenderness and love. To do this, he had to show his brothers that he was not only the *mashbir* (provider), but the *shallit* (ruler) too.[12] He had the absolute power to destroy them but would not do so. Instead, he exercised the greatest restraint. This would rid them of their erroneous attitude toward him. At the same time, he would have to see that the brothers rid themselves of their erroneous attitude toward him, that they would not sacrifice another son of Rachel, Benjamin, to satisfy their needs.

When Joseph revealed himself to his brothers, the quality of life was elevated. When we have the character of Joseph, we can expect a very bright future, the future of perfectionism and the Messiah.

Ma'aseh avot siman le-banim. The most invidious threat to us from Esau is perhaps not his evil but his good. We face the danger of accepting the good attributes of Esau and regarding them as absolute, unqualified good.

Freedom, for example, is one of the great virtues of American society. America has fought wars for it and to help foreign people to self-determination. This is all very fine, but if we adopt freedom as absolute

---

8. *Yalkut Shimoni*, Judges 5:51.
9. See Nahmanides to Genesis 42:9, s.v. "*va-yizkor Yosef et ha-ḥalamot asher ḥalem lahem*."
10. Genesis 42:7–27.
11. R. Samson Raphael Hirsch, Genesis 42:9.
12. Genesis 42:6 ("Now Joseph – he was the viceroy over the land. He was the provider to all the people of the land.").

good, we deal a crushing blow to our Tradition. We question everything, and we have a right, freedom of choice, to determine our own destiny. This could, God forbid, lead us to reject much of the Torah as it does not fit into our way of thinking.

The Mispronounced Name

November 28, 1987

Perhaps few things rankle man more than having his name mispronounced every time that he is introduced. And so it was the lot of Issachar. When a tender child, uninitiated in the arcane world of *dikdduk*, encounters Issachar for the first time in the printed medium, he undoubtedly tries to pronounce both *shin*s, which is the wrong pronunciation.[1] And when Issachar is read the first time it appears in the Torah, learned men hotly debate whether the name is pronounced with or without the second *shin*.[2]

---

1. *Da'at Zekenim* to Genesis 30:18; R. Jedidiah Solomon b. Abraham Norzi (*Minḥat Shai*, Mantua, ca. 1560–1626), *Minḥat Shai* to Genesis 30:18.
2. One reason for the pronunciation of only one *shin* in the name Issachar is that Issachar gave one *shin* to his son Yov to change his name to Yashuv when he discovered that Yov was the name of an idol. See *Da'at Zekenim* to Genesis 30:18; R. Hezekiah b. Manoah (*Ḥizkuni*, France, 13th cent.), *Ḥizkuni* to Numbers 26:24; R. Jacob Koppel b. Aaron Sasslower (Volhynia, 17th cent.), *Naḥalat Yaakov*, s.v. "*Inyan Keri'at Shem Yissakhar ba-Torah*." Based on that reason, one custom is to pronounce both *shin*s in the name of Issachar only until *Parashat Pinḥas*,

Va-Yetze

What did Issachar do to deserve this? Issachar's mission is presented to us by the Torah in very graphic terms. Issachar is described as a *ḥamar garem*, a "bony beast of burden."[3] He physically enervates himself, pushing himself to the very limits of his abilities. And he appreciates time. "He saw tranquility that it was good, and the land that it was pleasant" (Genesis 49:15). Time is used to monomaniacally pursue his goal of Torah scholarship. And he is very successful. His Tribe is recognized as *yod'ei vinah la-ittim*, "with understanding for the times" (I Chronicles 12:33).

Now, the man who is thrusting toward greatness may occasionally tread on someone's foot or ruffle someone's delicate feelings. So it behooves Issachar to look at himself and ask, Who am I? Why do we not preserve the second *shin*? What is the answer? As the Ḥatam Sofer puts it, the exchange of Jacob for the *duda'im* is a *kalon* (disgrace) for Rachel. Pronouncing the second *shin* would therefore constitute being *mitkabbed be-kalon shel ḥavero*, elevating oneself through the degradation of one's fellow.[4]

For Issachar, the challenge is to delineate the boundaries of assertive self-fulfillment and sensitivity to another's feelings in the process of pursuing one's self-fulfillment.

Does the prohibition against elevating oneself through the degradation of one's fellow prohibit us from competing? I dare say no! All who enter the arena of competition, such as in professional schools and the job market, know that failure is possible and fully accept the

---

Numbers 26:24, where the name of Issachar's son is recorded as Yoshuv, and subsequently to pronounce only one *shin*. *Naḥalat Yaakov*, ad loc. Another custom is to pronounce both *shins* only the first time Issachar is read in the Torah, at Genesis 30:18, and to pronounce only one *shin* in all subsequent portions of the Torah. R. Moses Sofer (Ḥatam Sofer, Hungary, 1762–1839), *Torat Mosheh, Va-Yetze*. For a discussion of the various customs in pronouncing the name of Issachar, see R. Shlomo Adler, "Keri'at Shem Yissachar ba-Torah," *Ha-Ma'ayan* 7 (Hebrew) (Jerusalem, 1967): 19–20.

3. Genesis 49:14.
4. Ḥatam Sofer, *Torat Mosheh, Va-Yetze*. According to the Ḥatam Sofer, one *shin* represents Leah's statement to Jacob, "*sakhor sekhartikha*" (lit., "I have hired you"), signifying Rachel's exchange of Jacob for the *duda'im* (Genesis 30:16), and the other *shin* represents Leah's statement "God has granted me my reward (*sekhari*) because I gave my maidservant to my husband" (Genesis 30:18). See also *Da'at Zekenim* to Genesis 30:18. One who elevates himself at the expense of another's degradation is said not to have a portion in the World to Come. Jerusalem Talmud, *Ḥagigah* 10a.

eventuality, so entry in the competitive marketplace implies forgiveness for any degradation. And if entrants are not prepared for the competition, they bring the degradation upon themselves.

Let's move to the world of advertising. Magnifying the attractiveness of one's product by pointing out the defects of a rival's product may constitute *mitkabbed be-kalon shel ḥavero*, but many caveats can be identified. One, suppose inadequacy of the competitor's product is conceded. What is claimed is merely superiority. This is not *mitkabbed be-kalon shel ḥavero*. There is no *kalon*. Then, what if the rival's product is selling at the same or a higher price? This too is a matter of "you shall not stand aside as your fellow's blood is shed" (Leviticus 19:16). And what of the defensive tactic and the preemptive strike of *mitkabbed be-kalon* when the legal environment permits this conduct?[5]

There are clear-cut examples of this conduct in other areas, such as the book reviewer who ostensibly is assessing an author's scholarship, but uses the occasion as a springboard to demonstrate his own erudition and, by contrast, the shallowness of the author. Take note also of the financier who gloated that he pulled out of the stock market at the peak while everyone else drowned in losses, "Too late!" *Mitkabbed be-kalon shel ḥavero*.

If Issachar is challenged to provide guideposts for Zebulun, he is even more challenged to provide guideposts for himself, i.e., guideposts for the field of Torah scholarship, for it is here that we hear echoes of R. Tarfon, "Woe is to me that I made use of the crown of the Torah."[6] We must be very concerned not to disgrace the honor of the Torah.

---

5. See R. Aaron Levine, *Case Studies in Jewish Business Ethics* (Hoboken, NJ: Ktav, 2000), 63–65.
6. *Nedarim* 62a. The Talmud records that R. Tarfon was eating figs in a field after most of the trimming knives had been put away. Although R. Tarfon was permitted to eat the figs under the circumstances, the owner of the field seized R. Tarfon upon discovering him eating the figs. The owner then placed R. Tarfon in a sack and took him to drown him in the river. To save himself, R. Tarfon wailed, "Woe to Tarfon that this man will kill you." When the owner realized the identity and stature of whom he had seized, he fled. R. Abbahu then notes that R. Tarfon was pained the rest of his life that he had used the crown of the Torah to save himself.

Va-Yetze

But, if Issachar would take the trouble to look at himself and discover the origin of the pronunciation of only one *shin*, he would find something very surprising. The name represents the correcting of a side-effect of someone else's initiative. What was the scenario that earned for Leah the reward of the birth of Issachar? It all began when Rachel saw that Leah had given birth to four children and she to none. What could she do? "Give me children – otherwise I am dead" (Genesis 30:1).

A creative solution was found by Rachel. Rachel would give her maidservant Bilhah to Jacob and raise the child.[7] But Leah was monitoring the events and saw that her maidservant Zilpah was jealous, so she gave Zilpah to Jacob also.[8] But this was for the sake of Heaven, because Leah did this only to still the jealousy of Zilpah, and not for herself.[9]

Yes, the man who everyone recognizes and admires may begin to believe that he has a monopoly over ideas because if an idea is good, he would have thought of it himself! To really achieve his identity, Issachar must be sensitive to the initiatives of other people, graciously participating in them and monitoring their progress. When this happens, we begin to read both *shins* in the form of *yesh sakhar le-pe'ulasekh*, "there is reward for your accomplishment" (Jeremiah 31:15).[10] This refers to Rachel's heroic action of doing the opposite of being *mitkabbed be-kalon shel ḥavero* by degrading herself for the purpose of elevating her sister. Rachel gave her sister the passwords that she had agreed upon with Jacob so that her sister should not be disgraced.[11] Then we achieve the connection with the Redemption in the form of *ve-shavu vanim le-gevulam*, "your children will return to their border" (Jeremiah 31:16).

---

7. R. Naphtali Tzvi Yehudah Berlin, *Ha'amek Davar*, Genesis 30:3, s.v. "*ve-seled al birkai*" (cross-referencing *Ha'amak Davar*, Genesis 16:2, s.v. "*ulai ibbaneh mimmennah*").
8. R. Berlin, *Ha'amek Davar*, Genesis 30:9.
9. Ibid.
10. *Rashi* to Jeremiah 31:14, s.v. "*Raḥel mevakah al baneha*." See also *Or ha-Ḥayyim* to Numbers 26:23. The *Or ha-Ḥayyim* notes that Issachar's name signifies reward for learning Torah. The *gematria* of *yesh* is 310. The Mishnah records that in the future, Hashem will grant a righteous person an inheritance of 310 worlds. Mishnah, *Uktzin* 3:12. The Mishnah is based on Proverbs 8:21, "I have [*yesh*] what to bequeath to those who love me, and I shall fill their storehouses."
11. *Rashi* to Genesis 29:25; *Megillah* 13b; *Bava Batra* 123a.

Thanksgiving

November 20, 1993

The story is told of a young accountant of insular *yeshivish* background. He was informed by a friend in the first year of his practice that his non-Jewish clients would expect a warm New Year's greeting. Torn between the desire to accommodate his non-Jewish clientele and the guilt of showing recognition to their Christian New Year, an inspiration hit him. He would wish them "happy new fiscal year."

This week, American society will be celebrating Thanksgiving. As religious Jews, it behooves us to evaluate whether participation in this holiday violates *be-ḥukkoteihem lo telekhu*, "do not follow their traditions" (Leviticus 18:3).

The mainstream understanding of the prohibition of *be-ḥukkoteihem lo telekhu* is not to follow a custom rooted in idolatrous practice. R. Nissim b. Reuben Gerondi opines that if a particular custom has no logic to it, it is a *ḥok*.[1] Then, it probably has its origin in idolatrous

---

1. R. Nissim b. Reuben Gerondi (*Ran*, Spain, 1320–1376), *Ḥiddushei ha-Ran, Sanhedrin* 52b, s.v. "*ve-rabbanan keivan de-khesiv sayyaf.*"

practice. R. Joseph Colon b. Solomon Trabotto adds that if the custom has no logic to it, following it constitutes conforming to the gentiles and is prohibited.[2] Also, if the practice departs from our standards of modesty and humility, it should not be followed.[3]

On the basis of these views, celebration of Thanksgiving seems to be a safe matter. It does not have any roots in idolatry and has a beautiful logic to it. Governor Bradford decreed the first Thanksgiving as a festival in 1623 to give praise to God for getting the Pilgrims through the bitter winter and all the attendant difficulties.[4] President George Washington declared it a national holiday in 1789 and emphasized that all religious denominations should spend the day in prayer and thanksgiving.[5]

But the *Gra* says that the relevant criterion is whether the custom would possibly emerge within the framework of Jewish values and tradition.[6] With respect to Thanksgiving, I would say, yes, this criterion is met. "Four are required to give thanks" (*Berakhot* 54b). One of them is a person who is released from prison.[7] For the length of the Diaspora, the Jewish people have been in prison, subject to systematic discrimination, persecution, pogroms, and genocide. So surely we owe thanksgiving to Hashem for placing us in a country that guarantees religious freedom.

I was in Washington, DC, recently in the Kesher Israel Congregation. Prominently displayed in the synagogue was a letter written by President Bush to the Jewish community. The letter congratulates the Jewish community on their *eruv*. In the letter, President Bush said that

---

2. R. Joseph Colon b. Solomon Trabotto (*Maharik*, Italy, ca. 1420–1480), *She'elot u-Teshuvot ha-Maharik, shoresh* 88. See also *Rema* to *Yoreh De'ah* 178:1 (citing *Maharik*).
3. Ibid.
4. Ralph Linton and Adelin Linton, *We Gather Together: The Story of Thanksgiving* (New York: Henry Schuman, 1949), 72.
5. James D. Richardson, ed., *A Compilation of the Messages and Papers of the Presidents, 1789–1897*, vol. 1 (Washington, DC, Government Printing Office, 1898), 64.
6. R. Elijah b. Solomon Zalman, *Be'ur ha-Gra* to *Shulḥan Arukh, Yoreh De'ah* 178:1, n. 7.
7. The other three categories of people who are required to give thanks for being saved are: (1) one who sails the seas; (2) one who travels in the desert; and (3) a sick person who is healed. *Berakhot* 54b. The four categories are alluded to in Psalms 107. See *Rashi* to Psalms 107:4, 107:10, 107:17; *Radak* to Psalms 107:1; Ibn Ezra to Psalms 107:2.

the secular authorities openly protect the Jews and allow them religious freedom. He quotes the *Ḥatam Sofer* in the letter.[8]

I hear a parallel of the words of the *rav ha-ḥovel*, "How can you sleep so soundly? Arise! Call to your God!" (Jonah 1:6). We hear the voice of *Ḥovot ha-Levavot* that *hakkarat ha-tov* is a very delicate sensitivity,[9] and we must do something dramatic and concrete to reinforce this feeling, to raise the national consciousness to this sentiment.

But I also hear the voice of Leah, our mother, pleading that we give a Jewish flavor to the sentiment, that we emphasize the future as well as the past. "This time let me gratefully praise Hashem" (Genesis 29:35).[10] As the *Torah Temimah* notes, the Torah records that Leah ceased giving birth after she said "this time let me gratefully praise Hashem" because she limited her praise to "this time" and did not pray then also about the future.[11]

And let me leave you with a thought that I say as both serious and light. If Thanksgiving is a vehicle to promote *hakkarat ha-tov*, then

---

8. President George H. W. Bush, Letter to Congregation Kesher Israel (1990). The portion of the letter quoting from the *Ḥatam Sofer* states:

    Indeed, there is a long tradition linking the establishment of *eruvim* with the secular authorities in the great political centers where Jewish communities have lived. In the words of a response of Rabbi Moses Sofer [*She'elot u-Teshuvot ha-Ḥatam Sofer, Oraḥ Ḥayyim*, no. 99.]: "Blessed the Lord, God of Israel, who has inclined the hearts of kings, rulers, and officers – under whose sovereign jurisdiction we, the Jewish people find protection – to grant permission to us to keep our faith in general, and specifically to establish *eruvim* in their thoroughfares, even on streets where the most important members of the government themselves live… in this city, there are places where we need to install a number of objects in order to create an *eruv* and we have not hidden our work, rather, it is publicized and open to all without doubt and permission has been granted."

9. R. Bahya b. Joseph ibn Paquda (Spain, 11th cent.), *Ḥovot ha-Levavot, Sha'ar Avodat ha-Elokim*.

10. The Mishnah states that when one gives thanks for the past, he should also cry out for the future. Mishnah, *Berakhot* 9:4; *Berakhot* 54a.

11. R. Baruch ha-Levi Epstein (*Torah Temimah*, Belarus, 1860–1941), *Barukh She-Amar: Le-Tefillot ha-Ḥol* (Tel Aviv: Am Olam, 1965), 186. See also R. Jacob b. Asher (*Tur*, Spain, 1270–1343), *Perush ha-Tur al ha-Torah le-Rav Yaakov ben Ha-Rosh* (Jerusalem: Feldheim, 2006), Genesis 29:35; R. Kalonymus Kalman ha-Levi Epstein (Poland, ca. 1753–1825), *Ma'or va-Shemesh* (Brooklyn, NY: Imrei Shefer, 2008), *Va-Yetze*, 150–151 (citing R. Jacob Isaac Horowitz [*Ha-Ḥozeh mi-Lublin*, Poland, ca. 1745–1815]).

it need not be produced only by means of turkey, cranberry sauce, and pumpkin pie. I believe this is in essence a *ḥok*. It is conforming to "*minhag* America." I would suggest that for the Jewish Thanksgiving, the hostess should offer a choice in the menu. Perhaps there should be a choice between *cholent* and turkey. Then, if we choose turkey, it is not because we are following *minhag* America but rather it is solely because we like turkey. Nothing wrong with that!

Rachel Weeps for Her Children

December 9, 2000

The Oral Law on today's *sidrah* records the most noble act of human self-sacrifice performed in the entire human history. The facts are familiar. In response to Laban's question, "What should be your wages?," Jacob responds, "I want your daughter in marriage." He formulates his marriage proposal in what has become for all future generations the idiom for the clearest and most precise terms, "I will work for you for seven years, for Rachel, your younger daughter" (Genesis 29:18).[1] After working seven years for Rachel, on the day of the wedding, Laban switches Leah for Rachel. Rachel is not only silent but gives Leah the passwords so that Leah should not be disgraced.[2]

What an act of self-sacrifice. When Manasseh brought an idol into the Sanctuary, Hashem made a decree to, God forbid, destroy the

---

1. See Genesis Rabbah 70:17; *Rashi* to Genesis 29:18, s.v. "*be-Raḥel bit'kha ha-ketannah*."
2. *Rashi* to Genesis 29:25; *Megillah* 13b; *Bava Batra* 123a.

Va-Yetze

Temple permanently. The entreaties of the Patriarchs were to no avail until "Rachel weeps for her children" (Jeremiah 31:14).[3]

But what of Leah's conduct? How does she allow herself to be part of the duplicity and deprive Rachel of her due?

A full appreciation of Rachel's righteousness and Laban's duplicity will put Leah's conduct in a much more favorable light.

Let's first take Rachel's conduct. Our Sages praise her for her *tzeniut*. When she first met Jacob, she wanted to marry him but told him that her father would not let it go through and would insist that he marry Leah. So then Rachel and Jacob made up passwords. Now, if Rachel had not been so modest, she would have told Laban that he should not try to interfere with her marriage and pull a switch because she made up passwords with Jacob. If she would have done so, she would have stopped Laban in his tracks. But she was a *tzanuah* and could not bring herself to take action to draw attention to herself.[4]

Now, Jacob sent gifts to Rachel the whole seven years. He sent them to Laban to give to Rachel, but Laban gave them instead to Leah.[5] Because Rachel was a *tzanuah*, she made no issue out of this either and apparently did not realize the danger this involved in making Leah think that she was the bride.

Imagine Laban sending out an invitation to everyone in town inviting them to the Haran Hilton for the wedding of Rachel to Jacob, and at the wedding he makes a switch. How could Leah go along with this?

It did not happen that way. Rachel's modesty allowed Laban to practice his craft of connivery. Only three people had first-hand knowledge of Jacob's marriage proposal to Rachel: Jacob, Rachel, and Laban. It was the best-kept secret in Haran. All three told no one of it, but for different reasons. Rachel and Jacob were motivated by *tzeniut*, while Laban intended to pull off his connivery. Laban tells everyone in Haran that Jacob's arrival blessed the well water and they experienced prosperity.

---

3. *Rashi* to Jeremiah 31:14; *Radak* to Jeremiah 31:14, s.v. "*ki einennu*"; *Eikhah Rabbah, pesiḥta* 24.
4. *Megillah* 13b.
5. *Midrash Tanḥuma, Va-Yetze* 6.

"Do you want him to leave?" he asks them. "No," they reply. "I hear that he wants to marry my younger daughter, but I think I can maneuver him to marry my older daughter, Leah." "Do what you need to do," they say. He then takes pledges from them to guarantee their silence.[6]

At the wedding, Rachel was shocked and sheepishly asks her father, "What of Jacob's explicit stipulation that he would work for 'Rachel, your younger daughter' (Genesis 29:18)?" Laban says, "I never agreed to it. I answered, 'It is better that I give her to you than that I give her to another man; remain with me' (Genesis 29:19)." I don't want you to work. I'll give my daughter to you without working. I'll even support you in *kollel*. Remain with me. All conditions now become null and void.[7] Rachel, how can you be so noble when Jacob, after all, made an overly generous proposal because he knew that the proposal to marry the younger daughter was unethical? He tried to compensate with an offer of seven years of work. Rachel, in the moment of truth, painful as it was for her, realized that Laban had outsmarted Jacob. And so, she felt that Leah was not taking what was hers. So she did something cosmic and gave Leah the passwords.[8]

What our Sages are telling us is that compassion is a great attribute, but it is magnified a hundred-fold if it accompanied by *tzeniut*. *Tzeniut* not only magnifies one's own righteousness, but transforms the moral climate as well. Yes, it opens the floodgates for the wicked to ply their deceptions, but it also changes the reality for everyone. Leah's yearning was legitimate and she was not guilty of *hassagat gevul*. Rachel's *tzeniut* actually changed Jewish history. Who knows if the righteous woman Leah would have accepted Rachel's offer had Rachel not been a *tzanuah*.

"Rachel weeps for her children" (Jeremiah 31:14), for all her children, because she is the mother of Israel.

---

6. Genesis Rabbah 70:19.
7. *Malbim, Ha-Torah ve-ha-Mitzvah*, Genesis 29:19.
8. *Rashi* to Genesis 29:25; *Megillah* 13b; *Bava Batra* 123a.

The Exchange between Rachel and Leah

(Undated)

To satisfy a whim, a capricious person will often do something that, in time, will be regretted severely. And such is our judgment with respect to Rachel's offer to her sister Leah. Rachel apparently made a foolish mistake of grave proportions, offering to temporarily exchange Jacob for accepting the *duda'im* (wild flowers) of Leah's son, Reuben.

Yet, when the Sages scrutinized this transaction, in all its implications and profundity, they made the following assessment: Both parties to the transaction gained and lost. For Leah's part, she gained two more sons, Issachar and Zebulun, and the privilege to be buried with Jacob in the Cave of Makhpelah, but lost the *dudai'm*. As for Rachel, she lost the possibility to bear an additional two sons as well as her place in the Cave of Makhpelah, but she gained the *duda'im*.[1]

---

1. Genesis Rabbah 72:3.

The Exchange between Rachel and Leah

Is this assessment that the *duda'im* represented a gain for Rachel and a loss for Leah not utterly astonishing? How can the fleeting pleasures of the moment be reckoned as anything of any value against the eternity of bearing tribes for the Jewish people and the privilege of being buried in the Cave of Makhpelah? Would the Sages assess that Esau's stew of lentils represented any value in the sale of the birthright?

But what we are seeing here is the unfolding of the story of the heroics of Jacob's sons. In the story of Reuben, "Reuben went out in the days of the wheat harvest" (Genesis 30:14), we are seeing a four-year old child re-creating the drama of two thousand years earlier, the drama of the tragic fall of man from the sin of the Tree of Knowledge. What was the setting of that sin? Man and woman were surrounded by permissible matter and only one tree was prohibited, and they could not resist temptation.

But the four-year old boy leaves his home, a home of poverty, by choice, as Jacob had asked of Hashem only for "bread to eat and clothes to wear" (Genesis 28:20), and a home kept that way by the machinations of a stingy grandfather, Laban.[2] The deprived child is exposed to the world beyond the supervision of his parents for the first time. He is surrounded by the opportunity for theft. Who will know the difference, young lad? Why don't you fill your stomach with all the delicacies of the field?

But no! "The righteous do not stretch out their hands to robbery."[3] But there is the permissible also, the wild flowers. Those you can grab and enjoy to your heart's content. But no, he denies himself this pleasure to preserve the flowers for his mother, to make a gesture of his eternal indebtedness to her. He owes her everything.

---

2. See *Midrash Lekaḥ Tov*, Genesis 31:15. Whenever Laban would see a beautiful object in his daughters' home, he would take it.
3. *Sanhedrin* 99b. See also *Sotah* 12a; *Ḥullin* 91a. The Torah records that Reuben went out "in the day of the wheat harvest," to praise Reuben. Although it was a time when the farmers did not mind if one took a few stalks of wheat, Reuben did not take any wheat but only from what was ownerless. *Rashi* to Genesis 30:14, s.v. "*bi-yimei ketzir ḥittim.*"

Va-Yetze

What we are witnessing is not a Manasseh. The scorner saw a trivial story not worthy of recording.[4] Quite to the contrary, we see the greatness of the sons of Jacob. We see nothing less than the transformation of the Tree of Knowledge into the Tree of Life. The pristine act justifies creation itself. It represents immortality for the parents. When Reuben brings the delicious flowers home, Rachel immediately understands their significance, and although she is not his natural mother, she identifies with the grand triumph of character that the flowers represented. The *naḥat* of Leah is also her *naḥat* for, after all, who made possible Reuben's birth? Was it not Rachel? Her selfless devotion to her sister, aiding the perpetration of Laban's fraud, made possible Leah's marriage to Jacob.

She is saying to Leah, "Your *naḥat* is my *naḥat*. Therefore, please give me some of your son's *duda'im*."

But Leah does not see the enormous significance of the *duda'im*. She sees only flowers. She sees only an attempt by Rachel to steal away Jacob by the beautiful fragrance of the flowers. In a curt reply, Leah says, "Was your taking my husband insignificant?" (Genesis 30:15).

Now we can see the gains and losses of the transaction. Leah gained children and burial in the Cave of Makhpelah for she demonstrated her singular commitment to Jacob and her own children – the ideal mother. But Rachel, though she lost this, got something significantly more. She merited to be the mother of all Jewish children. "Rachel weeps for her children" (Jeremiah 31:14), which means that she cries and weeps over all Jewish children.

Now the dialogue between Leah and Rachel is not irrelevant today because it is not merely a dialogue between two rival wives, a circumstance impossible today. Every mother is faced with two extraordinary challenges. One is the challenge of raising her children who are helpless, directionless, and underdeveloped, identifying with their every triumph and every sorrow. But then there is the second challenge for a mother, when *"al ken ya'azov"* takes place.[5] Here, will the mother still

---

4. *Sanhedrin* 99b. The reference in the text is to Manasseh, King of Judah, who reigned for fifty-five years. See II Kings 21:1-18.
5. Genesis 2:24 (*"Al ken ya'azov* (therefore a man shall leave) his father and mother and cling to his wife, and they shall become one flesh.").

identify with the pain and suffering of her children and with the ecstasy of their triumphs too?

Well, she does this when she can paraphrase Leah's statement with a cry to her daughter-in-law, "Is it not enough that you have taken my son, but also my son's *duda'im*?" And to her son, she says, "Is it not enough that you have transferred your loyalty, energy, devotion, and affection to your wife, but you bask in her glory instead of mine?" Behind every great man is a great woman. This is the wife, not the mother.

Since Rachel felt so acutely the triumph of Reuben although she was not his natural mother, she would have been the ideal mother-in-law, though she would get nothing in return and would not even be associated with the greatness of Reuben by the world. Nevertheless, she shared in the triumph. She hence was not only the mother of her own children, she was the mother of a married son and daughter-in-law, which is the microcosm of the Jewish nation.

Va-Yishlaḥ

Let's Set the Record Straight

November 19, 1983

"Esau ran toward him, embraced him, fell upon his neck, and kissed him; then they wept" (Genesis 33:4). When a lifetime of bitter enmity is suddenly mollified into tears of genuine affection, the result is nothing less than magic. How did Jacob accomplish this reconciliation? He was a pragmatic man and prepared himself with three approaches in his dealings with his brother Esau: a gift, prayer, and war.[1]

But I would submit that Jacob did not intend to merely go through the motions in his approach. Rather, he fortified the gift approach with prayer, beseeching the Al-Mighty for assistance, and with war, i.e., being prepared to wage a battle within himself, to destroy himself, his pride and self-worth, so that the appeasement approach would succeed.

Persistence attests to a person's sincerity. Jacob is at first rebuffed but does not change course. Even after he defeats Esau's guardian angel,

---

1. *Rashi* to Genesis 32:9, s.v. *"ve-hayah ha-maḥaneh."*

Va-Yishlaḥ

he still does not change course. The stunning triumph does not infuse him with an arrogant confidence of invincibility and lead him to conclude that if he can defeat the guardian angel of Esau, he certainly can defeat the mortal Esau.

Extending the olive branch from a position of strength again proves sincerity. And it is sincerity that opens the channels of communication and touches the man of perfidy. Sincerity gives credibility to Jacob's original message "I have acquired oxen and donkeys" (Genesis 32:6). As the *Gur Aryeh* explains, Jacob tells Esau: I did not take anything that was your due.[2] If Father meant to bless you, I could not take away your blessing. And the blessing "be a lord to your kinsmen" (Genesis 27:29) was not fulfilled in me. I did not receive any additional blessings other than through my own effort. My intention was merely to latch on to the spiritual aspect of the blessing "may God give you of the dew of the heavens and of the fatness of the earth, and abundant grain and wine" (Genesis 27:28). The dew is Torah, the fatness of the earth is Mishnah, abundant grain is Talmud, and wine is Midrash.[3] My aspirations in the spiritual domain in no way detract from you.

The man of truth makes his impact on society not by a grand act of embarrassment of the evil man – by confronting the evil man and proving in his presence the internal inconsistency of his actions and the evil of his ways – but by directing society toward goodness, sincerity, and purity. This has a mellifluous effect. The man of truth must carefully choose his battles. Some battles must be passed up to win the war. He must resist the temptation to expose evil when this will divert society from the main thrust, pointing to purity and integrity.

An episode in the life of Jacob poignantly illustrates this point. Laban cried out, "Why have you fled so stealthily?" (Genesis 31:27). You deprive me of caressing my daughters and grandchildren. But Rachel and Leah had just earlier testified to Jacob, "Are we not considered by him as strangers?" (Genesis 31:15). Would this not be an ideal opportunity for sweet revenge? But responding here would divert Laban's emotional energy to a peripheral issue. This temptation had to be resisted.

---

2. R. Judah Loew b. Bezalel (*Maharal*, Prague, ca. 1525–1609), *Gur Aryeh, Va-Yishlaḥ*.
3. Genesis Rabbah 66:3.

For twenty years, Jacob had been trying to make his integrity objectively discernable to Laban. Now he must concentrate all his energies to make this point and not lose the focus. Now is no time to set Laban straight on the matter; the battle must be passed up. And indeed, Jacob responds to Laban by saying, "Because I was afraid, for I thought perhaps you might steal your daughters from me" (Genesis 31:31). You are such a possessive father. I feared that you would not allow me to take your daughters. Jacob did all this to prevent the diversion of Laban's emotional energy from the main issue.

When Jacob had to choose a son who was most like himself, a son who would be the King, he chose Judah. He passed over Reuben. He said of Reuben, "Water-like impetuosity – you cannot be foremost" (Genesis 49:4). You are impetuous, like a stream, and therefore you cannot get the "extras," the Royalty or Priesthood.

But Reuben, the son who disturbed the location of his father's bed,[4] showed the deepest contrition. He donned sackcloth and fasted.[5] Our Sages tell us, "Whoever maintains that Reuben sinned is mistaken."[6]

Now, did Jacob hold a grudge against Reuben? Certainly not. But because Reuben was by nature an impetuous person, he was not fit to rule.[7] The impetuous man with the purest motives may not be able to resist the temptation to expose evil as he confronts it. He could very well choose the wrong battles, win the battles, but lose the war. Judah demonstrated that he had the objectivity to select himself as the battlefield and promote the cause of justice and integrity, even with the consequence of destroying himself.

Observing the contemporary scene, we find an infatuation and obsession of the media with sensationalism, with exposing evil. But directing society's attention toward integrity and goodness seems to be taking a back seat. People who champion peace and other good callings often choose the wrong battle and hence divert society from the main thrust.

---

4. Genesis 35:22, *Rashi* ad loc.
5. *Rashi* to Genesis 37:29.
6. *Shabbat* 55b.
7. R. Samuel b. Meir (*Rashbam*, France, ca. 1080–1174), *Rashbam* to Genesis 49:3.

Va-Yishlaḥ

Jacob politely refuses to associate himself intimately with Esau. He opts not to accompany Esau to Seir.[8] Jacob realizes that truth will never have an uplifting effect on society unless the whole nation of Israel consists of Jacobs; one Jacob alone cannot lift up society. The development of a nation of Jacobs will be a process culminating in the coming of the Messiah. "Saviors will ascend Mount Zion to judge the Mountain of Esau, and the kingdom will be Hashem's" (Obadiah 1:21). "Hashem will be King over all the land; on that day Hashem will be One and His Name will be One" (Zechariah 14:9).

---

8. Genesis 33:14–15.

Preemptive War

December 8, 1984

In recent times, we have had to live through a nightmarish chapter in the history of the Jewish State, the episode of preemptive war, negotiations with terrorists, and the massacre of a civilian population. Many quarters have been quick to condemn the Jewish State on all accounts. These issues have, however, a halakhic morality. It behooves us to look for halakhic guidance in these matters.

The first preemptive strike of the Jewish people, the first negotiation with terrorists, and the first massacre of a civilian population all occurred in the incident of Shekhem. This story is particularly instructive because although Jacob registered his vehemence and outrage here, it was only on practical rather than moralistic grounds.

Now, was not the massacre and looting of the town of Shekhem a dark moment in Jewish history? Did it not represent a momentary lapse of Jacob's family, doing the work of Esau?

Maimonides, however, insists that the entire town of Shekhem deserved death because one of the Seven Noahide Laws is *dinim*. Maimonides understands this to mean a societal obligation to enforce the other six Noahide Laws by setting up a judicial system and enforcement procedure. The people of Shekhem failed to bring their Prince to trial. They failed to revolt against him for his heinous crime. This, in Maimonides' view, constituted a capital offense for the town of Shekhem.[1]

Quite a harsh judgment. What would Maimonides say today with regard to State-sponsored terrorism emanating from Libya, Iran, and Iraq? Yes, these countries are totalitarian states, but official terrorism cannot be tolerated by the population. Such toleration might constitute a capital offense.

Well, Maimonides' severe judgment is resoundingly disputed by Nahmanides. The latter posits that the requirement to set up a judicial system is an obligation of *dinim* and so is the obligation to legislate a whole code for civil conduct, a whole code for interpersonal relations. But *dinim* is a *mitzvat aseh,* and a Noahide does not incur the death penalty for failure to perform a *mitzvat aseh.* Nahmanides understands that the people of Shekhem deserved death because of their past decadence of being idol worshippers, and this represented the opportune time to mete out their punishment of death.[2]

The *Or ha-Ḥayyim,* disputing the two great luminaries Maimonides and Nahmanides, avers that the crime of the people of Shekhem was their complicity in the kidnapping of Dinah.[3] There is a *midrash* to support this, which the *Or ha-Ḥayyim* does not mention. This is the *midrash* that says that Shekhem asked his people to consort with him to entice Dinah, the modest girl and pure soul, to leave her tent. So he set up a circus outside her tent. The curious girl came out to watch and was snatched away by Shekhem.[4]

Following the *Or ha-Ḥayyim,* we can perhaps understand Simeon and Levi's plan of demanding that all the men of Shekhem circumcise themselves as a precondition to intermingling to determine the solidarity of the people of Shekhem with their leader. If they would submit to bodily pain for the sake of pleasing their leader, this would constitute

---

1. *Mishneh Torah, Melakhim* 9:14.
2. Nahmanides to Genesis 34:13.
3. *Or ha-Ḥayyim* to Genesis 34:25–26.
4. *Pirkei de-Rabbi Eliezer* 38.

an act of blind loyalty and would prove that they were co-conspirators, for it is indeed amazing how a people could submit themselves in this manner if not out of blind loyalty to their leader.[5]

Now, if blind loyalty is a strong indication of solidarity with a heinous crime, it could be enough of an indication that the town had the halakhic status of a *rodef*, and *ha-ba le-horgekha, hashkem ve-horgo*, "if someone comes to kill you, kill him first."[6] This principle applies even when the mortal threat can be avoided by submission to the demands of the enemy.[7]

Let us apply this today and concede that, yes, a civilized population can be intimidated and forced to go along with the unreasonableness of its leaders. But I would ask, is there not a limit to what someone submits to under intimidation? If a civilized population allows itself to be a shield for a terrorist group, turning homes into a battlefield and allowing the emplacement in its midst of the most sophisticated artillery and missiles,[8] and bringing mortal damage, not only to its military, but to its civilians and the destruction of its country, we may well ask, does this not constitute an act of blind devotion and loyalty, giving the civilian population the status of *rodefim*?

There is yet another lesson in the episode of Shekhem relevant to dealing with terrorists. As the great commentator R. Samson Raphael Hirsch points out, the princes of Mohar and Matan came to Jacob to ask for Dinah's hand in marriage while Shekhem was still holding Dinah captive.[9] It represents a pro forma means of giving an appearance of legitimacy to a vile and base act. Civility and reasonableness while Dinah

---

5. R. Samson Raphael Hirsch, Genesis 34:19–24.
6. Numbers Rabbah 21:4; *Midrash Tanḥuma, Pinḥas* 3; *Sanhedrin* 72a.
7. R. Yeruham Yehudah Leib Perlman (*Ha-Gadol mi-Minsk*, Minsk, 1835–1896), *Or Gadol: Teshuvot u-Ketavim* (Jerusalem, Makhon Yerushalyim, 1987), *siman* 1, p. 16; R. Shlomo Zalman Auerbach (Israel, 1910–1995), "*Beirurim u-Sefeikot be-Inyan Piku'aḥ Nefesh Doḥeh Shabbat*," Moriah: Yarḥon Torani le-Divrei Halakhah u-Maḥshavah, *shanah* 3:3–4 (Sivan/Tamuz 5731/1971): 22.
8. See Jillian Becker, *The PLO: The Rise and Fall of the Palestine Liberation Organization* (New York: St. Martin's Press, 1984), 204 ("PLO bases were defended with trenches and gun emplacements, many on top of schools and hospitals, and in the midst of houses.").
9. R. Hirsch, Genesis 34:8–12.

is still held captive and after commission of the vile deed cannot wipe it out or extenuate it in any way. What remains is still "he committed an outrage in Israel… such a thing may not be done!" (Genesis 34:7).

Terrorists may make what appear to be reasonable demands. But if they are holding hostages while making these demands, we cannot give them any countenance. "He committed an outrage in Israel… such a thing may not be done!" (Genesis 34:7).

We pray and we work as hard as we can to make sure that our leaders will have the prudence, with *da'at Torah*, to know when to exercise power. As Jacob said on his deathbed, "Accursed is their rage for it is intense, and their wrath for it is harsh; I will separate them within Jacob, and I will disperse them in Israel" (Genesis 49:7). The anger should be spread out, never allowed to coalesce with an intensity in a single area. The anger should also be invested only in the "Israel" elements of society, the elevated element, so that zealotry is given its proper perspective.

If a war, an urgent war, should, God forbid, break out, it would be a *milḥemet mitzvah* and we must defend our brothers, as Jacob did. "And as for me, I have given you Shekhem – one portion more than your brothers, which I took from the hand of the Amorite with my sword and with my bow" (Genesis 48:22). He took out his sword, ready to lay down his life in defense of his children. Once war breaks out, whether it was just or not, no dissension can be tolerated within our ranks. Unity is what the Jewish people need.

The Jewish Cold War Ethic

November 30, 1985

The recent Reagan–Gorbachev summit has raised hopes for an easing of tension between East and West and has generated expectations of significant progress in disarmament talks.[1]

The armaments race has been described by experts as the MAD strategy, Mutual Assured Destruction. That approach entails a belief on our part, as well as the Soviets', that our military prowess will never effectively deter our enemy unless we can respond to a first-strike attack, regardless of its magnitude, with a retaliatory strike that will truly annihilate our enemy. If each side feels that way, there is no advantage to a first strike. Such a situation hence represents a perfect balance of power. Ironically, the closer we move toward this direction, the more each side

---

1. See Judith Miller, "Summit Finale: Western Allies Seen Encouraged; Reagan Report Pleases NATO Leaders," *New York Times*, November 22, 1985, A13; Anthony Lewis, "There Should Be Hope," Abroad at Home, *New York Times*, November 14, 1985, A35.

Va-Yishlaḥ

will be tempted to initiate a preemptive strike, eliminating the threat permanently.[2]

Is there any alternative to MAD? We believe that our Torah is timeless and its insights into human nature provide the basis for our approach to any problem, be it personal, social, or international in scope. The relationship of Jacob to Esau, as recorded in today's portion, is perhaps the first instance of a Cold War. Jacob's reaction to this represents Judaism's Cold War ethic.

First and foremost, Esau represents a threat to Jacob. Rebecca had said of him, "Behold, your brother Esau is consoling himself regarding you to kill you" (Genesis 27:42). What type of threat he represented now is not known, but he must be dealt with. Rather than taking Jacob's flattery of Esau, referring to Esau as "my lord,"[3] and the prodigious gift that he sent him, with all the attention attached, as reflecting the fawning, cringing side of Jacob, it should be taken as the minimum force available to Jacob to diffuse or neutralize the threat of Esau.

Yes! "*Ha-ba le-horgekha, hashkem ve-horgo.*" If one launches an attack, anticipate his attack with an attack of your own![4] But you may only neutralize the threat with minimum force. If one could save himself by injuring one of the limbs of the attacker rather than by killing him, the killing is not justified.[5]

Now, one who cherishes human life, who believes in the redeemability of every human being, would be willing to pay a high price to diffuse a threat without resort to violence and bloodshed. Indeed, Jacob was willing to pay a high price in the form of flattery, compliments, and generous expenditure of his resources, all to avoid violence and possible death. "Jacob became very frightened, and it distressed him" (Genesis 32:8). He feared death for himself. But he also feared that he might harm Esau.[6]

---

2. See Joseph Grieco, G. John Ikenberry and Michael Mastanduno, *Introduction to International Relations: Enduring Questions & Contemporary Perspectives* (London: Palgrave, 2015), 213–222; Robert Jervis, "Mutual Assured Destruction," *Foreign Policy* 133 (November–December 2002): 40–42.
3. Genesis 33:8, 33:13–15.
4. Numbers Rabbah 21:4; *Midrash Tanḥuma, Pinḥas* 3; *Sanhedrin* 72a.
5. *Sanhedrin* 74a.
6. *Rashi* to Genesis 32:8; *Siftei Ḥakhamim* to *Rashi* ad loc., n. 8.

The Jewish Cold War Ethic

But Jacob is not naïve. He goes by the motto *"khabdehu ve-ḥashdehu,"* honor your enemy but be suspicious of him.[7] Hence, Jacob uses the bluff tactic. Even after Esau reconciles with him and kisses him, Jacob suspects him. He accepts Esau's offer to accompany him to Seir, but darts away when he reaches Sukkot, in accordance with the talmudic explanation that if you are traveling with a stranger and you fear that he will harm you, tell him that your destination is far off. He will think that he has plenty of time to harm you. In the meantime, you can slip away.[8] Also, Jacob used the threat of a secret weapon. He made the veiled threat "I have acquired oxen and donkeys" (Genesis 32:6) – I have the Messiah the son of Joseph and the Messiah the son of David.[9] He also flatters Esau – "As I have seen your face, which is like seeing the face of a divine being" (Genesis 33:10) – but wrapped in the flattery is the message that Jacob has powerful allies, angels.

It is therefore with great expectation that we look to the progress from the cultural exchange and increased trade relationships. But realistically, we will not get far with appeasement. History teaches us a poignant lesson. Chamberlain's appeasement of Hitler only brought the world into a Holocaust![10] We must look to an approach that will make a profound impact on people's attitudes. This we can find by focusing on one verse when Esau is active and Jacob passive – "Esau ran toward him, embraced him, fell upon his neck, and kissed him; then they wept" (Genesis 33:4). Here, Esau is profoundly affected. It is a known, given

---

7. *Kallah Rabbati* 9 ("Others should always be considered in your eyes as robbers, but honor them as if they were Rabban Gamliel."); *Derekh Eretz Rabbah* 3 (same). See also R. Aharon Levine (*Reisha Rav*, Poland, 1879–1941), *She'elot u-Teshuvot Avnei Ḥefetz* 29:12 (Munich: Vaad ha-Hatzalah, 1948), 55, and *Ha-Derash ve-ha-Iyyun*, vol. 2 (Biłgoraj: N. Kronenberg, 1931), *ma'amar* 34, p. 33 (noting that the concept of *"khabdehu ve-ḥashdehu"* is similar to the statement in *Derekh Eretz Rabbah* loc. cit., but he has searched for and not found the source for that exact phrase).
8. *Avodah Zarah* 25b.
9. Genesis Rabbah 75:6. Oxen refers to Joseph based on the verse "a sovereignty is his ox-like one" (Deuteronomy 33:17). The donkey refers to the Messiah the son of David, who is described as *"ani ve-rokhev al ḥamor,"* "a humble man riding upon a donkey" (Zechariah 9:9).
10. See Frank McDonough, *Neville Chamberlain, Appeasement and the British Road to War* (Manchester: Manchester University Press, 1998), 57–94.

fact that Esau hates Jacob, but Esau's mercy was aroused at that time, and he kissed Jacob with all his heart.[11]

Now, why was Esau so moved? We can imagine the scene that brings on the kiss and the tears. Jacob bowed earthward seven times until he reached his brother.[12] How much Esau must have lapped up the scene of Jacob's humiliation of bowing down to him.

But I would submit that when Esau looked at Jacob as he bowed down, he did not see a pitiful lackey in front of him. He did not even see weakness, temerity, trepidation. No! What he felt and experienced was humility, genuineness, and compassion. Why? Because Jacob had just returned from the triumph with the angel. He accomplished what no man in human history had ever accomplished. He defeated an angel. For this, he merited immortality, and certification of Isaac's blessings by the angel.[13]

With the power of Esau's grudge removed, Jacob should have all the capacity to defeat him decisively. He is in a position of strength. Yet he chooses to extend the olive branch. No one will mistake compassion for weakness. This made the impact of "he [Esau] kissed him" (Genesis 33:4).

An opportunity, once in a century perhaps, presents itself when a country achieves something that shakes the world. This happened when the United States landed a man on the moon. What if we had extended an invitation to the Russians for nuclear disarmament at that time? Would anyone have claimed that it was weakness?

The challenge today is to marshal our society's genius to offer a peace initiative, the olive branch, juxtaposed alongside our strength, so our olive branch will not be mistaken for weakness but will be looked upon as a grand gesture of nobility. We will then move out of the orbit of MAD into the arena of reconciliation and finally to the era of "saviors will ascend Mount Zion to judge the Mountain of Esau, and the kingdom will be Hashem's" (Obadiah 1:21). "Hashem will be King over all the land; on that day Hashem will be One and His Name will be One" (Zechariah 14:9).

---

11. *Sifrei*, Numbers 69; *Rashi* to Genesis 33:4. Each letter of the word *"va-yishikehu"* (he kissed him) is written with a dot above it. Some Sages believe that Esau's kiss was insincere. R. Shimon b. Yohai, however, says that Esau's mercy was aroused at this time and he kissed Jacob with all his heart.
12. Genesis 33:3.
13. *Rashi* to Genesis 32:29, s.v. *"lo Yaakov."*

The Jewish Attitude toward the Protectors of Terrorism

December 5, 1987

On November 25, Palestinian terrorism in the State of Israel assumed a new, ominous form when a sole assailant soared with his hang glider over the electrified fences of an Israeli military installation in the upper Galilee. When the suicidal mission was over, before the perpetrator was cut down, six Israeli soldiers were murdered and seven injured.[1] This incident instantly changed the image of the Palestinian terrorist from a coward who would attack only women and children to the image of a bold and sophisticated guerrilla who would take on even the invincible Israeli Defense Forces.

The reaction to this frightening event has centered mainly on the ill-preparedness of the IDF, reminiscent of the complacent environment

---

1. Thomas L. Friedman, "Syria-Based Group Says It Staged Israel Raid," *New York Times*, November 27, 1987, A1.

Va-Yishlaḥ

prevalent just before the Yom Kippur War.[2] Battle attacks, however, have turned to the forces that rule by the fostering of a climate that produces terrorist acts.

The incident of the violation of Dinah and the reaction of Simeon and Levi are a model of how we should view those who protect and abet terrorists.

In the story of the rape of Dinah, the villain with whom we perhaps most sympathize is Hamor, the father of Shekhem. He seems to be acting like a very responsible, contrite father. He appears to be trying to escape with some honor. He says, "I'll make the wedding. I'll arrange a huge dowry. Let's fix things." Yet Jacob acts deceitfully with him. As the *Akedat Yitzhak* points out, the man of integrity would never be a hypocrite.[3] He would not hide his true feelings. If he encountered a disdainful act, he would express outrage. To keep the outrage within himself is wrong.

Now, as the *Ha'amek Davar* notes, Jacob knew from the very beginning that the only way to deal with Hamor is with deceit.[4] An exception to his conduct of truthfulness must be made here. The solution of offering union with the men of Shekhem is wholeheartedly approved by Jacob. He publicly tells them that if they refuse the offer, Dinah will be returned. If not, she can be snatched away while they are in pain from circumcision. It is only the propriety of the massacre that is debatable.[5]

But why the deceit? It is because if Hamor were really an honorable man, he would have first returned Dinah and then made his proposal. Instead, he makes his proposal while Dinah is still being held against her will.[6] Nothing but deceit is necessary here.

---

2. Joshua Brilliant, "Glider Raid Warning Ignored; IDF Probes Lapses That Cost Six Lives," *Jerusalem Post*, December 5, 1987, 1; Thomas L. Friedman, "Israeli Army Assailed Over Glider Raid," *New York Times*, November 28, 1987, A3.
3. *Akedat Yitzhak, Va-Yishlaḥ, sha'ar* 27.
4. R. Naphtali Tzvi Yehudah Berlin, *Ha'amek Davar*, Genesis 34:13.
5. In the view of Maimonides, the people of Shekhem were liable to the death penalty by the sword because they violated one of the seven Noahide laws by not bringing Shekhem to justice. *Mishneh Torah, Melakhim* 9:14. Nahmanides, by contrast, avers that the people of Shekhem did not incur the death penalty for failing to bring Shekhem to justice. See Nahmanides to Genesis 34:13.
6. See R. Samson Raphael Hirsch, Genesis 34:8–12.

The Jewish Attitude toward the Protectors of Terrorism

The modern Hamor is Mubarak Awad. He is giving legitimacy to the Palestinian cause by proposing civil disobedience and attaching the name of Gandhi and King to the Palestinian cause.[7] He advocates cutting electrical and water lines, and that Arabs should throw themselves in front of buildings to so overburden the Israeli Administration's machinery that it will be paralyzed. This is nothing more than an incompetent form of terrorism. It must be met with cunning. We must always be one step ahead of them. They should never be able to figure out what we will be doing next. The model is Jacob's dealings with Hamor.

Now let us turn to the most difficult element of the story of Dinah, the massacre of the civilian population of Shekhem. How can we justify this? Well, perhaps the Torah is showing us where the line of innocent bystander ends and the line of conspirator and abettor begins. Were the people of Shekhem just innocent bystanders? I say, no! Who ever heard of such an outrageous thing, for them to agree to the self-affliction of pain and even to placing their lives in danger, just to help out Shekhem. How outrageous! What they should have done is to say, "Listen, this is your problem, Shekhem. Don't drag us in."

If this is how we treat those who abet the crime, then *a fortiori*, what should our attitude be toward those who finance terror and protect terrorists?

Finally, we need to have responsible journalism in reporting such incidents. The American press will always want to portray both sides, run feature articles on the daring attacks, and even express a begrudging admiration for them. Must we also note the gloating of our enemies over the attacks?

We must look to the story of Dinah again. Her family expresses their emotions – "The men were distressed, and were fired deeply with indignation" (Genesis 34:6). The feelings that they experienced of irretrievable loss as well as a sense of outrage were the proper responses. If Jacob disapproved of their action, it was only because their anger manifested itself in violence; their reaction was excessive.

---

7. Joel Greenberg, "It Depends on What's 'Non-Violence,'" *Jerusalem Post*, November 27, 1987, 8.

Va-Yishlaḥ

We must work collectively to produce a climate that will abhor terrorism, to the extent of what our Forefather Abraham accomplished when he was pursuing the terrorists who abducted his nephew Lot. He pursued them *ad Ḥovah*, "until Hobah" (Genesis 14:15), until the terrorists themselves confessed their guilt.[8]

---

8. *Rabbeinu Beḥaye al ha-Torah*, Genesis 14:15. Hobah is a location to the north of Damascus, and the Hebrew word *"ḥovah"* means guilt.

The Reproof of the Wicked and the Reproof of the Righteous

December 12, 1992

In today's *sidrah*, we are presented with a stark contrast between the reproof given by the righteous and the reproof given by the wicked. The reproof given by the wicked is Laban's reproof to Jacob, "Such is not done in our place, to give the younger before the elder" (Genesis 29:26).

Laban's intention was not just to defend his position, but to turn the tables on Jacob and tell him, "Maybe where you come from, society is morally bankrupt, and the younger daughter can displace the older daughter. But not here!" Reproof in the hands of Laban is merely a wedge to raise himself at the expense of someone else.

Jacob also engages in reproof, when he sees the shepherds idling about. But before he gives reproof, he establishes a relationship of love by calling them "my brothers" (Genesis 29:4). He was probably the first practitioner of Ḥavvot Yair's dictum that "you shall reprove your fellow"

(Leviticus 19:17) means that the object of your reproof must first become your "fellow" before you can give him reproof.¹ First you must elevate him. Find something redeeming in the evil person. Tell him that he is a righteous person.

There is also the question "Where are you from?" (Genesis 29:4). Get your facts straight. Maybe the shepherds are from a distant place, so their conduct would be explained. Jacob also provides no direct reproof, saying only, "The day is still long; it is not yet time to bring the livestock in" (Genesis 29:7). The double phrase hedges that the shepherds may in fact be *ba'alei battim* who own the flock, not hired workers who were idling on their employer's time.²

Laban is at once the *Arami*, the master deceiver,³ but everything he says is according to Jewish law. This is reproof to us. If we do not want our teaching and reproof to be perceived as the ranting of Laban – self-righteous, sanctimonious, holier-than-thou talk – we must make sure that our teaching and reproof have a liberal sprinkling of "my brothers" and "Where are you from?"

---

1. See R. Eleazar b. Eleazar Kallir (Hungary, ca. 1738–1801), *Ḥavvot Yair, Or ha-Ḥayyim* ¶ 3.
2. *Rashi* to Genesis 29:7; *Siftei Ḥakhamim* ad loc.
3. Genesis Rabbah 70:19.

I Will Not Let You Go Unless You Have Blessed Me[1]

November 27, 2004

Arguably, the most incredible battle in human history was the battle between Jacob and the guardian angel of Esau in the fords of the River Jabbok. Mortal man triumphed over an angel.[2]

We can all relate to the encounter because the prize that Jacob received was the name Israel,[3] and we are all called Israelites. Also, the battle was all about validation. Jacob wanted the guardian angel to acknowledge that he deserved Isaac's blessings.[4] So, too, we want to hear that what we have and what we do are good.

---

1. Genesis 32:27.
2. Genesis 32:25–30.
3. Genesis 32:29.
4. *Rashi* to Genesis 32:27, s.v. "*berakhtani*."

Va-Yishlaḥ

Permit me to suggest that the battle between Jacob and the angel is re-enacted the moment a Jewish child is born. Just before a Jewish child passes through the birth canal, an angel gives the child a charge: "Even if the entire world says that you are righteous, consider yourself wicked."[5] So, too, Jacob already had the validation of his mother Rebecca, "Your curse be on me, my son; only heed my voice" (Genesis 27:13), and the validation of his father, "Indeed, he shall remain blessed" (Genesis 27:33).

At this juncture, the shrieks of Esau – "he cried out an exceedingly great and bitter cry" (Genesis 27:34) – must have been drowned out and put in denial. And when the angel says "I'll acknowledge that you deserve the blessings when Hashem officially changes your name," which is also validation of the blessings, Esau's tears and shrieks must have been totally nonexistent. But Jacob wants to get validation even from Esau that he deserved the blessings.

How does he earn this validation? It is by saying *im Lavan garti*, "I have sojourned with Laban" (Genesis 32:5), *ve-taryag mitzvot shamarti*, "and I have kept the 613 mitzvot."[6] Jacob was not saying that I kept the Sabbath or that I never missed *Ma'ariv*. No. He is declaring, "It was with all my might that I served [Laban]" (Genesis 31:6). I never learned anything from the master deceiver. I always had integrity with *mitzvot bein adam le-ḥavero*.

Esau, remember the nadir, when Isaac said, "What can I do, my son?" (Genesis 27:37). I cannot do anything for you. I already made your brother master over you, so whatever you acquire will be his because whatever a slave acquires, his master acquires.[7] But during these thirty-four years, I never conducted myself in my material striving as your master. I came from a kind and gentle world. I am the absolutely faithful worker, the considerate boss, the magnanimous competitor. I never let you feel that the blessing "be a lord to your kinsmen" (Genesis 27:29) was fulfilled.

May it be our lot that people should feel that every time they bless us, they are blessing themselves.

---

5. *Niddah* 30b.
6. *Rashi* to Genesis 32:5 (noting that the word "*garti*" has the numerical equivalence of 613, signifying that Jacob kept the 613 commandments while he sojourned with Laban and did not learn from Laban's evil ways).
7. *Rashi* to Genesis 27:37, s.v. "*hen gevir*."

The *Kibbud Av* of Esau

(Undated)

It is rare if not unique that the actions of a biblical hero are on the one hand resoundingly condemned but at the same time used as a model for posterity. But this was the judgment of our Sages in regard to our Forefather Jacob's obsequious self-debasement in his encounter with Esau. For addressing and referring to Esau as "my lord" eight times,[1] Jacob incurs divine wrath. As a punishment for this self-debasement, Hashem proclaims that eight kings would reign in Edom before a king would reign in Israel.[2]

But at the same time, we are told that when R. Judah ha-Nasi corresponded with Antoninus, he was very careful to write the salutation "His Majesty Antoninus, from Judah your servant." Why "your servant"? Because Jacob used the term "your servant Jacob" when he communicated with Esau.[3]

---

1. Genesis 32:5–6, 19; Genesis 33:8, 13–15.
2. Genesis Rabbah 75:11.
3. Genesis 32:5.

Va-Yishlaḥ

I would submit that for the purpose of promoting goodwill and gaining the ear of government, self-debasement is permissible, even to the extent of being obsequious. But Jacob not only employed the phrase of self-debasement, he actually believed that Esau might be his spiritual superior. Our Sages are quite explicit here. Why was Jacob afraid of Esau? Because he feared that Esau had the mitzvah of honoring his parents.[4]

We can put ourselves in Jacob's place. It is thirty-four years since he last saw his parents, fourteen years of learning in Shem and Eber and another twenty years with Laban. During that time, Jacob never served or attended to his parents.[5] In contrast, Esau was in frequent contact with his parents and attended to them in formal attire, all to honor them. In this regard, Esau is cited as a paragon of the fulfillment of the mitzvah of honoring one's parents.[6] Jacob essentially thought that Esau had outdone him with respect to this mitzvah, and perhaps this mitzvah is equivalent to keeping the entire Torah.

Now, the purpose of the revelation to Jacob that eight kings would reign in Edom before a king would reign in Israel was precisely to show him that he vastly underestimated the value of his own *kibbud av ve-am* and blew out of proportion the value of Esau's *kibbud av ve-am*.

What begins to negate Esau's *kibbud av ve-em* is the genealogy of the eight kings. In the biblical description of Esau's wives, we are reminded that "they were a source of spiritual rebellion to Isaac and Rebecca" (Genesis 26:35). They were the exact opposite of Isaac and Rebecca with respect to everything that they stood for.

And when did Esau marry? When he was forty years old,[7] and a full twenty-three years before Jacob departed to Padam Aram to work for a wife.[8] Yes, if one is double-dealing, being an exemplar of *kibbud av ve-em* in the presence of his parents but a *tzayid be-piv* behind their backs,[9] the duplicity must eventually explode in his face and be

---

4. Genesis Rabbah 76:2; *Da'at Zekenim* to Genesis 32:8.
5. *Rashi* to Genesis 37:34; *Megillah* 16b–17a.
6. Deuteronomy Rabbah 1:15.
7. Genesis 26:34.
8. *Rashi* to Genesis 28:9. Jacob was sixty-three years old when he left for Padam Aram.
9. See Genesis 25:28. The phrase "*tzayid be-piv*" (lit., "trapping was in his mouth") is understood by the Midrash to refer to Esau's attempts to deceive Isaac through his

discovered. The double life is no longer possible when Esau marries. His wives are idol worshippers. Isaac becomes blind because of the incense that Esau's wives offered to idols.[10]

In contrast, Jacob fulfilled the mitzvah of *kibbud av ve-em* on a grand scale. Jacob is the exemplar of integrity and the laws of the *po'el ne'eman*, derived from Jacob's behavior in Laban's employ.[11] He was the type of person of whom people surely said "fortunate are the parents who bore him."[12] This is certainly honoring one's parents.

The next step tears into Esau's motive for being the exemplar of *kibbud av ve-em* in the presence of his parents. Was he motivated by elemental *hakkarat ha-tov*? If that were the case, he transmitted nothing of this sentiment to his children. His wife Oholibamah is described as both the daughter of Anah and the daughter of Zibeon the Hivvite.[13] How can a woman be a daughter of two fathers? The answer must lie in that, as *Rashi* points out, she was the product of incest.[14] Well, incest shows the greatest contempt for the honor of one's father. And if Esau could marry such a woman, he obviously had no respect for his own father. And the three of his children from Oholibamah were *mamzerim*,[15] which showed that his own children had the same contempt for him and did not have even elemental *hakkarat ha-tov* for him.

If we imagine for a moment that Esau's respect for his parents stemmed from a sentimental attachment to his roots, that is, he imagined

---

speech into believing that he was righteous. For example, Esau would ask Isaac whether one is required to tithe salt or straw, creating the false impression that he was meticulous in the performance of mitzvot. *Midrash Tanḥuma, Toledot* 8.

10. *Rashi* to Genesis 27:1.
11. See *Midrash Bereshit Rabbati*, ed. Hanoch Albeck (Jerusalem: Mekitzei Nirdamim, 1940), Genesis 30:29.
12. See Mishnah, *Avot* 2:8. In enumerating the praise of his primary disciples, R. Yohanan b. Zakkai described R. Joshua b. Hanina as "*ashrei yoladeto*," "praiseworthy is she who bore him." See also *Yoma* 86a.
13. Genesis 36:2.
14. *Rashi* to Genesis 36:2, s.v. "*bat Anah bat Tzivon.*"
15. *Rashi* to Genesis 36:5; R. Jacob Culi, *Me-Am Lo'ez*, Genesis 36:40–43, trans. R. Shemuel Yerushalmi, *Yalkut Me-Am Lo'ez: Sefer Bereshit* (Jerusalem: Mossad Yad Ezra, 1968), 653–654. See also R. Isaac b. Judah Abrabanel (Portugal, 1437–1508), Genesis 36:1.

that his self-image of greatness was somehow derived from his parents, he did not transmit this sentiment in any fashion to his children.

There were eight kings in Edom, but never a king who was the son of a prior king. Each new king came from a different city. There was no continuity or stability. It is nothing worth preserving or building on. It is just the law of the jungle.

In fact, nothing of the past is sacred and worth continuing. Anah is first described as the brother of Zibeon,[16] but then as the son of Zibeon.[17] This signifies that Anah was the product of incest between Zibeon and Zibeon's mother.[18] "He is Anah who discovered the mules in the desert while he was pasturing the donkeys for Zibeon, his father" (Genesis 36:24). He cross-breeds a she-donkey and a mare to produce a mule. What have we here? A symbol of the beast of burden is combined with the horse, the symbol of war, to produce a better war technology, a wild white mule with a deadly bite. Anah was unfit, and he brought tainted animals into the world.[19]

So what then motivated Esau's *kibbud av ve-em*? It was the philosophy that gave a veneer of legitimacy to his brutal lifestyle, which characterized all the generations of his family. It was the philosophy of giving in order to take. If Esau was exemplary in honoring his parents, he could demand the same from his children. He could demand loyalty.[20]

Ma'aseh avot siman le-banim. Throughout the millennia, when Jews found themselves in hostile host countries, in countries with closed political systems, they have been hesitant to press for their rights and promote causes out of fear that they would be accused of not being loyal to their country, out of fear of being found lacking in their honor of the fatherland.

Paradoxically, here in the golden *galut*, in America, where men of great vision have come up with creative ideas of how to control the political process to further Jewish objectives and goals, alas, we have

---

16. See Genesis 36:20.
17. Genesis 36:24.
18. *Rashi* to Genesis 36:24, s.v. "*hu Anah*"; *Pesaḥim* 54a.
19. *Rashi* to Genesis 36:24, s.v. "*et ha-yeimim*"; *Pesaḥim* 54a.
20. R. Eliyahu Eliezer Dessler (Lithuania, England, and Benei Berak, 1892–1953), *Mikhtav me-Eliyahu*, 2nd ed., vol. 3 (Bnei Berak, 1925), 97–98.

our beloved State of Israel, and the dread of being accused of dual loyalty hangs over us. And if we are holding back, not asserting with fullest vigor what we know is right because of the subconscious fear of being accused of lacking in *kibbud av ve-em*, let us take note of what became of Esau. All the kings, all the chieftains, disappeared. What remained was only Esau, without a title, who was *Avi Edom*. This signifies that the man was not capable of fathering anything good. He was the father of that infamous red thing, the stew of lentils, which he accepted in exchange for the birthright.[21]

---

21. See Genesis Rabbah 63:12.

Va-Yeshev

And Hashem Was Preparing the Light of the Messiah

November 26, 1983

How often is the dramatic impact of a narrative softened when a digression is introduced? Such appears to be the case in today's *sidrah*. Just as the character of Joseph is being developed, the Torah introduces a digression, the story of Judah and Tamar, and only then does the Torah resume the narrative of Joseph being brought down to Egypt.

Noting this interruption, *Rashi* comments that Joseph's brothers never imagined in their wildest dreams that Jacob would fall into such a profound sorrow over the presumed death of Joseph. As the Torah says, "he refused to comfort himself" (Genesis 37:35). This excessive anguish of Jacob made the brothers regret their treacherous act and they blamed Judah. Had he demanded that they return Joseph to their father, the brothers would have listened. They deposed him from his position of leadership. Judah subsequently went to find a wife.[1]

Noting the interruption, the Midrash turns the tables completely and claims in essence that the central message is the birth of Peretz, who, together with Zerach, was the result of the union of Judah and Tamar.[2] Peretz is the progenitor of the Final Messiah. The main point was that before Joseph was brought down to Egypt, symbolic of the birth of our first enslaver, the Final Redeemer was born.[3]

All the events concerning Joseph being bought down to Egypt are a necessary prelude to the birth of the Final Redeemer at that particular time. Hence, the Tribes were preoccupied with the sale of Joseph, and Reuben was involved in repentance.[4] Reuben stood up against the madness of the moment and said, "We will not strike him mortally" (Genesis 37:21), but dropped his vigilance, thinking that the crisis was over when the brothers sat down to eat their meal. When he returned, Joseph was no longer in the pit.[5] Now, if he would have been continuously on top of the situation, the sale of Joseph would never have occurred.

Joseph also was donning sackcloth and fasting at this time.[6] The extreme anguish that Joseph felt over the treatment he received from his brothers at Dothan was an essential ingredient leading to the birth of the Messiah. For, as the Midrash asks, how is it possible for such a beautiful, princely lad to be sold for twenty silver pieces? The answer given is that when he was cast into the pit, full of snakes and scorpions,[7] Joseph was so frightened that he became ghastly pale, losing his entire radiance.[8] Joseph was put through multiple sales, and because the original sale was for only twenty silver pieces, the Ishmaelites turned a deaf ear to Joseph's plea that they should return him to his father Jacob for

---

1. *Rashi* to Genesis 38:1.
2. Genesis 38:29–30.
3. Genesis Rabbah 85:1.
4. Ibid.
5. Genesis 37:29.
6. Genesis Rabbah 85:1.
7. *Rashi* to Genesis 37:24.
8. R. Jacob Culi, *Me-Am Lo'ez*, Genesis 37:28, trans. R. Shemuel Yerushalmi, *Yalkut Me-Am Lo'ez: Sefer Bereshit* (Jerusalem: Mossad Yad Ezra, 1968), 675–676.

a handsome ransom, as Jacob was very wealthy. They gave no credence to the claim when the original kidnappers paid only twenty silver pieces for him.[9]

If Joseph had not suffered so grievously from his brothers' abduction, he probably would have found his way home, and the sequence of the Servitude in Egypt would have been different. If Jacob had not grieved so much over the loss of Joseph, Judah would not have been deposed and the story of Tamar would not have unfolded as it did.

Now, the birth of the Messiah is certainly a glorious event. We would have thought that Hashem would scan human progress from above and focus on one moment of human history of genuine humaneness, of resplendent nobility, and turn the sentiment into a scenario that would produce the Final Redeemer.

Instead, what have we here? An act of treachery of "one who kidnaps a man and sells him" (Exodus 21:16), a capital offense, which would have to wait almost two thousand years before Hashem would exact punishment through the execution of the ten righteous people of the generation, the *asarah harugei malkhut*, who were regarded as equivalent in stature to the Ten Tribes.[10]

And what else formed an essential element? It was the miscalculation of a righteous man, Reuben, the extreme anguish of both victim and survivor, and the accidental good committed by Judah, *yibbum*, when his intention was *ma'aseh zenut*.[11] Does this combination of goals, objectives, and sentiments deserve to be woven into a comprehensive web so that the progenitor of the Messiah would be born?

---

9. R. Jacob Culi, *Me-Am Lo'ez*, Genesis 37:36, *Yalkut Me-Am Lo'ez: Sefer Bereshit*, 681.
10. *Elleh Ezkerah*, *Musaf* Prayer on Yom Kippur; *Midrash Elleh Ezkerah*; *Midrash Mishlei*, Proverbs 1:13; *Rabbeinu Behaye al ha-Torah*, Genesis 44:17, 50:17.
11. *Yibbum* (levirate marriage) is the requirement in Jewish law that if a man died without children, his brother is obligated to marry his widow. Deuteronomy 25:5–10. Judah's first-born son, Er, married Tamar and died childless. Judah's second son, Onan, then married Tamar. When Onan died too, Judah held back his youngest son, Shelah, from marrying Tamar, fearing that he might die also. Genesis 38:6–11. In the time of Judah, before the Torah was given to the Children of Israel, *yibbum* was also fulfilled by having the father, rather than the brother, of the deceased marry the widow. See Nahmanides to Genesis 38:8.

I would submit that Hashem set into motion that ludicrous and ignominious scenario to demonstrate in a spectacular way that redemption is part and parcel of the Jewish people. It is fated for us. It is our destiny. When something is a matter of destiny, it simply must happen, no matter what. Man is powerless to prevent its occurrence. His best efforts to subvert the outcome will fail. Hence, even if the Jew is, God forbid, involved in treachery, the antithesis of the ideals that the Messiah represents, the Al-Mighty in his infinite wisdom will set into motion a scenario that will inexorably produce the Messiah.

Redemption is our destiny, but there are two paths towards its achievement. One is the path of *be-ittah*, "in its time," and the other is *ahishennah*, "I will hasten it."[12] As far as the *be-ittah* path is concerned, whatever man will do, God in His infinite wisdom will set into motion a scenario to produce the outcome of redemption. A generation that is completely wicked could produce the Messiah.[13] But how painful this process would be. We have it in our hands through free will to set into motion the *ahishennah* scenario.

Indeed, our Sages tell us that a man should never single out one son among his other sons.[14] If Jacob had not shown favoritism, we would not have gone down to Egypt.[15] *Tosefot* on Tractate *Shabbat* point out that the Covenant between the Parts would have been fulfilled in other ways, with a minimum of servitude and torture, mostly carried out by a *gerut*.[16]

Now, had Judah had the courage to stand up against the madness and say "return him to his father," the sale would not have taken place.[17] What proceeds is that the action of every Jew affects not only the merits of the Jewish people as a collective, but the very scenario of the Messiah itself.

In our lifetime, we will surely encounter the test of Judah. Will we stand up to the murderers, or will we just be swept up in the brutality

---

12. Isaiah 60:22.
13. *Sanhedrin* 98a.
14. *Shabbat* 10b.
15. Ibid.; *Siftei Hakhamim*, n. 90, to Rashi to Genesis 37:3.
16. *Tosafot* to *Shabbat* 10b, s.v. "*nisggalggel ha-davar.*"
17. *Rashi* to Genesis 38:1.

of the moment? Will we make the error of Reuben and miscalculate the nature of a crisis?

You might ask, what does proceeding in the right direction have to do with the scenario of the Messiah? The answer is: What does the sale of Joseph have to do with the birth of the progenitor of the Messiah? Could it have ever been predicted by the most productive mind?

I would submit that the elements of treachery, miscalculation, the anguish of the victim and the survivor, and unintended goodness represent the elements of an ignominious scenario of the Messiah. What we have seen is the beginning of a complete turning upside down and inside out of the scenario. The Holocaust is an event unparalleled in the annals of human history in terms of the unmitigated anguish of both victims and survivors. This event was undoubtedly creating on its own accord, as did the anguish of Jacob and Joseph, a scenario that would bring the Messiah. But the Jewish people were not content with a passive role, to allow events to completely overwhelm them, as did Jacob, when twenty-two years of his life became a blank, and Joseph, whose hysterics contributed to his enslavement.[18]

The formation of the Jewish State changed all this. A new scenario was put into motion, the active role. Jews are no longer the objects of history, the passive objects of pogroms, persecution, and annihilation. We no longer will permit the anguish of the victims and the survivors to determine the scenario of redemption. It now remains for the Jewish nation as a whole to have the intense commitment of not falling into the tragic error of Judah of the selling out of brothers.

May the Al-Mighty give us the discernment and wisdom not to fall into the error of miscalculation. This will hasten the coming of the Messiah in our own time and our witnessing that the Messiah is "the breath of our nostrils, Hashem's anointed" (Lamentations 4:20).

---

18. See *Sefer ha-Yashar, Va-Yeshev*; R. Jacob Culi, *Me-Am Lo'ez*, Genesis 37:36, trans. R. Shemuel Yerushalmi, *Yalkut Me-Am Lo'ez: Sefer Bereshit* (Jerusalem: Mossad Yad Ezra, 1968), 681.

Compassion and Divine Justice

December 7, 1985

Deeply ingrained in our Tradition is the belief that our destiny as the Chosen People marches on inexorably toward redemption, royalty, and universal mission. Today's portion, whose major theme is Jewish destiny, has some powerful lessons to offer.

Joseph was to learn that he could not ram destiny down his brothers' throats. He also learned that he could not be the architect of his own destiny. For petitioning the Chamberlain of the Cupbearers to help him, his stay in prison was only lengthened another two years.[1]

Joseph's brothers learned that they could not frustrate Jewish destiny. They thought that they were selling Joseph into slavery. Instead, their very action was instrumental in elevating Joseph to royalty.

Potiphar thought that he was consigning Joseph to obscurity by throwing him in the dungeon. Instead, the imprisonment allowed

---

1. *Rashi* to Genesis 40:23, s.v. "*va-yish'keḥehu.*"

Joseph to make the connections that allowed him to become the Viceroy of Egypt, allowing him to attain fame and glory.

If there must be an interval between prophecy and fulfillment, if we cannot be the architects of our own destiny, how do we speed up destiny?

The story of Judah and Tamar, which appears irrelevant to the main theme of Joseph being sold into slavery, supplies us with the answer. Tamar is accused of the sin of harlotry. It was generally not a capital offense, but in Tamar's case it would be, as Nahmanides says, because she would be profaning the royal household of Judah.[2]

Now, she was innocent and she chose to make a grand gesture of compromise by not directly accusing Judah of being the father of her child. "Identify, if you please, whose are this signet, this wrap, and this staff" (Genesis 38:25). From this, our Sages derive the oft-quoted statement: "Better that a person should cast himself into a fiery furnace than shame his fellow in public."[3] The grand gesture of compassion evokes on the part of Judah the grand act of justice.

The situation was ripe for a cover-up. What a disgrace for the person who is the symbol of morality, who sits in judgment over other people's morality, to himself be found guilty of an immoral act. Judah could have well rationalized that a cover-up was in order to prevent a *ḥillul ha-Shem*. After all, what would happen to the moral climate of society when people would realize the level of morality of their symbols of morality?

But the grand act of compassion evoked the grand act of justice. Judah must confess simply because justice demands it, and he will accept the consequences, whatever they may be. Judah produced a kind of justice that was perfect, ridden of any scintilla of bias, self-interest, or taint. Indeed, Hashem manifests Himself to us *middah ke-neged middah*.[4] If we show a grand act of compassion that is so spectacular that everyone is

---

2. Nahmanides to Genesis 38:24.
3. *Bava Metzia* 59a.
4. *Sanhedrin* 90a. Cf. *Sotah* 8b. The doctrine of *middah ke-neged middah* is expressed in the maxim of Hillel, "He saw a skull floating on the water and said, 'Because you drowned someone, you were drowned, and the one who drowned you will eventually be drowned'" (Mishnah, *Avot* 2:6).

moved by it, Hashem will show us justice, His divine plan for the world, in the same crystal-clear manner.

Unfortunately, the opposite is also true. An act of *sin'at ḥinnam* evokes a kind of world order that is simply chaos, a state of affairs where we do not see the divine hand operating at all. The world has been shaken lately by the natural catastrophes in Mexico, Puerto Rico, and Columbia, with thousands of innocent people perishing in a matter of a very short time.[5] Why? It is because of the *sin'at ḥinnam* in the world. Senseless hatred evokes a feeling of chaos in the divine order.

We do not want that in the worst way. We want to move from "Identify, if you please: Is it your son's tunic or not?" (Genesis 37:32), the most ugly manifestation of *sin'at ḥinnam*, to "Identify, if you please, whose are this signet, this wrap, and this staff" (Genesis 38:25), which represents the most grand act of compassion. Only then will we really feel that we are part of a redemption process and the coming of the Messiah is indeed imminent.

---

5. See Richard J. Meislin, "Earthquake Rocks Mexico; Hundreds Are Feared Dead as Buildings Fall and Burn," *New York Times*, September 20, 1985, A1; Jeffrey Schmalz, "Hurricane Left Grievous Wounds to Land and Spirit of Puerto Rico," *New York Times*, October 1, 1989 (Hurricane Hugo), 1.1; William Long and Marjorie Miller, "20,000 Feared Dead in Colombia Eruption; Volcanic Blast Triggers Huge Mudslides," *Los Angeles Times*, November 15, 1985, 1.

Mi-Ketz

When Is a Security Measure Self-Restraint?

December 26, 1992

In the wake of the escalation of violence and terrorist actions committed by Hamas in the liberated territories, including the brutal kidnapping and murder of Staff Sargent Nissim Toledano, the Israeli Government took the extraordinary action of deporting 415 Islam Fundamentalist members of Hamas.[1]

In reporting these actions, the Jewish press highlighted Prime Minister Rabin's statement that such senseless slaughter goes on in Bosnia, and the Kuwaiti Government expelled more than 300,000 Palestinians, so the world should not cry on the shoulders of the Israelis.[2]

---

1. Statement by Prime Minister Rabin on the Removal of Hamas Activists, December 20, 1992, Israel Ministry of Foreign Affairs, vol. 13–14, no. 44 (1992–1994).
2. See "Israeli Government Stands Firm, Refusing to Let Deportees Return," *Jewish Telegraphic Agency*, December 22, 1992; Avrohom Shmuel Lewin, "Rabin Blasts Civil Rights Groups for Supporting Terrorists," *Jewish Press*, December 25, 1992, 58.

The implication of this is that Israel's action might be wrong, but there are plenty of evils going on in the world. Why selectively rant against this evil? It is hypocritical and self-righteous for the world to do so.

I, for one, feel that the emphasis is totally misplaced. What should be emphasized is that it was an agonizing decision for the Israeli Government after long and intensive interaction with Israel's Supreme Court. It is in the spirit of the *halakhah* of *ha-ba le-horgekha, hashkem ve-horgo*, "if someone comes to kill you, kill him first."[3] If, however, one could save himself by injuring one of the limbs of the attacker rather than by killing him, the killing is not justified.[4]

This is the case here. The action represents the least force to neutralize the threat to public safety. But what we feel is merely a security measure that should be characterized as self-defense and designed to deter aggression is regarded by our enemies as a hostile act, even an aggressive, war-like act.

What is the criterion to characterize an action as a defensive measure rather than a war-like act? I would propose that today's portion provides some guidance here. We find Joseph in today's *sidrah* involved in acts of restraint, which elicit diametrically opposite reactions.

When Joseph accuses his brothers of being spies, he initially has them imprisoned. But on the third day, he says, "Do this and live; I fear God. If you are a truthful people, let one of your brothers be imprisoned in place of your confinement while you go and bring provisions for the hunger of your household" (Genesis 42:18–19). The grand act of compassion. The brothers, despite their knowledge that the charge is a total fabrication, go along with Joseph's compromise of having only Simeon incarcerated. It was a reversible harm.

But when Joseph plants his silver goblet in Benjamin's satchel, the brothers, led by Judah, take a life-and-death stance. Why? Two points stand out. One is that the brothers had a *kal ve-ḥomer* to establish their trustworthiness and their honesty. They had earlier returned the silver that Joseph had placed in their sacks.[5] Also, Judah was obligated to

---

3. Numbers Rabbah 21:4; *Midrash Tanḥuma, Pinḥas* 3; *Sanhedrin* 72a.
4. *Sanhedrin* 74a.
5. Genesis 43:20–22.

take matters to brinkmanship because he said "for your servant took responsibility for the youth" (Genesis 44:32). This included watching Benjamin like a hawk to make sure that he did not get into trouble. So we have no right to reject what is on the surface an act of restraint and characterize it as an aggressive and a hostile act unless: (1) irreversible harm is threatened by the act; (2) they have made goodwill gestures and established their honesty; and (3) they are willing to take responsibility.

Hamas has no right to reject our action because first, it is reversible; the deportations can be appealed. Second, they have made no gesture of good faith that would enable us to ignore the brutality and killings. *Adderabba*, their charter calls for the destruction of the State of Israel, with no territorial compromise, and for the establishment of a Muslim State.[6] And third, neither the PLO nor any Arab State is assuming any responsibility to end the violence and terrorist government. Saudi Arabia is even still financing Hamas. So the PLO, the so-called "moderates," has no right to reap the dividends of Hamas' terrorism.

In light of this, we should take on the world's condemnation rather than accept the world's condolences!

---

6. See Michal Rotem, "Hamas: Driven by Ardor and a Global Mission," *Jerusalem Post*, December 18, 1992, 5.

Va-Yiggash

For It Was to Be a Provider That God Sent Me Ahead of You

December 10, 1983

When the man of great sensitivity and selfless devotion acts in an apparently egotistical manner, his behavior evokes nothing less than amazement.

From the very moment that Joseph set his eyes upon his brothers in his capacity as Viceroy and beheld their prostration to him, he poignantly remembered his dream of "Behold! The sun, the moon, and eleven stars were bowing down to me" (Genesis 37:9). Joseph held this dream, according to the *Netziv*, to be a *nevuah*.[1] For this reason, he made no attempt to contact his father during his servitude. Now with the brothers bowing down to him, Joseph's characterization of his dream as a prophecy was vindicated. He then devises an

---

1. R. Naphtali Tzvi Yehudah Berlin, *Ha'amek Davar*, Genesis 42:9.

Va-Yiggash

ingenious plan to have every detail of the dream fulfilled. A pretext that the brothers are spies is created to force the brothers to bring Benjamin to Egypt. Once Benjamin would be brought down, another pretext would be made, the pretext of the goblet, to make Benjamin a slave, which would in turn force Jacob to come down and plead on his knees for Benjamin's release.

But this plan just prolonged the agony. Is there not an egotistical element here, drawing out the masquerade to such lengths, all the while causing untold anguish to Jacob?

But when a person interprets his dream as a prophecy, it cannot possibly relate to his personal life. A *nevuah* is never related to an individual as an isolated being. A *nevuah* must relate to the Jewish people as a nation. Joseph regarded himself as a man of destiny. It would be his mission to transform treachery into the highest sentiment of nobility, for Joseph understood that the specter of his entire family bowing down to him represented the manner in which the Servitude would begin. Joseph was determined that the event that would mark the beginning of the Servitude be one that represented man in his finest hour. Such an act would form an indelible memory of the most glorious type. Such a memory would sustain a nation in the most difficult times. A divine promise can sustain an individual, but it takes a glorious memory of a human event to produce a truly divine spark.

An individual of grace and generosity does not require his foe to fall to his knees to achieve forgiveness. When Joseph overheard his brothers saying "indeed we are guilty concerning our brother inasmuch as we saw his heartfelt anguish when he pleaded with us and we paid no heed" (Genesis 42:21), what he heard was shallow contrition. They did not regret their treachery, but only the consequence of it, the anguish of the victim. Their attitude toward Joseph had not changed. They still viewed him as a threat. In any case, this shallow contrition was surely sufficient for Joseph, and was enough to end the anguish for his father. But personal considerations had to be put aside and the agony prolonged before a finer emotion would be produced, which would set off the Servitude.

For It Was to Be a Provider That God Sent Me Ahead of You

The next moment came when Joseph laid eyes on Benjamin. "Joseph rushed because his compassion for his brother had been stirred" (Genesis 43:30). Why was his emotion aroused? Benjamin told him that he had ten children, each named to mark Joseph's endearment to him.[2] As the *Gur Aryeh* explains, five names correspond to the glister and singularity that Joseph represented to Benjamin, while the other five names correspond to the void and emptiness that Benjamin felt over Joseph's current status as he imagined it to be.[3]

One child is called *Ehi*, a brother providing companionship and warmth. The void that his disappearance created is reflected in *Huppim*, neither shared each other's wedding celebration. Another child was named *Rosh*, in recognition of Joseph's spiritual superiority. Now he is *Bela*, swallowed up; no one will appreciate him and he goes unnoticed. *Bekher*, he was the firstborn of my mother, having visibly evident rights. Now Benjamin bemoans that Joseph is a *Gera*, treated as a second-class citizen, as a liar. *Naaman*, he appreciated his sweetness and pleasantness. Now, *Ashbel*, God sent him into captivity and his sweetness is a source of exploitation for evil people.[4] And finally, *Muppim*, he merited to be the repository of all Father's Torah learned from Shem and Eber.[5] Now he is, alas, *Ard*, descended among the gentiles, so that no one cares for his spiritual growth and development.[6]

Joseph indeed witnessed a sublime moment here, but the emotions were not sufficiently refined, for man is surely capable of such aesthetic conduct when he does not perceive any conflict between his own ambitions and those of his fellow man. Benjamin's selfless devotion was untested.

---

2. Genesis Rabbah 94:8; *Sotah* 36b; *Rashi* to Genesis 43:30.
3. R. Judah Loew b. Bezalel (*Maharal*, Prague, ca. 1525–1609), *Gur Aryeh*, Genesis 43:30, s.v. "*kullam al shem ahi*" (correlating the name *Gera* to *Ehi*; *Ard* to *Rosh*; *Huppim* to *Muppim*; *Ashbel* to *Naaman*; and *Bela* to *Bekher*).
4. *Ashbel* is a contraction of *sheva'o Kel*, i.e., Hashem made him a captive. *Rashi* to Genesis 43:30.
5. *Muppim* is related to *mi-pi* (lit., "from the mouth"), signifying that Joseph studied from the mouth of Jacob. *Rashi* to Genesis 43:30. See also *Rashi* to *Sotah* 36b, s.v. "*Muppim*" (noting that Joseph's mouth was like that of Jacob's in his fluency in the laws that Jacob learned from Shem and Eber).
6. The names of Benjamin's sons are recorded at Genesis 46:21.

Va-Yiggash

That glorious, unsurpassable moment finally did come when Judah was willing to have himself banished from two worlds.[7] He was willing to become an eternal slave to Joseph[8] and even fight a life-and-death battle with the whole land of Egypt,[9] all so that Benjamin should be returned to his father and Father should not be put to agony. This is man's finest moment, when he is ready to perform a heroic act, a glorious act, even when a direct conflict of interest is seen.

The Al-Mighty looked down at the glorious event and declared that never had one brother shown so much devotion and love for another until that moment. Therefore, the Temple should be built on the territory of both Judah and Benjamin.[10]

When a dream is merely a mundane event, some part of it is *devarim betelim*.[11] And so, the part of the dream in which the moon bowed down to Joseph was *devarim betelim*, as Rachel was no longer alive at that time.[12] But when a dream is a *nevuah*, every single element is true and holy.[13] Now, at that moment when the dream is totally fulfilled, Jacob comes down to Egypt, relishing in the selfless sacrifice of Judah. The spirit of Rachel was also bowing down to Joseph. For the same selfless act that Rachel performed for Leah, giving Leah the passwords so that she should not be disgraced,[14] Judah was now performing for Benjamin; the magnanimous gesture was now reciprocated. A lesson had been completely learned and internalized.

Every Jew is called Judah – "Judah, you your brothers shall acknowledge" (Genesis 49:8).[15] And every Jew is called Joseph – *edut*

---

7. *Rashi* to Genesis 44:32.
8. Genesis 44:33.
9. Genesis Rabbah 93:8.
10. See *Midrash Tanḥuma ha-Kadum ve-ha-Yashan, Va-Yiggash* 8; *Yalkut Shimoni*, I Samuel 126.
11. *Nedarim* 8a–b.
12. *Rashi* to Genesis 37:10, s.v. "*havo navo*"; Genesis Rabbah 84:11.
13. See Jeremiah 23:28; *Radak* ad loc., s.v. "*va-asher devari itto yidabber.*" Jacob was not aware that the moon in Joseph's dream referred to Bilhah, who had raised Joseph as if she were his mother. *Rashi* to Genesis 37:10, s.v. "*havo navo*"; Genesis Rabbah 84:11.
14. *Rashi* to Genesis 29:25; *Megillah* 13b; *Bava Batra* 123a.
15. *Targum Yonatan*, Genesis 49:8; Genesis Rabbah 98:6.

bi-Yosef shemo (Psalms 81:6).[16] So every Jew has it within him to dream the grand dream and work tirelessly to make it become a reality. And every Jew has the power to create the glorious memory that will sustain a nation, as Joseph said, "For it was to be a provider that God sent me ahead of you" (Genesis 45:5).

---

16. *Radak* to Psalms 81:6; *Ba'al ha-Turim* to Genesis 48:16.

Three Black Days

December 29, 1984

Three black days mar the Jewish calendar in the month of Tevet. On the tenth day of Tevet, Nebuchadnezzar's siege of Jerusalem began.[1] On the ninth day of Tevet, the great Jewish legislator and architect of the building of the Second Temple, Ezra, died.[2] And on the eighth day of Tevet, the Torah was translated into Greek.[3] The third event is likened by our Sages to the Sin of the Golden Calf.[4] Accordingly, when it happened, the world was shrouded in darkness for three days.[5]

---

1. II Kings 25:1–4.
2. R. Aaron b. Jacob ha-Kohen of Lunel (Provence, end of 13th and first half of 14th cent.), *Orḥot Ḥayyim, Hilkhot Ta'anit* 24; *Kol Bo*, no. 63; R. Joshua b. Alexander ha-Kohen Falk (*Sema*, Poland, 1680–1756), *Perishah* to *Tur, Oraḥ Ḥayyim* 580, n. 6 (noting that the *Seliḥot* for the Fast of the Tenth of Tevet specifies that Ezra died on the ninth day of Tevet); *Magen Avraham* to *Shulḥan Arukh, Oraḥ Ḥayyim* 580:2, n. 6 (similar).
3. *Masekhet Soferim* 1:7; *Megillat Ta'anit, Perek ha-Aḥaron; Tur, Oraḥ Ḥayyim* 580; *Shulḥan Arukh, Oraḥ Ḥayyim* 580:2.
4. *Masekhet Soferim* 1:7.
5. *Megillat Ta'anit*, loc. cit.; *Tur*, loc. cit.; *Shulḥan Arukh*, loc. cit.

Three Black Days

The poignancy of the tragedies that occurred on the ninth and tenth days of Tevet is very clear, but why was the translation of the Torah regarded as a tragedy? Historians theorize that the motive of Eleazar the High Priest was to make the Torah accessible to the many Jews who had so assimilated into the Greek culture.[6] Ptolemy II Philadelphus was a bibliophile. He had noble motives. His library of 200,000 to 700,000 volumes would, after all, not be complete without the translation of the Torah.[7]

Now, even Heaven assisted the translators, as the seventy-two Sages bidden to do the translation all independently arrived at the conclusion that fourteen changes had to be made to avoid a basis for the Greeks to attack our basic religion and the authenticity of the Torah.[8]

The question, I submit, is itself the answer. If a miracle was necessary, and miracles are wrought only if absolutely necessary,[9] it demonstrated that the Children of Israel at that time were indeed ill-prepared to deal with all the tensions, challenges, and ridicule that would have emerged from a faithful translation of the Torah. They were not up to the challenge. They were much more comfortable to sweep all the unpleasantness under the rug and be satisfied with an illusionary certitude of their belief system, demonstrating the same insecurity in wanting the Golden Calf as an intermediary.[10]

---

6. See, e.g., H. St. John Thackery, *The Septuagint and Jewish Worship: A Study in Origins* (London: Oxford University Press, 1921), 41; Ralph Marcus, "Jewish and Greek Elements in the Septuagint," in *Louis Ginzberg Jubilee Volume: On the Occasion of His Seventieth Birthday*, eds. Alexander Marx et al. (New York: American Academy for Jewish Research, 1945), 233; Nina L. Collins, *The Library in Alexandria and the Bible in Greek* (Leiden: Brill, 2000), 115–116.
7. See Flavius Josephus (37–ca. 100), *Antiquities of the Jews*, Bk. 12, ch. 2 (paraphrasing Letter of Aristeas [ca. 180–145 BCE], which indicates that Demetrius of Phaleron had collected 200,000 volumes for Ptolemy II Philadelphus [309–246 BCE]); E. A. Wallis Budge, *A History of Egypt from the End of the Neolithic Period to the Death of Cleopatra VII B.C. 30*, vol. 7 (London: Kegan Paul, 1902), 192 (recording one estimate of the number of volumes in Ptolemy II Philadelphus' time to be 700,000); Matthew Bunsen, *Encyclopedia of the Roman Empire*, rev. ed. (New York: Facts on File, 2002), 15, s.v. "Alexandria, Library of."
8. *Megillah* 9a–9b.
9. See *Berakhot* 58a; Nahmanides to Exodus 13:16.
10. Exodus 32:1.

Va-Yiggash

Most basically, the Jews were unprepared to prove to the Greeks the unity of Hashem, that the God that is the source of good is also the source of evil, and all is one, all is really good. So the Sages prevented the Greeks from posing this challenge by simply changing "Let us make man" (Genesis 1:26) to "I shall make man." Secondly, the Sages were afraid that the Greeks would question the awesomeness of Hashem by pointing to the statement that Moses sent the "youths of the Children of Israel" to bring sacrifices in preparation for the Revelation at Sinai. So they translated this verse to say that Moses sent the "*zaatutei*" of the Children of Israel, which denotes importance.[11]

They were afraid to expose the inferences that the Greeks would make of Moses. They feared that the Greeks would diminish Moses' status by claiming that he was not wealthy and that he was tainted. So they changed the statement that Moses mounted his wife and sons "on the donkey" (Exodus 4:20) to "on a carrier of men,"[12] and "I have not taken one donkey of theirs" (Numbers 16:15) to "I have not taken one desired object of theirs."[13] This cover-up indicated that the Jews were afraid to be exposed to the challenge of whether the inferences were correct as far as their own perception of their leaders was concerned, that is, whether they put too much stock in wealth and mistrusted their leaders.

They also did not want to expose themselves to the challenge of explaining the difference between Sarah's laughter upon hearing the divine promise that she would bear a son, "*va-titzhak Sarah be-kirbah*" (Genesis 18:12), and Abraham's laughter upon hearing the same promise, "*va-yitzhak*" (Genesis 17:17).[14] They were not

---

11. Exodus 24:5; Rashi to Megillah 9a, s.v. "*zaatutei*."
12. The Sages did not want Ptolemy to think that Moses did not have even one horse or camel but had to transport his family on a lowly donkey. The term "carrier of men" could be interpreted as a camel. Rashi to Megillah 9a, s.v. "*nosei benei adam*."
13. The Sages changed the term "donkey" to "desired object" to avoid an inference that although Moses did not take any donkey from the Children of Israel, he did take other things from them. Rashi to Megillah 9b, s.v. "*lo hemed ehad mehem nasati*."
14. The Sages changed the phrase describing Sarah as laughing "inwardly" (*be-kirbah*), to laughing "among her relatives (*bi-keroveha*), to distinguish the laughter of Sarah from that of Abraham. Megillah 9a; Rashi ad loc., s.v. "*bi-keroveha*."

Three Black Days

perceptive enough to distinguish the laugh of ridicule from the laugh of ecstasy.[15] And the dating of the Exile of 430 years was covered up because they did not feel on an emotional level that at the Covenant between the Parts, the Servitude had already begun when a father is told that his children would go into exile.[16] The father is vicariously living that exile already and it is as if the Children of Israel were already in the physical exile of Egypt, "in a land not their own" (Genesis 15:13). They evidently were not prepared for such refinement in human nature.

All this revealed the miserably low status of their spiritual level. They wanted their religion to avoid all the tensions, emotions, and challenges of life, and be confined to a sphere where they would be safe from attack.

But what a gigantic mistake this was! It was this recognition that spelled greatness for Ezra. While the Divine Presence, according to Tradition, did not dwell in Second Temple,[17] the majesty of the Torah was at its very zenith in the Second Temple. Ezra knew that the equivalent of prophecy could be produced from the Torah itself. That is the belief that prophecy could be produced from the learning of the Torah with equal measure. Ezra knew that only if the Torah were subject to the severest intellectual challenges could it emerge as universal and relevant for each age. How much *emunah* could this produce. It is unimaginable!

Just as the Halakhah states *"kullam ḥayyav patur"*[18] because truth that was never challenged is a lesser truth, Ezra set out to bring all the

---

15. Rashi to Genesis 17:17; Maharsha, *Ḥiddushei Halakhot ve-Aggadot, Megillah* 9a, s.v. *"va-titzḥak Sarah bi-keroveha."*
16. The verse states, "The habitation of the Children of Israel during which they dwelled in Egypt was 430 years" (Exodus 12:40). The Children of Israel were in Egypt 210 years. To avoid an accusation that the Torah recorded a false calculation, the Sages inserted the phrase "and in other lands" in that verse to indicate that the Exile began before the Children of Israel descended to Egypt, when Hashem told Abraham that his children would be exiled. Rashi to *Megillah* 9a, s.v. *"u-ve-she'ar aratzot."*
17. *Yoma* 9b–10a; Rashi to Genesis 9:27, s.v. *"ve-yishkon be-oholei Shem."*
18. *Sanhedrin* 17a; Maimonides, *Mishneh Torah, Sanhedrin* 9:1. If Sanhedrin opens a capital case with a unanimous guilty verdict (*kullam ḥayyav*), the accused is exempt (*patur*) until some merit is found to acquit him.

Va-Yiggash

tensions, conflicts, and challenges of life straight into the lap of the Torah. He expanded the public reading of the Torah and the court system, forcing the common man to come into close contact with Torah, forcing him to bring all his disputes to the Jewish court.[19]

Well, if Ezra understood that by dragging people off the streets and uniting them with the Torah, the brilliance of the Torah would emerge that much greater, then how much more so is this true for us today. We are living in an age of profound knowledge in all the disciplines, be it medicine, sociology, economics, finance, or biology. All these areas of knowledge have something to contribute to the clarification of the Torah, and the Torah has something to contribute to the direction and development of all these disciplines.

Today, there is no greater opportunity to challenge the Torah in every aspect of life and find profound answers with Torah itself. What is needed is a synthesis between the professionals and the pure Torah scholars. Each must respect the other. There must be a communication and deep dialogue between them so that the moral concerns in each discipline are brought to the attention of the Torah scholars and a new and higher level of relevancy of the Torah is produced.

Ezra managed to produce a level of faith by showing that the awesomeness of Hashem, which Jeremiah did not see as he watched the gentiles reveling in the holy places, is found in the mere survival of the Jewish people among a pack of wolves,[20] and that the great strength of Hashem, which Daniel did not see as he witnessed the Children of Israel being subjugated, consists of the restraint that Hashem exercises against the gentiles.[21]

---

19. *Bava Kamma* 82a.
20. *Yoma* 69b; *Tosafot Yeshanim* ad loc., s.v. "*hei'akh ummah ahat*" (noting the exchange between R. Joshua and Emperor Hadrian, recorded at *Midrash Tanhuma, Toledot* 5, in which Hadrian exclaims, "How great is the lamb that survives among the seventy wolves," to which R. Joshua responds, "How great is the Shepherd Who protects her.").
21. *Yoma* 69b. The Talmud *ad locum* records that the Men of the Great Assembly, led by Ezra, restored the crown of God's glory to its original luster. Moses had originally described Hashem as "the great, powerful, and awesome God" (Deuteronomy 10:17). Jeremiah, by contrast, omitted the description "awesome" because he saw gentiles reveling in the holy places. See Jeremiah 32:18 ("the great and powerful God,

Three Black Days

But we can do much more than just survive. With the power of Torah, we can turn the clock back. We can revitalize the great accomplishments of Ezra and then proceed to merit the prophecy that comes from Torah, culminating in the rebuilding of the Temple speedily in our days.

His name is Hashem, Master of Legions"). Subsequently, Daniel omitted the description "powerful" when he saw the gentiles enslaving the Jewish nation. See Daniel 9:4 ("I beg of You, O Lord, the great and awesome God"). Ezra, however, reinstated Moses' formulation, describing Hashem as "the great, powerful, and awesome God" (Nehemiah 9:32).

When the Idealist Bends to the Pragmatist

December 21, 1985

Throughout history, idealists have worked to change the present to conform to their vision of a brighter future for mankind. Idealism, however, often clashes with pragmatism, forcing the dreamer to change course. Today's portion has much to say about Jewish idealism and when it should bend.

If there was ever a dreamer in Jewish history, it was Joseph. He took Jewish destiny very seriously. His grandfather Abraham had been presented with the shocking vision, "Know with certainty that your offspring will be aliens in a land not their own – and they will serve them, and they will oppress them – four hundred years" (Genesis 15:13). Joseph was ready to assume the burden of the Servitude and more. His faith was unshakable. It would be better for him and his family to endure anguish to minimize the torture of future generations.

What a noble, altruistic sentiment! It was only when Divine Providence catapulted him to the position of Viceroy that his own dream had a connection with the Covenant between the Parts. Now, if he could draw out the drama to its logical conclusion and have his father come and bow down and ask for Benjamin to be free, think of the humiliation and suffering that the family would endure until the point when Joseph would reveal himself. So much suffering would be experienced that any further suffering for future generations would be unnecessary.[1] What a grand plan.

But alas, "Joseph could not restrain himself" (Genesis 45:1). His heart melts from the expression of genuine and acute anguish from Judah, "For how can I go up to my father if the youth is not with me?" (Genesis 44:34). This demonstrates that a cry for compassion from the present generation is sufficient to cause the idealist to bend.

We are presently moving toward a crisis of immense proportions. Rabbi Kahane and his supporters tell us that the security of Israel is threatened by the presence of one million Arabs, and the Jewish character of the State is threatened by the prospect of the exploding Arab population in contrast to the trickle of *aliyyah* and the much lower Jewish population growth rate. The solution that he proposes is forced resettlement of the Arab population.[2]

The solution Kahane offers is radical and not acceptable. Judah is crying, "How can I go up to my father if the youth is not with me?" The solution will at the very least create for the Jew a monstrous image in the world community. Moreover, God forbid, we risk war with the Arabs, as such an act constitutes clear intimidation. Compassion for the current generation demands a revision of the ideal.

But something much more basic is at issue here. Joseph's contribution to Egyptian society was so spectacular that it could not but evoke the profoundest admiration and generate the highest sense of gratitude. Without his ideas of a forced one-fifth tax in the years of plenty, when waste was rampant and no one was thinking in frugal terms, a whole nation would have perished.[3] Who could match his loyalty to the State? He accumulated all the silver and cattle, and nationalized the land, all in

---

1. See R. Naphtali Tzvi Yehudah Berlin, *Ha'amek Davar*, Genesis 42:9.
2. Meir Kahane, "Emigration Is the Only Solution," *Judaism* (Fall 1977): 393–404.
3. Genesis 47:24.

barter for food.[4] All the wealth was for Pharaoh.[5] And he was careful to pay his political debt to the Priests of Egypt who exonerated him in the matter of Lady Potiphar[6] by allowing the Priests to retain their land.[7]

But what did this accomplish for the Jews? Did it change the course of history for us? Did it prevent the slavery and the oppression portions of the Covenant between the Parts? Not only did the servitude and oppression come anyway, but, I would submit, the profound good of Joseph served ultimately as the basis for the Egyptians' cruel hatred for the Jews. It served as the basis for the Egyptian receptivity to establish the heinous decree of "every son who will be born, into the River shall you throw him" (Exodus 1:22).

And detached from the crisis of the time, many years later, Egyptians would think that Joseph converted a free enterprise economy into a socialist system in short shrift. A free people and independent Egyptians were taxed one-fifth of their produce for seven years. And he subjected them to extortion at the worst time. The food in the royal warehouses stockpiled by Joseph was theirs, after all, and it should have been distributed free. The economic policy certainly should not have culminated in the Egyptians proclaiming "We will become serfs to Pharaoh" (Genesis 47:19).

What an irony. The noblest, most ingenious ideas, which made everyone think of Joseph as divinely-inspired, served, with the passage of time, as the basis of the Egyptians' hatred for us.

What does this tell us? It says quite plainly that rearranging the secular society is completely irrelevant as far as Jewish destiny is concerned. Our best-laid plans in our relations with the gentiles will not change Jewish destiny one iota. And the resettlement plan in Israel is not like the one that Joseph had implemented – "as for the nation, he transferred it by cities" (Genesis 47:21). What has broken Arab political influence in the last five years is nothing more than the oil glut.[8] Events have been shaped for us.

---

4. Genesis 47:14–20.
5. Genesis 47:23.
6. *Midrash Aggadah*, Genesis 47:26; *Targum Yonatan*, Genesis 47:22. Potiphar would have killed Joseph rather than imprison him if the Priests had found Joseph guilty.
7. Genesis 47:22.
8. David Toufic Mizrahi, "If Oil Isn't Important, Who in the Middle East Is?," *Washington Post*, November 3, 1985, C1.

Joseph's legacy was not "by your command shall all my people be sustained" (Genesis 41:40), complete control of the gentiles, having them where we would like them. No, it is his cry to Judah, "I am Joseph. Is my father still alive?" (Genesis 45:3). As the *Beit ha-Levi* explains, there is an element of reproof.[9] Joseph demands consistency and says, "Yes, I am moved by your compassion, Judah, but I want consistency. How could Father have survived for twenty-two years without me?"

When we will channel the national will toward promoting greater internal harmony among Jews, not only will the vision of the idealist be shared by a larger consensus, but equally important, problems that now seem insurmountable will fall to the wayside, and our path to our unique destiny will proceed with all due speed.

---

9. R. Yosef Dov Soloveitchik, *Beit ha-Levi al Derush u-Milei de-Aggadata, Va-Yiggash*, (Jerusalem, 1985), 63.

Reunions

January 10, 1987

A reunion and reconciliation contain all the elements of a touching human experience. In this week's portion, we are confronted with three such events. One represents the very pinnacle of human relations, but the remaining two fall far short of our expectations.

When Joseph reveals himself to his brothers, he reaches out to them. He speaks mollifying and conciliatory words, reaching a crescendo of emotion with "he kissed all his brothers and wept upon them" (Genesis 45:15).

We expect reciprocity on the part of the brothers, an outpouring of contrition, warmth, and sentimentality. But what do we find? Joseph's soothing words just barely shake the brothers loose from their confusion and silence. "Afterwards his brothers conversed with him" (ibid.). We do not even know what they said to Joseph.

Our premonition that the beauty of the moment would not last is unfortunately confirmed in next week's *parashah*. There, we read that after Jacob's death, the brothers fear that Joseph will take revenge against them. They fabricate a lie that Jacob instructed Joseph to forgive them for their sin.[1] Well, the message hence is that, yes, guilt and fear are very powerful motivational forces bringing man to repentance. Without such feelings, there would never be any repentance. But when it comes to building enduring human relationships, fear and guilt are actually impediments. Guilt always biases us in interpreting our friend's action.

The brothers took Joseph's action of not inviting them to dinner after Jacob's death as a sign of smoldering hatred that he harbored against them.[2] Similarly, on their journey back to Egypt from burying Jacob in the Land of Israel, Joseph's pause at the pit into which he had been thrown to pronounce the blessing "Blessed is He who performed a miracle for me at this place" was also interpreted by the brothers as a sign that Joseph still harbored a grudge against them.[3]

Now, when Jacob reunites with Joseph, we anticipate the very height of an emotional rollercoaster, for after all, Joseph meant to Jacob nothing less than *Gan Eden* itself on this world, and without him, Jacob's life was a deep depression. When it came to Joseph's reaction, he indeed outdoes himself. "He [Joseph] appeared before him, fell on his neck, and he wept on his neck excessively" (Genesis 46:29). He weeps and weeps, and does not stop. But what about Jacob? He shows no emotion, no weeping, and no embracing of Joseph. In fact, Tradition has it that Jacob was saying *Shema* at that time.[4] He appears reserved, as if he is holding back!

I would submit that Jacob did this purposely. The report that Joseph sent back to Jacob emphasized his elevation in Egypt, that he was "father to Pharaoh, master of his entire household, and ruler throughout the entire land of Egypt" (Genesis 45:10). He wanted Jacob to know about every nuance of his power and sovereignty. "Tell my father of all my glory in Egypt" (Genesis 45:13). When Jacob went down to Egypt,

---

1. Genesis 50:16–17.
2. *Rashi* to Genesis 50:15. The Midrash explains that Joseph's intention of no longer inviting his brothers for meals was for the sake of Heaven. When Jacob was alive, he seated Joseph at the head of the table. After Jacob's death, Joseph did not want to take this position anymore because Judah was a King and Reuben was Jacob's first-born son. Genesis Rabbah 100:8.
3. *Midrash Tanḥuma, Va-Yeḥi* 17.
4. *Rashi* to Genesis 46:29, s.v. "*va-yevkh al tzavvaro od.*"

he knew that he was going not only as an old father, to reunite with his long-lost son, but also as the father of a nation, a nation that was going to begin a very different chapter in its history, the chapter of slavery. Indeed, the Midrash tells us that Jacob made a detour to uproot cedar trees to provide wood for the future building of the Tabernacle![5]

Is life that is associated with position, stature, and honor the only life worth living? If his children are slaves, should they simply roll over and die? Who was witnessing the reunion? It was the entire Egyptian nation, as the Midrash says.[6] Jacob could not allow it to be recorded that he was dazzled by Joseph's position. He had to hold back his emotions of a father to a son so as not to leave his reaction open to misinterpretation that he was dazzled by the glory of Joseph's position.

Moreover, even as a father, what moved Jacob the most was that his son was alive and was not corrupted by the pagan culture of Egypt. Joseph's position as Viceroy had nothing to do with Jacob's ecstasy. Jacob says that quite eloquently, "Now I can die, after my having seen your face, because you are still alive" (Genesis 46:30). The *Or ha-Ḥayyim* interprets this as saying that Jacob looked at Joseph's face and saw that he was not guilty of any sins.[7] This is what made Jacob ecstatic.

Which reunion was a scene of pure beauty? It was the embrace of Joseph and Benjamin. "Then he fell upon his brother Benjamin's neck and wept; and Benjamin wept upon his neck" (Genesis 45:14). This is the embrace of two people who longed for each other. Now they embrace in a relationship that is devoid of guilt and fear, and any extraneous matters.

But they resolve to do more. It is a relationship that echoes the beautiful words of the poet who said, "Grow old along with me. The best is yet to be."[8] Both took a bold step to lift their relationship one rung further up the ladder of nobility. They know that it was *sin'at ḥinnam* that caused the tragedy for the family, so now they set out symbolically to go in the opposite direction with a demonstration of *ahavat ḥinnam*.

---

5. Genesis Rabbah 94:4; *Etz Yosef* ad loc., s.v. "*le-heikhan halakh*."
6. R. Jacob Culi, *Me-am Lo'ez*, Genesis 46:29, trans. R. Shemuel Yerushalmi, *Yalkut Me-Am Lo'ez: Sefer Bereshit* (Jerusalem: Mossad Yad Ezra, 1968), 785.
7. *Or ha-Ḥayyim* to Genesis 46:30.
8. Robert Browning (1812–1889), "Rabbi ben Ezra."

What do they do? The neck is taken by our Sages to represent the Temple because just as the neck is a bridge between the head and the body, so, too, the Temple is the bridge between heaven and earth.[9] Benjamin weeps over the Tabernacle at Shiloh that would be destroyed, located in the portion of Joseph. He commiserates with the destruction of his brother although he knows that his own ascendancy, in the form of building the Temple in his portion, depends on the destruction of the Tabernacle in the portion of Joseph. So, too, Joseph commiserates with the destruction of the two Temples that are destined to be in the portion of the Tribe of Benjamin, and he does not weep over the destruction of the Tabernacle in his own portion.[10]

The highest nobility in human relations occurs when a beautiful moment of sentimentality is captured but there is simultaneously the firm resolve between the parties that "the best is yet to be."

---

9. *Megillah* 16b; *Rashi* to Song of Songs 7:5, s.v. *"tzavvarekh"*; R. Moses Sofer, *Torat Mosheh, Va-Yiggash*, s.v. *"va-yippol al tzavvarei Binyamin."*

10. *Rashi* to Genesis 45:14.

How to Produce an Emotional Impact

December 17, 1988

The Torah goes to extraordinary lengths to build up a dramatic expectation of a reunion between Jacob and Joseph. On Joseph's part, Jacob was always the center of his negotiations with his brothers. And so, with considerable excitement, Joseph instructs his brothers that they should tell their father of his glory and power in Egypt.[1] For Jacob's part, his spirits were revived upon learning that Joseph was alive, and he desperately wanted to see him before he would die.[2]

When the reunion takes place, however, we are disappointed. Yes, Joseph meets our expectations. As the Midrash fills in the details, Joseph comes attired in royal raiment and a gold crown, with all the Egyptian

---

1. Genesis 45:13.
2. Genesis 45:27–28.

noblemen following him.³ Joseph bows in front of Jacob, and weeps on his neck.⁴ But Jacob is passive. Adding to the difficultly is the Midrash's comment that Jacob was reciting *Shema* then.⁵ Had he no other time to recite *Shema*?

Rather than looking at Jacob's role in the reunion as marring the event, the *Maharal* says that it embellished the event.⁶ At the moment that Jacob's emotions were surging from his son, he also achieved a new level of love of God and fear of Heaven. He now saw the merging of the Attribute of Judgment and the Attribute of Mercy. All the anguish that Joseph had caused him was for the good. "*Kol de-avid Raḥmana, le-tav avid*."⁷ He actually lived the first verse of *Shema*. "Hear O Israel, Hashem is our God, Hashem is the One and Only" (Deuteronomy 6:4).

Some would attach little significance to the demands that the Torah places on the emotions of the Jew. But this is the essential difference between the Jew and the Noahide. For the Noahide, we do not make demands on his emotions. He is prohibited from worshiping idols, but he is not commanded to have *emunah* or *bittaḥon*, or to love or fear God. *Lo tignov*, "you shall not steal" (Exodus 20:13), but not *lo taḥmod*, "you shall not covet" (Exodus 20:14). And *dinim* (lit., "laws"),⁸ but not "you shall love Hashem your God" (Deuteronomy 6:5).

We cannot rely on *emunah* to come by itself. We must do something to produce it. Jacob did this. How? He used a moment of beauty in his relationship with his son and attached Hashem to it. This produced *emunah*. Just imagine the strength that this meeting would provide to Jacob's descendants in their suffering in Egypt. At a time when *emunah* would weaken, they could point to Jacob, who acknowledged his greater

---

3. R. Jacob Culi, *Me-am Lo'ez*, Genesis 46:29, trans. R. Shemuel Yerushalmi, *Yalkut Me-Am Lo'ez: Sefer Bereshit* (Jerusalem: Mossad Yad Ezra, 1968), 785.
4. Genesis 46:29.
5. *Rashi* to Genesis 46:29.
6. R. Judah Loew b. Bezalel, *Gur Aryeh*, vol. 1, *Va-Yiggash*, p. 239.
7. *Berakhot* 60b. The phrase means that all that the All-Merciful does is for the good.
8. Maimonides understands *dinim* as a societal obligation to establish a judicial system to enforce the other six Noahide Laws. *Mishneh Torah, Melakhim* 9:14. In Nahmanides' view, *dinim* also requires the enactment of legislation governing civil conduct and interpersonal relations. Nahmanides to Genesis 34:13.

awareness of Hashem at the time of the reunion, and they could also believe that the Redemption would ultimately come.

If attaching Hashem to a moment of beauty between man and his fellow preserves that moment and suffuses it with meaning, the converse is also true. Attaching a pious moment, a moment when we feel that we have been rescued from certain death, to thanksgiving and love of our fellow Jew also preserves the moment and suffuses it with meaning, allowing it to exert an impact. As an example, if a peace offering is brought as a *todah* (thanksgiving offering), bread is to be brought with it. As the *Sforno* explains, through the increased number of loaves, more people eat from the offering and the miracle is publicized.[9]

Ḥinnukh of faith will make an impact only when parents are personally involved. A meaningful sharing of the parent-child relationship must accompany the acceptance of the yoke of Heaven. This is the basis of the position of *Rashi* in *Berakhot* 20a that the father is exempt from the obligation of ḥinnukh regarding the recitation of *Shema* because he is not present when his son gets up and goes to sleep.[10] It is not ḥinnukh at all if the father is not personally involved.

We must be synthesizers to produce an emotional impact on society. The greater the unity we achieve in our actions, the greater the emotional impact we will produce.

---

9. *Sforno, Kavvanot ha-Torah*, ch. 10.
10. *Rashi* to *Berakhot* 20a, s.v. "*ketannim.*"

The Balance between Freedom and Restraint

December 22, 1990

We would be hard put to identify a more surprising event in world affairs over the last century than the sudden demise of Communism. Just as we have become complacent in our celebration of the superiority of our system, the U.S. economy has suddenly been hit with a recession, the first in eight years.[1] This indicates that our system is far from perfect; it too is fallible!

Both the massive collapse of Communism and the failure of our own system reflect man's groping to discover the ideal blend between freedom, on the one hand, and restraint, on the other.

Permit me to suggest that the model for the ideal blend is the Torah, for the essence of the Torah is, after all, a collection of duties and prohibitions. Any time that we go considerably beyond this and impose

---

1. Robert D. Hershey, Jr., "Industrial Output Declines 1.7% in Latest Indicator of Recession," *New York Times*, December 15, 1990, 1.1.

Va-Yiggash

constraints on freedom in areas that Halakhah never intended to constrain, we are unleashing unhealthy forces. So, too, when we encourage freedom of conduct in areas where the Torah prohibits it, we are again unleashing unhealthy forces of instability in society.

Communism abolished private ownership of property. But the Torah society calls for private ownership. Communism represses the basic liberties of freedom of speech, assembly, and press. But the Torah does not call for this. Man's spirit is irrepressible. If he is denied freedom of expression and a feeling of self-worth in the economic sphere and in the creative sphere, his spirit and need for self-expression will only make their way elsewhere, and in the form of denying Hashem or in international and military adventure, in exerting control over other peoples.

And so, too, the present recession is due to government encouragement of bankers to be reckless, the deregulation of the banking industry while still protecting deposits with FDIC insurance up to $100,000.[2]

The demise of Communism was presaged by the failure of the first great social experiment in Communism. The architect of the experiment was Joseph. In dealing with the distribution of food during the famine, the institution of private property was for all intents and purposes abolished. First, people gave up their specie, then their cattle, then their land, becoming only share croppers.[3] Only their own enslavement was rejected by Joseph.[4] And also, Joseph implemented mass transfers of people so that they should notice that the change to Communism was real, not just for show.[5] No one could claim ownership of the land by dint of a long-standing presence. Then he created a privileged class, the Priests, who kept ownership of their land and were also guaranteed a subsidy.[6]

---

2. Seth A. Klarman, "Blundering Down Wall Street; How Trading Wisdom for '80s Greed Has Put Us in '90s Trouble," *Washington Post*, November 25, 1990, C3; Michael C. Keeley, "Deposit Insurance, Risk, and Market Power in Banking," *American Economic Review* 80, no. 5 (December 1990): 1183–1200.
3. Genesis 47:14–20.
4. Nahmanides to Genesis 47:19.
5. Genesis 47:21; *Rashi* ad loc., s.v. "*ve-et ha-am he'evir*."
6. Genesis 47:22. The Priests were given a stipend of a fixed amount of bread per day. *Rashi* ad loc., s.v. "*ḥok la-kohanim*."

This system was a total failure. Joseph should have restored free enterprise when the crisis passed. But instead, he kept the system permanently a Communist one.[7] This explains, I would submit, how the attitude of the Egyptians toward Joseph and his family changed so radically from admiration to such intense hatred. How could this be? Even to the point of genocide?

The answer is that Joseph himself unwittingly created the social order that would make the masses the pliable pawns of the hatemongers. He abolished private property, which gives man a sense of self-worth, and created a privileged class, which invites invidious comparisons. The hatred and the frustration just need a governmentally-approved outlet in the form of hating Jews. This is the grass roots anti-Semitism that is emerging today in the wake of the lessening of the grip of the Communist regimes.[8] Joseph himself created the mechanism for "a new king arose over Egypt, who did not know Joseph" (Exodus 1:8). Free enterprise should have been restored.

We are quite confident that we are living in the era of the Messiah because the most salient feature of the Messianic era is the tyranny in the world. "This World differs from the Messianic era only with respect to the servitude of the Diaspora" (*Sanhedrin* 91b). So now all the governments of the world are converging. From this convergence, it will be realized that the Torah is the best model for the ideal blend of restraint and freedom.

---

7. Genesis 47:26.
8. See Trudy Rubin, "Glasnost Has Brought a New Type of Antisemitism to the Soviet Union," *Philadelphia Inquirer*, January 26, 1990, A.19.

Va-Yeḥi

From There He Shepherded the Stone of Israel

December 17, 1983

Our Forefather Jacob suffered grievously from the favoritism that he showed Joseph. Now, at his deathbed, when all his children surround him in an intimate circle and he gives his blessing to each one, we would expect that he would do his utmost to promote harmony and filial devotion among his children and to prevent dissension and discord at all costs.

Yet, Jacob clearly reserves his most tender and magnanimous sentiments for Joseph. He says, "The blessings of your father surpassed the blessing of my parents to the endless bounds of the world's hills. Let them be upon Joseph's head and upon the head of the exile from his brothers" (Genesis 49:26). I was given a boundless blessing, "You shall spread out powerfully westward, eastward, northward, and southward" (Genesis 28:14), and these boundless blessings are all for you, Joseph, the crown of your brothers.[1] This appears as outright favoritism to Joseph.

---

1. *Rashi* to Genesis 49:26, s.v. "*ad ta'avat givot olam.*"

Va-Yeḥi

The answer seems clear. This is the crescendo of a blessing, and the blessing begins "But his bow was firmly emplaced and his arms were gilded" (Genesis 49:24). Not only did Joseph keep his bow emplaced, showing restraint in not taking revenge against his brothers, but he showered them with gold, with appreciation.[2] A lesser man would develop a sharper feeling of hatred toward his brothers with each incident that transpired. Being placed in a dungeon would be blamed on the brothers. Moreover, when someone is persecuted, he will either withdraw or fight back. He will not seek to bring about love and a filial sentiment.

Joseph was not driven merely by an attribute of kindness. Someone may heap kindness on a stranger, but never to correct a misconception of his love. He was driven by *ḥesed shel emet*.[3]

In exile, Jews are compared to dust,[4] and the nations of the world to water – "Many waters [of heathen tribulation] cannot extinguish the fire of this love" (Song of Songs 8:7). If every Jew is separate, he is a speck of dust that is easily destroyed. But if the particles of dust are cemented together, a stone is formed. Although the stone can be kicked and can tumble, it cannot be destroyed by the flood waters.[5]

Joseph is the one who made the stone. It is therefore appropriate that his portion be one of "an inheritance without borders,"[6] because only a man of *ḥesed shel emet* can heighten and intensify the blessings of his brothers. Each will find fulfillment in his mission of promoting peace, harmony, and profound understanding. When peace and harmony prevail in a nation, infinite possibility of accomplishment and elevation abounds. Joseph's blessing would never detract from his brothers. It would only add in a magnificent manner.

---

2. *Malbim* to Genesis 49:24.
3. See R. Solomon b. Moses ha-Levi Alkabetz (Safed, ca. 1505–1584), *Manot ha-Levi*, Esther 3:7 (noting that Haman rejected the month of Tevet as a time to attack the Jews when he studied the astrological sign of that month, a bow, and saw the *ḥesed* of Joseph, which is alluded to in the phrase "his bow was firmly emplaced" [Genesis 49:24]).
4. Hashem told Jacob, "Your offspring shall be as the dust of the earth" (Genesis 28:14).
5. See R. Naphtali Tzvi Yehudah Berlin, *Ha'amek Davar*, Genesis 49:24, s.v. "*mi-sham ro'eh even Yisrael*."
6. *Shabbat* 118a.

Such a personality, Joseph, would not only be a model of how to survive in Exile, but would be the paragon of how to be impervious to the Exile. Joseph was a man of charm,[7] and a man of charm can never be enslaved!

---

[7]. Genesis 39:4.

By You Shall Israel Bless

January 5, 1985

Jacob's reaction to the report of his children that Joseph was still alive can be described in terms no less grand than ecstatic. A morose individual was metamorphosed into one who enjoyed the bliss of the Divine Presence.[1] Yet, when Jacob, on his way to Egypt, stops off at Be'er Sheba to offer sacrifices, God appears to him in a dream and tells him, "Have no fear of descending to Egypt" (Genesis 46:3). This indicates that Jacob was indeed afraid. What happened to transform the ecstasy into cold fear?

Jacob's first reaction was that of a father, ecstasy. When the import of what his children told him, that Joseph was still alive and that "he is ruler over all the land of Egypt" (Genesis 45:26), sank in, he realized that the very reason that he was ecstatic could pose a terrible danger for his children in their development as a nation. The response of fear hence was the reaction of the father of a nation.

---

1. *Midrash Tanḥuma, Va-Yeshev* 2; *Targum Onkelos* to Genesis 45:27; *Rashi* to Genesis 45:27, s.v. "*va-teḥi ru'aḥ Yaakov.*"

Why was Jacob afraid? He was very confident that his moral teachings would be upheld and the Children of Israel would not be influenced directly by the decadence of the Egyptian society. He was afraid of the impact of the dazzle of Egypt. Joseph had not only survived and succeeded to reach dizzying heights, but was the Viceroy of Egypt. "He is ruler over all the land of Egypt" (Genesis 45:26). The spectacular always has the ability to secretly evoke emulation. This constituted the greatest fear, that the Children of Israel would be dazzled by something in the decadent society, maybe power or wisdom, and the lifestyle of a person with those qualities would subliminally be imitated. This is a form of idol worship.

It was this terrible fear that perhaps consumed Jacob on his deathbed. He looked at Joseph's two children, Ephraim and Manasseh, and realized that it was in these two lads that the amelioration of the dazzle would be accomplished. They were very different children. Ephraim was the *ben Torah*, who was frequently in Jacob's presence to study Torah,[2] and Manasseh was the interpreter[3] and the one appointed in charge of Joseph's house.[4] He was really the glitter overshadowed now by his father Joseph.

Manasseh was one way to counteract the glitter of Egypt, the product of Jewish glitter, Jewish magic. Gideon, the incarnation of Manasseh, represented the consummate dazzle. It would be Gideon who would display the stunning boldness of taking the bullock that was fattened for seven years for the honor of the Baal and sacrificing it for Hashem. It would be Gideon who would tear down the altar of the Baal and the *asherah* and use the wood to build an altar for Hashem.[5]

What was the reaction to Gideon? Unmitigated anger. The people wanted nothing less than to execute him. They demanded that his father turn him over.[6]

But what was the response? If the Baal is so powerful, let him avenge himself.[7] The momentum began to build up. Gideon summons

---

2. *Rashi* to Genesis 48:1, s.v. "*va-yomer le-Yosef.*"
3. *Rashi* to Genesis 42:23, s.v. "*ha-melitz*"; Genesis Rabbah 91:8.
4. *Targum Yonatan* to Genesis 44:1.
5. Judges 6:25–30.
6. Judges 6:30.
7. Judges 6:31.

the forces of the Jewish nation and a tremendous battle against Midian and Amalek develops. A band of three hundred warriors defeats a great host by means of brilliant military stratagems. They take torches and hide them in pitchers and bring along trumpets. While the first watch changes hands, and the fresh soldiers watching the outer perimeter are still drowsy from their sleep, these bands, in unison, smash the pitchers, make their torches visible, and sound the trumpets. Pandemonium ensues, and the enemy is resoundingly defeated.[8]

But there is another way to defeat the glitter of the decadent society, the method of Joshua. Joshua was the lad who "would not depart from within the Tent" (Exodus 33:11). With such a profound attachment to his *rebbe*, he observed all the multitudinous questions that people would ask in the ordinary course of everyday living. He witnessed a level of relevance of the Torah to which no one else was privy. And he observed the emotional reaction of his *rebbe* to everything, the whole continuum of human emotions. He even had to be at the slope of Mount Sinai when his *rebbe* would return from receiving the Torah to observe him in his triumph.[9] And his portion of the manna fell there, signifying that he belonged there.[10] Indeed, he was a good student and he was able to anticipate situations of national concern. Joshua instituted ten ordinances in inheriting the Land of Israel, anticipating circumstances where the interests of the individual would conflict with the interests of society.[11]

How did he prepare for war? He learned Torah in depth the night before.[12] This reduced the enemy to a mere abstraction. The only reality was Torah, the intellectual world of Torah.

---

8. Judges 7:16–25.
9. See *Rashi* to Exodus 24:13.
10. *Yoma* 76a; *Rashi* ad loc., s.v. *"zeh Yehoshua."*
11. *Bava Kamma* 80b–81a.
12. *Sanhedrin* 44b (statement of R. Yohanan); *Megillah* 3a–b; *Rashi* to Joshua 8:13, s.v. *"Va-yelekh Yeshoshua ba-lailah be-sokh ha-emek."* In preparation for the conquest of the city of Ai, the Torah records that "Joshua went that night into the midst of the valley (*ba-emek*)." The word *"emek"* is understood to mean that Joshua spent the night engaged in the study of *umkah shel Halakhah*, i.e., the profundities of Jewish law.

We certainly need both qualities – the glitter of Gideon as well as the profound attachment to Torah of Joshua – to counteract the glitter of the decadent world. But which is greater and needs more emphasis? Jacob felt that it was Joshua's approach. Why? If we look at the story of Gideon, symbolic of Jewish glitter, we find that it has its limitations. There perhaps was no biblical hero who was more consumed with self-doubt than Gideon. He must be reassured by Hashem every inch of the way. He asks Hashem to produce a second sign after Hashem had already given him one sign at his request that he would be successful.[13]

Gideon receives divine instruction that he should do battle against Midian and Amalek, and he will win.[14] In the frenzy of the moment, 32,000 soldiers respond to his call. But when he announces "Whoever fears and trembles, let him turn back and depart" (Judges 7:3), what happens? Twenty-two thousand soldiers withdraw.[15] When he is victorious and asks the people of Penuel and Sukkot for food for his famished soldiers, they respond, "Is the palm of Zebah and Zalmunna already in your hand that we should give bread to your legion?" (Judges 8:6).[16] We are not certain of your ultimate victory. We might be accused of treason if ultimately you are defeated. When he captures the Kings and asks his son Yether to kill them, the lad cannot do it because he is afraid.[17] The symbol that Gideon erects to commemorate the miracle of deliverance from the Midianites is also misunderstood and becomes a snare for idolatry.[18]

Yes, the greatest contribution of the Gideons is the climate that they create for the nurturing of fear of Heaven. But what really allows fear of Heaven to grow is the Joshua of society. The Joshua can demand

---

13. Judges 6:36–39. The first sign was that dew should fall only on the fleece of wool that Gideon set out on the threshing floor. The second sign was that the dew should fall only on the ground and the fleece should be dry.
14. Judges 6:36.
15. Judges 7:3.
16. Judges 8:5–8.
17. Judges 8:20.
18. Judges 8:24–27. To commemorate the miracle, Gideon made an *ephod*, a lavish garment or belt, from the golden nose rings that the Israelites collected as booty in their victory against the Midianites, but subsequent generations deified the *ephod*.

Va-Yeḥi

a miracle – "Sun, stand still at Gibeon, and moon in the Valley of Aijalon" (Joshua 10:12).

The dazzle of society changes from one generation to another. Today, the dazzle is scholarship, technology, and devastating military might. It is only the dedication to Torah on Joshua's level that can counteract it. We would make a big mistake to think that the profundity of the Torah is only for the intellectual elite but not for everybody. It is only those who are exposed to the dazzle of the Torah who will not fold under the dazzle of the secular society.

When the magic of Gideon embraces the sparkle of Joshua, Joseph himself is reconstituted and the Messiah the son of Joseph is produced. May it happen speedily in our days.[19]

---

19. The arrival of the Messiah the son of Joseph will precede the arrival of the Messiah the son of David. See *Sukkah* 52a. According to the *Malbim*, the Messiah the son of Joseph will be the future leader of the Ten Lost Tribes when they return. *Malbim* to Ezekiel 37:19 and Micah 5:1.

The Limits of Loyalty

December 28, 1985

The Jewish king, whose primary mission is to rally the Jewish people to accept full-heartedly the yoke of Heaven, has today an important message of Jewish loyalty and commitment. David singles out the sons of Barzillai for recognition. When David was fleeing Absalom, in the thick of the rebellion, Barzillai comes forward to provide food and provisions for David and his men.[1] At the time, he had no way of knowing that David would be restored to his position. What he did therefore was a *ḥesed shel emet*, a deed of kindness for which he had no hope of recompense.[2]

But there must be something more to Barzillai's kindness than meets the eye, for David instructs Solomon that the sons of Barzillai should be intimate associates, that they should eat at his table.[3]

---

1. II Samuel 17:27–29.
2. *Malbim* to I Kings 2:7.
3. I Kings 2:7.

Va-Yeḥi

Scripture records the motivation behind Barzillai's good deed – "For they said, 'The people are hungry and exhausted and thirsty in the desert'" (II Samuel 17:29). Surely he understood that he had a responsibility to the King. But what motivates his action is not duty but compassion to a group of people famished in the wilderness. David found this attribute precious and genuine, worthy of being drawn to the attention of the Jewish people.

Barzillai, according to our Sages, was not a man of strong moral fiber.[4] But there are many people who are learned and idealistic. They understand duty and obligation from an idealistic standpoint. But this supplants rather than supplements their humanity and compassion. As the Sabba of Slabodka said, "love your fellow as yourself" (Leviticus 19:18) means that just as you love yourself naturally, not for the sake of a mitzvah, so, too, love your friend naturally, not for the sake of a mitzvah.[5]

David also had something to say about disloyalty. He condemns Shimi b. Gera.[6] Shimi was what we would call a bandwagon loyalist; his loyalty shifted with the tides. When David was down, fleeing from Absalom, Shimi was quick to curse him and tell him that his downfall was due to his wickedness and sins. "He cursed me with a powerful curse" (I Kings 2:8). And David takes it to heart for, after all, Shimi was the head of the Sanhedrin.[7]

But when the tide changes and David returns triumphant to Jerusalem, Shimi is among the first to greet him, declare his loyalty, and beg for forgiveness.[8] He comes with an entourage of a thousand men.[9] He says to David, "If you show everyone that you can forgive me, then you will have support, for people will say that you are forgiving and compassionate."[10]

---

4. *Shabbat* 152a.
5. R. Nosson Tzvi Finkel (*Ha-Sabba mi-Slabodka*, Lithuania, 1849–1927), cited in R. Aharon Yaakov Greenberg, *Iturei Torah: Likkut, Nisaḥ u-Biur*, vol. 4 (Tel Aviv: Yavneh, 1971), 114.
6. I Kings 2:8–9.
7. II Samuel 16:10–11; *Rashi* to II Samuel 16:10, s.v. "*Hashem amar lo.*"
8. II Samuel 19:17–21.
9. II Samuel 19:18.
10. *Rashi* to II Samuel 19:21.

The Limits of Loyalty

What is the test of loyalty for such a man? David leaves it to the shrewdness of Solomon to devise that test.[11] Solomon decrees that Shimi must remain in Jerusalem, and the day that he leaves and passes the Kidron Valley, he will be guilty of a capital crime.[12] The man who is really loyal does not look for loopholes. After three years, Shimi leaves Jerusalem to a foreign country, Gath, to retrieve his slaves.[13] He rationalizes that he is not violating the agreement because he is not going in the direction of the Kidron Valley to organize his fellow tribesmen. Instead, he went innocently to a foreign country to retrieve his slaves and returned immediately, forgetting that he was forewarned not to leave Jerusalem and especially the Kidron Valley.

Finally, David condemns Joab b. Zeruiah, not only for using deceit to kill the two generals, Abner and Amasa, but for "what Joab the son of Zeruiah did to me" (I Kings 2:5). What is this that Joab did to David? He revealed the secret of why he sent Uriah to the front line, that David had instructed him to do so. By doing this, he made it look as though David purposely had Uriah killed. Why? To satisfy his lust for his wife.[14]

Having Uriah killed was an *avlah*. He denied him due process. Uriah should have been tried. Our Sages condemn David for this.[15] But establishing the story under a fake link between Bath-sheba and the order to send Uriah to the front line magnified the sin of David. And when Jewish leaders fail, the whole moral climate of society is dragged down. Expose evil, but do not exaggerate or magnify the evil.

---

11. I Kings 2:9.
12. I Kings 2:36–37.
13. I Kings 2:40.
14. *Rashi* to I Kings 2:5.
15. *Shabbat* 56a.

Peace: At What Price?

January 17, 1987

In a recent Gallup Poll reported in yesterday's *New York Times*, it was revealed that paradoxically, as the Iran-Contra affair drags on, not only has the President regained some of his lost popularity, but a significant backlash is developing against both the press and Congressional committees for coming down so hard on the President.[1]

Realists are quick to point out that we are living in a world political environment characterized by aggressive and conspiratorial evil, capable, God forfend, of unleashing catastrophic destruction on the world. The Presidency hence must have a dark side to it. We must be prepared to condone occasional departures from the strict letter of the law, provided that these violations are motivated by the desire to preserve or promote world peace.

This attitude apparently finds some support in our Tradition as an aspect of the talmudic dictum that it is permissible to alter the truth

---

1. Alex S. Jones, "Poll Finds Iranian Affair Hurt Credibility of U.S. Journalism," *New York Times*, January 16, 1987, A1.

for the sake of promoting peace.[2] An application of this principle of *darkhei shalom* appears in today's portion. When Jacob dies, Joseph's brothers fear that Joseph will wreak vengeance against them. In anticipation of this possibility, the brothers fabricate a story, that Jacob instructed Joseph to forgive them for the iniquity that they hurled against him.[3]

The now familiar game of the intelligence community of inventing cover stories to lend a veneer of legitimacy to its designs apparently also finds support in our Tradition, in another nuance of the dictum that it is meritorious to alter the truth for the purpose of promoting peace. When Hashem instructs Samuel to go to Beit Lehem Yehudah to anoint David King of Israel, he hesitates at first and protests, "How can I go? If Saul finds out, he will kill me" (I Samuel 16:2). Hashem tells him that his fears are well-founded. He creates a pretext for Samuel. He tells him to take along a young calf. If anyone stops him and asks him what he is doing in the area, he should respond: "I have come to bring an offering to Hashem" (ibid.).

It behooves us to look at the matter more closely. Is peace the ultimate value? Is it more important than integrity? Should integrity always be sacrificed to preserve peace? Examination of a caveat that the Sages attach to the *darkhei shalom* principle is most revealing.

It seems that Rav's wife caused him anguish. When he asked her to prepare lentils, she instead prepared peas. When he asked for peas, she prepared lentils. Hiyya, their son, was bent upon restoring domestic harmony. When his father would ask him to go to his mother and request a dinner of lentils, Hiyya would instead present a request for peas, whereupon his mother would prepare lentils, just what Rav wanted! After a while, Rav commented to his son that his mother had improved. Then Hiyya took credit. Rav scolded him gently, applying to him the verse "they train their tongue to speak falsehood" (Jeremiah 9:4).[4]

Now, all the commentators are up in arms. Why did Rav scold his son? Could there be a bigger mitzvah than restoring peace between his parents?

---

2. *Yevamot* 65b.
3. Genesis 50:16–17.
4. *Yevamot* 63a.

Va-Yeḥi

R. Solomon b. Jehiel Luria explains this by positing that yes, for the purpose of restoring peace, occasional lies are permitted, but even to preserve peace, habitual lies are prohibited.[5] Habitual lies corrupt man's character. What he is saying is that if falsehood is the basis for peace, peace itself becomes devoid of meaning. Life without virtue, without justice, integrity, and kindness, is not life at all. If what we mean by peace is merely a ceasefire, a respite from violence, then the quality of life itself has terribly deteriorated. What incentive is there to pursue peace when all we get is a temporary cessation of violence?

And what gives us the clue that we have overstepped the boundary from an occasional lie to a habitual lie? It is clearly when we begin to lose our credibility. And yes, we are beginning to lose our credibility when the President proclaimed with righteous indignation that he would never negotiate with terrorists, and now he has done exactly that![6] What damage this does for our broader goal of achieving disarmament and a reduction of world political tensions. The success or failure of these talks revolves entirely around credibility, whether we can be counted on to make good on our commitments.

And there is another insight into why Rav rebuked Hiyya. This is the understanding of R. Jacob b. Joseph Reischer.[7] Rav knew that he could not possibly hope that Hiyya's lie would remain undisclosed. Because he could not always rely on his son to act in the capacity of an intermediary in his request to his mother, the masquerade would eventually explode in Rav's face. What he is saying is that if lies only buy time, then we are selling out future generations. We cannot secure peace on the backs of future generations.

We are blessed to be living in a country with a free press and a system of checks and balances with a ravenous appetite to discover illegal acts. Can the government ever think that its illegal acts will forever remain a secret?

---

5. R. Solomon b. Jehiel Luria (*Maharshal*, Poland, ca. 1510–1574), *Yam shel Shelomoh*, Yevamot 6:46.
6. Michael Wines and Doyle McManus, "U.S. Sent Iran Arms for Hostage Releases; Weapons Were Supplied for Aid in Freeing 3 in Lebanon, Government Sources Say," *Los Angeles Times*, November 6, 1986, 1.
7. R. Jacob b. Joseph Reischer (Prague, ca. 1670–1733), *Iyyun Yaakov*, Yevamot 63a.

Peace: At What Price?

I confess that I am a bit confused. What is our policy and what is the cover story? Is our policy to trade arms for hostages, and the cover story the need to reach out to Iranian moderates? Or are things reversed? Or perhaps we have no policy at all! But a few venal arms brokers induce us to make a policy because they saw an opportunity to earn a quick profit?

And what of the role of Israel? What has become of our law prohibiting us from selling weapons of any sort to a gentile?[8] Could he not use them for violent crimes? I am not questioning the legitimacy of the armaments industry in Israel. Selling a defensive shield to a gentile is permissible.[9] And when we sell arms to a legitimate, responsible State, I do not care how it is organized, whether Communist, Socialist, or Democratic, as we are selling arms to a responsible government, and a government, as opposed to an individual, can be relied upon to use the weapons only for defensive purposes. But a terrorist State, a State that our own government has proclaimed many times is run by a group of madmen, or lunatics? How can we be a party to selling arms to them?

What we are witnessing here is the Iron Casket Syndrome. When Joseph died, we are told, he was embalmed and placed in an iron casket, which was sunk to the very depths of the Nile.[10] One opinion has it that the intent was to secure a blessing for Egypt, that the Nile would overflow and irrigate the fields because of Joseph.[11] But another opinion ascribes a vicious motive to the Egyptians. The man who requested that his bones be brought up to the Land of Israel would never have his request fulfilled, for what technology could possibly bring him up? And if he would not be brought up, the Children of Israel would also not be brought up.[12]

There is no dispute between the two opinions, I submit; they are two sides of the same coin. When does our enslavement begin? It

---

8. *Avodah Zarah* 15b; Maimonides, *Mishneh Torah, Rotzeaḥ u-Shemirat Nefesh* 12:12; *Shulḥan Arukh, Yoreh De'ah* 151:5.
9. *Avodah Zarah* 16a; Maimonides, *Mishneh Torah, Rotzeaḥ u-Shemirat Nefesh* 12:12.
10. *Sotah* 13a.
11. Ibid.
12. R. Asher b. Jehiel (*Rosh*, Germany, ca. 1250–1327), *Tosafot ha-Rosh, Sotah* 13a.

is when we perceive ourselves as mere instruments to bring about a blessing to the host country.

Let us not be put into an iron casket. Rather, let us retain our identity, our uniqueness, and our spirit!

Two Contrasting Views of the Host Country

January 2, 1988

Throughout the millennia of Jewish suffering in the exiles, we have been caught between two contrasting views of our attitude toward our host country. On the one hand, it is represented in Jacob's view, "Please do not bury me in Egypt" (Genesis 47:29). Jacob is saying, "You, children, are quite comfortable living here. I do not even want to be buried here." This is the defensive posture, ever sensitive and attuned to the assimilationist threat and ever prepared to take measures to deal with it. Not only is there a need to uphold tradition, but to keep the vision alive as well.

But then there was Joseph. He entered Egypt as a slave, but in a short while, he was running the country! "By your command shall all my people be sustained" (Genesis 41:40).

Today, living amidst affluence and unprecedented economic and political freedom, we are tempted to follow Joseph's route and try to shape the social, economic, and political institutions of society in a manner that would best suit Jewish values. But why expend this energy beyond the concerns of Jacob? It is because we are bidden, "Walk before Me and be *tamim*" (Genesis 17:1).

Tamim, as R. Hirsch points out, has two meanings. It means "the end" and also "perfect." What constitutes the perfect Jew? It is the one who will go the entire boundary of permissibility.[1]

Now, we know that the 613 commandments represent a yoke. The Torah constrains our freedom. If we live in a repressive society, where our economic and political freedoms are constrained, then in addition to abiding by the restraints of the Torah, we are forced to submit to other restraints. But the human spirit craves freedom of expression. If we are forced to submit to restraints in addition to the restraints of the Torah, we may very well rebel against the yoke of the Torah. We may very well take the path of least resistance.

We live in a society that glorifies freedom and gives its citizens license in economic and political arenas. The free spirit may spill over to our obligations *bein adam le-ḥavero* and *bein adam la-Makom*. We may view them with levity and lightness and again reject the yoke of the Torah.

What therefore is ideal is a socio-political environment that is most consistent with the Torah. It is a society that allows us freedom of action when the Torah does so and restrains conduct when the Torah does so as well.

We get a glimpse of the damage inherent in an economic and political environment veering far off the model that the Torah regards as ideal. This is in reference to Joseph's handling of the famine. Joseph taxes the Egyptians twenty percent and stores the produce in public granaries. Then, in the years of famine, he sells the grain to the public. In no time, the money is gone. Then the chattel is sold for food. The people are so desperate that they offer themselves as slaves to Pharaoh.[2] Joseph, as Nahmanides points out, does not take them up on this offer, but instead, expropriates only their land.[3] The people become share croppers. Then Joseph imposes a twenty percent tax.[4]

---

1. R. Samson Raphael Hirsch, Genesis 17:1.
2. Genesis 47:19.
3. Nahmanides to Genesis 47:19.
4. Genesis 47:24.

Now, the plan was a stroke of genius to deal with an emergency situation. It was divinely inspired. But why did he not return society to free enterprise when the emergency was over?[5]

In a repressive environment, where there is no private ownership of land and no one can make a fortune, the possibilities to aggrandize wealth are very limited. The environment is more repressive than the Torah would call for. Perhaps it was the continuation of unnecessary restraints on the Egyptians that sowed the seeds of discontent and engendered their hatred towards the Children of Israel.

According to the *Maharal mi-Prague*, we know theoretically that the physical oppression could never have taken place unless the Children of Israel experienced spiritual decline.[6] The economic repression created an injurious environment for the Jewish people as well and perhaps contributed to their assimilation.

We are living today in an American society where there is an increasing force pulling us in the opposite direction. Instead of repression, we have license – no need for truth in advertising, no need for product safety or regulation, no need for licensing of professionals, and no laws against abortion.

Our challenge is to set up the societal institutions to conform to the model of the Torah and have an alliance with the State of Israel, where we can so dedicate our efforts.

---

5. See Genesis 47:26.
6. R. Judah Loew b. Bezalel, *Gur Aryeh*, Exodus 2:14.

I Will Separate Them within Jacob

January 13, 1990

In perhaps the most pious moment of his life, Esau, after realizing that the blessing of Isaac that was meant for him was stolen by Jacob, shrieks, "Have you but one blessing, Father?" (Genesis 27:38).

If this was the pain of Esau upon being deprived of a blessing, we can well imagine the anguish of a son who was twice denied a blessing. This is Simeon.

All Jacob's children gather around his deathbed. At this time, he confers blessing and recognizes the singular qualities of his children. But Reuben, Simeon, and Levi are condemned.[1] Reuben is restored by Moses – "May Reuben live and not die" (Deuteronomy 33:6). And Levi is somewhat vindicated. The very trait for which he is condemned, his zealotry and fury, is praised in a different context. Moses praises Levi for responding to the clarion call "Whoever is for Hashem, join me"

---

1. See Genesis 49:4–7.

after the Sin of the Golden Calf.[2] And Levi massacred all the idolators – "The one who said of his father and mother, 'I have not favored him'" (Deuteronomy 33:9).[3]

But poor Simeon. He gets no vindication. He is condemned by Jacob and omitted entirely by Moses!

Moreover, Jacob's displeasure with Simeon leads him to proclaim, "I will separate them within Jacob" (Genesis 49:7). *Rashi* understands this to refer to the aspiration that Simeon be the *melammed tinnokot*.[4]

Now, if Jacob could find nothing redeeming in Simeon, why did he assign him the exalted mission of being the Jewish educator? Did our Sages not warn us, "If the teacher is like an angel of the Lord of Hosts, they should seek the Law from his mouth; if not, they should not seek the Law from his mouth"?[5] "The world endures only because of the breath of school children" (*Shabbat* 119b). "School children should not be made to neglect their studies even for the building of the Temple" (ibid.).

Permit me to suggest that the answer lies in turning the tables completely and picking up on the approach of Nahmanides, who contends that "I will separate them within Jacob" is a blessing, not a curse![6]

Yes, Jacob cursed the anger and the fury of Simeon and Levi, but only on account of the way in which their anger manifested itself. But the basic sentiment of "Should he treat our sister like a harlot?" (Genesis 34:31) was very precious and merited emulation. "I will separate them within Jacob." Every Jew should have a piece of Simeon and Levi in his heart.

Two wrongs were perpetrated against Dinah. Even if Shekhem's liaison with her were voluntary, it would be a tragedy because Shekhem

---

2. Exodus 32:26.
3. The Levites followed Moses' command to kill even their relatives who participated in the Sin of the Golden Calf, such as an Israelite father of a Levite's mother. *Rashi* to Deuteronomy 33:9. The term "his father" at Deuteronomy 33:9 is thus interpreted to mean the Levite's maternal grandfather rather than his father.
4. *Rashi* to Genesis 49:7, s.v. "*aḥallekem be-Yaakov*."
5. Ḥagigah 15b (expounding Malakhi 2:7, "For the lips of the Priest should safeguard knowledge, and people should seek teaching from his mouth; for he is an angel of Hashem, Lord of Hosts.").
6. Nahmanides to Deuteronomy 33:6.

was a gentile and this is an "outrage in Israel" (Genesis 34:7). This evoked a sense of mourning. "The men were distressed" (ibid.). But more fundamentally, the relationship was forced on Dinah and this action assaulted their fundamental sense of decency. It was an act of theft, plain and simple. This aspect of the sin evoked rage.

Simeon and Levi were capable of sorting out their emotions. The two sentiments of mourning and anger did not mingle or become jumbled within them. This is a virtue, to react to an assault on decency and feel the pain acutely in all its dimensions, *haron* (anger) and *itzavon* (distress).

But there was something else to praise about their actions. In their negotiation with Hamor and Shekhem, Simeon and Levi would not be moved one bit by the generosity and grace of Hamor and Shekhem. "Inflate exceedingly upon me the marriage settlement and gifts, and I will give whatever you tell me; only give me the maiden for a wife" (Genesis 34:12). When it came to Jewish identity, their attitude towards intermarriage was uncompromising.

And so if we read in the social column of the *New York Times* about an intermarriage and our heart does not jump with sadness, and if we witness an assault on decency, whether it is in the workplace, in our personal lives, or on a communal level, and we do not feel outrage, then Simeon is not residing in our heart.

"I will separate them within Jacob" provides us with the ideal test for the success of the religious educational enterprise. Yes, we must embrace the philosophy of *sefei leih ke-sora* (lit., "stuff him as an ox").[7] We must gorge our children with Torah and mitzvot. But if this does not result in inculcating in our children a basic sense of decency and a strong Jewish identity, and they are not aroused by Simeon's emotions when they encounter the circumstances that should trigger these emotions, then the educational process has failed, regardless of the number of pages of *Gemara* that were turned and assimilated!

---

7. *Ketubbot* 50a (recording Rav's opinion that when a boy is six years old, one should stuff him with Torah knowledge, as one stuffs an ox with food to fatten it); *Rashi* to Mishnah, *Avot* 5:21, s.v. "*ben hamesh shanah le-mikra.*"

Moreover, there is the challenge of producing the balanced Simeon. Within the context of the inner world of Simeon and Levi, they indeed sorted out their emotions well. They knew what to reserve *ḥaron* for, and what to reserve *itzavon* for. But when they implemented their plan of revenge, their emotions got distorted.

As the *Malbim* asks, how was it possible for two men to massacre a whole city? What put the people so off guard and made them so vulnerable? The answer, posits the *Malbim*, is that when Simeon and Levi spoke to Shekhem, they focused not on the forced aspect of the relationship or even on the fact that Dinah was still being held against her will while the discourse was taking place. No, they focused their anguish on the fact that Shekhem was not one of them, that he was uncircumcised. Instead of focusing on the causes for fury, they focus on a secondary issue. This signals to Hamor and Shekhem that the sons of Jacob are really not exalted people, caring about principles and decency. They are just interested in expediency, and perhaps will be inveigled by the dangling of wealth in front of their eyes. This puts them off guard and allows the massacre to take place.[8]

Well, within the context of war, there is plenty of room for deceit. But when we choose our battles, surely we should not be guilty of expressing outrage over issues for which Halakhah could possibly support a position opposite to the one that we are taking and at the same time displaying relative silence when it comes to assaults on basic decency.

Let us take to heart Nahmanides' insight. Because Jacob blessed Simeon "I will separate them within Jacob," Moses found it unnecessary to bless Simeon.[9] Simeon enjoys the blessings of all the Tribes. Let all the Tribes embrace Simeon and with that find the building blocks to create *malkhut Shamayim* on this earth!

---

8. *Malbim, Ha-Torah ve-ha-Mitzvah*, Genesis 34:13.
9. Nahmanides to Deuteronomy 33:6.

The Issachar and Zebulun Partnership

December 29, 1990

The most celebrated partnership in Jewish life is the Issachar–Zebulun partnership. Zebulun gives Issachar half of his portion in This World and Issachar gives Zebulun half of his portion in the World to Come.[1]

While the Issachar–Zebulun partnership plays a paramount role in fundraising campaigns for religious institutions, permit me to suggest that it has practically disappeared from Jewish life today.

The Torah assigns Levi and those who want to take on his role the mission of "they shall teach Your ordinances to Jacob and Your Torah to Israel" (Deuteronomy 33:10). If the transmission of Torah from one generation to the next is to be accomplished in all its power and beauty, with thoroughness and profundity, Levi and those who take on his role

---

1. See *Rema* to *Shulḥan Arukh, Yoreh De'ah* 246:1; R. Shabbetai b. Meir ha-Kohen (*Siftei Kohen* or *Shakh*, Lithuania, 1621–1662), *Siftei Kohen* ad loc., n. 2; R. Mosheh Feinstein, *Iggerot Mosheh, Yoreh De'ah* 4:37.

must be professionalized. Levi's existence is hence guaranteed. Support for Levi is simply *ḥalef avodato*, "in exchange for the service that he performs,"[2] and the great mitzvah of strengthening Torah in no way detracts from Levi's reward for learning. Both the learner and supporter fulfill mitzvot. One does not detract from the other.

In what way then is Issachar's Torah different? It is set apart in at least two essential ways. One is that the deal is valid only if it is made before Issachar learns Torah, as a means of enabling him to learn.[3] If it is made after, it is not valid. Second, it involves a special type of learning. Issachar is a "*ḥamar garem*," a "bony beast of burden," not a nine-to-five man.[4] His extraordinary diligence is evident in his bony body structure. Also, he is a total-content person. "He rests between the boundaries" (Genesis 49:14). His feet are planted in This World, but his heart is in the World to Come.[5] And he is completely content. "He saw tranquility that it was good" (Genesis 49:15). Moreover, his outstanding character trait is his humility – "and the land that it was pleasant" (ibid.).[6]

And most importantly, "He became an indentured laborer" (ibid.). Issachar is perceived as paying a tax for the entire nation.[7] His agenda is the highest level of scholarship. Most of the members of the Great Sanhedrin came from Issachar.[8] The Supreme Court's agenda is the very vision of the Jewish people, *einei ha-edah*.[9] His Tribe is recognized as *yod'ei vinah la-ittim*, "with understanding for the times" (I Chronicles 12:33).

---

2. The tithes given to the Tribe of Levi are described as "*ḥalef avodatam*," in exchange for the service that they perform. Numbers 18:21.
3. *Sotah* 21a; R. Joseph Caro (Safed, 1488–1575), *Avkat Rokhel*, no. 2; Rema to *Shulḥan Arukh*, *Yoreh De'ah* 246:1.
4. Genesis 49:14.
5. R. Ze'ev Wolf of Zhitomir (Ukraine, d. 1800), *Or ha-Me'ir*, *Va-Yeḥi*.
6. The reference to "the land" denotes humility. See *Rashi* to Ecclesiastes 1:4, s.v. "*ve-ha-aretz le-olam omadet*." See also *Zohar* 1:242a (noting that Issachar does not exhibit arrogance); *Rabbeinu Beḥaye al ha-Torah*, Genesis 49:15 (interpreting the phrase "he bent his shoulder to bear" as signifying Issachar's humility).
7. *Or ha-Ḥayyim* to Genesis 49:15.
8. *Rashi* to Genesis 49:15, s.v. "*le-mas oved*"; *Genesis Rabbah* 72:5, 98:12.
9. Numbers 15:24. Cf. Leviticus 4:13 (referring to Sanhedrin as "*einei ha-kahal*," "the eyes of the congregation").

Va-Yehi

Yod'ei ittim signifies the integration of astronomy and Torah for determining leap years, and determining war and peace.[10]

Indeed, it is only such an ambition and aspiration coming from a man of humility that makes it understandable why Issachar is willing to offer half of his portion in the World to Come to enable him to learn. Why? It is because his ambition aims for a goal that he clearly understands he can never achieve naturally, *ke-minhago shel olam* (lit., "according to the custom of the world"), by working and learning part-time. Instead, it can be hoped for only by a monomaniacal dedication to the task. Even then, his goal can be achieved only if a community of scholars reinforces the environment of learning. And perhaps it can be achieved only after many generations of hard work. It is truly an investment for the future.

If the great *tzaddik*, the Berdichever Rav (Ukraine, 1740–1809), would come down here now, I think that he would find much cause of merit for the Jewish people. Why? Today, there is a blurring of the Torah of Levi and the Torah of Issachar, yet no *ba'al ha-bayit* demands half of Issachar's portion in the World to Come for supporting Torah. But neither does Issachar offer this. It represents the highest level of *Torah le-shemah* and the highest aspiration of achievement, which can be hoped for only by a monomaniacal pursuit of the goal.

The partnership between Issachar and Zebulun is however not obsolete. It is made every day by the *ba'al ha-bayit*, a deal between his body and soul. We all have sparkles of the Twelve Tribes within us. We are all Issachars and Zebuluns at the same time. Residing within us is the conflict between the restless nature of Zebulun, who shall settle by the seashores,[11] and the sedentary nature of Issachar, who "saw tranquility that it was good" (Genesis 49:15).

Moses treats Issachar and Zebulun as one person. Both were given just one verse, "Rejoice, O Zebulun, in your excursions, and Issachar in your tents" (Deuteronomy 33:18). You, Zebulun, can already rejoice when you set out on your far-flung business ventures because you recognize the tranquility of Torah in your *own* tent.

---

10. *Rashi* to Deuteronomy 33:18; *Rashi* to I Chronicles 12:32; *Radak* ad loc.; R. Jehiel Hillel b. David Altschuler (Galicia, 18th cent.), *Metzudat David* ad loc.; Genesis Rabbah 72:5.
11. Genesis 49:13.

Exodus

Shemot

What Is Justice?

January 12, 1985

For the past two months, we have been following with fascination the saga of the "Subway Vigilante," Bernhard Goetz. Public opinion surveys seem to indicate that our attitude toward him is formed not so much by a detached, objective analysis of the unique circumstances surrounding the incident, but rather by an emphatic identification with him. Every mugging victim identified with him. The collective rage and frustration of a society against a lax criminal justice system found a rallying point in this man, Bernhard Goetz.[1]

Well, ironically, twenty years ago, at the peak of the Civil Rights Movement, Goetz might not have been viewed as a hero. Rather, the focus would have been on the wretched black man, lying in a corner. The four blacks who approached Goetz for money would have been viewed as driven to crime because of the callous neglect of society, a

---

1. Esther B. Fein, "Angry Citizens in Many Cities Supporting Goetz," *New York Times*, January 7, 1985, B1; David E. Sanger, "Callers Support Subway Gunman," *New York Times*, December 25, 1984, 1.1.

society of overt discrimination, a society that perpetuated the vicious cycle of poverty. In the bygone era, Goetz would have been vilified and regarded as an exploitative symbol.

The attitude toward Goetz has brought about an unfortunate equation between justice and heroism. If we can anticipate that society will regard our act as heroic, we feel that we are doing justice. If we anticipate vilification, the act is unjust. This makes justice a matter of swaying public opinion. It was this type of justice that represented the highest nobility in Egyptian society.

In today's portion, we are overwhelmed by the tyranny and wretchedness of Egyptian society, but we are also given a glimpse of an isolated example of its nobility. The daughter of Pharaoh has pity on Moses. Why? Because of a confluence of so many factors that evoked sentiments of admiration toward the Jewish people.

Moses was lying in a basket with a garland, as Yoheved, his mother, was overtaken by emotion at the thought that she may never see his wedding canopy.[2] The fact that he was a child of three months indicated the desperation of his parents, holding him until no other course was open to them. Pharaoh's daughter must have thought, these people who we are persecuting have real spunk; they resist their fate in the most violent way. And Moses was filled with a radiant glow of the Divine Presence.[3] He was a beautiful creature to behold. When she touched the basket, she was healed of her leprosy.[4]

Working to pull her in the other direction was her handmaid's protestation, "How can you defy your father's command? How can you, of all people, be disloyal to him?"[5] The force of good won out. She rescued the child and did not turn him over.

But is it not mind-boggling that she did not perceive the whole concept of casting newborn babies into the Nile as anathema, as an intolerable evil of the highest magnitude? Her attitude toward Moses

---

2. Exodus Rabbah 1:24; *Etz Yosef* ad loc., s.v. "*ḥuppat ne'urim*"; Sotah 12b.
3. R. Solomon b. Isaac (*Rashi*, France, 1040–1105), *Rashi* to Exodus 2:6.
4. Exodus Rabbah 1:23.
5. Ibid.

was formed entirely by extraneous factors and had nothing to do with the evil that was done to him. That is not justice.

What is justice? It is the revulsion against the power element in human relations. And what is the most fundamental abuse of power? It is when power is used to destroy innocent life, the newborn infant, undisputed innocence. It is for this abuse of power that we must reserve our greatest revulsion and reaction. This is represented in the action of the midwives. They defied Pharaoh and did not kill the newborn male children.[6] But they wanted their defiance to be blatantly evident, so they prayed that no child should be stillborn or even defective, so that they should be above suspicion![7] And when the midwives kept the boys alive, they took extra pains to take care of them after they were born.[8]

Three episodes in Moses' life also show how the Jewish concept of justice is qualitatively different from the concept of justice in Egypt at its best. In the first episode, Moses said in effect, "Remove excess power or violence from a relationship that is inherently a power relationship, that of slavery." As *Ha'amek Davar* points out, Moses saw that the Jewish slave was doing his work diligently, so he questioned why the slave was arrested.[9] Within the framework of the institution of slavery, this represents an abuse of power.

Next, he observes a relationship of equals, two Jews. He sees strife and asks the wicked one, "Why would you strike your fellow?" (Exodus 2:13). Removing the power element in a relationship of equals is justice. There is an element of power in a friendship and in a marriage. It is injustice for it to be there!

Finally, he shows in his intervention of the daughters of Jethro and the shepherds, without knowing the nature of the dispute, that even in a relationship of inherent conflict, the power element should be removed. As R. Samson Raphael Hirsch points out, the verse describing the

---

6. Exodus 1:17.
7. Exodus Rabbah 1:15.
8. The midwives would collect food and water for poor Jewish woman to help them sustain the children that the midwives saved from Pharaoh's decree. Exodus Rabbah 1:15. In addition, when the children were born, Yoheved would beautify them and Miriam soothed them from crying. Ibid., 1:13.
9. R. Naphtali Tzvi Yehudah Berlin, *Ha'amek Davar*, Exodus 2:11, s.v. "*makeh ish Ivri.*"

Shemot

conflict uses the masculine form, *va-yirgareshum*, "they drove them away" (Exodus 2:17), rather than the feminine form, *va-yigareshun*, signifying that the shepherds treated the women roughly, as if they were one of the boys.[10] This represents the highest understanding of justice, that even when power is pitted against power, restraint is in order. Prisoners of war are entitled to rights. Nuclear disarmament pacts are restraint on the use of power.

It is only after one develops a refined sensitivity that power in human relations is wrong that one begins to cultivate a hatred for some of the power institutions of society itself; it is only then that one begins to question the status quo itself. It is only after Moses lived through these three experiences that he cried out to Hashem, "Why have You done evil to this people?" (Exodus 5:22). It is only then that he reacted to the bondage itself with such a revulsion that any excess in the form of the intensification of the Servitude was the catalyst for him to cry out against the whole institution itself.

Pharaoh's response to the defiance of the midwives was that "he made them houses" (Exodus 1:21). Pharaoh set up a spy network to know the exact whereabouts of the midwives.[11] But the commentary says that the "houses" refer to houses of royalty and priesthood that Hashem granted to the midwives as a reward for fearing Hashem and defying Pharaoh.[12] The reaction of the Children of Israel and the house of Levi to the nadir of the Servitude formed the foundation of all the institutions of authority of the Jewish people.

It is only when our lawmakers and educators develop and internalize the concept that power in human relations is evil that they will have the wisdom to formulate laws that will be able to mediate between instances of abuse of power, to strike a delicate balance between the rights of the accused and the interests of the victims of crime.

---

10. R. Samson Raphael Hirsch (Germany, 1808-1888), Exodus 2:17.
11. Tobiah b. Eliezer (Balkans, 11th cent.), *Midrash Lekaḥ Tov*, Exodus 1:21. According to this interpretation of the phrase "he made them houses," Pharaoh set up Egyptian homes adjacent to Jewish homes to detect whether the midwives were defying his orders. When a Jewish baby would cry, a neighboring Egyptian baby would also cry and thus reveal the presence of the hidden Jewish baby.
12. *Rashi* to Exodus 1:21. Yoheved was given the house of priesthood through her son Aaron, and the Tribe of Levi through her son Moses. Miriam was an ancestress of King David. *Sotah* 11b.

Welcoming the Sabbath

1980s

What one generation regards as emancipation may be regarded by another generation as a form of enslavement. A case in point is the crushing labor that our ancestors experienced in the Egyptian bondage. Many Sages interpret this to mean that women were assigned men's labor and men were assigned women's labor.[1] Modern feminists would find nothing tyrannical *per se* in this arrangement, except that the assignments were forced.

The blurring of the distinction between men's and women's work in modern society has had a profound effect on Modern Orthodoxy today. In a recent article, Joel Wolowelsky hints at a very provocative proposal.[2]

---

1. *Midrash Tanḥuma, Va-Yetze* 9; *Sotah* 11b. The men were ordered to knead dough and bake bread, while the women were ordered to chop wood and draw water.
2. Joel B. Wolowelsky, "Modern Orthodoxy and Women's Changing Self-Perception," *Tradition: A Journal of Orthodox Thought* 22, no. 1 (Spring 1986): 65–81.

Shemot

The division of mitzvot between men and women in ushering in the Sabbath seems arbitrary. The holiness of the day is ushered in with two mitzvot. One mitzvah, the kindling of the Sabbath candles, is traditionally performed by the woman of the household. The basis of the commandment is to perform an act that honors the Sabbath and at the same time contributes to the delight of the Sabbath.[3] But a man is equally obligated to perform these commandments. So why is candle lighting the purview of the woman of the household? Similarly, it is a mitzvah to usher in the holiness of the Sabbath with the recitation of *Kiddush*. The man of the household does this. But women are equally obligated in this regard.[4]

Why not reverse the division of mitzvot between men and women? At the very least, some approval, the author argues, should be given to the Modern Orthodox custom of the man of the household reciting the *Kiddush*, but the woman being honored with the *birkhat ha-motzi*.[5]

We should welcome such proposals because they have the effect of challenging us to delve into the symbolism and significance of the mitzvot and ask ourselves why the Sages enacted the division of mitzvot on Friday night in the way they did and not in reverse. The arrangement, I submit, encapsulates the complementary nature of the roles of the two sexes in Jewish thinking.

Man has taken very seriously his biblical mandate of *ve-kivshuha* (Genesis 1:28), to subdue the earth. *Ish darko le-khvosh*, "it is man's nature to subdue the earth."[6] He subdues nature, pushes out the frontiers of knowledge, and advances civilization in every manner he knows how. In his preoccupation with mastering nature, man often fails to recognize

---

3. *Rashi* to *Shabbat* 25b, s.v. "*ḥovah*" (*kavod*); *Tosafot* to *Shabbat* 25b (*oneg*), s.v. "*hadlakat ner be-Shabbat*"; Maimonides (*Rambam*, Egypt, 1135–1204), *Mishneh Torah, Shabbat* 5:1 (*oneg*), 30:5 (*kavod*); R. Jehiel Michal Epstein (Belorus, 1829–1908), *Arukh ha-Shulḥan, Oraḥ Ḥayyim* 263:2 (*oneg*).
4. *Mishneh Torah, Avodat Kokhavim* 12:3; R. Jacob b. Asher (*Tur*, Spain, 1270–1343), *Tur, Oraḥ Ḥayyim* 271; R. Joseph Caro (Safed, 1488–1575), *Shulḥan Arukh, Oraḥ Ḥayyim* 271:2.
5. Wolowelsky, "Modern Orthodoxy," 76–77.
6. *Kiddushin* 35a.

the Divine in the natural order of things. He is therefore called upon to testify that he perceives Hashem in Creation. This is the testimony of the Sabbath, that by pronouncing *va-yishbot* (Genesis 2:2), that Hashem rested on the Sabbath, that is, Hashem routinized the processes that He set into motion on the first six days of creation, we recognize Hashem in the cycle of nature.[7]

But such a pronouncement could very well prove to be an empty statement if man is not sensitized always to the spiritual realm. It is therefore necessary to complement the testimony with the reinforcement of the woman's role to direct man's strivings inward, to the perfection of his character to the point of emulation of Hashem. This is symbolized by the kindling of the Sabbath lights, bringing enlightenment and peace into the world. Indeed, our Sages say that if one has sufficient funds only for either the wine for *Kiddush* or the Sabbath lights, it is preferable to use the funds for the kindling of the Sabbath lights.[8] Why? Because of *shalom*.

Why does the woman kindle the Sabbath lights? Our Sages tell us that it is because Eve extinguished the lamp of the world, *Adam ha-Rishon*.[9] Now, does this mean that every Jewish woman in succeeding generations must suffer on account of Eve? Does this not reinforce the question that it would seem more appropriate for the man of the household to perform this commandment?

Far from making every woman share in the guilt of Eve's sin, the purpose of this commandment is to impress upon the woman her enormous power to influence man for good or evil. Every man is, after all, *Adam ha-Rishon*, standing in a very delicate state of "from every tree of the garden you may freely eat; but of the Tree of Knowledge of Good and Evil, you must not eat" (Genesis 2:16–17). It is for a woman to reject what Eve did, that is, influencing her husband to do evil, to act contrary to the will of Hashem. Thus, on Friday night, the woman reinforces her

---

7. R. Yosef Dov Soloveitchik (*Beit ha-Levi*, Belarus, 1820–1892), *Beit ha-Levi al Derush u-Milei de-Aggadata, Bereshit* (Jerusalem, 1985), 5–7.
8. *Shabbat* 23b; Rashi ad loc., s.v. "*shelom beito*"; *Tur, Oraḥ Ḥayyim* 263; *Shulḥan Arukh, Oraḥ Ḥayyim* 263:3.
9. *Midrash Tanḥuma, Noaḥ* 1; Jerusalem Talmud, *Shabbat* 2:6; *Tur, Oraḥ Ḥayyim* 263; *Magen Avraham* to *Shulḥan Arukh, Oraḥ Ḥayyim* 263:3, n. 7.

role to sensitize man to direct his strivings inward, and man bears testimony that he perceives Hashem in the cyclical order.

There was no time in the history of our people when the religious and secular education of Jewish women was higher than it is today. At the same time, the potential for women to accomplish their mission of erasing the darkness in the world has never been greater. It is therefore incumbent upon us to encourage women to become full-fledged partners in the halakhic society. This requires us to give due recognition to milestones of the Jewish woman, to impress upon her the importance of the *ol ha-mitzvot*, to give recognition to the birth of a girl, and to encourage a guest to say *"be-reshut ba'al ha-bayit u-be-reshut ba'alat ha-bayit"* in the *birkhat ha-mazon*.

Another responsibility for the halakhic authorities and rabbis in the age of sophistication is not to use Halakhah as a wedge to rebuff innovation just for the sake of preserving the status quo, just to assert authority over women because they are not in a position of power and they look to us as arbiters of their inquiries. In the month of *ge'ullah*, we must go to other extreme and provide logic and reasoning beyond what our inquirers demand of us.

We must remove the familiar notion that the sexes are in an intense competition. We must remove the *esh* element of the relationship so that the *yud* and *heh* will not be erased in the name of the man and the woman.[10] The Divine Presence will rest in the Jewish home and this will usher in the *ge'ullah shelemah*.

---

10. *Sotah* 17a; *Rashi* ad loc. The Hebrew word for man is *ish* (איש), consisting of the letters *aleph* (א), *yud* (י), and *shin* (ש). The Hebrew word for woman is *ishah* (אשה), consisting of the letters *aleph* (א), *shin* (ש), and *heh* (ה). The *yud* from the man and the *heh* from the woman form the Divine Name. If those letters are omitted, the remaining letters of each of the man and woman are *aleph* and *shin*, which form the word *esh* (אש), fire.

The Defeat of Deep Thought

January 20, 1990

In a recent article, Brad Leithauser described the most fascinating chess game ever.[1] The contest pitted the current world champion, Gary Kasparov, by all accounts the best player ever, against a state-of-the-art chess computer called Deep Thought. The chess game represented, at present, the last arena where man could meet machine in an all-out struggle and it could be called a fair fight. And this is because both contestants have sufficiently similar skills to make competition between them meaningful. But at the same time, their skills are diverse enough not to make the outcome a foregone conclusion.

I read this article for my own amusement and certainly not with the purpose of drawing source material for a sermon. But the more I reflected upon Leithauser's brilliant insight and vivid description, the

---

1. Brad Leithauser, "Kasparov Beats Deep Thought," *New York Times*, January 14, 1990, A32.

more I felt that he had captured in the language of the millennium some of the struggles of the Exodus experience.

In the chess game, Deep Thought's advantage consisted of its crunching ability to examine 1,500,000 positions per second. Given that the rules called for the game to be completed within ninety minutes, many onlookers feared that the champion would feel time-pressured. And yes, he might even be intimidated by the machine and play below his strength. The computer is oblivious to time, unaware that actual physical objects occupy the board. It is not aware that it is only a game! In short, Deep Thought is a monstrous engine of efficiency, relentlessly pursuing its goal to win, with no sensitivity to its human opponent's anxieties, hopes, or anguish. The possible humiliation that the champion might suffer on account of ignominious defeat will not prompt the machine to allow Kasparov to lose with dignity!

Perhaps this description gives us an insight into Moses' anguish, "But they will not believe me" (Exodus 4:1). Why was he so pessimistic? He was situated in the eighty-third year of the last stage of Jewish servitude under the yoke of the Egyptians, the stage of *avodat perakh*, crushing labor. But it was also useless labor of no advantage to the enslavers. This represented the ultimate in time pressure, because what it means to be human, as R. Joseph B. Soloveitchik (New York, 1903–1993) puts it, is to have a mooring in time.[2] Man can engage in reflection on the past, appreciation of the present, and anticipation of the future. With life reduced to continuous crushing labor of no value to anyone, however, there is nothing worth reminiscing about, nothing to appreciate in the present, and nothing to anticipate. This *avodat perakh* stage of the Servitude, after it was routinized, represented a total dehumanization of the Jewish people. With such a climate of dehumanization, Moses thought, "They will not believe me" (Exodus 4:1).

Moreover, Moses said, "They will say, 'Hashem did not appear to you'" (Exodus 4:1). Moses thought that the Children of Israel would never believe that Hashem appeared to him. After all, he was the living symbol of the victim of the ultimate in Jewish persecution, the concerted

---

2. R. Abraham R. Besdin, *Reflections of the Rav: Lessons in Jewish Thought* (Jerusalem: World Zionist Organization, 1979), 200–202.

effort to destroy Jewish life at its very beginning – "She could hide him no longer" (Exodus 2:3). Yes, Moses escaped this dragnet, but not for the purpose of going "from a deep darkness to a great light,"[3] but rather just to be persecuted again, driven from Egypt as a criminal fugitive, as if to make the hunt interesting for the enemy.[4]

But Moses was incorrect. "The people believed, and they heard that Hashem had remembered the Children of Israel and that He saw their affliction" (Exodus 4:31).

We can never underestimate the power of faith! What allowed Kasparov to win against the monstrous computer? Deep Thought examined 1,500,000 moves per second. This is brute search. Kasparov's intuition allowed him to narrow his evaluation to several moves, with each thoroughly traced out. Deep Thought lost because it decidedly lacked any long-range planning. It was incapable of looking deeply into the ramifications of any one of the 1,500,000 moves.

Herein lies the power of faith, to look at the very circumstance that is for some a cause of demoralization and find in it a source of strength. Yes, Moses was the prototype of the victim of the ultimate in persecution, but his very survival proved that Hashem was setting into motion the redemption process. What an irony it was that when Pharaoh heard that the savior of Israel was to be born, he marshalled all the resources of the Egyptians to make a dragnet and kill every male child, even the Egyptian ones, who would be born on that day.[5] Not only did he not succeed, but he raised the savior of Israel in his own palace!

The man of faith will not be fazed by "let the work be heavier on the men" (Exodus 5:9), in the manner of Kasparov, who decisively defeated Deep Thought with a Queen's gambit, sacrificing material in exchange for a superior position on the board.

And if Pharaoh's fatal flaw was his conviction that he was in control, that the entire world was his chess pieces to manipulate, his final defeat evokes more than anything else the shattering of that illusion in the poignant imagery of chess.

---

3. Mishnah, *Pesaḥim* 10:5.
4. Exodus 2:15.
5. Exodus 1:22; *Rashi* ad loc.; Exodus Rabbah 1:18; *Midrash Tanḥuma, Va-Yak'hel* 4.

Just before the Splitting of the Sea of Reeds, the Children of Israel turn backwards and seem lost and confused. "The enemy declared, 'I will pursue, I will overtake, I will divide plunder'" (Exodus 15:9). I will come in for checkmate! But the tables are entirely reversed. Pharaoh and his hoards are drowned. We break out in *shirah*, whose essence is expressed by "horse with its rider [Hashem] hurled into the sea" (Exodus 15:1). This is the most important part of the *shirah* because it is repeated by Miriam.[6] Within the context of war, the horse is surely only a pawn, to be driven by its rider to serve his purposes. But the rider is the pawn of the man next up in the military hierarchy, all the way up to the King, to demonstrate to the Children of Israel that Pharaoh was merely a pawn. The horse and the rider were glued together and yo-yoed up and down from the highest heavens to the lowest depths.[7] The rider and the horse were all one, merely pawns, instruments to manifest the Divine Glory.

The article ends on a very somber note. In just a few years, a new model of Deep Thought will be capable of examining ten million moves a second! This will render any contest with humans a foregone defeat for man.

But what will become of the human advantage of intuition? Well, if the selective search will be confined to positions that only human logic can think of, the dark forces of evil will overwhelm us. Only if the selective search is moored to the acceptance of the divine plan and blueprint will we be able to mimic Kasparov when he was asked how he could defeat the power of brutal search. His answer was that the art of chess playing at the highest level is the ability to prevent one's opponent from showing what he can do!

---

6. Exodus 15:21.
7. *Midrash Tanḥuma, Be-Shallaḥ* 13.

The Dual Morality

January 5, 1991

One of the shocking aspects of government, even in a democratic society, is the tendency for those at the helm to operate under rules of conduct and an ethical system that fall far below the standards they would be subject to as private citizens. Witness the Nixon Presidency. Nixon and his inner circle engaged in or were involved in sordid crimes such as burglary, wiretapping, and obstruction of justice to perpetuate the power of the President, which Nixon equated with national security.[1] More recently, in the Reagan Administration, another inner circle created an off-the-shelf government that advanced Reagan's goals, though they were at odds with official U.S. foreign policy.[2]

---

1. See generally Congressional Quarterly Inc., *Watergate: Chronology of a Crisis*, ed. William B. Dickinson, Jr. (1973); Fred Emery, *Watergate: The Corruption of American Politics and the Fall of Richard Nixon* (New York: Touchstone, 1995).
2. See generally Theodore Draper, *A Very Thin Line: The Iran-Contra Affairs* (New York: Hill & Wang, 1991); Report of the Congressional Committees Investigating the Iran-Contra Affair, H.R. Rep. No. 100–433 (1987).

This is nothing new. The transformation of the Egyptian government from one that adulated Joseph to one of genocide can be found in the creation of this duality. It all begins with the premise that the individual is myopic and cannot objectively perceive the national interest. It is for them that we need a government, to be the eyes of the country to provide clear, unobstructed vision. This is how enslavement and genocide begin, as Pharaoh said to his people, "It may be that if a war will occur, it, too, may join our enemies and wage war against us" (Exodus 1:10). If we are attacked by a foreign invasion, the Jews will be a fifth column, joining the enemy. National security requires the persecution of Jews.

In hindsight, we can well appreciate the mesmerizing pressure and compulsion of a direct plea by the King to the midwives. "The King of Egypt said to the Hebrew midwives" (Exodus 1:15) and again, in the next verse, "he said" (Exodus 1:16). When one is approached directly by the King, his invisible misconduct is perceived as a legitimate act performed as an agent of the government.

If we need to have a glimpse of the duality, we can see it encapsulated by Hashem's call to Moses in Midian, "Go, return to Egypt, for all the people who seek your life have died" (Exodus 4:19). Our Sages tell us that Moses' accusers, Dathan and Abiram, were still alive, but they were referred to as "dead" because they had become impoverished and lost their influence.[3] But what kind of a system of justice is this? When the accusers are no longer influential, is the crime suddenly not a crime? This is how the government worked. It responded only to pragmatic pressure and had no sense of values independent of those pressures.

We are presented with a glaring contrast. Unlike the duality of Egyptian society, no such duality existed in Jewish society. Moses was given the helm for Jewish destiny, but no distinction was made between the standard of morality that would apply to him as an individual or as the leader of Jewish destiny and the standard that applied to the community. Moses' persistent rejection of the mission until "the wrath of Hashem burned against Moses" (Exodus 4:14) is explained by the Midrash as proceeding from his unwillingness to encroach on the prerogative of Aaron, who was the established prophet for eighty

---

3. Exodus Rabbah 5:4; *Rashi* to Exodus 4:19.

years.⁴ Moses thought that the whole process of redemption must follow the logical steps of private life and be under the constraint of *hassagat gevul*.⁵

And there is the second mystery of "Hashem encountered him and sought to kill him" (Exodus 4:24) on his way to Egypt. The *Meshekh Ḥokhmah* explains that Moses thought that he would add something convincing to show the Children of Israel if they did not believe him.⁶ He would put his wife and children in danger by taking them down to Egypt. This would demonstrate that he truly believed in Hashem's promise of the Redemption because otherwise he would not bring his wife and children to a place of slavery and hardship. But this was wrong. The sanctity of human life does not change whether one is operating as an individual or as a leader of Jewish destiny. If Moses was not commanded to bring his wife and children, they must be left in Midian, despite all calculations that bringing them to Egypt would help the cause.

Permit me to suggest that the *sine qua non* of a corrupt society is being perfectly at ease with a huge gap between the moral standards of the government and those of the general populace. No tension is felt. People are totally comfortable with it and do not question it.

The exalted and elevated society, on the other hand, is the society that consciously tries to narrow the gap and feels very uncomfortable with duality, and, yes, overthrows government that is taking duality too far.

A clear-cut application of this is that the world community should force Iraqi society to answer the question of whether they are willing to tolerate the madness of Saddam or are they going to overthrow him. If they do not remove him, they deserve to perish along with him. This supports the basis of economic embargo.

---

4. Exodus Rabbah 3:16; *Rashi* to Exodus 4:10.
5. *Hassagat gevul* (lit., "removal of boundary") refers to the prohibition against trespassing on economic, commercial, or incorporeal rights of others. See *Bava Batra* 21b; *Makkot* 24a.
6. R. Meir Simhah ha-Kohen of Dvinsk (*Or Same'aḥ* or *Meshekh Ḥokhmah*, Latvia, 1843–1926), *Meshekh Ḥokhmah*, Exodus 4:20, s.v. "*va-yikaḥ Mosheh et ishto*."

Hakkarat Ha-Tov

January 20, 2001

The pure, timid, and meek are never comfortable with power. They never seek it and surely do not campaign for it. But when leadership is handed to one on a silver platter, the authority behind it is unimpeachable and a mandate of nobility attaches itself to it. Then the resistance to the assumption of power breaks down.

How far removed was Moses from all this. When Hashem charged Moses with the mission of being the Redeemer of Israel, Moses resisted with "Who am I that I should go to Pharaoh?" (Exodus 3:11). Then, according to the Midrash, a dialogue of seven days with Hashem ensues.[1] It starts with "Who am I that I shall go to Pharaoh?," continues with "they will not believe me" (Exodus 4:1), and ends with "Please, my Lord, send through whomever You will send" (Exodus 4:13).

"How could Moses decline?" ask the commentators.[2] Refusing Hashem's command is a *ḥillul ha-Shem*. The Midrash answers that

---
1. Exodus Rabbah 3:14; *Rashi* to Exodus 4:10.
2. See, e.g., *Rashi* to Exodus 4:10; Nahmanides to Exodus 4:1.

Moses felt that he would be encroaching on the honor of Aaron.[3] Aaron was the established prophet for eighty years in Egypt. Moses appeared only briefly. "Moses grew up and went out to his brethren and observed their burdens" (Exodus 2:11). Then he became a fugitive. He was King of Kush, ancient Ethiopia, for forty years.[4] But Aaron prophesized for eighty years. What did his prophecy consist of? He did his thing, "loving peace, pursuing peace, loving people, and bringing them closer to the Torah."[5] His work prevented the Children of Israel from falling to the fiftieth level of impurity.

Now, if we are going to leap to redemption, Aaron should lead the charge. We owe it to him, out of *hakkarat ha-tov*. He has done so well as the spiritual inspiration. We cannot pass him over. People will say that he was dumped because it was his fault that we sank to the forty-ninth level of impurity. It is not until "the wrath of Hashem burned against Moses" and Hashem tells Moses that "when he sees you, he will rejoice in his heart" (Exodus 4:14) that Moses recanted.

Moses understood the need for alacrity in fulfilling his mission once it was given to him. He passed through Midian on his way to Egypt and decided against circumcising his son.[6] But why did he go to Midian altogether? It was to get permission from Jethro to leave.[7] Why? *Hakkarat ha-tov*. "I must ask Jethro for permission. I was a fugitive. He gave me refuge, a wife."[8]

Hakkarat ha-tov is not just a virtue. It is the fundamental value in our religion. Moses, "the man of God,"[9] must instinctively know how fundamental it is that Hashem should say "I am Hashem, your God, Who has taken you out of the land of Egypt, from the house of slavery" (Exodus 20:2). The verse does not say "I am Hashem, your God, Who created the heaven and earth" but rather "I am Hashem, your God, Who took you out of the land of Egypt" to teach us the importance of *hakkarat*

---

3. Exodus Rabbah 3:16; *Rashi* to Exodus 4:10.
4. *Yalkut Shimoni* 1:168.
5. Mishnah, *Avot* 1:12.
6. *Rashi* to Exodus 4:24; *Nedarim* 31b.
7. *Rashi* to Exodus 4:18.
8. Exodus Rabbah 4:2.
9. Deuteronomy 33:1.

Shemot

ha-tov.[10] *Hakkarat ha-tov* must be an integral part of one's decision-making process. It must at the very least be the tie breaker.

In organizations, big and small, when the top officer retires or resigns, invariably a search committee is assembled to find a successor. This is so even when the second-in-command is superlative and contributed much to the success of the organization. Now, if the organization agonizes over its choice for a successor, it might decide to add insult to injury and pass over the second-in-command, reasoning that it needs to infuse new blood and new horizons into the organization.

Take another example. A *yeshivah* appoints a *kollel yungerman* to the position of *Rosh Mesivta*. People scream "inbreeding" instead of recognizing the element of *hakkarat ha-tov*. The young man built up the spirit of the *yeshivah*.

Now we come to the big things, the Land of Israel. "We thank You, Hashem, our God, because You have given as a heritage to our forefathers a land desirable, good, and spacious."[11] Let us hear what our lips enunciate.

When we integrate *hakkarat ha-tov* to Hashem and to our fellow man into our lifestyle and way of thinking, we feel the footsteps of the Messiah approaching.

---

10. *Rashi* to Exodus 20:2; R. Shabbetai b. Joseph Bass (*Siftei Ḥakhamim*, Prague, 1641–1718), *Siftei Ḥakhamim* ad loc., n. 20; Abraham b. Meir ibn Ezra (Ibn Ezra, Spain, 1089–1164), Ibn Ezra to Exodus 20:1.
11. Grace After Meals, Second Blessing (Blessing for the Land).

Mosheh Rabbeinu's Ten Other Names

December 28, 2002

One of the mystiques surrounding Moses is his name itself. The *Midrash Rabbah* tells us that besides the name *Mosheh*, the most exalted person in the history of the Jewish people had ten other names.[1] All the other names recall Moses' cosmic mission and accomplishments. For example, *Ben Netanel*, Hashem gave the Torah through him; *Avi Sokho*, Moses was the head of all the Prophets; and *Yekutiel*, Moses taught the Children of Israel to put their trust and hope in Hashem. Yet, only the name that the daughter of Pharaoh gave stuck. Why?

R. Mordechai Gifter suggests that the name *Mosheh* recalls that no one can thwart Hashem's will.[2] Pharaoh mobilized his whole country

---

1. Leviticus Rabbah 1:3. The ten other names attributed to Moses are: Yered, Avidgor, Hever, Avi Sokho, Yekutiel, Avi Zanoah, Toviah, Shemayah b. Netanel, Ben Evyatar, and Levi.
2. R. Mordechai Gifter (Ohio, 1915–2001), *Pirkei Torah*, vol. 1 (Wickliffe, OH, 1992), Exodus 2:10, p. 180, s.v. "*va-tikra shemo Mosheh.*"

Shemot

to make sure that there would be no savior of Israel. But what happened? Not only did he not thwart it, but he nurtured the savior himself, raising him in his own household.

Let's take this further. R. Zadok ha-Kohen says that Hashem gives every Jew a special mission.[3] Each and every one of us is unique. We are not interchangeable. Whether we want to or not, during our lifetime, we will advance this mission. The issue is only whether we will do this as merely an instrument of the divine will or in a different way, exuberating in our *tzelem Elokim*. At the end of Moses' life, Hashem proclaimed, "Never again has there arisen in Israel a prophet like Moses" (Deuteronomy 34:10). This included all Moses' ten names.

But his mission began in the microcosm of the fateful scene on the banks of the River Nile, with Batyah sizing up Moses' mission. It is the mission of *hatzalah* (rescue). She says, "*ki min ha-mayim mishisihu*," "for I drew him from the water" (Exodus 2:10). As the *Sforno* notes, she does not call him *Mishisihu*, "I drew him," but rather *Mosheh*, "he will save," because I drew him from the water.[4] It would be Moses' mission to draw the people from the water, to save. This is what she drummed into him every time that she enunciated his name. And indeed, this was Moses' special mission. "He went out to his brethren and observed their burdens" (Exodus 2:11). This is the most fundamental *hatzalah*, when one is driven to lighten the burden of a fellow Jew, to save a Jew from an enemy or a wicked person.

"Moses is equivalent to 600,000 Israelites,"[5] so Moses is everyone. Our mission is clear. The Evil Inclination has seven names: *Ra*, "evil"; *Arel*, "uncircumcised"; *Tamei*, "unclean"; *Sonei*, "enemy"; *Mikhshol*, "obstacle"; *Even*, "stone"; and *Tziponi*, "hidden."[6] "One should always incite the

---

3. See R. Zadok ha-Kohen Rabinowitz (Lublin, 1823–1900), *Peri Tzaddik, Parashat Shekalim*.
4. R. Obadiah b. Jacob Sforno (*Sforno*, Italy, ca. 1470–1550), *Sforno* to Exodus 2:10.
5. Song of Songs Rabbah 4:2.
6. *Sukkah* 52a. Hashem called the Evil Inclination "Evil," as it is said, "For the imagination of man's heart is evil from his youth" (Genesis 8:21). Moses called it "Uncircumcised," as it is said, "Circumcise therefore the foreskin of your heart" (Deuteronomy 10:16). David called it "Unclean," as it is said, "Create a pure heart for me, O God" (Psalms 51:12), which implies that there is an unclean one. Solomon called it "Enemy,"

Good Inclination to fight against the Evil Inclination."[7] Our mission is one of *hatzalah*, to drive away the evil forces within one's self and the evil forces that envelop the world.

What is most fundamental in the mission of *hatzalah*? It is to rid oneself of *even*. If we do not do that, we prevent our *tzelem Elokim* from being felt by us. This was the fundamental reason that Moses was selected for leadership for the big *hatzalah* mission. He demonstrated compassion for a lamb when he was a shepherd and carried it on his shoulders, and was sensitive to theft.[8]

If we can all behave in the manner of "he observed their burdens," the First Redeemer is reborn in the process. So is the Final Redeemer.

---

as it is said, "If your enemy is hungry, give him bread to eat, and if he is thirsty, give him water to drink, for you will heap coals of fire upon his head, and Hashem will reward you" (Proverbs 25:21–22). Isaiah called it "Obstacle," as it is said, "Pave, pave. Clear the way. Remove the obstacle from the path of My people" (Isaiah 57:14). Ezekiel called it "Stone," as it is said, "I will remove the heart of stone from your flesh and I will give you a heart of flesh" (Ezekiel 36:26). Joel called it "Hidden One," as it is said, "I will distance the hidden one from you" (Joel 2:20).

7. *Berakhot* 5a (R. Levi bar Hama in the name of R. Simeon b. Lakish).
8. Exodus Rabbah 2:2–3. Moses avoided theft by grazing his flock in the desert.

Va-Era

Defense Mechanisms

January 19, 1985

One of the cardinal tenets of Judaism is the tenet of free will.[1] Yet this principle apparently is violated in Hashem's conduct with Pharaoh. When Pharaoh responds to divine retribution in the first five Plagues with the hardening of his own heart, persisting in his obstinacy, after the conclusion of the fifth plague, Pharaoh's heart is hardened by Hashem.[2]

One approach to the dilemma, of relevancy to the contemporary scene, is the understanding of Maimonides. In the final analysis, it is man, and man alone, who chooses between good and evil. But sin acts as a barrier to repentance. At first, the opportunities that present themselves are equally balanced. But if one sins, the next decision will be weighted or skewed toward choosing evil. In modern terminology, defense mechanisms will build up, rationalizing the evil. Once a certain

---

1. R. Saadiah Gaon, *Ha-Emuot ve-ha-De'ot*, *ma'amar* 4; Maimonides, *Mishneh Torah*, *Teshuvah* 5:1.
2. Exodus 9:7.

Va-Era

point is reached, it is the point of no return; there is certainty that evil will be chosen over good.[3]

Pharaoh is not therefore merely a historical figure who lived many thousands of years ago, but rather the prototype of the alienated Jew. Analyzing the defense mechanisms that Pharaoh built up in resisting the impact of the first five Plagues gives us therefore a clue into the process of becoming completely lost to Jewishness.

For a man who was obsessed with knowing the meaning of a dream, he surely delved into the meaning of the Plagues. The meaning of the Plague of Blood was glaringly blatant. It represented punishment for the spilling of innocent Jewish blood.[4] The Plague of Blood therefore represented the worst aspect of the Servitude, the spilling of Jewish blood for self-serving purposes, i.e., the prevention of the birth of the savior of Israel and the cure for Pharaoh of his leprosy.[5]

Since the *middah ke-neged middah* was so glaring, why does the Torah say in connection with this Plague "he did not take this to heart" (Exodus 7:23)? I would suggest that, very simply, it is because the first defense mechanism is to ascribe to the reproofer the very same characteristic for which he is chastising us. The meaning of the blood was self-serving exploitation. Well, Pharaoh just had to look to the fact that the Children of Israel became rich because of the Plague of Blood by selling water to the Egyptians.[6] He must have said, "They are no better than we are."

Then comes the Plague of Frogs. What does this represent? It is exploitation that is done just for the purpose of exerting mastery over someone. Although the frog is a timorous and remote creature that usually retreats to the water, here it showed arrogance to follow man and even Pharaoh everywhere. The most astonishing aspect of the plague was that the frogs lost their instinct for self-survival, jumping into ovens,

---

3. Maimonides, *Shemoneh Perakim* 8; Maimonides, *Mishneh Torah, Teshuvah* 6:3.
4. Tobiah b. Eliezer (Balkans, 11th cent.), *Midrash Lekah Tov*, Exodus 7:17.
5. See *Rashi* to Exodus 2:23, s.v. "*va-yamat melekh Mitzrayim*"; *Targum Yonatan*, Exodus 2:23; Exodus Rabbah 1:34.
6. Exodus Rabbah 9:10. If the Egyptians did not pay for the water taken from a Jew, the water would turn into blood in the hands of the Egyptians. Ibid.

not for any gain for themselves, but only to torment the Egyptians.[7] Well, the *middah ke-neged middah* was blatant here too. The Egyptians had tortured the Jews by requiring them to collect insects that were of no use to the Egyptians.[8]

Why did Pharaoh not respond to this Plague? The answer, I would submit, is that this plague evoked a more subtle form of the defense mechanism of ascribing to our enemies the same character trait that they ascribe to us. We find that Pharaoh recapitulates and says that he will send away the Jewish people as Moses requests, only Moses should pray to Hashem to remove the frogs.[9] Moses asks Pharaoh, "For when should I entreat for you, your servants, and your people to excise the frogs from you and your houses?" (Exodus 8:5). Pharaoh says, "For tomorrow" (Exodus 8:6). As a result, Pharaoh hardened his heart.[10]

Why did Pharaoh harden his heart? Pharaoh should have been impressed by Moses' sign. It could very well be that Pharaoh was convinced that by Moses agreeing to remove the plague a day after Pharaoh had already agreed to send out the Jewish people, Moses was in effect going along with Pharaoh and saying that if you desire it, I will allow your people to suffer unnecessarily for another day, just for the purpose of showing you that I have the power to remove the plague when I say so. Pharaoh seized upon this as evidence that the Children of Israel were capable of exploiting others for the sake of exerting power, just as he did.

Then came the Plague of Lice. This was also a paradoxical plague because it was the first plague where the Egyptians admitted "it is a finger of God" (Exodus 8:15). So why did Pharaoh continue to harden his heart? The answer is simple. No warning preceded the plague, so, paradoxically, even though it was the "finger of God," it was irrelevant to the struggle at hand.

The next test is the Plague of Wild Beasts. It is here that Pharaoh made his first overture of compromise. This tells us that chaos, the

---

7. Exodus 7:28 ("The River shall swarm with frogs, and they shall ascend and come into your palace… and into your ovens"); Exodus Rabbah 10:2; *Pesaḥim* 53b.
8. *Midrash Tanḥuma, Va-Era* 14; R. Benzion Yadler (Jerusalem, 1871–1962), *Tiferet Tziyyon* to Exodus Rabbah 10:4, s.v. "*va-yet Aharon et yado.*"
9. Exodus 8:4.
10. Exodus 8:11.

breakdown of the natural order, is something that Pharaoh could not cope with. Nothing is predictable. He desperately wants to open communications and offers "only do not go far off" (Exodus 8:24). Two days is far enough. Moses agrees. But then Pharaoh wants to compromise on his own terms. He does not send out the Children of Israel but lightens their work.[11] This response of spurious compromise is, of course, not acceptable.

Finally, we have the Plague of the Epidemic. The aspect of *middah ke-neged middah* was that invisible culprit, covering his tracks so that evil would not be traced to him. Pharaoh finds that "of the livestock of Israel not even one had died" (Exodus 9:7). He again is obsessed with finding the sinful trait in the Jews, and lo and behold, as the *Ha'amek Davar* tells us, he thinks that not every one of the Egyptians was harmed by the plague.[12]

Now, we must do our part so that the alienated Jew is not pushed to the sixth plague, the Plague of Boils. This is the plague of complete social alienation. To prevent this, first and foremost we must make sure that there is no Plague of Lice in our camp. We must demonstrate *tzelem Elokim* in our love of our fellow Jew, in our wisdom of the Torah. Another thing is to compromise when possible, and to build trust, so that no one can say that there is a breakdown in communication. Third, we must end the plague of self-serving exploitation, of using other people and organizations to serve our ends, and the plague of pride, especially organizational pride and the obsession to receive credit, and the Plague of the Epidemic, the cowardly sniping behind the scenes to make sure that we get our way and the other person is pushed into oblivion, without any trace to us.

What we need is to go back to the beginning of the scenario, when "the staff of Aaron swallowed their staves" (Exodus 7:12). This entailed a miracle within a miracle. Not only did Aaron's staff swallow all the staves of Pharaoh's magicians, it did not become any thicker from swallowing them.[13]

---

11. Ibn Ezra to Exodus 8:18; R. Naphtali Tzvi Yehudah Berlin (*Netziv*, Russia, 1816–1893), *Ha'amek Davar*, Exodus 8:28.
12. *Ha'amek Davar* states that an animal that belonged to an Egyptian but was rented to a Jew did not die because the Jew derived benefit from the animal in the form of milk and cheese. *Ha'amek Davar*, Exodus 9:7.
13. Exodus Rabbah 9:7.

How to Negotiate with a Tyrant

January 16, 1988

Brute force need not rely on deception!

One aspect of the Exodus experience strikes us as a glaring paradox. On the one hand, both our ancestors and Egyptian society were made to absorb the lesson that Hashem is omnipotent. Hashem indeed controls and manipulates every element of nature. We would therefore imagine that an unequivocal demand for complete liberation would accompany this display of devastating divine power. Yet, the demand placed on Pharaoh from the very beginning was merely "let us now go for a three-day journey" (Exodus 5:3).

Commentators are indeed perplexed by the demand.[1] One approach to the dilemma is advanced by R. Isaac b. Judah Abrabanel[2]

---

1. See, e.g., *Or ha-Ḥayyim* to Exodus 3:18.
2. R. Isaac b. Judah Abrabanel (Portugal, 1437–1508), Exodus 3:16.

and R. Isaac b. Moses Arama.[3] Hashem never demands of us more than we are capable of fulfilling. The severest demands are made of the saint. But of the man of feeble faith, only minimal demands are made.

Pharaoh was a cruel despot who deified himself.[4] The only reasonable approach toward him would be to make a minimalist plea of letting the weary slaves have a short vacation! If Pharaoh would have heeded this minimal request, Jewish history would have taken a different turn. The Master of the Universe, in His infinite wisdom, can generate infinite scenarios to achieve his purpose of ultimate redemption of the Jewish people.

To this we should add the bold comments of R. Samson Raphael Hirsch, who posits that the pronouncement of Moses and Aaron to Pharaoh "the God of the Hebrews happened upon us" (Exodus 5:3) smacks of idolatry because it descends to the level of the addressee. It implies that Hashem is just another deity in a society that worships many gods. Also, it says that the encounter was by mere chance.[5]

The negotiation with the tyrant Pharaoh has much relevance for us in these modern times with respect to the struggle of Soviet Jewry. The model tells us that we have achieved a prudent policy by not denouncing the Soviet totalitarian system and not linking our demands to Cold War politics. Instead, we link the right of Jewish emigration to human rights in general and the repatriation of the Jewish people to their homeland, a demand that the Soviet system can handle.

Most basically, the model asks us, how do we perceive the Soviet regime? Do we view it as an evil empire bent upon causing chaos in the world? Then we can derive hope from more posturing without flexibility, and we might even rejoice in the grant of visiting visas and in the shift in emphasis from human rights to humanitarian concerns in the form of allowing the sick and those separated from their families to emigrate. Tolerable.

---

3. R. Isaac b. Moses Arama (*Akedat Yitzhak*, Spain, ca. 1420–1494), *Akedat Yitzhak*, *Shemot, sha'ar* 35:9.
4. *Rashi* to Exodus 7:15; Exodus Rabbah 9:8; *Midrash Tanhuma, Va-Era* 14.
5. R. Samson Raphael Hirsch, Exodus 5:3.

But let us not forget that we just signed a nuclear disarmament treaty with Russia.[6] We indeed view them more highly. We trust them. If we trust them, we should not satisfy ourselves with mere crumbs. We need to escalate our demands.

What the model tells us is the utter folly and paradox of the position of dealing with the Soviet government itself and taking them up on an offer to distribute religious artifacts for us in exchange for silence during public protests.[7] What folly. If we are afraid of incurring the ire of the Soviet regime by demonstrating a lowly opinion of them, how do we expect the highest response to do something, granting religious freedom, that is totally contrary to the Soviet system?

Moses' success before the Ten Plagues is most instructive. He negotiated with Pharaoh the release of the Jewish slaves for the Sabbath.[8] Moses argued to Pharaoh that the productivity of the slave will increase by giving him a day off! So appealing to naked self-interest is the best approach.

In the 1970s, the Russians were forced to give something for every trade concession that they wanted. When they enacted the infamous "diploma tax,"[9] we countered with the Jackson–Vanik

---

6. The Treaty between the United States of America and the Union of Soviet Socialist Republics on the Elimination of their Intermediate-Range and Shorter-Range Missiles was signed in Washington, DC, by President Ronald Reagan and General Secretary Mikhail S. Gorbachev on December 8, 1987. The treaty was ratified by the U.S. Senate on May 27, 1988, and went into effect on June 1, 1988. See *International Legal Materials* 27 (January 1988): 90–97; John Walcott and Gerald F. Seib, "Reagan and Gorbachev Sign Ban on Intermediate-Range Missiles; They Promise to Seek Cuts in Long-Range Arsenal as 3-Day Summit Starts," *Wall Street Journal*, December 9, 1987, 1; Adam Pertman, "INF Treaty Ratified in Time for Summit," *Boston Globe*, May 28, 1998, 1; Don Oberdorfer, "Summit Brings Better Ties but No Arms Breakthrough; INF Pact Activated; Delay Is Seen for Treaty on Long-Range Missiles," *Washington Post*, June 2, 1988, A1.
7. See Paul F. Scotchmer, "Glasnost, God and Gorbachev," *Chicago Tribune*, January 21, 1988, 19.
8. Exodus Rabbah 1:28. This is why the Sages instituted that we say in the *Shemoneh Esrei* of the Sabbath morning prayer *"yismaḥ Mosheh be-matnat ḥelko,"* "Moses rejoiced in his gifted portion." *Etz Yosef*, ad loc., s.v. *"ve-tikken lahem"*; R. Issachar Berman b. Naphtali ha-Kohen (Poland, ca. 1520–1590), *Mattenot Kehunnah*, ad loc.
9. In 1972, the Soviet Union imposed a schedule of increased exit fees on Soviets with higher education who wished to emigrate. Laws 572, 573, adopted August 3, 1972, by

Va-Era

Amendment.[10] So the most fruitful approach is to exert political pressure to force the emigration of Soviet Jewry onto the agenda of the American government.

---

the Presidium of the Supreme Soviet and Council of Ministers (effective August 14, 1972). The fees ranged from approximately $5,000 for a graduate of a teacher's institute to over $25,000 for the Soviet equivalent of a Ph.D. Although the fees were applicable to any Soviet citizen who sought to emigrate to a non-Socialist country, the measure disproportionately affected Jews, who were emigrating from the Soviet Union in large numbers at that time. See generally Mitchell Knisbacher, "*Aliyah* of Soviet Jews: Protection of the Right of Emigration under International Law," *Harvard International Law Journal* 14, no. 1 (1973): 89.

10. The Jackson–Vanik Amendment to the Trade Act of 1974 was a provision of U.S. federal law that denied trade and other economic benefits to countries with non-market economies that restrict freedom of emigration and other human rights. 19 U.S.C. § 2432(a)–(e) (1974), repealed by the Russia and Moldova Jackson–Vanik Repeal and Sergei Magnitsky Rule of Law Accountability Act of 2012, Pub. L. No. 112–208, 128 Stat. 1496, on December 14, 2012.

The World Community's Spectacular *Dai*

January 12, 1991

In the teaching of R. Mosheh Feinstein, redemption takes two forms.[1] One form is when society reaches a refinement to the extent that it is repulsed by oppression, tyranny, and injustice, and rises in righteous indignation as it says "*dai!*" This is indeed a glorious phenomenon because it represents emulation of the divine attribute of *Shakkai*.[2] Just as when Hashem created the physical universe, He endowed each being

---

1. R. Mosheh Feinstein (New York, 1895–1986), *Derash Mosheh: Ḥiddushei Aggadah al ha-Torah* (Benei Berak, 1988), *Va-Era*, p. 40.
2. The Name of Hashem of *Shakkai* is explained by the Sages as a compound of "*She-amar le-olam dai,*" that Hashem said to the world "enough." *Ḥagigah* 12a; *Rashi* to Genesis 43:14. For additional commentary on the Name of *Shakkai*, see *Rashi* to Genesis 17:1 (interpreting *Shakkai* as a compound of *she-yesh dai*, that there is enough in Hashem's divinity for every creature) and *Rashi* to Genesis 28:3 (interpreting *Shakkai* as a compound of *she-dai be-virkhotav*, that Hashem's blessings are sufficient for those who are blessed by Him).

with limitations, parameters, and definite potential, in short, a *dai* element, so, too, man, in the moral sphere, can emulate Hashem and stand up and say "*dai*" to wickedness.

The second variety of redemption is when society lacks the will to stand up to oppression, so Hashem must intervene with supernatural events. This was the nature of the dialogue between Hashem and Moses. Hashem told Moses, "I appeared to Abraham, Isaac, and Jacob as *Kel Shakkai*" (Exodus 6:3). I foretold them that the redemption from Egypt would occur naturally, by means of the *dai* process. But if I rely on this, waiting four hundred years until the Egyptians will say *dai*, the Children of Israel will have already sunk to the fiftieth level of impurity.[3] So Hashem in his mercy says, "I will bring the Redemption with the Name of Hashem," which is intervention with the Ten Plagues.[4]

The Future Redemption will be with the attribute of *dai*. If we have any doubts that we are hearing the footsteps of the Messiah, we can set aside those doubts because for the past five months, the world has experienced a spectacular *dai* to the evil tyrant of Baghdad.[5] But the world is fearful that the *dai* is not a sufficient *dai*, that it has failed and war is almost inevitable. The crux of the problem is how to make a credible threat to the dictator so that actual use of force will be unnecessary.

---

3. R. Isaac b. Solomon Luria (*Arizal* or *Ha-Ari*, Safed, 1534–1572), *Siddur ha-Ari, Seder Haggadah*, s.v. "*matzah zu*"; R. Moses Alshekh (*Alshekh*, Safed, 1508–1593), *Torat Mosheh*, Exodus 12:41; R. Isaiah ha-Levi Horowitz (*Shelah ha-Kadosh*, Prague, ca. 1565–1630), *Shenei Luḥot ha-Berit, Masekhet Pesaḥim, Matzah Shemurah*, ¶ 158, s.v. "*ve-illu lo hotzi ha-Kadosh Barukh Hu*"; R. Hayyim b. Moses ibn Attar (*Or ha-Ḥayyim*, Morocco, 1696–1743), *Or ha-Ḥayyim* to Exodus 3:7, s.v. "*va-yomer Hashem*".
4. *Or ha-Ḥayyim* to Exodus 6:2; R. Ephraim Solomon b. Aaron of Luntshits (*Keli Yakar*, Łęczyca, 1550–1619), *Keli Yakar* to Exodus 6:3.
5. On August 2, 1990, Iraqi forces invaded Kuwait. Within a few hours of the invasion, the United Nations Security Council condemned the invasion and demanded a withdrawal of the Iraqi troops. On August 6, 1990, the United Nations Security Council instituted economic sanctions against Iraq. The next day, President George H. W. Bush deployed U.S. forces into Saudi Arabia. Over the next few months, many other nations joined the coalition of forces against Iraq. See Lawrence Freedman and Efraim Karsh, *The Gulf Conflict 1990–1991: Diplomacy and War in the New World Order* (Princeton, NJ: Princeton University Press, 1993), 67–102, 110–127.

The Exodus from Egypt is the blueprint for the Future Redemption, and the Exodus from Egypt provides us with the insight into how to make a tyrant back down and fall to a humiliating defeat.

"See, I have made you a deity to Pharaoh" (Exodus 7:1). Why was it necessary that Moses be a deity to Pharaoh? The answer is that this is the response to Moses' worry of *ve-ani aral sefatayim*, "I have sealed lips" (Exodus 6:12), his fear of garbled communication. The worry is that since Pharaoh's self-image is that of a deity, how then can a dialogue and channel be open to one who represents the Jewish people?

Two elements were given as a gift to Moses so that he would be perceived by Pharaoh as a deity. One was the element of compassion. Each Plague represented an escalation of punishment. A more severe measure was instituted only when a lesser one failed to bring Pharaoh to repent. The escalation conveyed to Pharaoh that at any moment, he could be destroyed but was spared because "'Do I desire at all the death of wicked man?' says the Lord Hashem Elokim. Is it not rather his return from his ways that he might live?" (Ezekiel 18:23). And the second gift is that Moses was the only person that Pharaoh dealt with, the single voice.

Our challenge in dealing with the tyrant is to assume the deity elements to match his self-image of a deity. If through pure aggrandizement he is accommodating to no one, our channel is through the democratic process. Make one voice speak for the whole world. This is happening with the U.N. Security Council resolution[6] and today with the resolution of the U.S. Congress to authorize force.[7] One voice.

And second, the element of compassion of the Ten Plagues is here. Many said that we should start with the Plague of the Firstborn, that the CIA should devise an assassination plot against Hussein,

---

6. On November 29, 1990, the United Nations adopted a U.S.-sponsored resolution authorizing member states to use force against Iraq if Iraq did not withdraw from Kuwait by January 15, 1991. S.C. Res. 678 (Nov. 29, 1990), reprinted in *International Legal Materials* 29 (1990): 1565.
7. Authorization for Use of Military Force against Iraq Resolution, Pub. L. No. 102–1, 105 Stat. 3 (1991).

putting Iraq into disarray.[8] But instead we started with the Plague of Blood, which is equivalent to cutting off the water supply. Hence the cutting off of the pipeline in Turkey.[9] But then we are also seeing the Plague of Frogs, the outcry of world indignation.[10] We could have made the Plague of Blood into the Plague of Darkness for them by really tightening the embargo, but instead we built up a military offensive capability.[11]

Well, for our part, we carried forward the *dai* outcry to its limit. Now we beseech Hashem to do His part in effecting the defeat of the tyrant. Please Hashem, let us see fulfillment of the promise in today's *haftarah*, "they will dwell upon it in security" (Ezekiel 28:26)!

---

8. Mark Falcoff, "Head Hunting: Assassination as a Policy," *National Interest* 24 (Summer 1991): 103; J. Craig Crawford, "Why Doesn't U.S. Just Assassinate Saddam Hussein," *Seattle Times*, August 20, 1990, A1.
9. On August 7, 1990, Turkey banned ships from loading Iraqi crude at offshore terminals in the eastern Mediterranean Sea, effectively ordering a shutdown of vital Iraqi oil pipelines in Turkey. Clyde Haberman, "The Iraqi Invasion; Quick Action by Turkey on Sanctions a Startler," *New York Times*, August 8, 1990, A10.
10. One aspect of the Plague of Frogs was the loud noise caused by the croaking of the frogs, which continued even after the frogs entered the stomachs of the Egyptians. Exodus Rabbah 10:6; *Midrash ha-Gadol*, Exodus 8:4; *Rashi* to Exodus 7:29. See also *Siftei Ḥakhamim* to Exodus 8:6, n. 50.
11. R. W. Apple, Jr., "Confrontation in the Gulf; U.S. Says Its Troops in the Gulf Could Reach 100,000 in Months," *New York Times*, August 11, 1990, A1. For a discussion of the sanctions imposed by the international community against Iraq, see generally Christopher C. Joyner, "Sanctions, Compliance and International Law: Reflections of the United Nations' Experience against Iraq," *Virginia Journal of International Law* 32, no. 1 (Fall 1991): 1–46.

I Shall Bring You to the Land

January 27, 2001

We are all familiar with the talmudic dictum that our Sages established four cups of wine to correspond to the four expressions of Redemption: *ve-hotzeti*, "I shall take you out"; *ve-hitzalti*, "I shall rescue you"; *ve-ga'alti*, "I shall redeem you"; and *ve-lakahti*, "I shall take you as a people."[1] The question is asked: Why not a fifth cup to correspond to *ve-heveti*, "I shall bring you to the Land" (Exodus 6:8)?

Perhaps the answer is that the Sages knew the limits of our intake of wine. By the time we reach the fifth cup, the wine generates levity

---

1. Jerusalem Talmud, *Pesaḥim* 10:1; Genesis Rabbah 88:5; Exodus Rabbah 6:4; *Rashi* to *Pesaḥim* 99b. The First Cup corresponds to "I shall take you out (*ve-hotzeti*) from under the burdens of Egypt" (Exodus 6:6), the Second Cup corresponds to "I shall rescue you (*ve-hitzalti*) from their service" (ibid.), and the Third Cup corresponds to "I shall redeem you (*ve-ga'alti*) with an outstretched arm" (ibid.), each denoting freedom from physical oppression. The Fourth Cup corresponds to "I shall take you (*ve-lakahti*) as a people" (Exodus 6:7), denoting spiritual redemption.

and giddiness instead of joy. This makes us lose our composure and our perspective on the Land of Israel.

R. Samson Raphael Hirsch's perspective on *ve-heveti* is that it is secondary to *ve-lakaḥti*.² The Land of Israel is the setting that Hashem gave us to allow us to realize our potential. It is "a land that Hashem, Your God, seeks out" (Deuteronomy 11:12). It provides us with the inspirational energy to achieve our potential. The Torah permeates the legal, social, and economic environments, the political process, and international relations. The blessing that we make on the fourth cup therefore applies also to *ve-heveti*.

The correspondence between the Four Cups and the four expressions of Redemption is disputed, but the interpretations are nuanced, not radically different.

Take the *Netziv*. In his view, *ve-hotzeti* corresponds to the end of the crushing labor with the Plague of Wild Beasts. "But Pharaoh made his heart stubborn even this time, and he did not send out the people" (Exodus 8:28). Then, *ve-hitzalti* corresponds to the Plague of Hail. "Pharaoh's heart became strong and he did not send out the Children of Israel, as Hashem had spoken through Moses" (Exodus 9:35). V*e-ga'alti* corresponds to the Plague of the Firstborn, and *ve-lakaḥti* to receiving the Torah.³

There is a common denominator here. The Sages wanted to be sure to achieve "I will raise the cup of salvations, and the Name of Hashem I will invoke" (Psalms 116:13). So the center is an event that is clearly a miracle. And we know that the more that we delve into it – "Whoever tells the story of the Exodus from Egypt at length is praiseworthy"⁴ – the more *yir'at Shamayim* we will produce with it. The Plague of Wild Beasts signifies the *hashgaḥah peratit* of *ve-hefleti*, that Hashem set apart the Children of Israel in Goshen and they did not experience the Plague.⁵ The Plague of Hail signifies the Unity of

---

2. See R. Samson Raphael Hirsch, Exodus 6:7–8; R. Hirsch, Deuteronomy 32:9.
3. R. Naphtali Tzvi Yehudah Berlin, *Ha'amek Davar*, Exodus 6:6.
4. *Haggadah, Maggid* (paragraph beginning with "We were slaves to Pharaoh in Egypt").
5. See Exodus 8:18 (stating that the Plague of Wild Beasts did not occur in Goshen, where the Jews lived). See also Nahmanides ad loc. (noting that even if a wild beast would find a Jew outside Goshen, it would not harm him); *Keli Yakar* to Exodus 7:17.

I Shall Bring You to the Land

the Creator.⁶ The Plague of the Firstborn is the moment of truth.⁷ And *Mattan Torah* is replete with the miracles of the Revelation at Sinai.

No wonder our Sages did not make a fifth cup for the Land of Israel. It is quite true that the Book of Joshua is full of miracles for the conquest and division of the Land. But conquest of the Land entails blood and tears, and the more removed we are from it, the more likely it is that we will say "my strength and the might of my hand made me all this wealth" (Deuteronomy 8:17). So there is a grave danger of designating a separate cup and blessing for *ve-heveti*. We might deflect from the theme of "the Name of Hashem I will invoke" (Psalms 116:13).⁸

Historically, the government of our beloved State has played a very positive role in keeping *ve-heveti* moored to *ve-lakaḥti*. It is in deferring to the *Rabbanut* on matters of *ishut*. It is by subsidizing Torah education and the family, and catapulting the mitzvah of settling the Land of Israel to new heights.

It is therefore with great consternation that we take the secular revolution that the Israeli government is trying to effect.⁹ What they are doing is breaking the nexus between *ve-heveti* and *ve-lakaḥti* and smashing the Four Cups, eliminating them and replacing them with one *ve-heveti*. This *ve-heveti* has no blessing and it has no *seder* either.

May we move in the direction of fortifying the connection between *ve-heveti* and *ve-lakaḥti* so that we can hear Elijah bringing tidings of the Redemption.

---

6. See *Keli Yakar* to Exodus 7:17.
7. See *Rashi* to Exodus 12:30.
8. See R. Judah Loew b. Bezalel (*Maharal*, Prague, ca. 1525–1609), *Kitvei Maharal mi-Prague*, ed. Abraham Kariv, vol. 1 (Jerusalem: Mossad HaRav Kook, 2001), 232, s.v. "*nes Ḥanukkah*" (stating that for every miracle of salvation for which one is required to give thanksgiving to Hashem, the emphasis is on the salvation rather than on the miracle through which the salvation was effected).
9. See Etgar Lefkovits, "Meimad Threatens to Leave Coalition over Secular Reform," *Jerusalem Post*, January 22, 2001, 3; Haim Shapiro, "Haredim Conflicted over Secular Candidates," *Jerusalem Post*, December 11, 2000, 3.

Bo

The Son Who Got Squeezed Out

January 14, 1989

As the watershed event in history, the Exodus demands of us a comprehension and multi-faceted educational obligation to our children. All four sons of Israel must be reached, the Wise Son, the Wicked Son, the Simpleton, and the One Who Does Not Know How to Ask.

All four sons are addressed in today's portion. But the son who we most eagerly want to hear from, because he has something important to say, the Wise Son, is left out. He must be patient. His voice will not be heard until *mishneh Torah, Parashat Va-Et'ḥanan*, and even there, it is "if your child asks you tomorrow" (Deuteronomy 6:20). "There is a tomorrow that occurs after a prolonged period of time."[1]

I would submit that the omission of the Wise Son from today's portion is not a slight, but rather the highest compliment to him.

---

1. *Rashi* to Exodus 13:14.

Bo

One who is driven by wickedness cannot contain his evil. Even while the Children of Israel experience the prophecy and the Divine Presence, he must shout his heresies, "What is this service to you?" (Exodus 12:26). And the man who is driven by curiosity, the Simpleton, cannot ask but "What is this?" (Exodus 13:14). And God fated that we should get so caught up in the spirit of the Redemption that we should forget that there are those among us who do not know how to ask, who require our patient attention. *Ve-at pesaḥ lo,* you must initiate the dialogue with him.[2]

But the Wise Son is patient and will wait to speak at the right moment. Why? Because the wisdom of the Wise Son is not just an intellectual trait. In the thinking of our Sages, the Wise Son embodies a moral character, evident in the seven traits found in a wise person.[3]

In *Parashat Bo*, as the Redemption unfolds, the Wise Son realizes that he should deny himself the role of a *sho'el*, one who asks questions. He acknowledges the truth that the Redemption is being orchestrated by the rabbinic leaders of the generation and the Children of Israel have a profound glimpse into Divine Providence. They all feel this, so "he does not speak before those who are greater than he in wisdom."[4]

The Wise Son is an *anav* too, feeling that speaking up now with pointed questions would perhaps upstage Moses and Aaron. This he cannot and will not do. In this context, he assumes the role of a *meshiv*, one who responds to questions. Someone must knock out the teeth of the Wicked Son. This person, I submit, is the Wise Son. The Wise Son in *Parashat Bo* assumes the role of the responder. And he is *meshiv ka-halakhah* by knocking out the teeth of the scorner, recognizing the harm that such a man does to the moral climate of

---

2. *Haggadah, Maggid.*
3. Mishnah, *Avot* 5:7. The seven traits are that the learned person (1) does not begin speaking before one who is greater than he in wisdom or in years; (2) does not interrupt the words of his fellow; (3) does not answer impetuously; (4) questions with relevance to the subject matter and replies accurately; (5) discusses first things first and last things last; (6) says "I have not heard" with respect to something that he has not heard; and (7) acknowledges the truth.
4. Mishnah, *Avot* 5:7.

society, even amidst a climate where everyone is soaring the very heavens in *emunah*.

And amidst this climate, when he abrogates his role as a *sho'el*, he hones his skills as a *meshiv* and realizes that the climate must be optimal for the question "What is this?" We cannot discourage questions, so we cannot answer impetuously. A teacher who responds impetuously discourages and suppresses questions, even on a subliminal level.

When does the Wise Son burst into action, assuming the mantle of a *sho'el*? It is in an entirely different climate. It is the climate that the Torah portrays in *Parashat va-Et'hanan*, "when Hashem, your God, brings you to the Land that Hashem swore to your forefathers" (Deuteronomy 6:10), and we encounter wealth for which we did not toil and are faced with the trial of prosperity. Then we are told, "Beware for yourself lest you forget Hashem Who took you out of the land of Egypt, from the house of slavery" (Deuteronomy 6:12). On a *derush* level, the *parashah* is understood to refer to the seven-year period of war when the Children of Israel conquered the Land of Israel, when *koslei da-hazirei* are permitted to be eaten, and there is a general deterioration of the moral climate of society.[5]

When we get a little closer to the question of the Wise Son, we are told, "You shall not test Hashem, your God" (Deuteronomy 6:16). Perhaps this refers to a period of persecution of our people, God forbid, to the Holocaust, when people say, "Where now is their God?" (Psalms 115:2).

It is in this climate that the Wise Son bursts forth and prods the *gedolei Torah*, who are what is meant by *etkhem*, "you" (Deuteronomy 6:20). And here he is *sho'el ke-inyan*. He asks the right question, a historical question, one that he knows the answer to. But he points us in the right direction to "What are the testimonies, and the decrees, and the ordinances that Hashem, your God, commanded you?" (Deuteronomy 6:20). Instead of imploring Hashem to produce miracles to prove that He is there and we are under His guidance, he tries his utmost, by utilizing his wisdom, to demonstrate testimony of the Divine Providence. If he is a scientist, he can point to the proof of God's existence

---

5. Hullin 17a. See also Nahmanides to Deuteronomy 6:10. The term *koslei da-hazirei* refers to bacon that is found as booty.

from the wonders of nature. "How abundant are Your works, Hashem; with wisdom You made them all" (Psalms 104:24). And if he is a computer expert, he can show that the Torah contains unmistakable patterns that make it impossible for the Torah to be of human authorship.[6] And he is the man who will use his wisdom for *tikkun olam* so everyone will see the divine image in him. "For in the image of God He made man" (Genesis 9:6).

To what extent will the Wise Son be committed to evidence? *Edut*. It will be then with the letters *ayin* and *dalet*, with the objective of producing the certainty that cannot be shaken by the seventy nations or the four winds![7]

And then he will surprise everyone. He will call for the rabbi to enumerate the *ḥukkim*, those mitzvot that have no logic or rationality to them. When the man of logic and rationality shows commitment to the *ḥukkim*, this has a vast impact on society, and the level of commitment rises. Only then does he move to *mishpatim*. Hence, "he discusses first things first and last things last."[8] He has his priorities set straight.

Whether the Wise Son is operating in the *ge'ullah* environment or the darkness of *hester panim*, he is never an elitist. "With respect to a matter that he has not heard, he says, 'I have not heard.'"[9] Even when he hears something from a child that he never heard before, he will say this. This unifies the Jewish people.

Lastly, he is always *modeh al ha-emet*, acknowledging and being thankful for the truth, not only when he is bested but, as *Midrash Shemuel* points out, even when the dialogue he establishes makes him realize on his own that he is wrong![10]

---

6. See Robert M. Haralick, Eliyahu Rips, and Matityahu Glazerson, *Torah Codes: A Glimpse into the Infinite* (New York: Mazal & Bracha, 2005); Doron Witztum, Eliyahu Rips, and Yoav Rosenberg, "Equidistant Letter Sequences in the Book of Genesis," *Statistical Science* 9, no. 3 (1994): 429–438.
7. See *Ba'al ha-Turim* to Deuteronomy 6:3. The letter *ayin* has the numerical equivalence of seventy, and the letter *dalet* has the numerical equivalence of four.
8. Mishnah, *Avot* 5:7.
9. Ibid.
10. R. Samuel b. Isaac de Uçeda (Safed, 16th cent.), *Midrash Shemuel* to *Avot* 5:7, reprinted in R. Ezra Batzri, ed., *Midrash Shemuel: Otzar Perushim al Pirkei Avot* (Jerusalem: Haktav Institute, 2001), 382. The term "*modeh*" in the phrase "*modeh al*

The Son Who Got Squeezed Out

It is only the Wise Son who is capable of unifying the Jewish people because it is only the person who can sweep up every element of society and make an impact on them who can be a unifying force. The Wise Son can therefore expand the family element in the Jewish people to ever-increasing circles of people.

---

ha-emet" can be interpreted as deriving from the verb *le-hitvadot*, "to acknowledge," and *le-hodot*, "to give thanks." The wise person is grateful to Hashem because he realizes that Hashem executes true judgment. Ibid.

Bottling Up *Emunah*

February 3, 1990

The spectacular signs and wonders through which Hashem brought about the Redemption from Egypt set straight the nonbelievers, doubters, and heretics of that time. Indeed, there was a God, and He was intimately involved in the governance of His world. But, as Nahmanides puts it, Hashem will not make miracles, signs, and wonders in each generation just for the purpose of silencing the wicked and the heretics.[1] How then can we bottle up or preserve for posterity the intense dosage of *emunah* that we acquired at the time of the Exodus?

It was perhaps this very concern that led the Wise Son of the Four Questions to stay out of the *parashah*, resisting the temptation to join the other sons who speak Torah, i.e., the Simpleton, the One Who Does Not Know How to Ask, and the Wicked Son. While the Redemption is unfolding, the Wise Son finds no role for himself. But in the end of an era, the dying out of the Generation of the Wilderness, there is a need to preserve the faith for posterity. It is here that the Wise Son activates

---

1. Nahmanides (*Ramban*, Spain, 1194–1270) to Exodus 13:16.

himself. His piercing question is: "What are the testimonies, and the decrees, and the ordinances that Hashem, your God, commanded you?" (Deuteronomy 6:20).

This question, permit me to suggest, is an elaboration on the theme of Nahmanides. Nahmanides answers his question by stating that *emunah* is preserved when Hashem institutes a plethora of commandments all designed to remind us of the Exodus experience.[2]

The Wise Son's search on the most obvious level takes him to an investigation of the *ḥukkim*. The paschal offering is called *ḥukkah*.[3] This exotic ritual is designed to re-enact the Exodus experience.[4] Throughout the ages, our Sages have read into this ritual the minutiae of the *ge'ullah* experience. And yes, we have a whole Festival of Passover, which is designed to re-create the Exodus experience for us – *pesaḥ*, matzah, *maror*, *afikoman*.

The Jew who is imbued with the *ḥok* personality wants to pronounce "so that you will know that I am Hashem in the midst of the land" (Exodus 8:18). And the *ḥok* personality speaks further. The *ot* of the Exodus dances to the *ot* of ritual that re-enacts the Exodus experience and finds its final point of settlement on the *ot* of the *tefillin shel yad*,[5] which is the submission of the Jew to Hashem to do everything commanded, even though he might not understand it.[6]

But the Wise Son is very demanding. He goes further, wanting to know how we should demonstrate that "I am Hashem in the midst

---

2. Nahmanides to Deuteronomy 6:20. See also Nahmanides to Exodus 13:16.
3. Exodus 13:10.
4. See R. Aaron b. Joseph ha-Levi (*Ra'ah*, Spain, ca. 1235–1300), *Sefer ha-Ḥinnukh*, eds. R. Yitzhak Yeshayah Weiss, R. David Zicherman, and R. Yitzhak Weinstein (Jerusalem: Makhon Yerushalayim, 1992), mitzvah no. 5.
5. Exodus 13:16 ("It shall be a sign (*ot*) upon your arm, and an ornament between your eyes."); Deuteronomy 6:8 ("Bind them as a sign (*ot*) upon your arm and let them be ornaments between your eyes.").
6. The Midrash records that the Children of Israel were successful in their war against Midian because the Jewish warriors did not precede the donning of the *tefillin shel yad* with the donning of the *tefillin shel rosh*. Song of Songs Rabbah 4:5. This *midrash* is understood to convey that the men performed the mitzvot before inquiring into the meaning of the mitzvot. See R. Simeon Sofer (Cracow, 1820–1883), *Mikhtav Sofer*, vol. 2, *Shemot*, *derush* 7 (Jerusalem, 1952), pp. 15a–b.

of the land." How can we re-create the feeling of *hashgaḥah peratit*, the individualization and personalization of *ge'ullah*?

The Jew who yearns for this level of re-creation of the Exodus experience focuses on the mitzvot that the Torah connects to the Exodus from Egypt. These are the prohibition against *ribbit*,[7] the commandment to wear *tzitzit*,[8] the law of honest weights and measures,[9] and the prohibition against eating *sheratzim*.[10] All are interpreted at Bava Metzia 61b to refer to the test of invisible misconduct.[11] The Jew who is the champion of "I am Hashem in the midst of the land" will be aware that Hashem observes his conduct, as there is no such thing as invisible misconduct.

But the Wise Son is very demanding. He wants nothing less than *edut*. How can we feel that we were there? How can we obtain first-hand testimony of the Exodus from Egypt? The answer is that we get a clue to this level that corresponds to "so that you shall know that there is none like Me in all the world" (Exodus 9:14) from the observation that there is no exhortation in the Torah that is repeated more times than

---

7. Leviticus 25:37–38 ("You shall not give him your money on interest nor for increase shall you give your food. I am Hashem, your God, Who has taken you out of the land of Egypt.").
8. Numbers 15:41 (stating at the chapter that addresses the laws of *tzitzit* "I am Hashem Who has taken you out of Egypt").
9. Leviticus 19:36 ("You shall have honest scales, honest weights, honest dry measures, and honest liquid measures; I am Hashem your God Who has taken you out of the land of Egypt.").
10. Leviticus 11:44–45 ("You shall not contaminate your souls by [consuming] creeping things that crawl on the ground. For I am Hashem Who brought you up from the land of Egypt to be your God."). *Sheratzim* are animals that slither along the ground or appear to do so because they have short legs and their movement is not readily noticeable. See *Rashi* to Genesis 1:24 and Leviticus 11:41.
11. Invisible misconduct with respect to *ribbit* entails deceiving the borrower that he is borrowing money that belongs to a gentile, which may be borrowed on interest. With respect to *tzitzit*, the potential deception is that the blue dye on the *tzitzit* is from an indigo plant rather than from the *ḥilazon*. *Rashi* to Bava Metzia 61b, s.v. "*kala ilan*." With respect to honest weights, invisible misconduct is possible by burying the weights in salt, which affects their weight. *Rashi* ad loc., s.v. "*le-tomen mishkelotav*." *Sheratzim* are not easily distinguishable from kosher fish. Consequently, an unscrupulous fishmonger could deceive customers into believing that a mixture of kosher fish and *sheratzim* is completely kosher.

Bottling Up Emunah

the prohibition against vexing and oppressing a convert and the positive duty to love him.[12] Why? "You know the feelings of a stranger, for you were strangers in the land of Egypt" (Exodus 23:9). Note the demands of the Torah to be sensitive to the feelings of alienation, to say nothing of the deeper anguish of the widow and the orphan.[13]

How can we create a feeling of *edut*? This is accomplished by doing the work of Hashem of "I have heard the groan of the Children of Israel" (Exodus 6:5), taking up the cause of the oppressed, the destitute, the abandoned, and the bereaved when these suffering ones feel that there is no salvation in sight, when no one cares for their plight. If someone takes up their cause, then it is nothing less than a re-creation of the Exodus for them, and the recipient is the witness of the Exodus. The savior is the one who makes possible an *edut* in the testimony of the one who is saved.

---

12. See *Bava Metzia* 59b. The Talmud notes that the Torah includes three prohibitions against wronging a convert (Exodus 22:20, Leviticus 19:33, and Leviticus 25:17), and three prohibitions against oppressing a convert (Exodus 22:20, Exodus 23:9 and Exodus 22:24). According to a *Baraita*, R. Eliezer the Great said that the Torah warns about offending a convert in thirty-six places, and some say in forty-six places. *Bava Metzia* 59b. For an analysis of the computation of these warnings, see R. Dovid Cohen (Brooklyn, contemp.), *Ohel David*, vol. 2 (Brooklyn, NY: Mesorah, 1987), 150–158. The Torah also requires a Jew to love the convert. Deuteronomy 10:19 ("You shall love the convert because you were strangers in the land of Egypt.").
13. Exodus 22:20–21.

The Public and Private Sign

January 19, 2002

A *ba'al musar* with an impish sense of humor once said that Hashem understands our need to show off or flaunt in our observance of the commandments so He was both accommodating and sympathetic.[1]

Accommodating? He gave us the mitzvah of the Four Species to be performed in full view of our fellow Jew amidst *Hallel* and *hoshanot*. Hence, the Evil Inclination hides in the mandate of "this is my God and I will adorn Him" (Exodus 15:2)[2] and tells us, "Go for it!" So we incur great expense to buy an *etrog* that is *hadar*. It must be big,[3] have a nice yellow color,[4] and be

---

1. See R. Aharon Yehudah Grusman, *She'elot u-Teshuvot Ve-Darashta ve-Ḥakarata* (Jerusalem, 1996), 205.
2. See *Shabbat* 133b (interpreting the verse to mean "adorn yourself before Him in the performance of the commandments").
3. See Mishnah, *Sukkah* 3:7; *Sukkah* 34b; Maimonides, *Mishneh Torah, Lulav* 7:8; *Shulḥan Arukh, Oraḥ Ḥayyim* 648:22.
4. See Mishnah, *Sukkah* 3:6; *Sukkah* 34b; *Tosafot* to *Sukkah* 31b, s.v. "*ha-yarok ke-kharti*"; *Shulḥan Arukh, Oraḥ Ḥayyim* 648:21; R. Israel Meir ha-Kohen Kagan (*Ḥafetz Ḥayyim*, Radin, 1838–1933), *Mishnah Berurah* 648:65.

spotless,⁵ and its stem must be symmetrical with its *pitam*.⁶ Moreover, we bring the *etrog* to the synagogue in an ornate case made out of gold or silver.

Just imagine if we would be commanded to perform the mitzvah of the Four Species privately. What would become of the mitzvah? The *etrog* would be tiny, with a radius the size of an egg's.⁷ It would not be very pretty. We would keep the *etrog* in some cheap protective material, and the most frequent question the rabbi would get is: "If I freeze the *etrog* and it remains intact next year, is it still kosher?"

Sympathetic? Hashem does not bid us to perform the mitzvah of *maror* amidst a public ritual such as the recitation of *Hallel* or *hoshanot*. If we were so required, we would not be able to control ourselves. We would use only horseradish and a *Ḥazon Ish shiur*.⁸ Gastronomical problems, with heartburn the least of them, would proliferate. Hatzalah would be busy the whole night.⁹ Mercifully, we eat *maror* in the confines of our private homes. Many of us opt for romaine lettuce, for some all the better. Many more say, "Plain Iceberg lettuce will suffice. If it was good enough for R. Aharon Kotler, *zt"l*, it's good enough for me."¹⁰

---

5. See *Shulḥan Arukh, Oraḥ Ḥayyim* 648:12, 16.
6. R. Israel b. Gedaliah Lipschutz (Germany, 1782–1860), *Tiferet Yisrael, Yakhin Sukkah* 3:6; R. Shalom Shachna Czerniak, *Ḥayyim u-Verakhah: Arba'at Minim* ¶ 65 (citing *Tiferet Yisrael*); R. Yehiel Michel Stern, *Kashrut Arba'at ha-Minim* (Jerusalem: Makhon Imrei David, 1992), 8.
7. See Mishnah, *Sukkah* 3:7 (opinion of R. Judah); *Sukkah* 34b; Maimonides, *Mishneh Torah, Lulav* 7:8; *Shulḥan Arukh, Oraḥ Ḥayyim* 648:22.
8. For the mitzvah of *maror*, one is required to eat at least a *ke-zayit*, a volume equivalent to the size of an olive. *Shulḥan Arukh, Oraḥ Ḥayyim* 475:1. The prevailing view is that a *ke-zayit* is an amount in volume equivalent to the size of half of an egg. See *Shulḥan Arukh, Oraḥ Ḥayyim* 486:1; R. Israel Meir ha-Kohen Kagan, *Mishnah Berurah* 486:1. The *Ḥazon Ish*, based on the opinion of R. Ezekiel b. Judah Landau (*Noda bi-Yehudah*, Prague, 1713–1793) that the size of an egg today is half the size of an egg that existed in the times of the Talmud, is of the opinion that a *ke-zayit* is equal to two-thirds the volume of a modern-day egg. R. Abraham Isaiah Karelitz (*Ḥazon Ish*, Belarus and Israel, 1878–1953), *Ḥazon Ish, Oraḥ Ḥayyim* 39:17. According to R. Yaakov Yisrael Kanievsky (*Steipler Gaon*, Russia and Benei Berak, 1899–1985), the volume of a modern-day egg for purposes of halakhic measurements is approximately forty-five to fifty grams. R. Yaakov Yisrael Kanievsky, *Shiurin shel Torah* (Benei Berak, 1990), 65.
9. Hatzalah is a voluntary emergency medical service.
10. See R. Shimon D. Eider, *Halachos of Pesach* (Jerusalem: Feldheim, 1998), 234n23 (stating that R. Aharon Kotler used Iceberg lettuce to fulfill the mitzvah of *maror*).

Well, today's *sidrah* has something to say about flaunting the performance of mitzvot. "I shall go through the land of Egypt on this night, and I shall strike every firstborn in the land of Egypt, from man to beast... The blood shall be a sign for you upon the houses where you are" (Exodus 12:12–13). We are bidden to smear the blood of the paschal offering on the doorposts and the lintel, but inside, not outside.[11] The climactic moment of the Redemption is not a moment to gloat or to experience revenge. No, it is a sign "for you" (Exodus 12:13). It is a moment for silent reflection.

The difference between us and them is only the blood, the loyalty to Hashem and courage that we demonstrated by slaughtering the deity of the Egyptians.[12] By repudiating the deity of the Egyptians, we became worthy of redemption. "Then I passed you and saw you wallowing in your blood, and I said to you, 'In your blood you shall live'; I said to you, 'In your blood you shall live'" (Ezekiel 16:6).

We are also bidden to make *tefillin shel yad*, the sign for the lesson of the Exodus from Egypt. Again, it is not an external sign but rather a sign "for you" (Exodus 13:9).

What is the nature of this sign? It is a means of re-creating the *emunah* of the Exodus from Egypt. Sure, there is great value to history. Keep the memory fresh. But it is too far in the past to accomplish this directly. First we must re-create *emunah*.

How do we do this? It is by channeling the energies of "my strength and the might of my hand" (Deuteronomy 8:17) to Hashem. It is all the mitzvot of the firstborn. This is the sign of *tefillin shel yad*.

If flaunting makes the performance of a mitzvah a defining experience, then it is virtuous because it is *yir'at Shamayim be-galui*, "fear of Heaven in public." Public *yir'at Shamayim* is important because of its educational impact. "The hidden [sins] are for Hashem, our God, but the revealed [sins] are for us and our children forever" (Deuteronomy 29:28).[13]

---

11. *Rashi* to Exodus 12:13.
12. Exodus Rabbah 16:2.
13. See R. Hayyim Meir Yehiel Shapira, *Tiferet Hayyim* (Warsaw: Kleiman, 1920), 32 (explaining the verse to mean that public performance of mitzvot enables one to teach righteousness to one's children and grandchildren).

The Public and Private Sign

How do we maximize the educational impact of *yir'at Shamayim be-galui*? We get the hint of how to do it by the very last verse of this week's *sidrah*. "It shall be an ornament between your eyes" (Exodus 13:16). "Then all the peoples of the earth will see that the Name of Hashem is proclaimed over you, and they will revere you" (Deuteronomy 28:10).

Why will the nations fear us when they look at the *tefillin shel rosh*? It is the *tefillin shel rosh* that is a curiosity for the gentiles. It could lead the gentiles to mock us, or it could lead them to view it as part of our mystique and be driven to emulate us.

Which way will it go? It all depends on how they perceive us *before* they see us wearing *tefillin shel rosh*. If they see us as a people that exudes integrity and warmth in our family, social, commercial, and professional dealings, they will look upon the *tefillin shel rosh* as a mystique and then will delve deeper into our ways and emulate us. If this is not so, they will use the *tefillin shel rosh* as a vehicle to mock us.

May we achieve ever higher levels of fear of Heaven in private. The more we achieve in private, the more we will achieve in public.

Be-Shallaḥ

The Sea Saw and Fled

January 14, 1984

Throughout the ages, in times of national crisis, the Jewish people have always managed to summon up tremendous strength of character, bordering on the superhuman. Such was the case in our first crisis of national existence, at the Sea of Reeds. With the hosts of Pharaoh in fierce pursuit at the rear and the terrifying depths of the sea in front of them, the Children of Israel, following Moses' command, plunged into the Sea. When the water reached their nostrils, *ba'u mayim ad nafesh*,[1] the miracle of the Splitting of the Sea of Reeds took place.[2] Yet, the Midrash, in commenting on the verse "the sea saw and fled" (Psalms 114:3), says, "What did the Sea see?... It saw the casket of Joseph." The Sea split in the merit of Joseph.[3]

---

1. See Psalms 69:2 ("Save me, God, for the waters have reached until the soul."). Psalm 69 was recited by those who sanctified Hashem's Name by jumping into the Sea of Reeds. R. Samuel Eliezer b. Judah ha-Levi Edels (*Maharsha*, Poland, 1555–1631), *Ḥiddushei Halakhot ve-Aggadot, Sotah* 37a, s.v. "*ve-alav mefaresh ba-kabbalah*."
2. See *Sotah* 37a.
3. *Midrash Shoḥer Tov*, Psalms 114. The Midrash draws a parallel between the term used to refer to the sea in Psalms 114:3 ("The sea saw and fled (*va-yanos*)") and the term

Now, why is the superhuman courage and devotion to the command of Hashem of the multitude ignored and the merit ascribed to Joseph?

Rachel called Joseph that name for two reasons. One, *asaf Hashem et ḥerpati*, "Hashem has taken away my disgrace" (Genesis 30:23). *Rashi* comments that Hashem laid her disgrace up somewhere where it could not be seen.[4] Rachel had the ability to selectively blot out the unpleasantries and pain of the past and focus on a single delightful event in her life.

Second, *yosef Hashem li ben aḥer*, "may Hashem add on for me another son" (Genesis 30:24). Her focus on the past provided the sustenance and striving for her future. She had a prophecy that Jacob would be the progenitor of twelve sons.[5] Joseph was the eleventh son to be born to Jacob. With her disgrace swept aside, Rachel now aspired that the remaining son would be hers.

A beautiful fusion between the past and future was accomplished. The present did not exist for her. The selected event of her past provided the basis for her striving.

Throughout his life, Joseph was true to his name. He never lost his ebullient spirit, regardless of the circumstances in which he found himself. Thrown together with the dregs of society in a dungeon, he did not lose his spirit. The Divine Presence still rested on him.[6] He was able to interpret the dreams of the Chamberlain of the Cupbearers and the Chamberlain of the Bakers. In this respect, Joseph surpassed Jacob. For the twenty-two years during which Jacob was separated from Joseph, the Divine Presence departed from Jacob.[7] He fell into a state of melancholy.

What was at the base of Joseph's ebullience? It was his ability to selectively blot out the pain of his past and forget it. "God has taken away my disgrace" (Genesis 30:23).

---

    used to describe Joseph's fleeing from Lady Potiphar in Genesis 39:12 ("he fled (*va-yanas*)").

4. *Rashi* to Genesis 30:23, s.v. "*asaf.*"
5. *Rashi* to Genesis 30:24.
6. *Pirkei de-Rabbi Eliezer* 39.
7. *Midrash Tanḥuma, Va-Yeshev* 2; *Pirkei de-Rabbi Eliezer* 38.

What event did he focus on? It was his dream of "Behold! The sun, the moon, and eleven stars were bowing down to me" (Genesis 37:9). This was not an egotistical dream. It was the prophecy, as he took it, that he would unite his brothers. He would be, as Jacob called him, "the stone of Israel" (Genesis 49:24). This event allowed him to have a very optimistic view of the future. "May Hashem add on for me another son" (Genesis 30:24).

At the Sea of Reeds, the Children of Israel exhibited the dual character of Joseph. In that moment of desperation, the Children of Israel had to blot out their deep feeling of crushing servitude of 210 years. This part of their nature could naturally produce a cringing instinct in them, which would manifest itself in either surrender or paralysis. But instead, the Children of Israel had the power to focus on the past year, the year of the Ten Plagues, the year of miracles. These forces gave them enormous strength to believe that just as the first two expressions of redemption had been fulfilled, the second two would also be fulfilled. "May Hashem add on for me another son" (Genesis 30:24).

If the past was linked to the future when the Children of Israel plunged into the Sea, this link was further solidified and enhanced when the Children of Israel saw the Egyptians dead on the seashore. When they saw that, they said *shirah*.[8]

What is the main thrust of the *shirah*? It is the first verse. This is the verse that is repeated by Miriam, "I shall sing to Hashem for He is exalted above the arrogant, having hurled horse with its rider into the sea" (Exodus 15:1).

The *Midrash* comments that the horse and rider are glued together, with the horse advancing above the rider.[9] Both the horse and the rider are thrust into the very depths of the Sea and catapulted to the very heavens, and then cast to the very depths again and again. This conveys that Pharaoh and his men are no more than horses. Just as a horse is merely a weapon or tool for the rider, so, too, Pharaoh and all his might were merely instruments through which the Divine Glory was revealed. The idea was reinforced by the fact that after the Ten Plagues, Pharaoh and

---

8. Exodus 14:30, 15:1.
9. *Mekhilta* to Exodus 15:1; *Midrash Tanḥuma, Be-Shallaḥ* 13; *Rashi* to Exodus 15:1, s.v. "*sus ve-rokhvo*."

his people said, "What is this that we have done that we have sent away Israel from serving us?" (Exodus 14:5).

And why did he pursue them in the Sea of Reeds? If the surface of the Sea froze, perhaps it would soon melt and Pharaoh and his hosts would drown. If the Children of Israel walked out of the Sea through a miracle, did Pharaoh not know that miracles happen only for the Jewish people and not for him?

His pursuit of the Jewish people and his downfall were for no reason other than to demonstrate that Hashem is "exalted above the arrogant" (Exodus 15:1), that it is Hashem Who "extends a hand to sinners."[10]

When the Children of Israel understood that Pharaoh was merely a medium through which the Kingdom of Heaven was revealed, they transcended the present and acquired an unquenchable thirst for redemption. No longer were the Children of Israel tied to the present. A striving developed. They had been given a glimpse into Divine Providence. Now they wanted nothing less than the entire Kingdom of Heaven. "You will bring them and implant them on the mount of Your heritage, the foundation of Your dwelling-place that You, Hashem, have made – the Sanctuary, my Lord, that Your hands established" (Exodus 15:17), culminating in "Hashem shall reign for all eternity!" (Exodus 15:18).

When an individual connects the past with the future, with "Hashem shall reign for all eternity" as the vision of the future, he transcends his own individuality and has only one desire, that he should merit that the Glory of Heaven should increase through him.

Until now, no one said *shirah*. Abraham was saved from the burning furnace and did not say *shirah*. Isaac was saved from the knife at the *Akedah* and did not say *shirah*. Jacob was saved from the angel, from Esau, and from the people of Shekhem but did not say *shirah*.[11]

As the *Shem mi-Shemuel* explains, the Patriarchs felt that they were the medium through which the miracles occurred, that the miracles were wrought to save their lives. Now for the first time, the Children of Israel realized that the revelation of *malkhut Shamayim* does not need any human medium at all. The miracles that the Children of Israel

---

10. *Ne'ilah* Prayer on Yom Kippur.
11. Exodus Rabbah 23:4.

experienced on a personal level, miracles that demonstrated the love of Hashem for His people, were really undeserved and unnecessary. They therefore were inspired to say *shirah*.[12]

The Splitting of the Sea of Reeds imparts a universal message. Our Sages tell us, "*kashin le-zavvugan ke-keri'at Yam Suf,*" "the matching of a man and woman into a married couple is as difficult as the Splitting of the Sea of Reeds."[13] Now, this refers to both the matching of a man and woman into a pair and then their remaining as a couple. The only way that the Jewish home can produce *shirah* is when both partners bring with them to the marriage the same mental framework that the Jewish people had at the Splitting of the Sea. That framework is the dual character of Joseph, the expressions "God has taken away my disgrace" (Genesis 30:23) and "May Hashem add on for me another son" (Genesis 30:24). There is the need to sweep aside all the pettiness and disputes into an unseen corner and concentrate on the delight of the marriage, the children, and shared goals. Marriage is a metaphysical union of souls. What must serve as the vision of the couple, the element of "May Hashem add on for me another son," is the Kingdom of Heaven, the element of "Hashem shall reign for all eternity."

And our Sages tell us that whoever gladdens the bride and groom is considered as if he built up a ruin of Jerusalem.[14] Now, the *ḥatan* and *kallah* are very happy living in their little world of enjoying each other, living in the blissful present. But our role is to channel the happiness in the proper direction. We must channel the joy into *binyan*, and the *binyan* is nothing less than the Kingdom of Heaven.

When each Jewish home will begin to exude *shirah*, the whole national character will change. We will begin to realize that we are, thank God, living in an era when the four expressions of redemption have already been fulfilled. We only need to take decisive action so that each element of redemption is embellished, so that each element reaches its fullest potential, and we will merit to greet the Messiah speedily in our days!

---

12. R. Shmuel Bornsztain (*Shem mi-Shemuel*, Poland, 1855–1926), *Shem mi-Shemuel: Al Seder Parshiyyot ha-Torah u-Mo'adei Kodesh*, 9th ed., vol. 2 (Jerusalem, 1992), *Be-Shallaḥ* (5671/February 1911), pp. 170–171.
13. *Sotah* 2a.
14. *Berakhot* 6b.

Justice and Mercy

February 2, 1985

Several years ago, the Bitachon Women of America honored their National Chairperson, Zlata Mellglut, at their annual banquet. Just before the presentation ceremony, a photographer from *Newsweek* stepped up to the dais and asked Zlata permission to take her picture. Nervously, after tidying up her *shaitel*, Zlata smiled sheepishly and said, "Young man, be sure to do me justice." Looking at her with a puzzled glance, the photographer retorted, "Madam, what you need is mercy, not justice."[1]

One of the great tragedies of the contemporary scene is the confusion we often make between the concepts of justice and mercy. Often, we demand of Hashem and our fellow man nothing less than the highest order of justice, but we call it elemental justice. At the same time, we are willing to offer no more than what, in the wildest stretch of the imagination, is justice, but we call it mercy of the highest order.

---

1. The story is fictional.

Justice and Mercy

Witness the automobile executive. When it comes to his own employment contract, he will settle for nothing less than golden handcuffs and a golden handshake. But when it comes to negotiating with his workers, he will not budge an inch. And when he finds that a particular model is defective and could not sustain a rear-end collision, he will not recall it because cost-benefit analysis indicated that it should not be recalled.

Well, at the Sea of Reeds, the concepts of justice and mercy were really set straight. Perhaps after the Ten Plagues, the Children of Israel began to feel that the immunity that they had experienced was something that they fully deserved. At the Sea of Reeds, they realized that this was not so. Everything did not proceed as smoothly as in the past. Moses commands the waters to split, but they do not. In the momentary hesitation of the water, *ba'u mayim ad nafesh*, there was a crisis of national existence. Suddenly, the waters do split, just in the nick of time! And Moses proclaims, "What ails you, O sea, that you flee?" (Psalms 114:5). But what happened was that obstructionist forces demanded, "*Halalu ovdei avodah zarah ve-halalu ovdei avodah zarah*," the Egyptians are idol worshippers, and so are the Children of Israel.[2]

Paradoxically, it was at the rebellion of the Sea of Reeds, the first of the ten trials with which our ancestors tested Hashem in the Wilderness,[3] that the Children of Israel experienced their greatest notice of divine grace and Revelation and arrived at the insight that Hashem is merciful in judgment. Even Pharaoh, who was the personification of evil itself, experienced a profound moment of repentance and was spared![4] *Mi khamokha ba-elim, Hashem*, "Who is like You among the heavenly powers, Hashem!" (Exodus 15:11). *Mi khamokha* does not have a *dagesh* in

---

2. The Midrash records that at the time that Hashem wanted to split the Sea of Reeds, the *sar* (angel) of Egypt objected, arguing that the Children of Israel worshipped idols as did the Egyptians. *Yalkut Re'uveni, Be-Shallaḥ*, s.v. "*va-yet Mosheh et yado*"; Exodus Rabbah 21:7; *Yalkut Shimoni, Be-Shallaḥ* 234. According to the *Zohar*, Hashem invoked the merit of Abraham and split the Sea for the Children of Israel. *Zohar* 2:170b.
3. Mishnah, *Avot* 5:4.
4. R. Jacob Culi, *Me-Am Lo'ez, Be-Shallaḥ* 15, trans. R. Shemuel Yerushalmi, *Yalkut Me-Am Lo'ez: Sefer Shemot* (Jerusalem: Wagshal, 1968), 345.

the first letter, *khof*, because Pharaoh was inundated by the waters; he was gasping for breath and could not pronounce the *kof*.[5]

But most of all, the Children of Israel acquired a new concept of Hashem's mercy. This is *rahamim she-be-rahamim*, "mercy within mercy." For us, our grandest concept of mercy is an interventionist one. If a friend is found in disaster, we intervene and help, and perhaps even in a grand manner. But in ordinary life situations, there is no place for mercy.

But at the Sea of Reeds, the Children of Israel learned differently. They understood that the miracle was completely unnecessary to effect their survival. Most basically, they could have been led by means of a shorter, land route to the Land of Israel, such as "by the way of the land of the Philistines" (Exodus 13:17). Then, what gave Pharaoh the effrontery and the strength to pursue the Children of Israel when he was previously crushed and pulverized and he himself had chased them out? Now he leads the army rather than staying at the back. How could the Egyptians in their sane minds follow the Children of Israel into the Sea? Did they not know that miracles never happened to them, but only to the Children of Israel? This was irrational, reflecting a bout of insanity. Their free will was taken away from them.[6]

What is the most important part of the *shirah*? It is the phrase "horse with its rider [Hashem] hurled into the sea" (Exodus 15:1).[7] This is the part of the *shirah* that is repeated by Miriam.[8] What does this mean? The horse is the soldier's implement of war and the soldier is merely the general's pawn, and the general is the king's pawn. Both the rider and the horse were glued together, gyrating up and down.[9] The rider and the horse are really one. Pharaoh was merely a pawn of Hashem, to demonstrate to the Children of Israel their singularity as a people, the special relationship that Hashem has with them, a relationship of

---

5. Ibid.
6. See R. Jacob Culi, *Me-Am Lo'ez*, Exodus 15:1, trans. R. Shemuel Yerushalmi, *Yalkut Me-Am Lo'ez: Sefer Shemot*, 329; *Shem mi-Shemuel*, vol. 2, Be-Shallah (5677/February 1917), pp. 208–209.
7. R. Naphtali Tzvi Yehudah Berlin, *Rinah shel Torah*, Song of Songs 1:9.
8. Exodus 15:21.
9. *Mekhilta* to Exodus 15:1; *Midrash Tanhuma*, Be-Shallah 13.

love. We were not bestowed the miracle of the Splitting of the Sea of Reeds to extricate us from our affliction. It was the other way around. We were afflicted so that Hashem could demonstrate His miracles and His special closeness to us![10]

The Splitting of the Sea of Reeds generates a special spirit of generosity on the part of the Children of Israel. "This is my God and I will adorn Him" (Exodus 15:2). "Adorn yourself before Him in the performance of the commandments."[11]

How can we reproduce the generous spirit? It is by emulating the lesson that the Children of Israel learned at the Sea of Reeds, that justice consists of tempered demands on others but expectations from ourselves, and of mercy in ordinary life, mercy in the form of imparting a singular feeling of specialness to someone else. This is produced only when a crisis of existence is not the motivating force behind the act of kindness.

Imparting a feeling of singularity and specialness to others and maintaining a tempered expectation from them are also the ingredients for the ideal marriage. "It is as difficult to pair them as the Splitting of the Sea of Reeds."[12] This refers not only to the matching of people, but also to the keeping of them together.[13]

---

10. See R. Shmuel Bornsztain, *Shem mi-Shemuel*, vol. 2, *Be-Shallaḥ* (5671/February 1911), p. 171.
11. *Shabbat* 133b.
12. *Sotah* 2a.
13. See Genesis Rabbah 68:4.

The Song of Deborah

January 25, 1986

In the annual cycle of the Torah and *haftarah* readings, *Shirat Mosheh* and *Shirat Devorah* are always parallel.[1] Historically, the cataclysmic event of the Splitting of the Sea of Reeds and its accompanying *shirah* occurred on the seventh day of the Exodus and are commemorated for posterity on the seventh day of Passover. The day of the week on which the seventh day of Passover falls unfailingly predicts the day of the week on which Israeli Independence falls, the fifth day of Iyyar. Hence, *Shirat Devorah* must have some relevance for the State of Israel.

Permit me to suggest that the life of Deborah and her times not only capsulate the history of the State since its inception, but also evoke the mission of the modern Jewish State at its highest potential.

We are told that Deborah was a prophetess, but a somewhat unique prophetess. She prophesized not for *aḥarit ha-yamim*, but rather for her own time. And what did Deborah do? "She judged Israel at that time" (Judges 4:4). The role of a judge is a very unnatural role for a

---

1. Maimonides, *Mishneh Torah, Seder Tefillot Kol ha-Shanah*.

The Song of Deborah

woman. Jewish law disqualifies a woman from serving as a judge in a civil suit.[2] Deborah's role as a judge can therefore be understood, as is the *Arukh ha-Shulḥan*'s position,[3] only as the litigants involved willingly accepted her authority, in accordance with the principle *davar she-ba-mamom, tenai kayyam*.[4] A woman judge hence symbolizes the limits of creative legislation in a secular state through the institution of a political democracy, the consent of the people, when those who stand to lose by means of a certain arrangement waive their rights in the matter.

Deborah was *eshet Lappidot*, "the wife of Lappidoth."[5] Lappidoth was not a learned person.[6] She made thick wicks and told him to donate them for the Tabernacle so that the light of the Menorah would shine brightly.[7] This action symbolized that she had a profound love for Torah. She was rooted in the highest awe of Torah. When she was inspired to say *shirah*, we would imagine that she would combine the wonders of the past, including the Exodus from Egypt, in her praises of the deliverance that she witnessed. But she mentions only Sinai[8] because the awesome experience of Sinai was uppermost in her mind, and that is what ensured that her rulings were in accordance with the letter and the spirit of the Torah.

And Deborah assumed another very unnatural role; she was a great military leader.[9] This is unnatural, as our Sages tell us, "*nashim lav benot milḥamah ninhu*"; women were not warriors.[10] And there would

---

2. Jerusalem Talmud, *Shevuot* 4:1; R. Asher b. Jehiel (*Rosh*, Germany, ca. 1250–1327), *Rosh, Shevuot* 4:2; *Shulḥan Arukh, Ḥoshen Mishpat* 7:4.
3. *Arukh ha-Shulḥan, Ḥoshen Mishpat* 22:1.
4. The principle is that in a monetary matter, a stipulation of the parties is given effect even it is contrary to what is written in the Torah. See *Bava Metzia* 51a; R. Aaron b. Joseph ha-Levi, *Sefer ha-Ḥinnukh*, mitzvah no. 77; R. Yom Tov Ishbili (*Ritva*, Spain, ca. 1250–1330), *Ḥiddushei ha-Ritva, Shevuot* 30a.
5. Judges 4:4.
6. *Tanna de-vei Eliyahu, Seder Eliyahu Rabba* 9.
7. *Megillah* 14a; Rashi to Judges 4:4.
8. "Mountains melted before Hashem – as did Sinai – before Hashem, the God of Israel" (Judges 5:5).
9. See Judges 4:6–9.
10. See *Kiddushin* 2b; R. Aaron b. Joseph ha-Levi, *Sefer ha-Ḥinnukh*, mitzvah no. 603. The phrase "*nashim lav benot milḥamah ninhu*" is used by commentators in describing the *Sefer ha-Ḥinnukh*'s discussion of mitzvah no. 603. See, e.g., R. Israel Joshua Trunk of Kutno (*Yeshuot Malko*, Poland, 1820–1893), *Yeshuot Malko, Oraḥ Ḥayyim* 50.

be two victories, one against the hosts of Sisera, and then another and separate episode of the defeat of Sisera himself, for even after the hosts are decimated, if the General remains alive, he can reorganize the people and incite a new war![11] The defeat of Sisera himself after his hosts were decimated is given what seems an inordinate amount of attention.

In the times of the Jewish State, military battle is an everyday occurrence. Unlike the other nations, for whom war is an aberration, for the Jewish State, it is an incessant affair. The Jewish State has achieved a stunning military victory, only to be set back diplomatically. That is why so much attention is given to Yael's victory, how she marshaled every ounce of her resourcefulness to defeat Sisera. "He asked for water, she gave him milk; in a stately saucer she presented cream" (Judges 5:25). This denotes that the defeat of the enemy outside the battlefield should not be taken for granted. It may very well call for innovation and new political institutions to assure the defeat of the enemy.

But it is more than the enemy's propaganda and cause that must be defeated; it is his way of life and the values that he espouses. It is only these circumstances that can explain why *Shirat Devorah* dignifies the bewailing of the mother of our arch nemesis! Why is the poetry of the wicked given importance? The answer is very simple. The enemy is more than a propaganda threat. He is a culture and a way of living – a promiscuous life, a barbaric existence, a pleasure-seeking animal! A way of life is idolized and immortalized by many people. International terrorism is regarded by many governments simply as a spectator sport!

Deborah was indeed a spectacular woman of achievement and inspiration, but she had a critical side to her as well. She cries, "*Lammah yashavta bein ha-mishpetayim?*" (Judges 5:16), "Why did you sit between the boundaries" and not really help your brothers?

We are not guilty of this. Every time Israel is in a crisis, world Jewry rallies to the aid of the Jewish State with the highest level of commitment. But are we equal to Deborah's challenge? What is her challenge? We feel a stark contrast between the Splitting of the Sea of Reeds and *Shirat Devorah*. The Splitting of the Sea of Reeds called for action. The Children of Israel were in a desperate crisis. They faced the

---

11. Judges 4:12–23.

deep sea in front on them and were being pursued from behind by the hosts of Pharaoh. "Why do you cry out to Me? Speak to the Children of Israel and let them journey forth" (Exodus 14:15).

But Deborah manufactures a crisis. She tells Barak b. Abinoam, "Go and convince the people to go toward Mount Tabor" (Judges 4:6). Draw the people to the high mountain. The ten thousand soldiers of Naphtali and Zebulun will have no inclination to go on their own. They were not being attacked at that time. They will be reluctant to go. They will regard this action as pure provocation of Sisera. Then Deborah continues, "I will then draw Sisera to the Kishon Brook" (Judges 4:7). He will have no inclination to respond to the threat. His advisers will tell him not to do battle at that time. But unnaturally, he will come to the valley and he will not respond proportionately. Instead, he will bring thousands more troops than are necessary to neutralize the threat, and he and his hosts will be decimated. She creates the challenge of producing a grand action that will be worthy of *shirah*.

There is no prophecy today, but the establishment of the State of Israel is unmistakably a sign of divine favor for the Jewish people, especially after the world chanted our death tune at the Holocaust and claimed that God had abandoned us. Our challenge is to hear the call to produce the grand act of sanctifying God's name, ascend Mount Tabor, and produce our own act of *kiddush ha-Shem* worthy of *shirah*. "So may all Your enemies be destroyed, O Hashem! And let those who love Him be like the powerfully rising sun" (Judges 5:31).

The PLO and Amalek

January 21, 1989

In its waning moments, the Reagan Administration launched two major policy initiatives in the Middle East. First, it refused to grant Arafat a diplomatic visa for the purpose of delivering a message to the United Nations.[1] But, in an apparent about-face several weeks later, after analyzing Arafat's Geneva speech wherein he repudiated terrorism and became a sudden convert to the ideology of peaceful co-existence, the United States declared that those statements minimally met its standards for initiating dialogue.[2]

Many observers regard the two actions as inconsistent and contradictory.[3] Be it as it may, we now are faced with a new reality. The dual

---

1. U.S. Department of State, "Statement Denying Visa for Arafat," November 26, 1988, reprinted in *New York Times*, November 27, 1988, A5.
2. Robert Pear, "U.S. Agrees to Talks with P.L.O., Saying Arafat Accepts Israel and Renounces All Terrorism," *New York Times*, December 15, 1988, A1.
3. Walter Reich, "A Tactical War of Words; Talks Will Determine Value of What Arafat Says," *Los Angeles Times*, December 24, 1988, M4; David Bar-Illan, "What PLO Tells Faithful, Not What It Says to U.S., Shows Folly of Recognition," *Los Angeles Times*,

actions of our government represent a challenge of strategy towards our mortal enemy, the PLO.

The PLO is not only our sworn enemy, but it is the manifestation of Amalek today.

In his analysis of the commandment to wipe out Amalek, the *Netziv* asks, what is it that the Torah wants us to obliterate? Is it the nation of Amalek? It does not exist today, anywhere. Is it the memory of Amalek? This is impossible because the Torah speaks of Amalek, so it cannot be forgotten. What the Torah wants us to obliterate is the ideology of Amalek, a nation fanatically bent on the mission to deny God's law and role in human society. The righteous must suffer and the wicked prosper, and the innocent perish.[4]

In shocking imagery, the mission of Amalek is described as "*ki yad al kes Kah*," "for the hand is on the throne of God" (Exodus 17:16). It is the hand of Amalek. Brazenly, he puts his hand on the throne of Hashem and wants to partially cover His holiest name. He concedes only the first two letters, *yud* and *heh* – Hashem created This World and the World to Come – but as far as governance is concerned, there is complete denial. The *vav*, which is the *tiferet*, the open miracles that Hashem brings about, is denied. And the second *heh*, which is the operation of the divine image of man in human society, is also denied by Amalek.[5]

Since its inception, the PLO has been bent on denying and trying to undo the miracle of the establishment of the State of Israel. This is an open miracle of our time. The PLO brazenly is taking a *sefer torah* and burning it, with special emphasis on the Book of Genesis. The words of R. Yitzhak in particular are scorned – "Hashem need not have begun the Torah but from 'This month shall be for you [the beginning of months]' [Exodus 12:2] because it is the first commandment that Israel was given."[6] The whole story of the Book of Genesis, as the *Maharal* points out, is to

---

December 22, 1988, M7; John M. Goshko and David B. Ottaway, "U.S. Reassures Israel, Sets Talks with PLO; Reagan Says 'We Have Not Retreated' from Ally," *Washington Post*, December 16, 1988, A1.
4. R. Naphtali Tzvi Yehudah Berlin, *Ha'amek Davar*, Exodus 17:14.
5. Ibid., Exodus 17:16.
6. *Midrash Tanḥuma ha-Kadum ve-ha-Yashan*, Bereshit 11; Rashi to Genesis 1:1, s.v. "*bereshit*."

tell us and the world why the Land of Israel was given to us and taken away from the other nations of the world.[7] "The strength of His deeds He declared to His people to give them the heritage of the nations" (Psalms 111:6). Why? Because *asarah dorot hayu makh'isim lefanav*, "ten generations angered Him." There was a succession of ten generations of wickedness from Adam and Eve to the Generation of the Flood,[8] then the Generation of the Dispersion, an exile of four hundred years, and finally we deserved to be the Chosen People to receive the Land of Israel.

Arafat and his cohorts are tearing up the Book of Genesis and spitting at the words of R. Yitzhak. For this, we hate them.

And there is an element of Amalek in the PLO that the whole world can understand. That is its dedication to terrorism in the form of throwing fire bombs into crowded shopping malls,[9] training the terrorists of the entire globe,[10] and ordering assassinations.[11]

Moses was aided in the fighting of Amalek with the support of Aaron and Hur. Each held up one arm of Moses.[12] The only other time that the pair of Aaron and Hur appears in the Torah is in the opposition to the Sin of the Golden Calf. There, Hur seems to be uncompromising.[13] But Aaron is not the peacemaker. Rather, he is the master of dilatory tactics, feigning cooperation when he is in fact in opposition.[14]

We should approach the PLO in the manner of both Aaron and Hur. We should use our government recognition of the PLO as a means

---

7. *Maharal, Gur Aryeh*, Genesis 1:1.
8. See Mishnah, *Avot* 5:2.
9. Barry Rubin, *Revolution until Victory?: The Politics and History of the PLO* (Cambridge, MA: Harvard University Press, 1996), 48; "PLO Unit Takes Credit for Jerusalem Bombing," *New York Jewish Week*, March 2, 1984, 18; William J. Drummond, "13 Die in Jerusalem Terrorist Bombing; 46 Hospitalized in Explosion, Fire: PLO Claims Responsibility for Attack," *Los Angeles Times*, July 5, 1979, A1.
10. Jillian Becker, *The PLO: The Rise and Fall of the Palestine Liberation Organization* (New York: St. Martin's Press, 1984), 190–193; Bruce Hoffman, *Inside Terrorism*, 2nd ed. (New York: Columbia University Press, 2006), 76–80.
11. Rubin, *Revolution until Victory?*, 37–38; "Study Says PLO Murdered 1,131 in Last 10 Years," *New York Jewish Week*, February 11, 1979, 3.
12. Exodus 17:12.
13. Leviticus Rabbah 10:3; *Rashi* to Exodus 32:5, s.v. "*va-yomer ḥag la-Hashem maḥar*."
14. Exodus 32:5; *Rashi* ad loc.

to be ready to pounce upon them and show that if terrorism actually occurs, we can say that Arafat does not speak for the Palestinians. He cannot control them and therefore we have no reason to deal with him. Or perhaps we can do better if we strain ourselves a bit and show that there is a connection between Arafat and the terrorist-advocating splinter groups. This will expose Arafat's duplicity.

But besides emulating Aaron and Hur to fight evil, there must simultaneously be the counterweight against Amalek in the form of building an altar and calling it *Hashem nisi*, "Hashem is my banner" (Exodus 17:15). We must not only support organizations that attend to the disadvantaged and disenfranchised elements of society, but also have a higher level of consciousness of the plight of the disadvantaged. This will bring about "Hashem will be King over all the land; on that day Hashem will be One and His Name will be One" (Zechariah 14:9).

The Day the *Pardes* Resonated

January 26, 1991

The richness and multi-dimensional nature of the Torah is expressed by *pardes* – *peshat, remez, derash,* and *sod*.[1] Often, each of these dimensions of the Torah offers its insight and interpretation but keeps its distance from the other dimensions; each goes its separate way. But today, *Shabbat Shirah,* the *pardes* resonates in harmony.

---

1. *Peshat* is the literal interpretation of a verse; *remez* (lit., "hint") is a veiled reference, such as *gematria*; *derash* is homiletical interpretation; and *sod* (lit., "secret") is a mystical interpretation. The use of the word "*pardes*" as an acronym for *peshat, remez, derash* and *sod* dates to the late thirteenth century. See Albert van der Heide, "PARDES: Methodological Reflections on the Theory of the Four Senses," *Journal of Jewish Studies* 34 (1983): 147–159. See also *Oxford Dictionary of the Jewish Religion,* ed., Adele Berlin, 2nd ed. (New York: Oxford University Press, 2011), 552, s.v. "Pardes." For examples of references to the acronym *pardes*, see R. Hayyim Vital (Safed, 1542–1620), *Sha'ar Ru'aḥ ha-Kodesh, hakdamah* 3; R. Abraham Samuel Benjamin Sofer (*Ketav Sofer,* Germany, 1815–1871), *Ketav Sofer, Kedoshim*; R. Joseph Hayyim b. Elijah al-Hakam (*Ben Ish Ḥai,* Baghdad, 1833 or 1835–1909), *Rav Pe'alim, ḥelek* 1, *Sod Yesharim, siman* 5.

The Day the Pardes Resonated

The inquisitive voice asks with considerable astonishment: After the ancient Egyptians were pulverized and demoralized with the Ten Plagues to the point that "there was not a house without a corpse" (Exodus 12:30), how did they summon the willpower and the appetite to pursue the Children of Israel?

Peshat answers triumphantly. We feel the answer in the *shirah*. "The enemy declared, 'I will pursue, I will overtake, I will divide plunder'" (Genesis 15:9). Pharaoh promised his people that if they would follow him, he would retrieve the gold and silver that the Egyptians had given to the Children of Israel.[2]

But is this enough of an incentive? *Derash* offers to help out by producing the *midrash* that says that Pharaoh made a magnanimous offer. Usually, the king takes half the booty. Now, the offer was to divide the spoils equally.[3]

But the *pardes* droops in disappointment with the answer. *Derash* presses on with a big discovery. Pharaoh offered to open his treasury and divide it, if only the people would follow. He also appealed to their base instincts, telling them that in Egypt, we oppressed the Jews, but I imposed restraint. I did not order you to rob them, to kill them, to rape them. But now, I am removing all restraints. You are not accountable to me at all. You can devour them with abandon.[4] "I will satisfy my lust with them, I will unsheathe my sword, my hand will impoverish them" (Exodus 15:9).

Just as the *pardes* begins to nod approval to *derash*, *peshat* once again rises and queries why the verse "the enemy declared, 'I will pursue, I will overtake'" (Exodus 15:9) is not in the beginning of the *shirah*. *Remez* answers that it is because of the principle that the events recorded in the Torah are not necessarily presented in chronological order.[5]

This left the *pardes* somewhat unhappy, until it approached *sod* and said to it, "You have contributed nothing to the dialogue. What do you say?" And *sod* answered, "I'll tell you why it is in the middle of the

---

2. *Mekhilta* to Exodus 15:9.
3. Ibid.
4. Ibid.
5. Ibid. The principle is *"ein mukdam u-me'uḥar ba-Torah."*

shirah. It is because our lot is that 'in every single generation, they rise up against us to destroy us.'[6] And therefore, even when we are exulting in *shirah* for a triumph, an evil tyrant might be lurking in the background, plotting against us."

And there is a tyrant in 5751 (תשנ"א). The year is indicated by the first letters of the verse "*ahalek shalal timla'emo nafshi*" (אחלק שלל תמלאמו נפשי), "I will divide plunder; I will satisfy my lust with them" (Exodus 15:9).[7] This is Iraq's invasion of Kuwait. The Arab nations placed high hopes on Saddam because they thought that he would redistribute the wonderful profits of oil.[8] The Kuwaitis, who have a $100 billion investment portfolio in the West, should have plowed their funds back into the Gulf States.[9] And the prospects of "I will divide plunder" grew because of "I will satisfy my lust with them," the lust and desire for honor was unlimited. Their imagination took off. He would proceed to Saudi Arabia and control fifty percent of the world's exports of oil.[10] He would attack Israel and set up a Palestinian State.[11]

But what actually happened after the January 15 deadline passed?[12] It was only "I will unsheathe my sword," the brandishing of the sword. Their military could not fight. They could only dispatch terror in the form of firing scud missiles at Israel, causing everyone to put on gas masks and fear acts of terror all around the world.[13]

---

6. Haggadah, *Maggid*, *Ve-Hi she-Amedah*.
7. See Yoel Schwartz, *Ha-Tekufah be-Aspaklaria Toranit: Meura'ot 5750–5751 u-Milhemet ha-Mifratz* (Jerusalem: Devar Yerushalayim, 1991), 72.
8. See Fred Halliday, "The Crisis of the Arab World: The False Answers of Saddam Hussein," *New Left Review* 184 (November–December 1990): 71.
9. See Abner Katzman, "Kuwait Leaders-in-Exile Run Vast Financial Empire," *Philadelphia Inquirer*, October 18, 1990, B9.
10. See H. W. Brands, "George Bush and the Gulf War of 1991," *Presidential Studies Quarterly* 34, no. 1 (March 2004): 118.
11. Lawrence Freedman and Efraim Karsh, *The Gulf Conflict 1990–1991: Diplomacy and War in the New World Order* (Princeton, NJ: Princeton University Press, 1993), 101.
12. On November 29, 1990, the United Nations adopted a U.S.-sponsored resolution authorizing member states to use force against Iraq if Iraq did not withdraw from Kuwait by January 15, 1991. S.C. Res. 678 (Nov. 29, 1990), reprinted in *International Legal Materials* 29 (1990): 1565.
13. Spencer C. Tucker, ed., *Encyclopedia of Middle East Wars: The United States in the Persian Gulf, Afghanistan, and Iraq Conflicts*, vol. 3 (Santa Barbara, CA: ABC-CLIO, 2010), 635, 831;

The Day the Pardes Resonated

The brandishing of the sword made many decent people who had thought that "sanctions only" was the right course realize the error of their ways. His tactic shocked the decent man of the entire world community, but he still had support in Jordan and Egypt amidst those evil elements who rejoice with every scud missile hitting Tel Aviv.[14]

Then he committed the self-destructive error of "my hand will impoverish them" by dumping millions of barrels of oil in the Persian Gulf.[15] Those who had placed such high expectations on him to spread the wealth of oil were betrayed. He had taken the plunder and destroyed it. What a betrayal!

We get the imagery of the time of the attack with "You blew with Your wind" (Exodus 15:10), the whizzing Tomahawk Cruise Missiles, the awesome air power. Hashem used these instruments of destruction as divine agents of retribution, blowing the evil empire with a devastating destruction, which brought the mighty military establishment to go underground into hardened bunkers and dug-in positions. This evokes the imagery of *kisamo yam*, "the sea enshrouded them" (ibid.), but instead of the enemy being covered by the sea, it was covered by earth. And permit me a poetic license here, as *yam* (sea) and *adamah* (earth) have the same *gematria* of fifty.[16]

Now we are awaiting a re-enactment of "the mighty sank like lead in water" (Exodus 15:10). *Ḥizkuni* tells us that lead is different from other metals. When other metals are placed in dust, they disintegrate. But lead acts as a magnetic force, attracting substance to it.[17] When Iraq will go down, it will take the PLO with it. The PLO hitched its wagon to an evil

---

Jack Nelson, "Iraqi Missiles Strike Israel; Others Reported Fired at Saudi Arabia Bases," *Los Angeles Times*, January 18, 1991, 1; William Clairborne, "New Scud Missile Attack Deepens Fears of Israelis," *Washington Post*, January 19, 1991, A1; Eric Schmitt, "Scud Missiles; An Arsenal of Terror," *New York Times*, January 19, 1991, 15; David Treadwell, "Brisk Sale of Gas Masks in U.S.," *Jerusalem Post*, January 27, 1991, 7.

14. Christopher Lockwood, "Jordanian Joy at Strike on Israel," *Jerusalem Post*, January 21, 1991, 5. See also "The PLO Missiles," *Jerusalem Post*, January 30, 1991, 4.
15. Freedman and Karsh, *The Gulf Conflict 1990–1991*, 342; Richard A. Schwartz, *Encyclopedia of the Persian Gulf War* (Jefferson, NC: McFarland, 1998), 64–66.
16. *Yam* consists of the letters *yud* (י = 10) and *mem* (ם = 40). *Adamah* consists of the letters *aleph* (א = 1), *dalet* (ד = 4), *mem* (ם = 40), and *heh* (ה = 5).
17. R. Hezekiah b. Manoah (*Ḥizkuni*, France, 13th cent.), *Ḥizkuni* to Exodus 15:10.

monster. They hitched their wagon to a sinking star that is disintegrating, as their depravity sank to ever lower depths. The PLO never repudiated terror and monstrosity. They never even distanced themselves from it.

We are told that the spoils of the Sea of Reeds were greater than the spoils of Egypt.[18] Similarly, we are already experiencing good surprises. The accursed people wanted desperately to insert a wedge between the United States and Israel. Instead, just the opposite happened; the bond between the countries has never been so close and warm. Even Germany has come forward with a multi-million dollar offer of humanitarian aid.[19]

But the biggest spoils will be that when evil of such dimensions is revealed, there is a spontaneous cry from the whole world and some level of "Hashem shall reign for all eternity!" (Exodus 15:18). And out of all this havoc and wreckage, we believe that what will emerge is "You will bring them and implant them on the mount of Your heritage" (Exodus 15:17). It will be the Messiah himself who will pronounce the Third Temple, the one that Hashem Himself will build, "the Sanctuary, my Lord, that Your hands established" (ibid.).[20] May it happen speedily in our days.

---

18. *Mekhilta, Bo* 13.
19. On January 23, 1991, Chancellor Helmut Kohl announced that Germany would send $165 million to Israel as "immediate humanitarian aid" after the Iraqi missile attacks, and subsequent aid would be sent to support the anti-Iraq alliance in the Persian Gulf. See Stephen Kinzer, "War in the Gulf: Germany; Kohl Is Sending $165 Million in Humanitarian Aid to Israel," *New York Times*, January 24, 1991, A15.
20. See *Mekhilta, Be-Shallaḥ* 10; *Rashi* to Exodus 15:18, s.v. "*mikdash*."

The Public Woman and *Tzeniut*

February 6, 1993

The ideal for the Jewish woman is succinctly expressed in the oft-quoted phrase *"kol kevuddah bat melekh penimah"* (lit., "every honorable princess dwelling within") (Psalms 45:14). For the Woman of Valor, this mandate is felt ever more intensely when she assumes a public role. This was so for Deborah. She was a public person, a judge. And when Barak refused to gather up ten thousand men without her assistance, she said, "Indeed, I will go with you" (Judges 4:9). In executing the double task of gathering up the men and leading the war against Sisera, she probably became the most public woman in Jewish history.

But she did not betray *tzeniut*. She never used her position to attract attention to herself. Instead, she catapulted the Jewish nation to a new dimension of *tzeniut*.

A sharp contrast proceeds from the Song at the Sea of Reeds and the Song of Deborah. The Song at the Sea of Reeds is unmitigated glory. One cannot find a hint of failure, of something unseemly or even mundane regarding the Jewish experience or conduct at the Splitting of the Sea of Reeds. For all the failure and shortcomings, one must resort to the Oral Law. "The Sea saw and fled" (Psalms 114:3).[1] *Halalu ovdei avodah zarah ve-halalu ovdei avodah zarah.*[2]

But Deborah explicitly mentions setbacks of the Jewish people – "when vengeances are inflicted upon Israel and the nation dedicates itself to God" (Judges 5:2). In a time of breach and lowly stature, both physically and spiritually, if the people respond, the inspiration and courage is also a divine gift. You cannot take any credit at all – "Bless Hashem" (ibid.).

And the ideal of the Tribe of Judah is also missing – "This one said, 'I will enter [the Sea of Reeds] first.'"[3] With respect to this, Deborah openly censures and excoriates the Tribe that did not voluntarily join Zebulun and Naphtali, who were instructed to fight,[4] in particular Reuben. "In the indecision of Reuben, there was great deceit" (Judges 5:15).

Why? Reuben's separation of itself is subject to much analysis and speculation. The *Me-Am Lo'ez* says that retrospectively, this verse casts aspersions on the Tribe of Reuben regarding their true motive for preferring to settle in the east of Jordan.[5] Was their motivation really to take advantage of the grazing land? Or perhaps it was to stay far away from the rest of the Jewish people so that they would not have to join them in battle? The Tribe of Dan is also criticized openly.[6] Excuse is

---

1. See *Midrash Shoher Tov*, Psalms 114:3. According to one interpretation of the phrase "the sea saw and fled," the sea saw that the Children of Israel rebelled at the Sea of Reeds. The sea then refused to split until Hashem rebuked it and made it split.
2. Lit., "these [i.e., the Children of Israel] are idol worshippers, and these [i.e., the Egyptians] are idol worshippers." The Midrash records that at the time that Hashem wanted to split the Sea of Reeds, the *sar* (angel) of Egypt objected, arguing that the Children of Israel worshipped idols as did the Egyptians. *Yalkut Re'uveni, Be-Shallah*, s.v. *"va-yet Mosheh et yado"*; Exodus Rabbah 21:7; *Yalkut Shimoni, Be-Shallah* 234. According to the *Zohar*, Hashem invoked the merit of Abraham and split the Sea for the Children of Israel. *Zohar* 2:170b.
3. *Midrash Shoher Tov*, Psalms 114:2, s.v. *"hayetah Yehudah le-kadsho."*
4. See Judges 4:6.
5. R. Jacob Culi, *Me-Am Lo'ez*, Judges 5:16, trans. R. Shemuel Yerushalmi, *Yalkut Me-Am Lo'ez* (Jerusalem: Wagshal, 1974).
6. Judges 5:17 ("Dan – Why did he gather [his valuables] onto ships?").

found for the Tribe of Asher, but their behavior does not reflect well on them either.[7]

Deborah's song focuses on the inner world of the Jew, and she bids us to purify our motives and sense of duty and integrity.

The public women in history have raised our conscience to the treasures of our inner world. From Hannah we learn about *tefillah*[8] and *tehiyyat ha-metim*.[9] From Abigail, we learn about *olam ha-ba*.[10]

Deborah was *eshet Lapidot*, a fiery woman.[11] But her inner yearning was to bring the Jewish people closer to Hashem – let reward and punishment truly reflect *tzaddik ve-tov lo* and *rasha ve-ra lo*. "So may all Your enemies be destroyed, O Hashem! And let those who love Him be like the powerfully rising sun" (Judges 5:31).

---

7. Ibid. ("But Asher lived by the shores of seas and remained [to protect] his open [borders].").
8. *Berakhot* 31a. The Talmud notes that many important laws can be learned from Hannah regarding prayer. For example, from the verse "Hannah spoke in her heart" (I Samuel 1:13), we learn that one who prays must direct his heart to Hashem. In addition, the verse "only her lips moved" (ibid.) signifies that the supplicant must frame his words distinctly with his lips.
9. Hannah referred to *tehiyyat ha-metim* in her prayer for a child. See I Samuel 2:6 ("Hashem brings death and gives life; He lowers to the grave and raises up."); *Rosh ha-Shanah* 17a.
10. Abigail said to David, "May my lord's soul be bound up in the bond of life, with Hashem, your God" (I Samuel 25:29). This phrase is interpreted to refer to the World to Come. See *Targum Yonatan* ad loc.; *Shabbat* 152b.
11. Judges 4:4.

They Will Leave with Great Wealth

(Undated)

Expounding the verse in *Mishlei* "the wise of heart will seize good deeds" (Proverbs 10:8), the Midrash teaches that this refers to Moses at the moment of the Exodus from Egypt.[1] Everyone was preoccupied with borrowing ornaments and clothing from the Egyptians, which would constitute the spoils of Egypt, but Moses was wise and busied himself with the mitzvah of retrieving the remains of Joseph and carrying them out of Egypt.

The Midrash's choice of describing Moses' conduct as "wisdom" is very puzzling. A more fitting description would apparently be *ḥasidut* (piety) or *tzidkut* (righteousness), imparting the message that everyone else was preoccupied with amassing material goods, but Moses was preoccupied with something spiritual. Instead of reflecting wisdom, Moses' action reflected piety.

---

1. Exodus Rabbah 20:19.

Moreover, the Midrash seems to imply that only Moses' action entailed a mitzvah, but not the action of the Children of Israel. But how can this be in the face of Hashem's command "let each man request of his fellow and each woman from her fellow silver vessels and gold vessels" (Exodus 11:2)?

Perhaps the answer lies in an insight that the *Me-Am Lo'ez* offers regarding the Covenant between the Parts. After Hashem relates to Abraham the terrible exile that his descendants will suffer, Hashem offers him consolation, "and afterwards they will leave with great wealth" (Genesis 15:14).[2]

If "great wealth" is taken to mean material spoils, it is difficult to see how Abraham, who was extremely noble and compassionate, and a giant of the spirit, would regard the exile of his children as worthwhile because it would conclude with them acquiring some trinkets and baubles. This leads the *Me-Am Lo'ez* to postulate that "great wealth" means a spiritual legacy. The suffering that his children would endure would cultivate in them personality traits that would ready them to receive the Torah.

The wisdom of Moses then consisted of realizing that occupying himself with the remains of Joseph was part of the mitzvah of the spoils of Egypt. His wisdom consisted of his broadened conceptualization of a mitzvah that explicitly dealt only with the command to borrow ornaments and clothing.

By busying himself with the remains of Joseph, Moses aroused the Children of Israel to the sentiment that the servitude of the Jewish people was a "great wealth." Beyond that, the remains of Joseph evoke the image of the progress and advance of the *ge'ullah* personality. Just as Joseph's experience as a dream interpreter when he was a slave both recommended and elevated him to royalty, so, too, we must believe that the Servitude in Egypt prepared us to be the Nation of Hashem. In his life experience, Joseph identified with all five expressions of Redemption. By resisting the wiles of Lady Potiphar, Joseph demonstrated that he would not surrender or submit to his baser instincts, that is, he would not be a slave to his passions, hence personifying release from slavery.

---

2. R. Jacob Culi, *Me-Am Lo'ez*, Exodus 6:1, trans. R. Shemuel Yerushalmi, *Yalkut Me-Am Lo'ez: Sefer Shemot* (Jerusalem: Wagshal, 1968), 78.

Yitro

Re-Creating the Revelation Experience in Our Time

January 28, 1989

Among the events of Jewish history that the Torah requires us to recount vividly and keep uppermost in our memory is the Revelation. "Make them known to your children and your children's children – the day that you stood before Hashem, your God, at Horeb" (Deuteronomy 4:9–10).

This command relates both to the experience and the content of Sinai. *Rabbeinu Beḥaye* posits that transmitting the experience is more important than relaying the content, for he who forgets the experience is prone to deny the content.[1]

But how can we preserve the experience of Sinai? It took place more than 3,300 years ago. The transmission of the experience through hundreds of generations surely dilutes the experience to the point of emasculation.

---

1. R. Bahya b. Asher (*Rabbeinu Beḥaye*, Saragossa, 1255–1340), *Rabbeinu Beḥaye al ha-Torah*, Deuteronomy 4:9.

Addressing himself to this question, *Rabbeinu Beḥaye* posits that the essence of the mitzvah is not to take action that would erase the significance of the experience. With this, we fulfill our obligation to remember the experience of Sinai.

Rabbeinu Beḥaye's words at once speak against the mechanical performance of the commandments and the compartmentalized personality. If the Revelation gripped our attention, mesmerized us along with the totality of creation, then we may never allow ourselves to feel distracted from Torah. If we feel that we are experiencing something that is not a Torah experience, we are tearing ourselves away from Sinai!

Rabbeinu Beḥaye's insight gives a new twist to an old story. The preface of *ma'amad har Sinai* tells us, "Moses ascended to God" (Exodus 19:3). Then unfolds the drama of the angels saying, "What is one born of a woman doing among us?" Hashem tells them, "He has come to receive the Torah." The angels protest, "Do you desire to give that secret treasure, which has been hidden by You for 974 generations before the world was created, to flesh and blood! What is man that You should remember him, and the son of man that You should be mindful of him?[2] Hashem, our Master, how mighty is Your Name throughout the earth, Who places Your majesty upon the heavens!"[3] Hashem tells Moses that he must provide an answer. Moses captures the Torah for the Jewish people by showing that for the angels, the Torah is only an abstract doctrine, but for the Children of Israel, it is a relevant and living doctrine.[4]

When the era of *leḥem avirim* ended, Joshua demonstrated a new level of relevance of the Torah when he devised ten ordinances that mediated conflicts between the individual and society.[5]

But we are not in the position to be like Moses or Joshua. We can however relate to another legislator, Ezra. His ten ordinances are very relevant for the modern man who finds himself in a society surrounded by Torah institutions. Ezra revitalized and reinvigorated the Torah institutions, the institutions of family purity, Torah, the Sabbath,

---

2. Psalms 8:5.
3. Psalms 8:2.
4. *Shabbat* 88b–89a.
5. *Bava Kamma* 80b–81a.

Re-Creating the Revelation Experience in Our Time

and *tzedakah*. Also, he proceeded to move a little beyond the entrenched position of doing things. He instituted that for the public reading of the Torah, three men should be called to read the Torah and that ten verses should be read. This went beyond Moses' ordinance, which required that one man should read three verses or that three men together should read three verses.[6] And finally, he created the opportunity for the Jew to make a grand statement attesting to the relevance and centrality of the Torah. He instituted the reading of the Torah on the Sabbath during the Afternoon Prayer.[7]

"As for me, my prayer to You, Hashem, be at an opportune time" (Psalms 69:14).

---

6. *Bava Kamma* 82a.
7. Ibid. This ordinance was intended to enable the shopkeepers to hear the Torah on the Sabbath because they could not come to the synagogue during the week. Ibid.

Profundity in Simplicity

(Undated)

The story is told of the Rabbi of the Young Israel of Eden Park. Once upon a time, a brainstorm hit him. Whereupon, he enthusiastically called up his congregants urging them to attend the forthcoming Sabbath services, promising to deliver an unforgettable and powerful message in his sermon. His contagious enthusiasm convinced the President of the *shul* to order a *kiddush* and engage a *ḥazan* and two choirs to mark the event with the appropriate trappings.

Well, the fateful day arrived. Some congregants who had not attended services for years attended out of curiosity. Can you imagine their disappointment and annoyance when the promised thunder of the sermon turned out to consist of self-evident truths and concepts that were familiar to all? Needless to say, the Rabbi paid dearly for his escapade. When last heard, he was serving the Young Israel of Saratoga Springs.

Profundity in Simplicity

This precise story, with a few slight variations, leads to the great biblical commentator the *Me-Am Lo'ez*[1] to the following shocking query: The Al-Mighty built up the event of *Mattan Torah* to such a spectacular drama. Immediately after the Exodus, *sefirat ha-omer* began, the forty-nine-day count to create excitement in anticipation of the great event of *Mattan Torah*. For three days before the event, the Children of Israel sanctified themselves and their clothing.[2] No one was allowed to come in contact with Mount Sinai.[3] Just prior to the Revelation, thunder, lightning, and the sound of the *shofar* were heard.[4] After such a spectacular demonstration, the Children of Israel would have expected to become privy to, and be mesmerized by, the mysteries and secrets of the Torah.

Instead, what was revealed to them was self-evident truths and principles of morality that were absolutely necessary for the survival of civilization. Did a people that had witnessed the Ten Plagues, the Splitting of the Sea of Reeds, the manna, the Clouds of Glory, and the war against Amalek need to be reminded "I am Hashem, your God" (Exodus 20:2)? They had touched Divine Providence with their own hands! Was it necessary to promulgate the prohibition against murder, robbery, adultery, and bearing false witness? Civilization cannot live without these laws!

But the answer is that in the realm of morality, profundity is not arrived at by rejecting the simple. Quite to the contrary, profundity is discovered by delving into the simple. By developing a delicate and refined sense of morality, the ethical concerns of an individual expand tremendously. The Midrash's interpretation of "one ladle of gold, its weight ten shekels, filled with *ketoret*" (Numbers 7:20) illustrates this point.[5] In the *gematria* system of "*at bash*," the *dalet* and *kuf* are interchangeable.[6] When the *kuf* of *ketoret* is replaced with a *dalet*, the *gematria*

---

1. R. Jacob Culi (Constantinople, ca. 1685–1732), *Me-Am Lo'ez*, Exodus 20:17, trans. R. Shemuel Yerushalmi, *Yalkut Me-Am Lo'ez: Sefer Shemot* (Jerusalem: Wagshal, 1968), 477, 516–518.
2. Exodus 19:10–11.
3. Exodus 19:12–13.
4. Exodus 19:16.
5. Numbers Rabbah 13:16.
6. Sabbath 104a. In the *at bash* system, the first letter of the Hebrew alphabet, *aleph*, is replaced with the last letter of the alphabet, *taph*; the second letter, *bet*, is replaced with the second-to-last letter, *shin*, and so forth.

Yitro

of the resulting letters, *detoret*, is 613. This imparts the message that the Ten Commandments contain the entire Torah of 613 mitzvot. The Midrash also notes that there are 613 letters from the beginning of the Ten Commandments, "*Anokhi Hashem*," until the last two words, "*asher le-re'akha*," signifying the 613 mitzvot. And the additional seven letters of "*asher le-re'akha*" allude to the Seven Days of Creation – the whole world stands only in the merit of the Torah.[7]

The Tablets were "inscribed on both their sides; they were inscribed on one side and the other" (Exodus 32:15). The letters bore through completely the three *tefaḥim* in thickness of the Tablets,[8] but miraculously had the appearance of being engraved on whichever side of the Tablets one looked.[9]

The man of delicate moral sensitivity comprehends "I am Hashem your God" to the level of *ein od mi-levaddo*, "there is none beside Him" (Deuteronomy 4:35), and therefore *lo sa'aseh lekha pesel*, "you shall not make for yourself a carved image" (Exodus 20:4). Do not make *yourself* into an idol.[10] There is no more independent force in the universe, save the Al-Mighty.

For the man of delicate moral sensitivity, *lo tirtzaḥ*, "you shall not murder" (Exodus 20:13), relating to the sanctity of human life, extends to *malbim penei ḥavero be-rabbim*. Embarrassing a friend in public, changing the color of his complexion to a ghostly white, amounts to murdering him.[11] The doctrine of indirect responsibility is understood by the man of moral sensitivity. As the Jerusalem Talmud explains, the verse "our hands have not spilled this blood" (Deuteronomy 21:7) means that we did not create the conditions that turn an individual to crime.[12]

---

7. Numbers Rabbah 13:16. See also *Rashi* to Numbers 7:20.
8. *Bava Batra* 14a.
9. *Rashi* to Exodus 32:15; *Shabbat* 104a and *Rashi* ad loc., s.v. "*ve-nikra mi-ba-ḥutz*"; R. David b. Samuel ha-Levi Segal (*Turei Zahav* or *Taz*, Poland, ca. 1586–1667), *Divrei David*, Exodus 32:15.
10. *Sanhedrin* 61a; *Rashi* ad loc., s.v. "*bo'u ve-ivduni*. R. Meir b. Todros ha-Levi Abulafia (*Ramah*, Spain, ca. 1170–1244), *Yad Ramah*, Sanhedrin 61a; Maimonides, *Mishneh Torah, Avodat Kokhavim* 5:5.
11. *Bava Metzia* 58b.
12. Jerusalem Talmud, *Sotah* 9:6. The elders declare that they did not send him away without food, which could have led him to turn to robbery for his sustenance and

The man of moral sensitivity understands that the prohibition of *lo tignov*, "thou shall not steal," extends even to the failure to return a greeting to a poor man,[13] and that *lo sin'af*, "thou shall not commit adultery," extends even to intangible property rights, the right to earn a living, and invasion of this right is akin to adultery.[14]

The words of the Tablets bore completely through and appeared to be engraved on either side. Sometimes, it takes a moral sensitivity to something that is not obviously written on the Tablets to arouse a moral sensitivity to the basic moral precepts of our religion. In a time of *hester panim*, when the Glory of the Al-Mighty cannot readily be seen, the feeling of helplessness on the part of the individual arouses the sentiment of *Anokhi Hashem Elokekha*. Similarly, in an era when mass murderers have inured us to violence, and human life seems cheap, it might take the anguished look of a victim of injustice to arouse our sensitivity to a revulsion to murder and robbery when it appears very distant from us. And it may take the obvious element of *hakkarat ha-tov* in the mitzvah of *kibbud av ve-em* to arouse *hakkarat ha-tov* on the abstract level in acknowledging "I am Hashem, your God, Who has taken you out of the land of Egypt" (Exodus 20:1).

---

thereby subject himself to the risk of being killed by one of his intended victims. They also declare that they did not send the victim from the town without an escort. See also *Sotah* 38b and *Rashi* to Deuteronomy 21:7.
13. *Berakhot* 6b; *Rashi* ad loc., s.v. "*gezelat he-ani.*"
14. *Sanhedrin* 81a.

Mishpatim

For the Children of Israel Are Servants to Me[1]

January 28, 1984

To the modern, twentieth-century mind, which craves relevance, particularly in the realm of morality, the choice of the Torah to begin its discussion of civil laws with the anachronistic institution of the Jewish servant is at the very least disturbing and puzzling. Moreover, why does the Torah, which imposes eternal and universal values, choose to give prominence to the institution of slavery, which is regarded as abhorrent by the civilized world for more than two hundred years?

An examination of the laws pertaining to the Israelite bondsman reveals that far from being irrelevant, these laws express the crux of Judaism's philosophy of interpersonal relations. Commenting on the phrase "it is good for him with you" (Deuteronomy 15:16), which speaks of why the Israelite bondsman wants to remain with his master after six years of service, our Sages derive the obligation on the part of the master to

---

1. Leviticus 25:55.

treat his Jewish slave with complete equality of living standards. The Talmud states that anyone who acquires an Israelite bondsman, rather than acquiring a slave, acquires a master for himself.[2]

Tosafot elaborate that the superior status follows in the instance when the master has only one pillow. Taking it for himself violates the equality condition. Denying it to himself and his slave is simply Sodomitic behavior. Therefore, the master is forced to give the pillow to the slave and deny it to himself.[3] What follows is the principle that in a subordinate relationship, the Torah favors the weaker vessel.[4]

Now, the principle is not unique to the Israelite bondsman, but rather permeates the entire gamut of interpersonal relations. Within the context of a market transaction, a highly leveraged position of a market participant is regulated.

Suppose one is traveling on an airplane and the pilot suddenly announces that the plane is about to crash. Someone begins running down the aisle selling parachutes. This is a highly leveraged situation for the seller. He could fetch any price he desires. But the Torah demands restraint here. He may charge only the price at which the parachute would sell without the desperate need hanging over the prospective buyer.[5] Similarly, a vendor of necessities is subject to a one-sixth profit-rate constraint.[6]

---

2. *Kiddushin* 20a.
3. *Tosafot* to *Kiddushin* 20a, s.v. "*kol ha-koneh.*"
4. See Ecclesiastes 3:15 ("God always seeks the pursued."); *Bava Kamma* 93a (noting the statement of R. Abbahu that one should always strive to be of the persecuted rather than of the persecutors, as none among the birds are more persecuted than doves and pigeons, yet the Torah made them alone eligible for the altar); *Midrash Tanḥuma, Emor* 9.
5. See R. Aaron Levine, "Discussion on Milton Friedman, Capitalism and the Jews," in *Morality of the Market: Religious and Economic Perspectives*, eds. Walter Block, Geoffrey Brennan, and Kenneth Elzinga (Vancouver, BC: Fraser Institute, 1985), 447.
6. *Bava Metzia* 40b. The profit constraint of one-sixth is widely understood to mean twenty percent of the cost base. Cf. R. Shneur Zalman of Liadi (Russia, 1745–1812), *Shulḥan Arukh ha-Rav, Ḥoshen Mishpat, ḥelek* 6, *Hilkhot Middot u-Mishkalot va-Hafka'at She'arim, se'if* 17. For a discussion of this profit constraint, see R. Aaron Levine, *Economic Morality and Jewish Law* (New York: Oxford University Press, 2012), ch. 4.

The relationship between a lender and a borrower is another unequal relationship where the law again imposes regulations in favor of the weaker party. The lender may not request favors of the borrower for the term of the loan, as this constitutes usury.[7] And he may not even pass by the borrower when he knows that the borrower has no money to repay his debt, as doing so will cause the borrower's heart to sink and make him feel his dependency intensely.[8]

Now, even when the feelings of subordination and inferiority are only imagined, the Torah favors the weaker vessel. In a judicial proceeding, if one of the litigants garbs himself in luxurious clothing while the other dresses himself in rags, the court will order the finely-dressed litigant either to dress his adversary as himself or dress in rags too. Without this equality of dress before the judge, we are afraid that the weaker vessel will simply forget his case![9]

Also, the convert always feels inferior and out of place. We must counteract this. The *halakhah* of *lo silḥatzennu*, "you shall not oppress him" (Exodus 22:20), tells us that we must conduct ourselves with respect to him *lifnim mi-shurat ha-din*, "beyond the letter of the law."[10]

Now, why are all these safeguards and counterbalances necessary for the weaker vessel? Perhaps the answer lies in another universal moral principle that the Torah tells us in connection with Israelite bondsman, "You shall not subjugate him through hard labor" (Leviticus 25:43). This deals with the prohibition of imposing work on the slave just to prevent him from being idle.[11] And then the Torah says, "You shall fear your God" (ibid.). Only the master will know for sure in his heart if the work that

---

7. *Bava Metzia* 75b; R. Isaac b. Jacob Alfasi (*Rif*, Algeria, 1013–1103), *Rif* ad loc.; *Mishneh Torah, Malveh* 5:12–13; *Rosh, Bava Metzia* 5:79; *Tur, Yoreh De'ah* 160; *Shulḥan Arukh, Yoreh De'ah* 160:12; R. Abraham Danzig (Prague, 1748–1820), *Ḥokhmat Adam* 131:11.
8. *Bava Metzia* 75b.
9. *Shevuot* 31a; *Rashi* ad loc., s.v. "*levush ke-moso*."
10. R. Eliezer b. Samuel of Metz (France, ca. 1115–ca. 1198), *Sefer Yere'im* 181; R. Moses b. Jacob of Coucy (France, 13th cent.), *Sefer Mitzvot Gadol, Lo Sa'aseh* 172–173; R. Isaac b. Joseph of Corbeil (France, 13th cent.), *Sefer Mitzvot Katan* 88.
11. *Rashi* to Leviticus 25:43. For example, the master may not ask the Israelite bondsman to heat a cup for him if the master does not need the cup heated. Ibid.

Mishpatim

he assigns his slave is really needed or is being assigned just to assert his mastery over him.

Business executives and government officials from the highest echelons to the most petty functionaries surround themselves with layers of inaccessibility just for the purpose of asserting their authority and sense of power, to make people feel their dependency. But the principle of "you shall not subjugate him through hard labor" is a universal one. In a judicial procedure of *dinei nefashot*, discussion of the case begins with the junior members of the court.[12] If we would hear first from the senior members, the junior members would feel a compulsion not to argue. The full weight of the power of the senior members would be felt by the junior members and then true opinions would not be voiced.[13]

Similarly, when R. Shimon and R. Yishmael, two of the *asarah harugei malkhut*, were led into martyrdom, R. Shimon asked R. Yishmael, "What did I do to deserve this?" R. Yishmael responded, "Did it ever happen that you made someone wait until you drank your cup or tied your shoelace before you answered a question or dealt with a *din Torah*, and you made him feel his state of dependency on you? The Torah adjures us, '*im anneh se'anneh*,' 'if you dare to cause him pain' (Exodus 22:22). One may not cause great pain, and one may not cause small pain."[14] R. Shimon said, "You have comforted me, *rebbe*."[15]

---

12. Mishnah, *Sanhedrin* 4:3; *Sanhedrin* 36a. The Sanhedrin was seated in a semicircle so that the members could see each other. The most eminent judge was seated in the middle and the other judges were seated next to him, with the most junior judge sitting furthest from the middle. In capital cases, the discussion began *min ha-tzad* (lit., "from the side"), i.e., with the less eminent judges.
13. *Sanhedrin* 36a; *Rashi* ad loc., s.v. "*lo sa'aneh al rav*." The procedure to begin the discussion in capital cases with the less eminent judges is based on the verse "*lo sa'aneh al riv*," "do not respond to a dispute" (Exodus 23:2). The word "*riv*" (dispute) is written without the letter *yud*. Consequently, the Sages interpret the verse to mean "*lo sa'aneh al rav*," "do not respond against a master." *Rashi* to Exodus 23:2. If the most eminent judge were to express his view first, arguing for conviction, the less eminent judges might be reluctant to express a contrary view. By beginning the discussion with the less eminent judges, those judges would not be placed in a position to have to express a view contrary to the most eminent member of the court.
14. This interpretation explains the repetition of the root word *anneh*, to cause pain, in the phrase "*im anneh se'anneh*." *Mekhilta* to Exodus 22:22, s.v. "*im anneh se'anneh*."
15. *Mekhilta*, op. cit.

For the Children of Israel Are Servants to Me

Now, if you say that the principle is applicable only to those in a position of authority, the *Tanna* in *Perek* says, *"ein lekha adam she-ein lo sha'ah,"* every man has his hour.[16] A circumstance or situation will arise for everyone where he is needed and can make someone feel his state of dependency. But the Torah says *"lo se'annun,"* "you shall not cause pain" (Exodus 22:21) and *"ve-yareta me-Elokekha,"* "you shall fear your God" (Leviticus 25:43).

---

16. Mishnah, *Avot* 4:3.

Distance Yourself from a False Word

February 4, 1989

We are all familiar with the words of R. Shimon b. Gamliel, "The world endures on three things: justice, truth, and peace."[1] We would therefore expect that when the Torah speaks of these values, it would attach equal importance to each value.

Not so! With respect to justice, a strong positive statement is made: "Righteousness, righteousness shall you pursue" (Deuteronomy 16:20). Similarly, with respect to peace, it says, "Seek peace and pursue it" (Psalms 34:15). But with respect to truth, a weak, hedging statement is made. Instead of apprising us of the value of truth in a positive statement, the Torah merely states, "Distance yourself from a false word" (Exodus 23:7).

Perhaps the question is itself the answer. Truth is not an absolute value in Jewish teaching. The extent to which we must embrace

---

1. Mishnah, *Avot* 1:18.

truth depends on the setting. Let's start with the pristine inner world of R. Safra. He personified one who "speaks truth from his heart" (Psalms 15:2).² Hence, when a customer barged into his store when he was reciting *Shema* and made a bid for his merchandise, R. Safra simply ignored him. The customer, thinking that R. Safra wanted more money for the article, increased his bid. Again, R. Safra did not react, as he was still immersed in reciting *Shema*. Upon completion of *Shema*, R. Safra confessed to the customer that he had heard the initial bid and resolved in his heart to accept it. R. Safra then sold the item to the customer at the initial bid price.³

For us, R. Safra's conduct represents *lifnim mi-shurat ha-din*. A resolve of the heart has no consequences other than in connection with *tzedakah*. It is only in that connection that we are required to carry out a resolve of our heart.⁴

Let's consider another setting where we can move a little closer to falsehood but still be in the clear. Let's examine the realm of innocent deception. A story is told of a farmer who went to a bank to borrow $100. The loan officer proceeded to explain to the farmer that there would be an eight-percent interest charge and also insisted on collateral. "Do you have any collateral?" asked the loan officer. The farmer presented a $100,000 State of Israel bond. The amazed banker grabbed the bond and went off with the application. In no time, the loan was approved. The same time next year, the farmer renewed the loan on the same terms. The loan officer, however, could not control his curiosity. "If you have a $100,000 State of Israel bond, why do you need a $100 loan?" The farmer replied, "Do you know of a cheaper way to rent a safe deposit box?"

Let's now consider the arena of securing a legitimate end. Here we move a little closer to falsehood yet still remain within the bounds of permissibility. Suppose an elderly person applies for a job that entails arduous physical labor. The applicant is, however, afraid that his appearance might give the impression that he cannot handle the job. To remove

---

2. *Makkot* 24a.
3. *She'iltot de-Rav Aḥai Gaon, Va-Yeḥi*, no. 36.
4. R. Moses Isserles, *Rema* to *Shulḥan Arukh, Yoreh De'ah* 258:13.

an unwarranted bias, the applicant, according to contemporary *posekim*, may dye his hair to present a youthful appearance.[5]

Let's now analyze the realm of negotiation. Here we move even closer to falsehood yet remain within the bounds of permissibility. Suppose a real estate tycoon is negotiating a deal to purchase a parcel of land. Since no such sale took place recently, a standard of value is missing. The negotiation process itself will determine the value. Open entry into the negotiation will, however, give away the identity of the tycoon, and the price of the parcel will be hiked up considerably. Hence it would be permissible for the tycoon to set up a smokescreen, to invent a diversionary tactic, so that it will not occur to his opposite number who is bidding on the land. Accordingly, the entrepreneur may set up a dummy corporation or send an agent to bid for him.[6]

Let's now turn to the realm of protecting one's legitimate rights in an immoral climate. Here we move closer to falsehood but still remain in the realm of permissibility. Suppose an employer hires a per diem worker for a job classified as a *davar ha-avud*, that is, if the worker does not give the work his immediate attention, he will cause a material loss for his employer.[7] Then the worker leaves the employer flat. As a means of dealing with the immoral conduct, it is permissible for the employer to offer the reneging worker a raise as an inducement to keep him on the job.[8] In the event the tactic is successful, the employer bears no

---

5. R. Moses Mordecai Epstein (Lithuania, 1866–1933), *She'elot u-Teshuvot Levush Mordekhai, Yoreh De'ah*, no. 24; R. Elazar Meir Preil (New Jersey, 1881–1934), *Ha-Ma'or* 1:26–27; R. Mosheh Feinstein, *Iggerot Mosheh, Yoreh De'ah* 2:61.
6. See R. Aaron Levine, *Economics and Jewish Law* (Hoboken, NJ: Ktav, 1987), 17–18.
7. An example of a *davar ha-avud* given in the Talmud is the hiring of a wagon driver to bring wood for the construction of a bridal canopy or to deliver flutes to a wedding to enhance the ceremony. Delay in the dispatch of the driver would defeat the purpose of the sender because the driver would arrive after the ceremony is over. Another example is the hiring of a worker to remove flax from its steeping waters. If the flax plant is soaked too long, it would no longer be possible to extract the fibers inside the plant to make linen. *Bava Metzia* 75b.
8. *Bava Metzia* 76b; *Rif,* ad loc.; *Mishneh Torah, Sekhirut* 9:4; *Rosh, Bava Metzia* 6:2; *Tur, Ḥoshen Mishpat* 333; *Shulḥan Arukh, Ḥoshen Mishpat* 333:5; *Arukh ha-Shulḥan, Ḥoshen Mishpat* 333:19.

Distance Yourself from a False Word

responsibility for the additional wages, and can even recover in a Jewish court the additional wages paid to the employee.⁹

Finally, let's consider a setting where our very survival is tested. An appropriate setting is the international arena. If a country perceives another country as in a state of readiness to attack it, then *ha-ba le-horgekha, hashkem ve-horgo*, "if someone comes to kill you, kill him first."¹⁰ Within this context, deception and cover stories, and dichotomizing the public view to promote stability, are all gentle tools because they must all be viewed as alternatives to nuclear holocaust.

Now, the arena of cloak-and-dagger tactics in international relationships seems so far removed from the pristine world of R. Safra. But in fact, we can easily leap from any setting very close to R. Safra. Why? Because truth has an incredible instinct to survive. When it is bludgeoned and pummeled, it really develops a will to somehow stay alive. Within an environment of extreme distrust, the United States and Russia were able to negotiate a nuclear disarmament of intermediate-range missiles, but submitting to an objectively verifiable standard. Each country would allow the other to witness the destruction of its missiles.¹¹

When truth is almost dead, it desperately seeks the achievement of justice and peace. Truth seeks allies and no longer operates in a vacuum. It knows no one will pay it any attention alone. It can survive only as a compound, together with justice and peace.¹² Within such a context, falsehood will be exposed because the standard of truth is that it must have some connection to justice and peace.

Now, if Arafat proclaims that he is no longer advocating terrorism and is suddenly converted to peaceful co-existence, then we must put him to the test.¹³ Is this statement objectively verifiable? Does it comport

---

9. *Mishneh Torah*, op. cit.; *Arukh ha-Shulḥan*, op. cit.
10. Numbers Rabbah 21:4; *Midrash Tanḥuma, Pinḥas* 3; *Sanhedrin* 72a.
11. See Treaty between the United States of America and the Union of Soviet Socialist Republics on the Elimination of their Intermediate-Range and Shorter-Range Missiles (signed on December 8, 1987, and went into effect on June 1, 1988).
12. See Zechariah 8:16 ("in you gates, judge with truth, justice and peace"); Mishnah, *Avot* 1:18.
13. Robert Pear, "U.S. Agrees to Talks with P.L.O., Saying Arafat Accepts Israel and Renounces all Terrorism," *New York Times*, December 15, 1988, A1.

Mishpatim

with justice? No! The PLO charter still states that Palestinians must be liberated by armed struggle, that Israel is illegitimate, fascist, fanatic, and racist, and that all people have a right to self-determination, except Israel.[14]

When something that is professed to be truth has no allies, that is, it is not a compound of justice and peace, it cannot survive and is exposed for what it is, falsehood.

May it be our lot to always mix our truth with a goodly measure of justice and peace.

---

14. The Palestinian National Charter, Resolutions of the Palestine National Council, July 1–17, 1968, translated into English in Leila S. Kadi, *Basic Political Documents of the Armed Palestinian Resistance* (Beirut: Palestinian Research Center, 1969), 137–141.

Balancing the Rights of the Victim and the Rights of the Accused

January 28, 1995

One of the greatest challenges to society's legal system today is to legislate and implement a criminal code that strikes a delicate balance between the rights of the victim and the rights of the accused.

A glimpse into how the Torah views this balancing act is provided in today's *parashah*. We are shocked to see that the Torah prescribes "an eye for an eye" (Exodus 21:24). It seems primitive and smacking of revenge. But our Sages say it means monetary compensation.[1] Now, why not say so explicitly?

Perhaps the answer is that when we hear of a crime of mutilation and certainly of murder, before we come into contact with an accused in any form, the appropriate reaction is undoubtedly a desire for retaliation

---

1. *Bava Kamma* 83b; *Rashi* to Exodus 21:24.

and death for the murderer. These are in fact the explicit punishments that the Torah prescribes. The reaction to crime in the abstract must capture all the anguish, anger, disgust, and ugly feelings of the victim. It is only this reaction that will galvanize society into letting no leaf go unturned in discovering the murderer and the mutilator. It is only later when we seize a suspect that the values of concessions, compromise, and compassion come into play.

But society's condemnation of the crime in its full blast would be empty indeed and even a mockery if the actual penalties imposed on a convicted felon were no more than a slap on the wrist. There must be some correspondence between what the statutes say and what the actual punishment is. Apropos are the words of the *Maharal*. In his view, it is for this reason that the Torah does not state explicitly that the punishment is the payment of monetary compensation because the punishment of the perpetrator must promote the attainment of forgiveness from the victim.[2] How far is American law removed from these objectives!

But it is not enough for the statutes to be given seriousness by having the actual punishments conform in some way to the statutes. The statutes must inspire laws themselves. There are Son of Sam Laws all around the country.[3] In Jewish law, we have the principle that a sinner should not profit from committing a sin.[4] But the laws must extend beyond not allowing the criminal to profit monetarily. A criminal's autobiography should not be a vehicle to enable the criminal to portray himself in the best light, deflating the monstrosity of his crime, with no rebuttal by the victim or statement by the prosecution regarding the evidence.

---

2. *Maharal, Gur Aryeh, Emor.*
3. "Son of Sam" laws restrict the ability of a criminal to profit from publicizing the crime. In 1977, New York State adopted a Son of Sam Law to prevent the serial killer David Berkowitz, popularly known as "Son of Sam," from profiting from his notoriety. 1977 N.Y. Laws 823 (codified at N.Y. Exec. Law § 632–a(1) (McKinney 1982)). Since then, many other Son of Sam laws have been adopted throughout the United States. See Michelle G. Lewis Liebeskind, "Back to Basics for Victims: Striking Son of Sam Laws in Favor of an Amended Restitutionary Scheme," *Annual Survey of American Law* 29 (1994): 29 (noting that as of March 30, 1993, the U.S. federal government and forty-three states had adopted Son of Sam Laws).
4. Mishnah, *Hallah* 2:7; Mishnah, *Shevi'it* 9:9; *Yevamot* 92b; *Ketubbot* 39b; *Sotah* 15a; *Gittin* 55b; *Bava Kamma* 38a, 38b–29a; *Avodah Zarah* 2b; *Menaḥot* 6a; *Niddah* 4b.

Balancing the Rights of the Victim and the Rights of the Accused

With respect to the rights of the accused, we have a stark contrast here. In Judaism, the model is the Sanhedrin of twenty-three judges. They serve a dual role as both prosecutors and defense attorneys.[5] The judges are authentic Torah scholars and people of impeccable integrity who are sharp-witted and "with it." The American legal system, by contrast, employs the jury of peers, who are too submissive to emotional appeal and stymied by complexity, and who filter facts by means of their prejudices.[6]

I do not think that the American legal system is moving now to adopt the Sanhedrin model. But what we need is "I will restore your judges as at first and your counselors as at the beginning" (Isaiah 1:26). We need ideas of how to improve a flawed system, such as Stephen Adler's idea of ending the peremptory challenge.[7]

---

5. See Mishnah, *Sanhedrin* 4:1.
6. Stephen J. Adler, *The Jury: Trial and Error in the American Courtroom* (New York: Times Books, 1994), 50.
7. Ibid., 220–224.

Terumah

Holy of Holies

February 4, 1984

Modern man understands well that for any good, accomplishment, or material possession to be surrounded by an aura of desirability and luster, exclusivity is an important factor. It is therefore no surprise that when it came to the Tabernacle, the holiest place, the Holy of Holies, where the Ark, symbolic of the Torah,[1] and the Staves of the Ark, symbolic of the supporters of Torah,[2] were located, an aura of exclusivity was conferred on it. Only one man of the entire Jewish nation, the High Priest, once a year, was permitted to enter the Holy of Holies, and only after separation from his family for seven days.[3] The office alone did not legitimize the entry. If the High Priest did not personify the values of the Ark, the Staves, and the Cherubim, he would

---

1. Exodus Rabbah 34:2.
2. *Midrash Aggadah, Terumah* 25; Tobiah b. Eliezer (Balkans, 11th cent.), *Midrash Lekaḥ Tov*, Exodus 25:13.
3. *Rashi* to Leviticus 8:34; *Torat Kohanim, Tzav, Mekhilta de-Miluim* 37; *Yoma* 3b.

Terumah

perish.[4] In the Second Temple, which lasted for 420 years, more than three hundred High Priests served.[5]

Yet, in contrast to this aura of exclusivity associated with the Holy of Holies, we find that Hashem commanded that the container of manna, the Oil of Anointment, the Staff of Aaron, and the priestly vestments be placed next to the Ark in the Holy of Holies.[6] Now, why were these objects placed there? Did they not detract from the desired aura of exclusivity?

I would submit that, quite to the contrary, rather than detracting from the aura of exclusivity, these articles were placed in the Holy of Holies to inculcate in us the elements necessary to create the aura and luster so that we will want to make the Ark, the Staves, and the Cherubim central to our life.

First, the container of manna. The manna symbolizes man's constant dependence on Hashem.[7] As the students of R. Shimon b. Yohai asked, "Why did Hashem not send down to the Children of Israel a gigantic mound of manna that could be drawn from as needed each day?"[8] Why was the manna parceled out so that it descended every day only in an amount that was needed to survive, a tenth of an ephah?[9] Anything extra spoiled.[10]

R. Shimon answers that it is analogous to a king who decided to dole out an allowance to his child every day rather than give him a lump sum, as the daily provision would force a need of interaction and

---

4. See Leviticus 8:35; *Rashi* ad loc.
5. *Yoma* 9a.
6. Exodus 16:33 (manna); *Rashi* ad loc., s.v. *"ve-hannah oto lifnei Hashem"*; Numbers 17:25 (Staff of Aaron); *Rabbeinu Behaye al ha-Torah*, Exodus 26:33. See also R. Aharon Levine (*Reisha Rav*, Poland, 1879–1941), *Ha-Derash ve-ha-Iyyun*, vol. 2 (Biłgoraj: N. Kronenberg, 1931), *ma'amar* 225, pp. 305–307 (commentary on *Rabbeinu Behaye* questioning whether the Oil of Anointment and the priestly vestments were placed by the Ark).
7. R. Samuel b. Meir (*Rashbam*, France, ca. 1080–1174), *Rashbam* to Exodus 16:4, s.v. *"lema'an annassenu"*; Nahmanides to Exodus 16:4; Ibn Ezra to Exodus 16:4; *Or ha-Hayyim* to Exodus 16:4.
8. *Yoma* 76a.
9. Exodus 16:36.
10. Exodus 16:20.

communication between the child and the father, and the child would have to see the father every day. Giving him a lump sum would mean that the child would never visit his father.[11]

Indeed, the most basic feeling that must be nurtured within us if the Ark, the Staves, and the Cherubim are to be central to our lives is our utter and constant dependence on Hashem, the realization that if He would withdraw His support for even one second, our existence would cease. *Ein od mi-levaddo*, "there is none beside Him" (Deuteronomy 4:35).

The Oil of Anointment was also in the Holy of Holies. Now, this oil was used to anoint Aaron and his sons,[12] the Kings,[13] and the Tabernacle and its appurtenances.[14] An astonishing miracle took place with regard to this oil. When Samuel came to Beit Lehem to anoint one of Jesse's children as King of Israel, he thought that the chosen one was Eliab. Accordingly, Samuel tried to anoint him. Miraculously, the canister of oil simply retreated from Eliab and refused to anoint him. The same thing happened with respect to the other children until he came to David. Then the oil jumped out of the canister.[15]

When the High Priest was anointed, all the Priests would walk around in a circle and the oil would miraculously jump out and anoint the High Priest.[16]

I ask you: Is there anything that could possibly generate more of a feeling of singularity and uniqueness than this, giving a person a sense of destiny, the feeling of *bishvili nivra ha-olam*?[17] No one else is suited for what the King or the High Priest is being anointed.

Another miracle in connection with the Oil of Anointment is that of the twelve *luggim* of oil made by Moses, not even a drop was missing after all these anointings took place.[18] In contrast to material

---

11. *Yoma* 76a.
12. Exodus 30:30.
13. I Samuel 10:1; *Horayot* 12a; *Keritot* 5b.
14. Exodus 30:26–29.
15. *Yalkut Shimoni*, I Samuel 124.
16. *Yalkut Shimoni*, Psalms 45:8.
17. See Mishnah, *Sanhedrin* 4:5; *Sanhedrin* 37a.
18. *Horayot* 11b; *Keritot* 5b; Rashi to Exodus 30:31. The twelve *luggim* of oil prepared by Moses are indicated by the word "*zeh*" in Exodus 30:31, "oil of sacred anointment shall

Terumah

striving, where one's achievement of uniqueness and singularity detracts from others, in the spiritual domain, one's singular achievement in no way detracts from that special feeling someone else can achieve. Every person is a child of destiny.

And there was also the Staff of Aaron, symbolic of the triumph of Torah over its detractors, even those who ostensibly also espouse Torah values.[19] The Staff of Aaron is symbolic of the ultimate triumph of Torah, which does not leave the victor battered, demoralized, or emasculated. Quite to the contrary, he emerges stronger than before. With regard to the Staff of Aaron, it is said, "It brought forth a blossom, sprouted a bud" (Numbers 17:23). Unlike the development of a fruit, in which the blossom is shed after the fruit emerges,[20] from the battle of Torah, the victor emerges with the blossoms intact.

Finally, the priestly vestments were deposited in the Holy of Holies. These vestments are symbolic of the fact that although the man personifying the values of the Ark, its Staves, and the Cherubim – the High Priest – is not there, the vestige of his triumph is there.

Now, in the time of the First Temple, King Josiah had a premonition that the Temple would be destroyed. Accordingly, he hid the Staff of Aaron, the container of the manna, and the Oil of Anointment to save them from desecration. What gave him this premonition? It was that the Staves of the Ark no longer protruded into the *parokhet*.[21]

---

this (*zeh*) be for Me for your generations," as the *gematria* of *zeh* is twelve. *Horayot* 11b; *Keritot* 5b; *Rashi* to Exodus 30:31.

19. See Numbers 17:21–23. After the rebellion of Korach and his assembly, the Staff of Aaron blossomed, showing that Aaron and his sons had been chosen by Hashem for the Priesthood.
20. See R. Jacob Culi, *Me-Am Lo'ez*, Numbers 17:23, trans. R. Shemuel Yerushalmi, *Yalkut Me-Am Lo'ez: Sefer Be-Midbar* (Jerusalem: Wagshal, 1969), 217.
21. *Yoma* 52b; *Rabbeinu Behaye al ha-Torah*, Deuteronomy 10:1. Previously, the staves of the Ark had miraculously protruded from the Holy of Holies into the *parokhet* as a sign of affection of Hashem toward the Jewish people. See *Tosafot* to *Menahot* 98b, s.v. "*dohakin u-voltin ba-pharokhet*." Another sign that Josiah saw that the Temple would be destroyed was that Hilkiah, the High Priest, found a Torah scroll in the Temple. II Kings 22:8. The scroll was rolled to the verse in the Reproof stating "Hashem will lead you and your king whom you will appoint over yourselves to a nation that neither

This is indeed frightening. It tells us that the first sign of decay of society is the loss of the exuberant enthusiasm of the supporters of Torah. When the supporters of Torah fail to see themselves as completely dependent upon Hashem, as people of destiny able to weather criticism and detractors with aplomb, then we are deep in trouble! This will inevitably demoralize the Ark itself, the *benei Torah* themselves, making them less certain of their singularity and uniqueness.

But the relationship is reciprocal. Any decline in the self-image and striving of the *benei Torah* will affect the attitude of the supporters of Torah.

All the elements that contribute to the special aura of what is central to our life – the Ark, the Cherubim, the Tablets, the Oil of Anointment, the Staff of Aaron, the container of the manna – are gone and hidden. What remains is only the *even ha-shesiyah*, the center of creation.[22] But we can re-create the Temple, including the Holy of Holies, when we begin to master the attitude embodied in these symbols!

---

you nor your ancestors have known" (Deuteronomy 28:36). *Yoma* 52b; *Rashi* to II Kings 22:13; R. David Kimhi (*Radak*, Provence, ca. 1160–ca. 1235) to II Kings 22:11.
22. See *Yoma* 54b; *Zohar, Va-Yeḥi* 1:231a.

The Crown of Torah

February 20, 1988

The Jew possessed of a sense of mission imagines himself a world-class Olympic athlete tenaciously pursuing the four crowns: the crown of Torah; the crown of Priesthood; the crown of Royalty; and the crown of a good reputation.[1] To inspire and remind us of the central importance of the four crowns in the Jewish life experience, three of the appurtenances of the Tabernacle were constructed with a *zer zahav*, a "gold crown."[2] The top of the cover of the Ark had a crown, corresponding to the crown of Torah. The Table had a crown, corresponding to the crown of Royalty. And the Golden Altar had a crown, corresponding to the crown of Priesthood.[3] The Menorah is associated with the crown of a good reputation.[4]

---

1. Mishnah, *Avot* 4:13.
2. Exodus 25:11 (the Ark); Exodus 25:24 (the Table); Exodus 30:3 (the Golden Altar).
3. Exodus Rabbah 34:2; *Yoma* 72b.
4. Numbers Rabbah 14:10.

The Crown of Torah

Which of the crowns should we pursue? Ironically, it is the crown of a good reputation, corresponding to the Menorah, which did not have a crown.[5] After all, the crown of Royalty and the crown of Priesthood are regarded as inaccessible,[6] and the crown of Torah is subsumed in the crown of a good reputation.[7]

How can someone acquire a wonderful reputation? It is only by looking at the Torah as the guidepost of how to become one who finds "favor and goodly wisdom in the eyes of man and God" (Proverbs 3:4). The attitude that the crown of a good reputation somehow subsumes the crown of Torah is apparently reinforced by the peculiar assimilation that our Sages make between a good name and the Menorah. The Menorah is the symbol of wisdom – *ha-rotzeh le-haḥ'kim yadrim*, "one who wants to become wise should go southward."[8] But the Menorah clearly symbolizes the man who subordinates his creative energy to the will of the Torah. "Toward the face of the Menorah shall the seven lamps cast light" (Numbers 8:2).[9]

When oil is set on fire, it is not destroyed, but rather sublimated to produce enlightenment. The Menorah hence represents good deeds that are produced from the holy Torah.[10]

But this attitude does much violence to the crown of Torah. According to Tradition, one aspect of the acceptance of the Torah of "we will do and we will obey" (Exodus 24:7) is *Torah le-shemah*, learning for the sake of learning.[11] So that there should be no mistake in confusing

---

5. See Mishnah, *Avot* 4:13.
6. See *Yoma* 72b; Maimonides, *Mishneh Torah, Talmud Torah* 3:1. Royalty is reserved for the descendants of David (Psalms 18:51, 89:37), and the Priesthood is reserved for the descendants of Aaron (Numbers 18:1, 25:13).
7. Mishnah, *Avot* 4:13.
8. *Bava Batra* 25b. The Menorah was located in the south corner of the Holies. Ibid.; *Yoma* 33b.
9. See R. Samson Raphael Hirsch, Numbers 8:2.
10. See Numbers Rabbah 13:16 (commenting on the phrase *"solet belulah va-shemen"* (flour mixed with oil) (Numbers 7:13), the Midrash states that oil symbolizes good deeds, which should be combined with the learning of Torah); Leviticus Rabbah 3:7 (stating that oil symbolizes good deeds).
11. See R. Yosef Dov Soloveitchik (*Beit ha-Levi*, Belarus, 1820–1892), *Beit ha-Levi al Derush u-Milei de-Aggadata* (Jerusalem, 1985), *Mishpatim*, Exodus 24:7, p. 69.

the Menorah with the crown of Torah, we focus on the crown of Torah and realize that it represents *Torah le-shemah*.

We first notice the Cherubim. They represent the Torah of *tinnokot shel beit rabban*.[12] "The world endures only because of the breath of school children" (*Shabbat* 119b). Then we look at the *talmid ḥakham* who is isolated, all alone in the Holy of Holies, as opposed to the Menorah, which exuberates in society in the company of the crown of Priesthood and the crown of Royalty. This is the *talmid ḥakham* of *tokho ke-baro* (lit., "his inside is like his outside," i.e., sincere).[13] Then we are reminded that the broken Tablets are resting in the Ark.[14] What do we think of the *talmid ḥakham* who has forgotten his learning?[15] Do we accord him the honor that is still due him?

R. Meir tells us, "Whoever engages in Torah study for its own sake merits many things... the secrets of the Torah are revealed to him; he becomes like a steadily strengthening fountain and an unceasing river."[16] If we ask ourselves, "Where is the power of Torah today?", R. Meir has not misspoken. Rather, there is not enough *Torah le-shemah*.

If we see that there is no ethical and righteous person, one who is "righteous, devout, fair, and faithful,"[17] it is because there is not enough *Torah le-shemah*. And if we see that there is no visionary – "[the Torah] makes him great and exalts him above all things"[18] – it is also because there is not enough *Torah le-shemah*. The crown of Torah is what invigorates the other crowns and expands their horizons.

---

12. See *Rashi* to Exodus 25:18, s.v. "*keruvim*"; *Sukkah* 5b and *Ḥagigah* 13b (noting in the name of R. Abbahu that the derivation of the word "*keruv*" (cherub) is *ke-rabia*, "like a child," because in Babylonia, a child is called a "*rabia*").
13. *Yoma* 72b.
14. *Bava Batra* 14a–b; *Rashi* to Numbers 10:33.
15. See *Menaḥot* 99b; R. Ezekiel b. Judah Landau (*Noda bi-Yehudah*, Prague, 1713–1793), *She'elot u-Teshuvot Noda Bi-Yehudah, Oraḥ Ḥayyim* 9.
16. Mishnah, *Avot* 6:1.
17. Ibid.
18. Ibid.

The Crown of Torah

Let it be our lot to imagine ourselves as world-class athletes playing out the drama of the High Priest on Yom Kippur. We take a spoonful of *ketoret*, symbolic of what is pleasant in life,[19] and bring it to the Holy of Holies, juxtaposing the *ketoret* with the crown of Torah, giving it its proper place in Jewish life, both studying Torah for its own sake and supporting such Torah.

---

19. See Proverbs 27:9; *Midrash Tanḥuma, Tetzavveh* 15.

Whoever Adds, Detracts

February 11, 1989

This past week, in a most provocative observation, Professor Burton Caine of the law faculty at Temple University, pointed out that of the entire U.S. Constitution, the only section that is written in quotation marks is Article II, section 1, clause 8, the portion relating to the formula of the oath of office of the President of the United States. The clear intent of the framers of the Constitution, according to Professor Caine, was that the President should recite the formula of the oath of office verbatim, nothing more, nothing less.[1]

When taking the oath of office, President Bush, however, after stating "To the best of my abilities, I will preserve, protect and defend the Constitution of the United States," added the words "so help me God." This addendum, in the mind of the Professor, violated the Constitution.[2]

By extension, one could argue that the addendum rendered the oath of office invalid. As far as I'm concerned, until such time as

---

1. Burton Caine, letter to the editor, *New York Times*, February 5, 1989, E24.
2. Ibid.

George Bush retakes the oath of office, Dan Quayle is President of the United States!

Unwittingly, the Professor stumbled upon a vital principle in Jewish law, *kol ha-mosif gore'a*, "one who adds to the prescriptions of the Torah, it is as if he diminished them."

Alluded to in today's portion,[3] the principle finds its most famous biblical source in the excessive precautions that Adam saw fit to make when he transmitted the divine command to Eve not to partake of the fruit of the Tree of Knowledge. Apprehensive that Eve needed extra distance from violating the divine command, he added the proscription "you must not touch it" to the command "you must not eat from it."[4] This addendum provided the Primordial Serpent with the fuel that it needed to ensnare Eve into eating the fruit of the Tree of Knowledge. The Serpent pushed her against the tree and said, "Just as there is no death from touching the tree, there is no death from eating from it."[5]

Underlying Adam's excessive precautions was an underestimation of the strength of the woman's moral fiber. Since time immemorial, this error brought calamity on humankind. Paradise lost!

Today, the clarion call of those who distort the Torah's perspective on women can be encapsulated in various perversions of *kol ha-mosif gore'a*. There are those who are troubled why women are given

---

3. The allusion is derived from the verse "*ammatayim va-ḥetzi arkho* (two and a half cubits, its length) (Exodus 25:10), which refers to the dimensions of the Ark in the Tabernacle. The word *ammatayim* (אמתים) means two cubits. If the first letter of *ammatayim* is removed, the resulting word is an alternative spelling of the word *matayim* (מתאים), which means two hundred. By adding the first letter to the word "*matayim*," the dimension is thus reduced from two hundred to two. *Sanhedrin* 29a; Rashi ad loc., s.v. "*ammatayim*."

Another source from *Parashat Terumah* mentioned by the Talmud *ad locum* is the verse "*ashtei esrei yeri'ot*" (eleven curtains) (Exodus 26:7), which refers to the goat-hair covering of the Tabernacle that was constructed from eleven curtains. *Ashtei esreh* (עשתי עשרה) means eleven. If the first letter of *ashtei* is removed, the resulting phrase is *shetei esreh* (שתי עשרה), which means twelve. By adding an additional letter to *shetei esrei*, the number is thus reduced from twelve to eleven. *Sanhedrin* 29a; Rashi ad loc., s.v. "*ashtei esreh*"; *Zohar, Terumah* 1:164b.

4. *Siftei Ḥakhamim* to Rashi, Genesis 3:4, n. 3; R. Enoch Zundel b. Joseph (Russia, d. 1867), *Etz Yosef* to Genesis Rabbah 19:3, s.v. "*amar lah*."

5. Rashi to Genesis 3:4.

Terumah

the special mitzvah of lighting the candles in honor of the Sabbath.[6] This mitzvah could have just as easily been given to men.[7] It seems that the purpose of giving this mitzvah to women is to constantly remind women of Eve's sin. Eve caused the candle of the world to be extinguished, so we require women to compensate for this by lighting candles in honor of the Sabbath.[8] Why should women today suffer on account of Eve's sin?

And then there are those who see in the Morning Blessings the blessing of "Blessed are You, Hashem, our God, King of the Universe, Who did not make me a woman" as another addition that diminishes the status of women. Those who are more sophisticated and learned probe into the reason that women are exempt from time-bound mitzvot. R. David b. Joseph Abudirham says that a woman is subject to her husband's will, so she is exempt from time-bound mitzvot.[9] But is this not insulting, saying that a woman must be at the beck and call of her husband? And then there is the *Maharal*,[10] who says that women's nature is more perfect, so they do not need so many mitzvot for the purpose of *le-tzaref bahem et ha-bri'ot*, to perfect themselves.[11] But is this not patronizing to women?

The quest for a multiplicity of reasons leads to a diminishing of the status of women, as the reasons offered are contradictory and irreconcilable.

But I would submit that *elu ve-elu divrei Elokim hayyim*, "these and these are the words of the living God."[12] If the Torah invests women with a mission to assume the role of the enabler and to create the Jewish home, we must equip women with the means to perform

---

6. *Tur, Orah Hayyim* 263; *Shulhan Arukh, Orah Hayyim* 263:3.
7. See *Shulhan Arukh, Orah Hayyim* 263:2.
8. *Midrash Tanhuma, Noah* 1; Jerusalem Talmud, *Shabbat* 2:6; *Tur, Orah Hayyim* 263; *Magen Avraham* to *Shulhan Arukh, Orah Hayyim* 263:3, n. 7.
9. R. David b. Joseph Abudirham (Spain, 14th cent.), *Sefer Abudraham, Tefillot shel Hol*, ch. 3.
10. *Maharal, Derush al ha-Torah ve-ha-Mitzvot* (Piotrków, 1913), 76–77.
11. Genesis Rabbah 44:1; Leviticus Rabbah 13:3; *Midrash Tanhuma, Shemini* 7–8, *Tazri'a* 5; *Midrash Shoher Tov*, Psalms 18:31, s.v. "*imrat Hashem tzerufah*."
12. *Eruvin* 13b.

their role. *Kol ha-mosif gore'a*. Therefore, there is a perfect matching of commandments to role assumption. Even single women are exempt from time-bound commandments because we must prepare them for their role.[13] Attitudes must be shaped from early childhood as to the role women will assume.

But at the same time, we are told that women have a superior moral fiber,[14] and therefore, the role of enabler and the creator of the Jewish home does not in any way preclude them from expending time and energy to find fulfillment in careers and intellectual growth. As a clear signal of their superiority, women are given the mitzvah of lighting the Sabbath candles. This mitzvah is not to remind women of Eve's original sin, but is a celebration of the power of women's influence. If a woman's influence brought the first man to the brink of disaster, then the woman's influence can equally catapult man to the giddiest heights and glory.

Yes, man takes too seriously his biblical mandate of *ve-kivshuha*.[15] He takes that to mean that he must subdue nature, advance civilization, and push the frontiers of scientific achievement.[16] But it is the job of the woman to suffuse the cosmic search with humaneness, integrity, and purpose, *le-hadlik et ha-nerot* (lit., "to light the candles").

Now, the Professor erred in his concept of *kol ha-mosif gore'a*. He takes Bush to task for not appreciating the diversity of our country, not appreciating that we have atheists and non-deits among us. He claims that Bush did not show sufficient respect for the separation of church and state. But this is a distortion of *kol ha-mosif gore'a*. In the modern era, when power and self-interest are the dominant forces in the international arena, how do we suffuse the oath to "preserve, protect and defend the Constitution" with sincerity, integrity, and meaning? It is

---

13. See R. Joseph Engel (Poland, 1859–1920), *Tziyyunim la-Torah* (Piotrków, 1904), *klal* 39, p. 118.
14. Maharal, *Derush al ha-Torah*, 76–77.
15. Hashem blessed Adam, "Be fruitful and multiply and fill the earth and subdue it" (Genesis 1:28).
16. See R. Joseph B. Soloveitchik (New York, 1903–1993), *The Lonely Man of Faith* (New York: Doubleday, 1965), 16–19.

with the phrase "so help me God." It will be only "so help me God" that will further the "kinder and gentler society."[17]

It so happens that since George Washington, there has never been another President with the first name George until George Bush. When it's all over and done, let it be said of you, George Bush, *"me-George ad George, lo kam ke-George."*[18]

---

17. George H. W. Bush, "Address Accepting the Presidential Nomination at the Republican National Convention in New Orleans," August 18, 1988.
18. From George [Washington] until George [Bush], there was no one like George [Washington]. This is a stylistic adaptation of the epitaph on Maimonides' tombstone, "From Moses [the Prophet] until Moses [Maimonides], there was no one like Moses [the Prophet]."

The Minimax Mitzvah of *Talmud Torah*

February 28, 2004

The most demanding mitzvah is the mitzvah of *talmud Torah*: *Lo yamush sefer Torah zeh mi-pikha*, "this Book of the Torah shall not depart from your mouth" (Joshua 1:8). It is a constant and continuous mitzvah. A contrast is set up between the mitzvah of *talmud Torah* and the mitzvah of *sukkah*. For *talmud Torah*, only one blessing, *birkhat ha-Torah* in the morning, is sufficient.[1] It will suffice for my discrete learning sessions. But each time we eat a meal in the *sukkah*, a new blessing of *leshev ba-sukkah* is required.[2] *Tosafot* explain the difference. There are fixed times for meals, so between meals, our minds wander. But *talmud Torah* is our natural activity. Should we be diverted momentarily, our

---

1. Berakhot 11b.
2. Shulḥan Arukh, Oraḥ Ḥayyim 639:8. Cf. Maimonides, *Mishneh Torah, Sukkah* 6:12 (stating that one must recite *leshev ba-sukkah* every time one enters the *sukkah*); Tur, Oraḥ Ḥayyim 639 (same).

Terumah

minds never wander and we never despair to return to *talmud Torah*, so one blessing suffices.[3]

Such a stringent formulation. So R. Jose's dictum in Menaḥot shocks us.[4] He tells us, "On the Table shall you place Showbread before Me, always" (Exodus 25:30). What does "always" mean? One answer is on the practical level, that the Showbread was constantly on the Table. The twelve loaves were baked on Friday and put on the Table on the Sabbath.[5] Only then was the old Showbread removed. Moreover, in the forty-two sojourns in the Wilderness, the Showbread was always on the Table.

But R. Yose tells us that minimally, we can be *yotze* the concept of "always" if the Showbread was removed on the Sabbath but replaced sometime before the Sabbath ended, so we can fulfill our obligation of *lo yamush* by learning something during the Morning Prayer and something during the Evening Prayer.[6] Moreover, R. Yohanan says that the recitation of *Shema* can serve double duty.[7]

We can well imagine that the exegesis is a devastating blow to the encouragement of *yeshivot*, *kollelim* and, for that matter, any learning groups. Indeed, R. Yohanan says that we must keep the exegesis a secret – "It is forbidden to say this in the presence of an *ammei ha-aretz*."[8] But Rava says the opposite – "It is a mitzvah to say it in the presence of *ammei ha-aretz*."[9] The Halakhah almost always follows Rava.[10] R. Yohanan is very understandable, but what is Rava telling us? The *Sefat Emet* provides the key by saying that the Sages knew that they would not promote the ideal of *lo yamush* by prescribing it outright.[11]

---

3. *Tosafot* to *Berakhot* 11b.
4. *Menaḥot* 99b.
5. Maimonides, *Mishneh Torah, Temidim u-Musafim* 5:10.
6. R. Yose as understood by R. Ammi. *Menaḥot* 99b.
7. *Menaḥot* 99b.
8. Ibid.
9. Ibid.
10. In talmudic debates between Rava and Abbaye, the Halakhah follows Rava except for six cases. *Bava Metzia* 22b; *Sanhedrin* 27a.
11. R. Yehudah Aryeh Leib Alter (*Sefat Emet*, Poland, 1847–1905), *Sefat Emet: Ḥiddushei Masekhtot mi-Seder Kodashim, Menaḥot* 99b.

The Minimax Mitzvah of Talmud Torah

Permit me to elaborate. The Sages, in their wisdom, knew that promoting *lo yamush* required a very creative motivational technique. This technique was combining shock with an appeal to curiosity, integrity and, most of all, the inability to live a lie. Our first reaction to the revelation that *lo yamush* can be fulfilled with the recitation of *Shema* during the Morning Prayer and Evening Prayer is that at least we should do the minimum requirement well. That means that when we get up in the morning, we cannot be mindless about *birkhat ha-Torah*. And when we say "Who selected us from all the peoples and gave us His Torah,"[12] we become very troubled with the notion that if our chosenness as a people depends on Hashem giving us the Torah, can our chosenness, in turn, depend on the minimal recitation of *Shema* in the morning and in the evening? This is unimaginable. There must be much more to it than just five minutes in the morning and five minutes in the evening.

Then, if we are to do the minimum requirement well, we must of course say *Shema* with *kavvanah*. In the *Shema*, we say, "You shall speak of them while you sit in your home, while you walk on the way" (Deuteronomy 6:7). Do we want to live a lie? This impels us to go to *shul*, do a little learning combined with prayer, and think a little about what we learned while we sit in our home and while we walk on our way. Now Torah takes on a life of its own. We are already hooked. Torah learning transforms us, and we yearn for more. "The orders of Hashem are upright, gladdening the heart" (Psalms 19:9).

Yes, by doing the minimal well and to perfection, a thousand points of light begin to emerge and we are well on our way to the ideal of *lo yamush*.

When we get up in the morning and say "Who selected us from all the people and gave us His Torah," we cannot say that in a mindless way. And we should feel troubled that our knowledge of Torah is so meager that we do not deserve our chosenness, and therefore we take action to increase our knowledge of Torah. And when we say "you shall speak of them while you sit in your home, while you walk on the way" (Deuteronomy 6:7), we feel that we are living a lie unless we fill our day with Torah learning.

---

12. Morning Prayer, *Birkhat ha-Torah*.

Titzavveh

Wiping Out the Federal Deficit

February 18, 1989

As President Bush delivered his first budget message to Congress, he evoked the image of an America drowning in a massive sea of red ink.[1] Yet he remained confident, optimistic, and upbeat. He must have derived solace from the fact that as he prepared and presented his budget message, Jewish congregations throughout the world were reading the portions of *Terumah* and *Titzavveh*, the portions that tell the story of the Tabernacle, which was probably the first communal project that entailed a big deficit.

As the Midrash puts it, when the Children of Israel heard the material requirements for the Tabernacle, they were confident that they could donate the necessary amounts of silver and copper. But when it came to the gold requirements, they were crestfallen. They knew that

---

1. George H. W. Bush, "Address on Administration Goals before a Joint Session of Congress" (February 9, 1989), 1989–1 Pub. Papers 74.

even if they donated their total holdings of gold, they could come up with but an insignificant fraction of the material demands. But God wrought a miracle. We gave what we had with purity and sincerity, and the material donation miraculously expanded to meet the structural requirements.[2]

I surely hope that President Bush will not rely on a miracle to narrow the budget deficit.

Amidst the desperation to deal with the deficit, implementing "flexible freezes" in every major category of spending, including national defense and social security, Bush, in a bold move, more symbolic than substantive, called for modest increases in education expenditures. Specifically, in the area of educational innovation, he proposed expanding coverage of the Head Start program and setting up an $8 million fund to give prizes to the best teachers in each State.[3]

Bush must have derived his inspiration from the Tabernacle. The single item in the Tabernacle contributing most to the deficit was the Cherubim, the golden cherub figures of children that were constructed atop the cover of the Ark. The gold required for the Cherubim alone was a hefty multiple of the gold actually contributed.[4] And there is something symbolic here, as R. Meir Shapiro of Lublin points out.[5] For all the appurtenances of the Tabernacle, if the means of society could not afford them, baser metals could be used, and the gold, silver, and copper requirements could be dispensed with.[6] Not so with respect to the Cherubim. They were required to be made out of gold.[7] This tells us

---

2. R. Isaiah ha-Levi Horowitz (*Shelah ha-Kadosh*, Prague, ca. 1565–1630), *Shenei Luḥot ha-Berit ha-Shalem*, vol. 3 (Haifa: Yad Ramah Institute, 2006), *Terumah*, p. 219, ¶ 10; R. Jacob Culi, *Me-Am Lo'ez*, Exodus 25:2, trans. R. Shemuel Yerushalmi, *Yalkut Me-Am Lo'ez: Sefer Shemot* (Jerusalem: Wagshal, 1968), 937.
3. George Bush, *Building a Better America* (1989) (supplement to the President's Message to the Joint Session of Congress, February 9, 1989), 53 (awards for teachers), 103–104 (Head Start), *reprinted in* H.R. Doc. No. 101-26, 101st Cong., 1st Sess. 101 (1989).
4. R. Eliyahu Kitov (Israel, 1912–1976), *Sefer ha-Parshiyyot*, vol. 4 (Jerusalem: Yad Eliyahu Kitob, 1985), 447.
5. R. Meir Shapiro (Poland, 1887–1933) on Exodus 25:18, quoted in R. Hayyim Yaakov Zuckerman, *Otzar Ḥayyim* (Tel Aviv, 1966), *Shemot*, 170.
6. *Mekhilta*, *Yitro* 10.
7. Ibid.

that the Torah education of the young is a matter of top priority. Every sacrifice must be made, even if a deficit must be incurred.

It is interesting to note that not only the clientele of the Torah educational enterprise is depicted in the form of angels, but also the transmitters of Torah education. "For the lips of the Priest should safeguard knowledge, and the people should seek teaching from his mouth; for he is an angel of Hashem, Master of Legions" (Malakhi 2:7). If the teacher is like an angel, then learn from his Torah.[8] Comparison of the *rebbe* to an angel at the very least bespeaks of Torah education not as a job or profession, but as a mission in life. One angel does not accomplish two missions.[9] The angel is monomaniacally preoccupied with a single task.

We lament that this concept is very far from us today. We do not invest the *rebbe* with the material resources so that he can assume an attitude of mission in his life's work. The career of the educator is so often marked by the need to juggle two or three jobs in order to eke out a living. The idealism and sense of mission that the *rebbe* brings with him has to inevitably be diluted by the practicalities of attending to the material needs of his family.

If Bush derived so much from the Tabernacle in terms of confidence and inspiration, perhaps that is also a hint of direction in the realm of education. Despite the fact that both the pupils and the teachers of Torah are depicted in the form of angels, which naturally evokes an image of docility and a pressure-free environment, nonetheless, our Sages state, *"kin'at soferim tarbeh ḥokhmah,"* "jealousy among scribes increases wisdom."[10] Halakhah generally approves of competition.[11] An

---

8. *Ḥagigah* 15b (statement attributed to R. Yohanan).
9. Genesis Rabbah 50:2. An application of the principle that one angel does not perform two missions is that Hashem sent three angels to Abraham: one to tell Sarah that she would give birth to a son, one to overturn Sodom, and one to heal Abraham. See *Rashi* to Genesis 18:2, s.v. *"ve-hinei sheloshah anashim"*; *Siftei Ḥakhamim* to Rashi ad loc., n. 9.
10. *Bava Batra* 21a.
11. *Rif, Bava Batra* 21b; *Tosafot* to *Bava Batra* 21b; *Mishneh Torah, Shekhenim* 6:8; *Rosh, Bava Batra* 2:12; *Tur, Ḥoshen Mishpat* 156; *Shulḥan Arukh, Ḥoshen Mishpat* 156:5; *Arukh ha-Shulḥan, Ḥoshen Mishpat* 156:6. For a discussion of the extent to which Halakah protects a firm from the competitive forces of the marketplace, see R. Aaron Levine, *Moral Issues of the Marketplace in Jewish Law* (Brooklyn, NY: Yashar Books, 2005), 95–138.

established firm is not entitled to protection from a new entrant unless the *beit din* is convinced that the new entrant would ruin the established firm.[12] The same rule generally applies to the Torah educational enterprise. But proceeding from the statement *kin'at soferim tarbeh ḥokhmah*, we go one step further. Ordinarily, an established firm is entitled to protection against an outside firm that does not pay taxes to the local government.[13] This does not apply to Torah education. The outsider is vouchsafed entry here too.[14]

What this glaring approach implies for secular society is that we should introduce more competition in the educational marketplace. Now, the public sector subsidizes education by providing free public schools. This makes the public school clientele captive, as the alternative of withdrawing from the public school is not viable. Instead of subsidizing producers, we should subsidize parents. The per-pupil expenditure should be given to parents in the form of educational vouchers. Providing the public subsidy to education in this form could very well prove a bonanza to *yeshivah* education as the voucher could be formulated in a manner that would not violate the doctrine of separation of church and state.[15]

One final observation: While it is generally true that one angel does not accomplish two missions, there is an exception. The angel that healed Abraham also rescued Lot from the destruction of Sodom.[16]

---

12. R. Eliezer b. Joel ha-Levi (*Ra'avyah*, Bonn, 1140–1225), quoted by R. Mordecai b. Hillel ha-Kohen (*Mordekhai*, Germany, ca. 1240–1298), *Mordekhai, Bava Batra* 2:516, and R. Meir b. Barukh of Rothenburg (*Maharam me-Rotenburg*, Germany, ca. 1215–1293), *Haggahot Maimuniyyot, Shekhenim* 6:8; R. Moses Isserles, *She'elot u-Teshuvot ha-Rema* 10; see also *Darkhei Mosheh* to *Tur, Ḥoshen Mishpat* 156, n. 4; R. Joseph ibn Migash (*Ri mi-Gash*, Spain, 1077–1141), *Bava Batra* 21b. See generally R. Levine, *Moral Issues of the Marketplace*, 96–100.

13. See sources cited in note 11 above.

14. *Bava Batra* 21b–22a. For a discussion of Halakhah's approach to competition in the Torah educational sphere, see R. Aaron Levine, *Economic Morality and Jewish Law* (New York: Oxford University Press, 2012), 138–141.

15. See Zelman v. Simmons-Harris, 536 U.S. 639 (2002) (upholding constitutionality of a voucher system employed by the State of Ohio where the financial aid was given directly to parents and not the schools, the vouchers were available to a broad class of beneficiaries consisting of all students enrolled in failing schools, and the vouchers could be used for either religious or non-sectarian schools).

16. *Rashi* to Genesis 18:2; Genesis Rabbah 50:2. Cf. *Bava Metzia* 86b.

When the angel assumes the role of removing the shackles from the *tzaddik*, allowing him to manifest his goodness, this will automatically benefit society at large, uplifting the moral climate and rescuing it from the decadence of Sodom. For our Tradition, this translates into the principle that when we give primacy to the education of our youth, it will be the breath of the *tinnokot shel beit rabban*, which is pure and innocent, devoid of sin,[17] that will enable the brilliance of mature adult Torah scholarship to influence society.

For the secular society, shifting society's focus away from a passive acceptance of the culture of violence and monstrous self-indulgence and self-interest toward the physical and intellectual needs of the pure and innocent children provides the necessary spurt to create the shocking contrast between the scourge of the drug culture and the ideal of a good society. The shift in focus will cultivate in us a revulsion and outrage against the drug society to the extent that we will have the willpower to finally do something about it. And the focus on children, those who require our care, will infuse society with a sense of responsibility, a sense that will spread from the bottom to the top of society. That focus will suffuse corporate America and the financial sector with a new sense of responsibility, which will minimize reckless loans to LDCs and LBOs.

When people of society are looking at each other, as the Cherubim, "their face toward one another" (Exodus 25:20), we are soaring upward and the deficit dissipates.

---

[17] See *Shabbat* 119b ("The world endures only because of the breath of school children.").

Ki Tissa

A Spectrum of Views of the *Klal*

February 25, 1989

Today's *sidrah* apparently assaults our sense of fairness. The lion's share of the verses in today's very long *sidrah* is taken up by the *Kohen* and the *Levi*, with very little left for us plain folk, the *Yisraelim*. Rather than constituting discrimination, the unequal distribution of *aliyyot* is taken by our Sages as reflecting a delicate sensitivity to our feelings. We are all presumed to have a profound identification with the community and therefore to feel a sense of shame for the Sin of the Golden Calf even though we did not commit it, and it was committed thousands of years ago. To spare us this ignominy, the part of the *sidrah* in which the episode of the Golden Calf unfolds is taken up by the *Levi*, who did not participate in the sin.[1]

---

1. *Yoma* 66b; *Rashi* to Exodus 32:26; R. Abraham Abele b. Hayyim ha-Levi Gombiner (*Magen Avraham*, Poland, ca. 1637–1682), *Magen Avraham* to *Shulḥan Arukh, Oraḥ Ḥayyim* 428:6; R. Samuel b. Nathan ha-Levi Kolin (Bohemia, 1720–1806), *Maḥatzit ha-Shekel* to *Magen Avraham* ad loc.

Ki Tissa

Perhaps there is no *sidrah* that provides us with such a spectrum of views of the community. We start off with the mystical. In taking a census, the Torah forewarns us not to count heads.[2] Instead, we must count *shekalim*.[3] Why? As *Rabbeinu Behaye* explains, Divine Providence manifests itself in two dimensions: the *hashgahah* of the *klal* and the *hashgahah* of the *perat*. Any time that we venture out by ourselves, we risk the danger of severing our connection with the *klal* and we are therefore in grave danger. We are exposed. Fear of being exposed is what motivated the Shunammite Woman to say "among my people I dwell" (II Kings 4:13).[4]

But there is a perversion of this. It is thinking that the *klal* is just a means of achieving anonymity, of hiding and escaping responsibility. An even greater distortion is the perversion of the *Erev Rav*, who wanted to be enveloped in the *klal* so that they would be protected.[5] From whatever glory would befall the *klal*, they would benefit. Because they would be protected, any sort of deviance would be tolerated.

But there is a noble view of the *klal*. This is Moses' view. Life without the *klal* is unthinkable. "And now if You would but forgive their sin – but if not, erase me now from Your book that You have written" (Exodus 32:32). And this is the intercession of *va-yihal*, "Moses pleaded before Hashem" (Exodus 32:11). When it comes to the survival of the *klal*, sin is minimized because the *klal* will exist for all eternity and any backsliding will of course be followed by rejuvenation. But finally Moses says, "If your Presence does not go along with the Children of Israel, do not bring us forward from here" (Exodus 33:15). Now, Moses will not be satisfied with an angel.[6] And why? How can this be reconciled with the principle of *she-lo yehei hote niskhar*, that a sinner should not profit from committing a sin?[7]

---

2. Exodus 30:12–13.
3. Exodus 30:13.
4. *Rabbeinu Behaye al ha-Torah*, Exodus 30:12.
5. See Exodus 12:38; Exodus Rabbah 18:10. The *Erev Rav* was a mixture of people from various nations who joined the Children of Israel during the Exodus from Egypt. *Rashi* to Exodus 12:38.
6. *Rashi* to Exodus 33:15; Exodus Rabbah 32:8.
7. Mishnah, Hallah 2:7; Mishnah, Shevi'it 9:9; Yevamot 92b; Ketubbot 39b; Sotah 15a; Gittin 55b; Bava Kamma 38a, 38b–29a; Avodah Zarah 2b; Menahot 6a; Niddah 4b.

The answer is that an angel is only a magician and witchcraft for the future. He has a monomaniacal mission. And this mission must go on. But the angel cannot heal the past. When one is weighed down by guilt and by failure and trauma, his goals and aspirations are lowered. This Moses could not tolerate. We must be under Hashem's Providence and nothing else.

Before the Sin of the Golden Calf, Hashem said that an angel would lead the Children of Israel. Exodus 23:20. After the Sin of the Golden Calf, Moses demanded that Hashem rather than an angel lead them. That request appears to violate the principle that a sinner should not profit from committing a crime. Nahmanides explains that the statement that an angel would lead them would not be fulfilled until after Moses' life, in the time of Joshua. By requesting that Hashem Himself lead the Children of Israel, Moses was seeking only to restore the Children of Israel to their prior level of connection to Hashem. See Nahmanides to Exodus 23:20 and Exodus 33:12.

The End Game of the Persian Gulf War

March 2, 1991

As the "mother of all military routs"[1] came to a climax, coincidentally with the reading of the Megillah, many of us began to wish that a Harbonah type would appear on the scene and finish the job, bringing down the evil tyrant.

For civilized man, Saddam is the incarnation of evil and the brute of boundless evil. His crimes against humanity began with the chemical weapons that he used against his own people, the atrocities he committed against Kuwait, the scorched-earth policy he inflicted as his army was ejected from Kuwait, the ecological disaster he created for the Persian

---

1. Saddam Hussein described the Persian Gulf War as "*umm al-ma'arik*" (lit., "the mother of all battles"), a metaphoric reference to the Battle of Al Qādisiyyah in 636 C.E., in which Islamic Arabs united to win their first decisive victory against the Sassanid (Persian) army. Spencer C. Tucker, ed., *Encyclopedia of Middle East Wars: The United States in the Persian Gulf, Afghanistan, and Iraq Conflicts*, vol. 3 (Santa Barbara, CA: ABC-CLIO, 2010), 844, s.v. "Mother of All Battles."

Gulf, the oil slick, and the scud attacks against the non-combatant, civilian population of Israel.[2] For us, he embraces the character traits of Amalek, for, as R. Hayyim Soloveichik points out, Amalek is not a racial concept, but any nation that behaves like Amalek, with wanton and boundless evil.[3] So we are sure that we should awake with a sense of mission. "You shall wipe out the memory of Amalek from under the heaven" (Deuteronomy 25:19).

But some thoughtful people point out that at present, the Iraqis believe that the United States should plan to avoid a continuation of heavy casualties. Assassinating Saddam could very well make him a martyr, turning a devastating military defeat into a political victory of ideology and hatred for Israel and America. Moreover, the iron grip that Saddam has had on Iraq for the past eleven years has put people who are blood relatives and totally loyal to him in all the key positions of the main media and the military, and they are perfect clones of him, vicious assassins.

The singular quality of Harbonah is his ability to bring to action a royal resolve and make sure that a resolve for action does not dissipate. But for the present situation, we need a Harbonah with special characteristics.

Four kings in Jewish history expressed their attitude toward war.[4] David proclaimed that he was working to pursue and destroy.[5] Asa said he had strength only to pursue, but not to destroy.[6] Yehoshafat said that he had no strength either to pursue or destroy, but he would recite *shirah*

---

2. Tucker, *Encyclopedia of Middle East Wars*, 701, 1416 (chemical attack against Kurds); 710–712 (atrocities against Kuwait); 421–422 (ecological disaster); 635, 831 (scud attacks against Israel).
3. R. Hayyim Soloveichik (*Rav Ḥayyim Brisker*, Brest-Litovsk, 1853–1918), cited in R. Joseph B. Soloveitchik, *Days of Deliverance: Essays on Purim and Chanukah* (New York: Toras HoRav Foundation, 2007), 16 (reproduced from manuscript of Tonya Soloveitchik Memorial Lecture presented at Yeshiva University on March 4, 1974). See also R. Mosheh Shternbukh (Jerusalem, contemp.), *Teshuvot ve-Hanhagot* 3:223 (Jerusalem, 1997), 244 (explaining how R. Hayyim Soloveitchik derived his concept of Amalek through a textual analysis of Maimonides, *Mishneh Torah, Melakhim* 5:4).
4. *Yalkut Shimoni*, II Samuel 163; Lamentations Rabbah 30.
5. Psalms 18:38.
6. See II Chronicles 14:12.

when it was all over.[7] Finally, Hezekiah said, "I have no strength for any of these matters, not to purse, not to destroy, and not to recite *shirah*. Only, I will sleep on my bed and You, Master of the Universe, do everything."[8]

Our Sages inform us that Sancheriv was destined to be Gog and Magog, and Hezekiah the Messiah, but because Hezekiah did not say *shirah*, all was lost![9] Now, I understand well why Hezekiah wanted no part of war. It was, after all, the golden age of Torah scholarship. "They searched from Dan until Beer Sheba, and no ignoramus was found."[10] War, development of technology and strategy, or any aspect of it, is anathema for the man whose delight in life is in the spiritual creativity of Torah scholarship. But why not recite *shirah*? Is it so difficult to say a *kapitel* of *Tehillim* after *Shaḥarit*?

But I would suggest that just as there is "the hard work of freedom," as President Bush put it,[11] there too is the hard work of *shirah*. *Shirah* is not merely the recitation of a few chapters of Psalms. The essence of *shirah* is universality. In the Song at the Sea of Reeds, not only the spiritual elite were moved to say *shirah*, but every segment of society to the lowliest recited *shirah*. "A slavewoman saw at the Sea what even Ezekiel b. Buzi did not see."[12] And the impact of *malkhut Shamayim* of "Hashem shall reign for all eternity" (Exodus 15:18) was felt by the future generations, even fetuses in the wombs of their mothers.[13] Even Pharaoh said, "Who is like You among the heavenly powers, Hashem!" (Exodus 15:11).[14]

Now, when President Bush said that we defeated the "village bully,"[15] this was a very apt phrase because when we do not allow naked

---

7. See II Chronicles 20:21–22.
8. See II Kings 19:19, 19:35.
9. *Sanhedrin* 94a; Song of Songs Rabbah 4:19.
10. *Sanhedrin* 94b.
11. State of the Union Address of President George Bush, January 29, 1991, reprinted in *New York Times*, January 30, 1991, A12.
12. *Mekhilta, Be-Shallaḥ* 3; Rashi to Exodus 15:2, s.v. "*zeh Keli*."
13. *Berakhot* 50a.
14. R. Jacob Culi, *Me-Am Lo'ez, Be-Shallaḥ* 15, trans. R. Shemuel Yerushalmi, *Yalkut Me-Am Lo'ez: Sefer Shemot* (Jerusalem: Wagshal, 1968), 345.
15. "The Persian Gulf War; Excerpts from the President's News Conference," *Washington Post*, March 2, 1991, A12.

aggression to stand, then we have attacked the village bully on the level of interpersonal relations.

Yes, it takes a Harbonah. We insist that we cannot trust Saddam. We must continue the economic embargo to ensure that he does not return. We should cut his oil pipeline in Turkey to ensure that he will pay reparations to Kuwait. But we must also reform and educate the Iraqi people. Now, they believe that there was the war, but there are eighty thousand Iraqi prisoners of war.[16] The Iraqis were indoctrinated that Americans would torture them.[17] The prisoners of war will return and put this big lie to rest. And surely we should identify and try those who were responsible for the atrocities in Kuwait. This will provide us with a propaganda platform to unmask Saddam and show his own people his ugly, monstrous hues.

But it is for us to take the revulsion against exploitation to its delicate limit as did R. Shimon in justifying the judgment of his death. He attributed the judgment to his causing minute anguish to litigants by making them wait momentarily before he adjudicated their case.[18]

There is a mother of all *shirah*. That is the *shirah* that begets a *shirah*, with no travail and no anguish to follow. The *shirah* is when the stellar knowledge of Torah scholarship penetrates every aspect of practical life, from the macrocosm of international relations to the microcosm of interpersonal relations, reflecting the integrated personality.

---

16. Spencer C. Tucker, ed., *Encyclopedia of Middle East Wars: The United States in the Persian Gulf, Afghanistan, and Iraq Conflicts*, vol. 1 (Santa Barbara, CA: ABC-CLIO, 2010), 368.
17. Tony Wharton, "Captive Audience Treated Well; POWs Can Be Tools of War or Friends for Life," *Virginian-Pilot & Ledger Star*, March 3, 1991, C1; Joan Lowy, "Iraqis Have It Better than US, GI Guards Say," *Pittsburgh Post-Gazette*, February 14, 1991, A11.
18. *Mekhilta* to Exodus 22:22, s.v. "*im anneh si'anneh*."

The Irrational Defense

(Undated)

The creative problem-solver never contents himself with addressing only symptoms. Instead, he penetrates to the root cause and devises a plan to ensure that the problem will not reoccur. Hence, when Moses descended the mountain, before he came close to the camp and beheld with his own eyes the Golden Calf, the idolatry, and the wild dancing, his perceptive mind and sensitive heart were in tune with the pulse of his people and he heard the *kol annos*, the "vexing voice" (Exodus 32:18). He realized that the moral climate of society had disintegrated. To restore sobriety, it was necessary to counter license and abandon with their extreme opposite, repressive judgment in its harshest form.

To counter the free spirit of self-indulgence, a cadre of loyalists had to be dispatched flaunting death by attempting to execute justice amidst a multitude of hostile elements. In instructing the Levites to gird their swords against the transgressors, Moses told them that the instruction was given by Hashem, "So said Hashem the God of Israel" (Exodus 32:27).

The Irrational Defense

But the Midrash points out that it was not.[1] *Torah Shelemah* compares this to the student who is permitted to give judgment in the name of a preeminent authority in order to make the judgment acceptable.[2]

The transgressors were meted out *misat sayyif,* "death by sword," as if they were an *ir nidaḥat,* but not as individuals whose death is effected through *sekilah,* "stoning."[3] Moses knew that idolatry took on many subtle forms. Nahmanides claims that the Sin of the Golden Calf was not actual idolatry.[4] The Children of Israel desired only to replace Moses. They wanted a new leader. But they wanted to replace a peerless leader with a calf, an immature cow, something that they could fatten with grass and teach how to be a leader. This was self-delusion. Moses showed them the error of their ways by burning the Golden Calf, pulverizing it into fine grains, and forcing everyone to drink it.[5]

I would submit that Moses was trying to drive home the point that in setting up the Golden Calf as their leader, they were not setting up an authority external to them, but merely an extension of themselves.

But when the same Moses, the champion of the Sinaitic Covenant and zealot, is told by Hashem that the Children of Israel sinned with the Golden Calf, we cannot even recognize him. His reaction cannot even be described as exhibiting forbearance for the sin. Nay, it begins with impudence, continues with irrelevancies, and ends with an escape from the realities of the situation.

Moses first declares, "Why, Hashem, should Your anger flare up against Your people?" (Exodus 32:11). How could Moses question why Hashem was angry? Moses, himself, had characterized the Golden Calf as a "disgrace among those who rise up against them" (Exodus 32:25). It was a sin of such gravity that it would be a source of scorn for the Jewish people for all generations. Our enemies would always point to it as a means of ridiculing us, saying that the sin was equivalent to a bride

---

1. *Tanna de-vei Eliyahu, Seder Eliyahu Rabba* 4.
2. R. Menachem Mendel Kasher (Israel, 1895–1983), *Torah Shelemah, ḥelek* 21 (Jerusalem, 1965), Exodus 32:27, p. 143, ¶ 222.
3. Rashi to Exodus 32:20, s.v. "*va-yashk et benei Yisrael.*"
4. Nahmanides to Exodus 32:1.
5. Exodus 32:20.

Ki Tissa

committing harlotry in her wedding canopy.⁶ Now, Moses says, "Why should your anger flare up against Your people?"

Another point in defense: Why did You, Master of the Universe, say "Go, descend, for the people that you brought up from the land of Egypt has become corrupt" (Exodus 32:7)? Why did you call the Children of Israel "my people"? They are Your people. As the Midrash puts it, it is analogous to a king who had a vineyard. When sweet grapes were produced, the king boasted of the superb quality of his vineyard. When the vineyard produced sour grapes, however, the king denounced the workers and said "your" vineyard produces sour grapes. We are Hashem's people, Moses argues, for better or for worse!⁷

Moses continues with "whom You have taken out of the land of Egypt, with great power and a strong hand" (Exodus 32:11). Now, is this not more of a reason for Hashem not to forbear the Sin of the Golden Calf? Does this not magnify the sin, rejecting His yoke after such magnificent miracles were wrought in the Exodus from Egypt?

But Moses was saying something very, very bold. Yes, Hashem, when You wrought Your great miracles, You already knew the future. You knew at that time that there would be a Golden Calf, yet You wrought your great miracles anyway. Therefore, You must forbear this sin.⁸

Then impudence continues into irrelevance: "Why should Egypt say, 'With evil intent did He take them out, to kill them in the mountains and to annihilate them from the face of the earth'?" (Exodus 32:12). But does public opinion make any difference to Hashem? Should justice be perverted on account of what people might say?

Finally, Moses moves to escape from reality. "Remember for the sake of Abraham, Isaac, and Israel, Your servants, to whom You swore by Yourself, and You told them, 'I shall increase your offspring like the stars of the heaven, and this entire land of which I spoke, I shall give to your offspring and it shall be their heritage forever'" (Exodus 32:13). But Hashem had told Moses, "I shall make you a great

---

6. *Shabbat* 88b.
7. *Pesikta de-Rav Kahana* 16, 128b (Buber ed.); *Yalkut Shimoni, Ki Tissa* 8.
8. Exodus Rabbah 43:8; R. Jacob Culi, *Me-Am Lo'ez*, Exodus 32:11, trans. R. Shemuel Yerushalmi, *Yalkut Me-Am Lo'ez: Sefer Shemot* (Jerusalem: Wagshal, 1968), 1131.

The Irrational Defense

nation" (Exodus 32:10). The promise to the Patriarchs would in fact remain inviolate, for Moses was also their descendant. Moreover, why does Moses use the terms "Israel" and "as the stars of the heaven" to describe the Children of Israel? The words "Jacob" and "as the sands of the sea" should have been used, as the exalted language applies only when the Jewish people are acting in accordance with the will of Hashem?[9] And why does Moses ask now that the Land of Israel should be as Hashem promised, "their heritage forever"? This is not at all relevant to the life-and-death issues at hand. It smacks of an escape from the present situation.

I would submit that Moses was only trying to restore the equilibrium with respect to Hashem's statement of, God forbid, "I will annihilate them" (Exodus 32:10). And Moses needs no logical basis for his entreaty.

Moses' approach, I submit, was not just for the case at hand. He was anticipating every crisis that would occur throughout our history. When we are demoralized by the severest crimes, we need not invoke logic as a basis for our survival. Indeed, in such times, logic will always make a compelling case for our certain annihilation. What keeps us alive and hopeful in these situations is a combination of blind belief and irrational confidence that we will persevere.

---

9. *Yoma* 22b; *Midrash Aggadah, Va-Yetze* 28:13; *Or ha-Ḥayyim* to Genesis 47:28.

Va-Yak'hel–Pekudei

You Will Find Favor and Goodly Wisdom in the Eyes of God and Man

February 25, 1984

Throughout the ages, countless Jews of simple faith have displayed a remarkable ability to suffer unspeakable horrors and to readily offer their lives in defense of our heritage. Yet, the suffering and sacrifice of people of simple piety often goes unnoticed and unrecorded. What captures our imagination is the spectacular, those few individuals who respond to a crisis of our national existence with spontaneous ingenuity and creativity. It is those heroes that history glorifies.

It therefore would seem to us only natural that the two heroes of the crisis of the Sin of the Golden Calf, Moses and Aaron, would assume center stage in the rebuilding after the sin. And, indeed, when Hashem speaks to Moses, telling him of the Tabernacle and its appurtenances, constantly using the phrase *ve-asita*, "you shall make,"[1] Moses thought that it would devolve upon him to build the Tabernacle. But, to his surprise, he was told that it would fall upon the shoulders of the grandson of the righteous Hur, who was killed by the mob at the scene of the Golden Calf.[2]

Hur, the Prophet, who together with Aaron was left in charge in Moses' absence, was approached by the mob with the request "make for us a god that will go before us" (Exodus 32:1). His instinct was to refuse to cooperate. In a flash, he was gone, a victim of the mob. Oh! Had he only had the spontaneous ingenuity of Aaron to feign cooperation while all along working to defeat the idolators. Were he only the master of the dilatory tactic, as Aaron was, and had the imaginativeness to say "A festival for Hashem tomorrow!" (Exodus 32:5), Hur would have been the hero of the moment instead of becoming a victim of the mob. The nation's focus was on Moses and Aaron. They were the spectacular actors who were the crisis managers.

But Hur's response to the mob reflected a pious instinct, a singular loyalty to Hashem. Would his sacrifice go unnoticed and be forgotten? No! To demonstrate how precious the life of Hur was to Hashem, his grandchild would be invested with singular qualities, qualities that would make even the biggest cynic and doubter admit that he was chosen by Hashem.[3] And hence, when Moses told the Children of Israel that Bezalel, Hur's grandson, would be the czar of the Tabernacle, the Children of Israel protested that it was nepotism.[4] Moses responded, "See, Hashem has proclaimed by name, Bezalel, son of Uri son of Hur, of the Tribe of Judah" (Exodus 35:30).

Now, did this statement that Hashem had selected Bezalel satisfy the scorners and doubters? But what Moses was saying was, look at this man and you will not doubt his divine election. Bezalel was the master crafter, consummate in all media, in gold, silver, copper, embroidery, and weaving.[5]

---

1. Exodus 25:11, 25:13, 25:17–18, 25:23–26, 25:28–29, 25:31, 25:37, 26:4, 26:6–7, 26:10–11, 26:14–15, 26:18, 26:26, 26:31, 26:36–37, 27:1–4, 27:6, 27:9.
2. Exodus Rabbah 48:3.
3. Ibid.
4. *Midrash Tanḥuma, Va-Yak'hel* 3.
5. Exodus 35:31–33.

How did he cultivate his delicate art? As Nahmanides points out, he was, after all, a product of the enslavement of the Children of Israel in Egypt, not part of the elite Levites.[6] A slave is occupied with crude labor. Moreover, all this talent resided in the delicate body of a thirteen-year old boy. There could be no doubt regarding his singularity. If his divine selection was not in doubt and his position free of contest, this did not automatically confer endearment upon him. In fact, singularity often evokes jealousy. But Bezalel took his divine gift one step further. "You will find favor and goodly wisdom in the eyes of God and man" (Proverbs 3:4). With reference to whom is this stated? Bezalel.[7]

How did Bezalel transform his singularity into a charm that made him beloved by both God and his fellow man? I would suggest that it was his quality of "He [i.e., Hashem] gave him the ability to teach" (Exodus 35:34). He was willing to share his esoteric art with others for the asking. He did not jealously guard his secret art and keep it to himself. This gained for him "favor and goodly wisdom" in the eyes of man.

But there was more. Of all the genius that Bezalel contributed toward the construction of the Tabernacle, there is no appurtenance that is ascribed to him more than the Ark, as the verse says, "Bezalel made the Ark" (Exodus 37:1). The Midrash explains that when Moses told Bezalel of the Tabernacle, Bezalel inquired about its purpose. Moses replied that the purpose of the Tabernacle is to provide a resting place for the Divine Presence and for the learning of Torah. Then Bezalel asked, "What is to be done with the Tablets?" Moses responded that first the Tabernacle would be built, then the Ark to house the Tablets. Bezalel protested that the Ark must be built first, whereupon Moses agreed.[8] Because Bezalel extended himself for the Ark, the Ark is ascribed to him.[9]

Now, was there ever anyone who extended himself for Torah more than Moses? He went to the heaven to accept the Torah and exerted every molecule of his being to understand it and teach it to the Children of Israel. We always ascribe the Torah to Moses. *Torah tzivvah*

---

6. Nahmanides to Exodus 31:2.
7. *Midrash Tanḥuma, Va-Yak'hel* 3.
8. Exodus Rabbah 50:2. Cf. *Berakhot* 55a; *Rashi* to Exodus 38:22.
9. Exodus Rabbah 50:5; *Midrash Tanḥuma, Va-Yak'hel* 10; *Rashi* to Exodus 37:1.

lanu Mosheh, "the Torah that Moses commanded us" (Deuteronomy 33:4). Why does the impassioned plea by Bezalel make the Ark ascribed to Bezalel more than to Moses?

The answer, I would submit, is that one who is the essence of Torah cannot assume the role of the champion of the honor of the Torah. When the Torah giant demands honor for the Torah, the cynics smirk and proclaim, "We are hearing self-glorification." Only the *ba'al ha-bayit* can demand honor for the Torah and be free of this charge. The champion of the honor of Torah can only be the *ba'al ha-bayit*. It is only he who makes an impact on society for the glory of Hashem. And hence Bezalel was one who found "favor and goodly wisdom in the eyes of God and man."

The instruction to build the Tabernacle is preceded by the commandment to observe the Sabbath.[10] Why? Our Sages tell us that it is to inform us that the work of the Tabernacle does not trump the prohibition of performing work on the Sabbath.[11] Now, is this not a simple matter? Why would I think otherwise?

The *Meshekh Hokhmah* answers that both the construction of the Tabernacle and the observance of the Sabbath involve acknowledging the Divine, but in the case of the Tabernacle, it is through action, spectacular action involving gifted talents, whereas on the Sabbath, it is through abstaining from action, from creative and useful work, the thirty-nine *melakhot*.[12] One might think that the glamorous action of acknowledging Hashem is greater than the invisible, unnoticed, unimaginative inaction. We are told otherwise. The Tabernacle is built only by the routine and unspectacular loyalty to Hashem in everyday life, rather than the few moments of magnificent public actions.

Many of us assembled here are either survivors of the Holocaust or children or grandchildren of victims of the Holocaust. Is Hur not the prototype of the whole generation of Jews who were perceived to have gone to their slaughter as obedient lambs, just because they were Jews? And we think that the sacrifices of all these people of simple piety,

---

10. See Exodus 35:2–3; Exodus 35:10–19.
11. *Rashi* to Exodus 31:13 and 35:2.
12. See *Meshekh Hokhmah*, Exodus 35:2.

people who could not in this crisis display guile and ingenuity, have gone unrecorded in history. Only Hashem could demonstrate that this is not so. People who showed wisdom in the sense of "the beginning of wisdom is the fear of Hashem"[13] must be given a grandchild of the Bezalel character.

And yes, the grandchildren of the Holocaust era are the Bezalel Jews, the Jews who have risen to the top of every branch of creative human endeavor. Unlike other minorities who have made their mark only in a few areas, the talent of the Jew knows no bounds. And all this talent resides in the delicate frame of a thirteen-year old boy. The Jew quickly masters all the intricacies of a new field and quickly rises to the top.

Our Bezalel character is now recognized to a greater extent by the nations of the world. The increasing incidents of anti-Semitism are more than eloquent testimony that our singularity as a people is recognized. Who but a Bezalel character could have built the State of Israel, a nation rising out of the ashes of the crematorium? Only the multi-talented could accomplish this.

We now only await refinement of the leap from singularity to finding "favor and goodly wisdom in the eyes of God and man." This will occur in its final stage when the Bezalel Jew shows a measure of generosity with his talent and when the *ba'alei battim* of the Jewish nation make a clarion call for the honor of Torah. Then we will merit fulfillment of the prophecy of Isaiah: "Many peoples will go and say, 'Come, let us go up to the Mountain of Hashem, to the Temple of the God of Jacob, and He will teach of His ways and we will walk in His paths.' For from Zion will the Torah come forth, and the word of Hashem from Jerusalem" (Isaiah 2:3).

---

13. Psalms 111:10.

Donations versus Total Commitment

March 8, 1986

The story is told of a devout but idiosyncratic Jew, Pinchas Peppernastel. Reb Pinchas had a pet chicken. Man and pet were inseparable. Once upon a time, Reb Pinchas was invited to a fund-raising *yeshivah* dinner. He eagerly wanted to attend, but alas, his pet chicken would hear nothing of it. When all gentle persuasion failed, Reb Pinchas angrily demanded an explanation from the chicken, to which the chicken responded, "For you, it is an easy matter. All they want is a donation. But from me, they will settle for nothing less than total commitment."

What is the difference between a donation and total commitment? The various contributions that were offered for the Tabernacle provide us with the answer. Standing at the bottom were the coercive levies, consisting of the *beka la-gulggolet,* small silver coins, one for the purpose of building the sockets for the wooden beams of the Tabernacle, and the second for maintaining communal sacrifices.[1]

If a Jew would claim that he is not interested in supporting a basic Jewish religious education or he is not concerned that the holy institutions of the community should be operative at least on a minimal level, we simply do not believe him. Deep down, every Jew wants these and hence harbors an intrinsic demand for them. Though outwardly the requirement to contribute looks like coercion, it amounts really to a voluntary contribution.[2]

Standing higher is the man who is swept up in the tide of the moment. This was the *nesa'o libbo*, the man whose heart inspired him.[3] The saintly *Or ha-Ḥayyim* understands this to describe the individual who is carried away and gives beyond his means for the cause.[4] How beautifully this character trait counteracts the mass hysteria displayed during the Sin of the Golden Calf, where the Torah states in connection with the donation of gold jewelry *"ve-yisparku,"* "they removed it," in *hitpa'el*, the reflexive form. It was as if the jewelry removed itself, with everyone being caught up in the frenzy of the moment.[5]

An even higher level of giving was demonstrated by the women. The Gaon of Reisha explains that the contribution of the women of their personal jewelry was beyond a mere donation of gold. They gave up

---

1. Rashi to Exodus 25:2, s.v. *"tik'ḥu et terumati."* The *beka la-gulggolet* (lit., "a beka for each head," i.e., per person) was a half-shekel. See Exodus 38:26 and *Rashi* ad loc., s.v. *"beka."*
2. See *Berakhot* 17a; R. Moses Joshua Judah Leib Diskin (*Maharil Diskin*, Russia and Jerusalem, 1817–1898), *Ḥiddushei Maharil Diskin al ha-Torah, Terumah*, s.v. *"Dabber el benei Yisrael ve-yik'ḥu li terumah"* (citing Maimonides, *Mishneh Torah, Gerushin* 2:20).
3. Exodus 35:21.
4. *Or ha-Ḥayyim* to Exodus 35:21. The *Or ha-Ḥayyim* distinguishes the *"ish asher nesa'o libbo,"* the man who gave beyond his means, from *"kol asher nadvah ruḥo,"* one whose spirit motivated him, who gave within his means. The one who gave beyond his means was on a higher spiritual level than the one who gave within his means, as signified by the mention of *nesa'o libbo* before *nadvah ruḥo* in Exodus 35:21 and the use of the term *"ish"* (man) in that verse only in connection with the *nesa'oh libbo* and not the *nadvah ruḥo*. Ibid.
5. R. David Kimḥi, *Perush Rabbi David Kimḥi (Radak) al ha-Torah*, ed. R. Moshe Kamelhar, 3rd ed. (Jerusalem: Mossad HaRav Kook, 1982), 233, Exodus 32:3.

something of sentimental value. They understood that the Tabernacle was more precious than their jewelry.[6]

But there is an even higher level than this. All too often, the tragedy of modern life is that a donor makes a generous contribution, but once the contribution is made, the donor becomes detached from the beneficiary. The latter is ignored and is not identified with at all. Are we interested in following the progress of a *yeshivah* to which we lent support? Do we identify with the achievements of an organization that we support?

Demonstrating this level of involvement with the recipient was the contribution of the Princes. Their name, *Nesi'im*, is spelled in today's *sidrah* without the letter *yud*. Their original approach to giving was indeed deficient. When they heard Moses' clarion call to build the Tabernacle, they proclaimed, "Let the people give what they can. We will make up the deficiency." What they did essentially was to project themselves into their donation. They were reaching for self-glorification.[7]

And what happened? The response of the people was so enthusiastic that nothing was lacking. The donation of the Princes was not needed.[8]

So how did they ameliorate the situation? They went to the other extreme and tried their best to elevate the recipient. How did they accomplish this? By donating the *shoham* stones and the filling stones.[9] The filling stones rested on the heart of the High Priest. Each stone represented the triumphs, successes, admirable qualities, and moments of failure of the entire Jewish nation.[10] The High Priest's heart was to be attuned to the entire gamut of human emotions. Their feelings were to be close to his heart.

Moments of triumph were represented. The *bareket*, the brilliant fiery-red stone, symbolized the dissemination of Torah by Levi, and the

---

6. R. Aharon Levine, *Ha-Derash ve-ha-Iyyun*, vol. 2 (Biłgoraj: N. Kronenberg, 1931), *ma'amar* 286, pp. 402–403.
7. See *Rashi* and R. Ephraim Solomon b. Aaron of Luntshits (*Keli Yakar*, Łęczyca, 1550–1619), *Keli Yakar* to Exodus 35:27; Numbers Rabbah 12:16.
8. See Exodus 36:7.
9. Exodus 35:27.
10. See *Rabbeinu Beḥaye al ha-Torah*, Exodus 28:15.

sapir, the sky-blue stone, represented the delving into the profundity of the Torah on the highest level by Issachar. And there was the *yahalom*, alluding to the success of the businessman, Zebulun, and the *tarshish*, signifying the national abundance in the territory of Asher. These moments the High Priest was not to ignore. They were to be close to his heart. He was to jubilate in the triumph of another Jew, nay, even in the windfall gain of another Jew. It is only of this heart that it was said "when he sees you, he will rejoice in his heart" (Exodus 4:14). Hashem told Moses, "Aaron will not be envious of you when you will be elevated to be the Redeemer of Israel but instead will rejoice in your triumph."[11]

But the heart of the High Priest did not resonate only with respect to moments of glory and attributes of admiration. No, it was associated with moments of failure too. The stone of the Prince of the Jewish people, Judah, was the *nofekh*, which had a greenish color, denoting that Judah's face became pale when he was confronted by his father, suspicious that he had murdered Joseph.[12] And so, too, his faced turned green when he was confronted by Tamar.[13] The man of the sensitive heart relates to the ignominy of his brother with empathy.

And even more than this was the *leshem*, the stone of Dan, which reflected an upside-down human image.[14] It was for the sensitive soul to take action to turn that image right-side up. This represents the activities and interventionism in the emotional realm, par excellence.

And there were the *shoham* stones that also formed part of the gift of the Princes. These stones were set in the Breastplate,[15] which is placed over the heart, and on each shoulder strap of the Apron to support the Breastplate.[16] Changing the letters around, *shoham* spells *Hashem*,

---

11. *Rashi* to Exodus 4:14, s.v. "*ve-ra'akha ve-samaḥ be-libbo.*"
12. *Rabbeinu Beḥaye al ha-Torah*, Exodus 28:15.
13. Ibid.
14. Ibid. The upside-down image intimates that the Tribe of Dan reversed their true goal of serving Hashem when they set up the image of Micah in their territory. See Judges 18:30–31.
15. Exodus 28:20.
16. Exodus 28:6–12; Maimonides, *Mishneh Torah, Kelei ha-Mikdash* 9:9. The *shoham* stones on the shoulders straps of the Apron were placed in gold settings. On each stone, the names of six of the Tribes were inscribed according to their order of birth.

representing the sanctification of the Name of Hashem in the inner recesses of our heart.[17] That is the invisible sanctification of Hashem, when we get absolutely no credit for our action.

But the *shoham* also represents the charm of grace, as it was the stone of Joseph.[18] During his entire life, Joseph always found favor in the eyes of his fellow man.[19] And we can never have too much charm.

Let the leaders of the Jewish people, who carry the burden of responsibility on their shoulders, have charm so that the people will respond to their appeals. And let charm be in the heart of every Jew so that we will always seek to elevate our fellow Jew and not project ourselves into our *ḥesed* for the purpose of self-glorification. Let them go with the Princes' gift of oil for lighting the Menorah, and the spices for the *ketoret* and for the Oil of Anointment.[20] These were for beautification and not atonement, for both the Menorah and the *ketoret* were purely outlets to demonstrate our love and joy in serving Hashem.[21]

The highest and most noble gift was embodied in Moses' donation. It was not a material donation, but rather that he put up the Tabernacle. He erected it. And this is what we should aim for, to put our fellow Jew on his feet, with the highest level of dignity and happiness!

---

17. *Rabbeinu Beḥaye al ha-Torah*, Exodus 28:15.
18. Ibid.
19. See Genesis 39:21.
20. Exodus 35:28.
21. See *Midrash Tanḥuma, Tetzavveh* 15; R. Shmuel Bornsztain (*Shem mi-Shemuel*, Poland, 1855–1926), *Shem mi-Shemuel: Al Seder Parshiyyot ha-Torah u-Mo'adei Kodesh*, 9th ed., vol. 1 (Jerusalem, 1992), *Toledot* (5676/November 1915), pp. 285–286.

The Generosity of Giving

March 28, 1987

Ever since the construction of the first synagogue, attitudes have proliferated regarding the appropriate degree of involvement in its affairs and high mission. Adopting the bloated self-image of a High Priest, some have applied to themselves the verse "he shall not come at all times into the Sanctuary" (Leviticus 16:2) – holiness is best appreciated at a distance. Others have adopted the strategy of carefully looking about themselves and limiting their involvement in the synagogue to the lowest common denominator, applying to themselves the verse "the wealthy shall not increase and the destitute shall not decrease" (Exodus 30:15).

There was once a group of Princes who thought that they hit upon the highest sentiment of magnanimity. When Moses issued the clarion call for thirteen materials to build the Tabernacle,[1] the Princes

---

1. Exodus 25:2–9; 35:5–9. See *Rashi* to Exodus 25:2; *Da'at Zekenim* to Exodus 25:3; *Midrash Tanḥuma, Terumah* 5. According to one grouping of the items enumerated at Exodus 25:2–9, the thirteen items are: (1) gold; (2) silver; (3) copper; (4) wool, consisting of turquoise wool, purple wool, and scarlet wool; (5) linen; (6) goats' hair;

proudly pronounced that they would complete anything that was missing. How noble and how generous. Yet, they were gently rebuked. When they were referred to, the letter *"yud"* in their name was missing. Their name was deficient because they did not properly connect themselves to the collective.[2]

Why was their generosity deficient? Formulating a commitment in terms of a willingness to complete what is missing sends a clear-cut message to everyone that they need not involve themselves in the holy work, for the collective efforts of everyone else will accomplish what is necessary. Rather than inspiring others, such a generosity dampens enthusiasm for the cause. Moreover, suppose the response of the general public turns out to be much weaker than expected. Then, the generous pledge turns into a begrudging gift, and even worse, maybe those who made the pledge will subconsciously want to retrieve what they gave to society without a full heart.

When people of elevated spirit are chastised gently, they rise to the heights and make amends. They then stretch the very imagination of generosity. The Princes did this by donating the *shoham* stones and the filling stones, and by bringing an offering of *ketoret*.[3]

If their commitment was less than definitive and even smacking of *asmakhta*, they corrected it by trying to capture the idealistic fervor of Sinai by donating the *sapir*, committing themselves to a primacy and innovative spirit,[4] an adventurous spirit, as symbolized in Zebulun's stone,[5]

---

(7) rams' skins; (8) goatskins; (9) acacia wood; (10) oil for the light; (11) spices for the anointing oil and for raising the smoke of the incense; (12) *shoham* stones; and (13) filling stones. *Siftei Ḥakhamim* to Rashi, Exodus 25:2, n. 6; R. Elijah Mizrahi (*Re'em*, Constantinople, ca. 1450–1526), *Sefer ha-Mizraḥi*, Exodus 25:2. Another grouping of the thirteen items counts each of the three types of wool separately and omits the oil and spices. See Song of Songs Rabbah 4:25.

2. *Rashi* and *Keli Yakar* to Exodus 35:27; Numbers Rabbah 12:16.
3. Exodus 35:27–28.
4. Exodus 28:18; *Rabbeinu Beḥaye al ha-Torah* loc. cit. The *sapir* was a sky-blue sapphire stone for Issachar, who was committed to the study of Torah.
5. Zebulun's stone was the *yahalom*, a white jewel. Exodus 28:18. The white color represented a merchant's chair, alluding to Zebulun's success in business. Zebulun engaged in commerce to support Issachar. *Rabbeinu Beḥaye al ha-Torah* loc. cit.

The Generosity of Giving

the courage of Gad,[6] and the intensity of Judah.[7] They even related to the failings of the Tribes, symbolized in the *odem* and *pit'dah*, using transgression as an energizing and driving force in their commitment.[8]

If their generosity failed to inspire, the *ketoret* would go to the other extreme and maximize inspiration. The *ketoret* symbolized exerting an influence on everyone, not only because the *ḥelbbenah* was included,[9] not only because its fragrance permeated the entire city of Jerusalem,[10] but because a tremendous contrast is set up between two of its ingredients. One of the ingredients was *tzari*.[11] What is *tzari* but sap dripping from the bark of a tree?[12] It is so accessible. But another ingredient was *tzippuron*.[13] The Oral Law had to be consulted to determine what it was. It turns out to be a plant that must be dredged up from the ocean depths. Then, when we finally extract it from the sea, we need the scientific community to verify what it is.[14] Even after all that, it is still not worthy of being included with the other ingredients of the *ketoret*. We need to add two more ingredients to ready the *ketoret*: the *boris karshinah*,

---

6. Gad's stone was the *aḥlamah*. Exodus 28:19. This jewel strengthens one's courage in battle, alluding to Gad's skill in warfare. *Rabbeinu Beḥaye al ha-Torah* ad loc.
7. Judah's stone was the *nofekh*, a greenish brilliant stone. Exodus 28:18. The *nofekh* symbolized that Judah's face turned green when he confessed in the matter of Tamar and when Jacob suspected him of having killed Joseph. In addition, one who carried this stone had the power to make the enemy retreat. *Rabbeinu Beḥaye al ha-Torah* loc. cit.
8. Exodus 28:17; *Rabbeinu Beḥaye al ha-Torah* loc. cit. The *odem* was a red stone selected for the Tribe of Reuben. It symbolized that Reuben's face turned red with shame when he admitted that he upset his father's couch. The *pit'dah* was a green stone selected for the Tribe of Simeon, signifying that the face of Zimri, the Prince of the Tribe of Simeon, turned green when he rebelled against Moses.
9. Exodus 30:34; *Rashi* ad loc.; *Keritot* 6b.
10. See *Yoma* 39b.
11. *Tzari* is referred to in the Bible as "*nataph*." Exodus 30:34; *Rashi* ad loc., s.v. "*nataph*."
12. *Rashi* to Exodus 30:34, s.v. "*nataph*"; *Keritot* 6a.
13. *Tzippuron* is referred to in the Bible as "*sheḥelet*." Exodus 30:34; *Rashi* ad loc., s.v. "*u-sheḥelet*."
14. See Nahmanides to Exodus 30:34; R. Abraham b. David II Portaleone (Italy, 1542–1612), *Shiltei ha-Gibborim*, ch. 79. For a discussion of the interpretations of the *Rishonim* of the nature of the *tzippuron*, see *Kovetz Peirushei ha-Rishonim al Bereitat Pitum ha-Ketoret* (Israel, 2005), 227–231.

for the purpose of bleaching the *tzippuron* so that it should be beautiful, and the Cyprus wine that is mixed in to make the *tzippuron* pungent.[15]

We see here that the *tzippuron*, even when extracted from the ocean floor, is two preparations away from being worthy of making a contribution. Inspired leadership must enlist not only those who are readily accessible and willing to serve, but in addition attract those who are far removed from a readiness to serve.

---

15. *Keritot* 6a.

Discovering the Gap

March 12, 1988

Human nature is such that we are capable of reading into the actions of our fellow man dramatically opposite motivational forces. Hence, when the Children of Israel requested of Moses an accounting of the materials that they contributed toward the construction of the Tabernacle, cynics read into this demand decadence of the first order.[1] The demand was, after all, an implied accusation that Moses might have mismanaged the donations, misappropriated the funds, or even embezzled them.

But Moses was beyond reproach! The Master of the Universe, Himself, testifies, "In My entire house, he is the trusted one" (Numbers 12:7).

And the timing of the demand is another disturbance. The Tabernacle project came immediately after Moses interceded on behalf of the Jewish people in the Sin of the Golden Calf and displayed his grandest gesture on the part of the nation, willing to give not only his life, but his place in history. "If not, erase me now from Your book that You have written" (Exodus 32:32).

---

1. Exodus Rabbah 51:6.

This same cynical attitude dredges up obscure *midrashim*, which claim that the amount of gold contributed for the Golden Calf was four times the amount of gold contributed for the Tabernacle.[2] Now, when Aaron cast the gold into the fire, what emerged? Was it a camel, a giraffe, a gigantic monster? No. It was merely a small golden calf. Here, no one demanded an audit of what became of all the gold. It seems that when it comes to a sacred matter, Jews demand an exact accounting, but when it comes to *havalim* (empty matters), they are not so exacting![3]

There is no end to the dark side of human nature. Cynics go on to point to the *midrash* that says that when Moses explained that the hundred talents of silver were all used for the sockets of the beams of the Tabernacle, he was at a loss to explain where the remaining 1,775 silver pieces were used until he was saved by remembering that they were used as hooks to attach the curtains to the pillars of the courtyard of the Tabernacle.[4] It seems that we cannot trust anyone!

Some, however, would distance themselves from this cynical attitude. The demand for a reckoning is not so bad! The soul of the Jew is pure. When it comes to contributions to the Golden Calf, the Jew regrets his action immediately and therefore is not really interested in an accounting. Secretly, he is hoping that the money that he gave for an evil purpose was diverted and was never put to use for that purpose.

But there are those who turn 180 degrees and read into the demand the highest nobility. R. Eliyahu Kitov points out that when the Jews heard Moses' clarion call for all the required material, not one of them, in his wildest imagination, could conclude that the collective entity of the Jewish people had the ability to supply even the minutest fraction of what was needed to meet the specifications of

---

2. The amount of gold contributed for the Tabernacle was twenty-nine talents and 730 shekels. Exodus 38:24. According to the Midrash, the amount of gold contributed in the Sin of the Golden Calf was 125 talents, corresponding to the *gematria* of "*massekhah*" (molten). *Midrash Tanḥuma, Ki Tissa* 21; Rashi to Exodus 32:4, s.v. "*massekhah*."
3. See R. Meir Shapiro of Lublin (Poland, 1887–1933), cited in R. Aharon Yaakov Greenberg (Israel, 1900–1963), *Iturei Torah: Likkut, Nisaḥ u-Biur*, vol. 3 (Tel Aviv: Yavneh, 1970), 294.
4. Exodus Rabbah 51:6.

the appurtenances. Much of their gold had already been used up for the Sin of the Golden Calf. Now, the *kaporet* of the Ark alone required three tons of gold. The gold available could plate only four boards, but a total of forty-eight boards had to be plated, to say nothing of the gold required for the Menorah.

The request for an accounting was therefore a grasping to discover the nature of the gap, the amount of blessing that they were receiving. They knew this on a theoretical level, but wanted to experience it and feel as intensely as possible their indebtedness to Hashem. Yes, each Jew now could have nothing to boast about. No one could say, if not for my contribution, there would be no Tabernacle. Quite the opposite, everyone knew that it was only through miracles that the appurtenances were produced in the prescribed manner. Everyone deliberately took action to make himself feel indebted to Hashem.[5]

We all bewail today the terrible rift in the Jewish community, the division between the secular and religious Jew on the one hand, and within the religious Jewish community on the other. Some point to a fruitful approach. If only those who are meticulous in their performance of mitzvot *bein adam la-Makom* would display a corresponding delicate sensitivity in interpersonal relations, a greater degree of harmony would be achieved in the Jewish community.

But the demand for an audit takes this approach a bit further. Surely we must excel in the mechanical act of a mitzvah. It must be done with precision and with all the nuances and stringencies so we can be sure that we fulfill the mitzvah. But mitzvot must produce a change in our character. It must make us feel that we are indebted to Hashem. Regardless of our economic and social condition, we must feel as debtors to Hashem. This is the direction for religious education and *ḥinnukh* of the home.

If mitzvot make us feel indebted to Hashem, our attitude is changed, our outlook on life is changed, for the good will drive us away from cynicism and will produce the beauty and harmony that comes from a unity of the Jewish people.

---

5. R. Eliyahu Kitov (Israel, 1912–1976), *Sefer ha-Parshiyyot*, vol. 4 (Jerusalem: Yad Eliyahu Kitob, 1985), 444–448.

Glossary

AFIKOMAN. Piece of matzah eaten at the end of the Seder.
AḤARIT HA-YAMIM. Lit., "end of the days." Messianic era.
AHAVAT ḤINNAM. Unwarranted love.
AKEDAH. The Binding of Isaac.
ALEPH. First letter of the Hebrew alphabet.
ALIYYAH. Ascent, particularly of a spiritual nature. Also denotes the immigration of Jews to the Land of Israel.
AM HA-ARETZ, (PL.) AMMEI HA-ARETZ. Common person.
AM SEGULLAH. The Chosen Nation.
AM YISRAEL ḤAI. The nation of Israel is alive.
ANAV. A humble person.
ARMAH. Insidious guile.
ASARAH HARUGEI MALKHUT. The Ten Sages who were martyred by the Romans in the period after the destruction of the Second Temple. The description of their martyrdom is set forth in *Elleh Ezkerah*, which is recited on Yom Kippur and Tish'ah be-Av.
ASHERAH. An idolatrous object constructed of wood.
ASMAKHTA. An agreement that lacks the presumption of firm resolve on the part of the obligor or fails to generate a presumption of reliance on the part of the party to whom the commitment was made.
AT BASH. A system in which the first letter of the Hebrew alphabet, *aleph*, is replaced with the last letter of the alphabet, *taph*; the

Glossary

second letter, *bet*, is replaced with the second-to-last letter, *shin*, and so forth.

AVODAH. Service.

AVODAH ZARAH. Idolatry.

AVODAT PERAKH. Crushing labor. Typically refers to the most difficult period of the Servitude in Egypt.

AYIN. Sixteenth letter of the Hebrew alphabet, with a numerical equivalence of seventy.

BA'AL HA-BAYIT, (PL.) BA'ALEI BATTIM. Householder.

BAR MITZVAH. Lit., "a son of commandment." A Jewish boy who has reached the age of thirteen, the age at which he is responsible for his actions and obligated to observe the commandments.

BARAITA. A teaching or tradition of the *Tannaim* that was excluded from the Mishnah and incorporated in a later collection complied by R. Hiyya and R. Oshaia.

BEIN ADAM LA-MAKOM. Lit., "between man and God." Refers to the obligations between man and God.

BEIN ADAM LE-ḤAVERO. Lit., "between man and his fellow." Refers to the obligations governing interpersonal conduct.

BEIT DIN. Jewish court of law.

BEKA. A measure of weight equivalent to the weight of a half-shekel.

BEKA LA-GULGGOLET. Lit., "a *beka* per head." Small silver coin equivalent to half a shekel. A coercive levy used for the building of the sockets for the wooden beams of the Tabernacle and to finance communal sacrifices.

BEN TORAH, (PL.) BENEI TORAH. A Torah scholar or moral individual.

BERIT MILAH. Circumcision.

BINYAN. Building.

BIRKHAT HA-MAZON. Grace after Meals.

BIRKHAT HA-MOTZI. Blessing over bread. The blessing is "Blessed are You, Lord our God, King of the Universe, Who brings forth bread (*ha-motzi leḥem*) from the earth."

BITTAḤON. Faith.

CHOLENT. Traditional Jewish stew, usually made of potatoes, meat, beans, and barley.

Glossary

DA'AT TORAH. Lit., "knowledge of Torah." Refers to the opinion of rabbinic scholars.

DAGESH. A point or dot placed within a Hebrew letter, which changes the pronunciation of the letter. The accent may be either weak (*dagesh kal*) or strong (*dagesh ḥazak*). The weak version is placed inside the consonants *bet, gimel, dalet, kaf, pe* and *tav*. The strong version may be placed in almost any letter and indicates a doubling of the letter.

DAI. Enough.

DALET. Fourth letter of the Hebrew alphabet.

DARKHEI SHALOM. Lit., "the ways of peace." Refers to the duty to end discord. To achieve this result, the use of lies is permitted under certain circumstances.

DERASH. Homiletical interpretation.

DEVARIM BETELIM. Meaningless matters.

DIKDDUK. Hebrew grammar.

DIN TORAH. Jewish court case.

DINA DE-MALKHUTA. Lit., "law of the Kingdom." Secular law.

DINEI NEFASHOT. Capital cases.

DINIM. Lit., "laws." One of the seven Noahide laws that requires the establishment of a proper system of justice in society.

DUDA'IM. Mandrakes. Wild flowers.

EDUT. Testimony.

EIN OD MI-LEVADDO. "There is none beside Him." Deuteronomy 4:35.

EMET. Truth.

EMUNAH. Faith.

EMUNAH SHELEMAH. Complete faith.

ERETZ YISRAEL. Hebrew name of the Land of Israel. The term is biblical, although its meaning varies, designating both the territory actually inhabited by the Israelites (I Samuel 13:19) and the Northern Kingdom (II Kings 5:2). Only from the Second Temple period onward, however, was the term used to denote the Promised Land. It was the official Hebrew designation of the area governed by the British mandate in Palestine after World War I until 1948.

EREV RAV. A mixture of people from various nations who joined the Children of Israel during the Exodus from Egypt.

Glossary

ERUV. Lit., "mixture." Ritual enclosure of a geographic area that permits residents of the area to carry certain objects on the Sabbath without violating rabbinic prohibitions. The enclosure is often created by stringing a wire around posts throughout an area to render the area a single domain in Jewish law.

ETROG. Citron. One of the Four Species that the Torah requires the Jew to hold in his hand on the Festival of Sukkot.

FOUR SPECIES. The four articles of plant life that a Jew is commanded to hold in his hand on the Festival of Sukkot, consisting of a branch of the date palm, a citron, willow branches, and myrtle branches.

GALUT. Exile. Dispersion of Jews from the Land of Israel.

GALUT EDOM. Exile of the Jews from the Land of Israel by the Romans. The exile began in 70 C.E. after the destruction of the Second Temple.

GAN EDEN. Garden of Eden.

GEDOLEI TORAH. Rabbinic leaders. Outstanding Torah scholars.

GEMARA. Aramaic for "completion" or "tradition." This term is popularly applied to the Talmud as a whole, or more particularly to the discussions and elaborations by the *Amoraim* on the Mishnah.

GEMATRIA. Exegetical method by which a word or phrase is associated with another word or phrase with the same numerical value.

GERUT. Conversion. Also refers to living in a foreign land.

GET. A divorce document in Jewish law that the husband must present to his wife to effect the divorce.

GE'ULLAH. Redemption.

GEVURAH. Strength. One of the ten *Sefirot*.

HA-BA LE-HORGEKHA, HASHKEM VE-HORGO. If someone comes to kill you, kill him first.

HAFTARAH, (PL.) HAFTAROT. Selection from the Prophets that is read in the synagogue after the Torah reading on the Sabbath and the Festivals. The theme of the selection is usually related to the Torah reading that precedes it.

HAGGADAH. Lit., "the telling." Book recited at the Passover Seder containing passages regarding the Exodus from Egypt. The reading of the Haggadah is based on the verse "You shall tell your son on that day, 'It is because of what the Lord did for me when I came forth from Egypt'" (Exodus 13:8).

Glossary

ḤAGIGAH. Type of sacrifice required to be brought on the Three Festivals. A special sacrifice of the *ḥagigah* was brought on the eve of Passover and was served before the paschal lamb was eaten so that the paschal lamb would be eaten in state of satiation.

HAKKARAT HA-ḤET. Acknowledgment of sin.

HAKKARAT HA-TOV. Gratitude.

HALAKHAH. Jewish law.

HALLEL. Praise. Recitation of Psalms 113 through 118 during the morning service on the first two days of Passover, Sukkot, Shavuot, and Hanukkah. On Rosh Ḥodesh and the last six days of Passover, Psalms 115:1–11 and 116:1–11 are omitted from the prayer.

ḤAMAS. Theft of less than a penny's worth. This sin sealed the fate of the Generation of the Flood.

ḤARON. Anger.

HASHGAḤAH PERATIT. Divine supervision of the individual.

HASHKAFAH. Outlook.

ḤASIDUT. Piety.

HASSAGAT GEVUL. Lit., "removal of boundary." Trespass on economic, commercial, or incorporeal rights.

ḤATAN. Bridegroom.

HATZALAH. Rescue. Also the name of an emergency medical service operating in Jewish communities around the world.

HATZLAḤAH. Success.

HATZLAḤAH RABBAH. Good luck.

ḤAZAN. Cantor.

HEH. Fifth letter of the Hebrew alphabet.

ḤELBBENAH. An herb with a putrid smell. One of the ingredients of the *ketoret*.

ḤEREV. Sword.

ḤESED. Kindness.

ḤESED SHEL EMET. True kindness. Kindness for which the person performing the kindness has no hope of recompense from the recipient.

HESEḤ HA-DA'AT. Lit., "removal of thought." Inattentiveness.

HESTER PANIM. Lit., "hiding of the face." Hidden nature of God's governance. May be a manifestation of divine judgment in response to sin or a test of worthiness.

Glossary

HILLUL HA-SHEM. Lit., "disgrace of the Name." Refers to an action that brings dishonor and disgrace to God.

HINNUKH. Religious training.

HOK, (PL.) HUKKIM. Divine decree for which the explanation is beyond human comprehension.

HOL. Secular matters.

HORA'AT SHA'AH. Extraordinary procedure outside the framework of the law in cases of emergency.

HOSHANOT. Poetic prayers recited on Sukkot during *hakkafot* (circuits) around the synagogue.

HUKKIM. See "Hok."

HURBAN. Lit., "destruction." Typically refers to the destruction of the First and Second Temples.

IR NIDAHAT. Condemned city. A Jewish city required to be destroyed as a result of its citizens having become idolators. No case of such a city has occurred.

ISHUT. Laws relating to personal status, such as marriage and divorce.

ITZAVON. Distress.

KADOSH. Holy.

KAL VE-HOMER. *A fortiori.*

KALLAH. Bride.

KANFEI NESHARIM. Lit., "wings of eagles." A description of the manner in which Hashem took the Children of Israel out of Egypt at Exodus 19:4 ("You have seen what I did to the Egyptians, and how I bore you on the wings of eagles, and brought you to Myself.").

KAPITEL. Yiddish for "chapter."

KAPORET. Cover of the Ark.

KASHRUT. Jewish religious dietary laws.

KAVOD. Honor.

KAVVANAH. Intention; concentration, particularly on the meaning of the words uttered during prayer.

KEDUSHAH. Holiness. Also the name of the third section of the *Shemoneh Esrei*.

KELEV. Dog.

KEREN. Horn.

KESHET. Bow.

KETORET. A mixture of aromatic herbs burnt twice daily on the Golden Altar in the Temple and as part of the ritual performed by the High Priest in the Holy of Holies on Yom Kippur.

KETUBBAH. A woman's marriage contract in Jewish law.

KEVOD HA-TORAH. Honor of the Torah.

KIBBUD AV VE-EM. Honoring one's father and mother.

KIDDUSH. Lit., "sanctification." A blessing recited over wine or grape juice to sanctify the Sabbath and Jewish holidays. The term is also used to refer to a reception held in the synagogue or a congregant's home after the morning Sabbath or holiday prayers where the blessing over wine is recited and refreshments are served.

KIDDUSH HA-SHEM. Lit., "sanctification of the Name." An observable and noble action that brings glorification to God.

KIN'AT SOFERIM TARBEH ḤOKHMAH. Lit., "jealousy between scribes increases wisdom." This dictum serves as a basis for allowing free entry of new teachers into a religious elementary school system.

KIPPAH. Skullcap. Also known as a "yarmulke."

KLAL. Community.

KODESH. Holy matters.

KOHEN. Priest. Principal functionary in the divine services. The special task of the Priests was to engage in rituals conducted mainly in the Temple. The post of the Priests is authorized by hereditary right, and they constitute a distinct class separate from the rest of the Jewish people.

KOL HA-MOSIF GORE'A. If one adds to the prescriptions of the Torah, it is considered as if he diminished them.

KOLLEL, (PL.) KOLLELIM. An institute of full-time, advanced study of the Talmud and rabbinic literature.

KORBAN, (PL.) KARBANOT. Sacrificial offerings prescribed by the Torah. The sacrifices were offered in the Tabernacle and the Temple at the hands of the Priests.

KORBAN PESAḤ. Paschal offering.

KULLAM ḤAYYAV PATUR. Judicial rule that if a Sanhedrin opens a capital case with a unanimous guilty verdict (*kullam ḥayyav*), the accused is exempt (*patur*) until some merit is found to acquit him.

LEḤEM AVIRIM. Lit., "bread of angels." The manna.

Glossary

LEKKET. Gleanings. Biblical commandment at Leviticus 19:9 that if one or two stalks of grain slip out of the reaper's hand while harvesting them, they must be left to the poor. If three stalks fall together, the owner may retrieve them.

LIFNIM MI-SHURAT HA-DIN. Beyond the letter of the law.

LO TAḤMOD. Thou shall not covet. The Tenth Commandment (Exodus 20:14). The prohibition is violated by pressuring another individual to sell a possession of his against his will.

LOMDISHE. Yiddish for "learned." Characterized by intricate and scholarly reasoning.

LOG, (PL.) LUGGIM. A liquid measure equal to the volume of six eggs.

LUGGIM. See "*Log*."

MA'AMAD HAR SINAI. Lit., "the standing at Mount Sinai." Divine revelation to the Children of Israel at Mount Sinai and the receiving of the Torah.

MA'ARIV. Evening prayer.

MA'ASEH AVOT SIMAN LE-BANIM. The life experience of the Patriarchs is indicative of the further course of Jewish destiny.

MAFTIR. The last verses of the weekly Sabbath and festival reading from the Torah. On a regular Sabbath, the last few verses of the weekly portion are repeated as the *maftir*. On special Sabbaths and the Festivals, the *maftir* is taken from a passage relevant to that particular day and is read from a second Torah scroll.

MAGGID. Itinerant preacher and skilled narrator of Torah and religious stories. Also refers to the portion of the Haggadah in which the story of the Exodus from Egypt is recounted.

MALBIM PENEI ḤAVERO BE-RABBIM. Lit., "whitening the face of his friend in public." Embarrassing someone in public. The Talmud relates that such an act is akin to murder.

MALKHUT SHAMAYIM. Kingdom of Heaven.

MAMZER, (PL.) MAMZERIM. Offspring of certain illicit relationships that are punishable by *karet* or capital punishment.

MAROR. Bitter herbs.

MASHIAḤ. Messiah.

MATTAN TORAH. The giving of the Torah to the Children of Israel on Mount Sinai.

Glossary

MEGILLAH. Lit., "scroll." Most commonly refers to the Book of Esther, one of the Five Scrolls, but may refer to one of the other four scrolls. The Five Scrolls are a portion of the Hagiographa, each of which is read publicly on a different festival during the year. The other four scrolls are: Song of Songs; Ruth; Lamentations; and Ecclesiastes.

MELAKHOT. Lit., "activities." Typically refers to the thirty-nine categories of creative labor that were performed in the construction of the Tabernacle and that are prohibited on the Sabbath.

MELAMMED TINNOKOT. Teacher of Torah to children.

MESIRUT NEFESH. Self-sacrifice.

MIDDAH KE-NEGED MIDDAH. Measure for measure. Retributive justice.

MIDRASH. Hebrew designation of a particular genre of rabbinic literature consisting mainly of exegesis of specific books of the Bible.

MILAH. Circumcision.

MILḤEMET MITZVAH. Obligatory war.

MINHAG. Custom.

MINḤAH. The afternoon prayer.

MINYAN. A quorum of ten men necessary for public synagogue services and certain other religious ceremonies.

MIRMAH. Outward boundary of permissible shrewdness.

MISHNAH. Designates the collection of rabbinic traditions redacted by R. Judah ha-Nasi at the beginning of the 3rd century. The purpose of the Mishnah is to elaborate, systematize, and concretize the commandments of the Torah.

MISHNEH TORAH. Lit., "repetition of the Torah." A name for the Book of Deuteronomy. Also a name for the code of Maimonides.

MISHPATIM. Law governing interpersonal conduct.

MITKABBED BE-KALON SHEL ḤAVERO. Elevating oneself at the expense of another person's degradation. A person who acts in such a manner is said to lose his share in the World to Come.

MITZVAH, (PL.) MITZVOT. A religious act or duty. The Bible contains 613 commandments, consisting of 248 positive commandments and 365 negative commandments.

MITZVAT ASEH. Positive biblical commandment. There are a total of 248 positive biblical commandments.

Glossary

MITZVAT ASEH SHE-HA-ZEMAN GERAMA. A positive time-bound commandment.

MUSAF. Lit., "supplement." Additional sacrifice prescribed for the Sabbath and the Festivals. In the liturgy, it is the name for the additional prayer recited on the Sabbath, Rosh Ḥodesh, the Three Festivals, and Yom Kippur after *Shaḥarit*.

MUSAR. Jewish ethics or moral philosophy.

NAḤALAT HASHEM. Lit., "possession of God." The Chosen Nation.

NAḤAT. Proud pleasure or satisfaction, particularly from the achievements of a child.

NASHIM TZIDKANIYYOT. Righteous women.

NE'ELAV. One who bears insults.

NEVUAH. Prophecy.

OLAH. Burnt offering. An offering that is entirely consumed by the Altar fire.

OLAH TEMIMAH. Lit., "a perfect burnt-offering." The term is used to describe Isaac.

OLAM HA-BA. The World to Come.

ONEG. Enjoyment. Refers to the mitzvah to enjoy the Sabbath.

PARASHAH, (PL.) PARSHIYYOT. Lit., "portion." Selection of a biblical book.

PARASHAN. One who explains the plain meaning of a text.

PARDES. Lit., "orchard." An acronym for *peshat, remez, derash,* and *sod. Peshat* is the literal interpretation of a verse; *remez* (lit., "hint") is a veiled reference, such as *gematria; derash* is homiletical interpretation; and *sod* (lit., "secret") is a mystical interpretation.

PAROKHET. Curtain of the Sanctuary that marked the division between the Holy and the Holy of the Holies.

PESAḤ. Passover.

PESHAT. Literal interpretation of a verse.

PITAM. Portion of an *etrog* that protrudes from the side opposite the one that connects the fruit to the tree.

PO'EL NE'EMAN. Faithful worker.

POSEK, (PL.) POSEKIM. A rabbinic scholar who renders practical halakhic decisions.

Glossary

RABBANUT HA-RASHIT. Chief Rabbinate of the State of Israel. The supreme rabbinic authority for Jewish law in the State of Israel, consisting of one Ashkenazi Chief Rabbi and one Sephardi Chief Rabbi, known as the *Rishon le-Tziyyon*.

RABBEINU. Our teacher.

RASHA. Wicked person.

RAV. Rabbi.

RAV HA-HOVEL. Captain of a ship.

REBBE. Religious teacher.

REMEZ. Lit., "hint." Veiled reference.

RIBBIT. The prohibition against charging or receiving interest on a loan between Jews.

RIBBONO SHEL OLAM. Master of the Universe.

RISHONIM. Early rabbinic authorities. The period of the *Rishonim* extended from the middle of the 11th century to the middle of the 15th century.

RODEF, (PL.) RODEFIM. Lit., "pursuer." According to Jewish law, if *A* pursues *B* with the manifest intent to kill him, everybody is under a duty to rescue *B*, even by means of killing *A*, if no lesser means are available to neutralize *A*.

ROSH HODESH. The first day of a Jewish month. Considered a minor Jewish festival on which fasting is prohibited but work may be done.

ROSH MESIVTA. Head of a Jewish high school for boys. Often abbreviated as *R"M* (pronounced "RoM").

SANHEDRIN. Assembly of ordained scholars that functioned both as the Supreme Court and Legislature before 70 C.E.

SEDER. Lit., "order." Ritual ceremony held on the night of Passover involving the recitation of the Haggadah.

SEFER TORAH. Torah scroll.

SEFIRAT HA-OMER. Counting of the forty-nine days between Passover and Shavuot, as prescribed at Leviticus 23:15-16.

SEFIROT. Ten creative forces that intervene between the infinite, unknowable God and our created world, as taught by the Kabbalah. The *Sefirot* are: *keter* (crown); *hokhmah* (wisdom); *binah* (understanding); *hesed* (loving-kindness); *gevurah* (power);

Glossary

tiferet (beauty); *netzaḥ* (eternity); *hod* (splendor); *yesod* (foundation); and *malkhut* (sovereignty).

SELIḤOT. Prayers for pardon recited a few days before Rosh Ha-Shanah and during the days between Rosh Ha-Shanah and Yom Kippur.

SHABBAT SHIRAH. The Sabbath when *Parashat Be-Shallah* (Exodus 13:17–17:6) is read, which contains the Song of the Sea of Reeds.

SHAHARIT. Morning prayer.

SHAKKAI. One of the names of God. Explained as a contraction of *she-amar le-olam dai*, that Hashem said to the world "enough"; *she-yesh dai*, there is enough in Hashem's divinity for every creature; or *she-dai be-virkhosav*, that Hashem's blessings are sufficient for those who are blessed by Him.

SHALOM. Peace.

SHEHITAH. Ritual slaughter.

SHEMA. Lit., "hear." Refers to the passage at Deuteronomy 6:4, "Hear, O Israel: The Lord is our God, the Lord is One." The term is used more generally to refer to the entire portion of the daily prayers that consist of Deuteronomy 6:4–9, Deuteronomy 11:13–21, and Numbers 15:37–41.

SHEMA YIGROM HA-ḤET. Lit., "lest some sin cause." Concern of the Patriarchs that perhaps some sin would cause Hashem's promises to them not to be fulfilled.

SHEMONEH ESREI. Jewish prayer recited in the morning, afternoon, and evening services. Also referred to as the *Amidah*, the "standing prayer." The weekday formulation of the prayer consists of nineteen blessings, although it originally had eighteen. For the Sabbath and festivals, the middle thirteen blessings are replaced with blessings specific to the occasion.

SHERATZIM. Animals that slither along the ground or appear to do so because they have short legs and their movement is not readily noticeable.

SHIDDUKHIM. Marriage matches.

SHIRAH. Song. A triumphant hymn in praise of Hashem, such as the Song at the Sea of Reeds.

Glossary

SHIRAT DEVORAH. Song of Deborah. Victory hymn at Judges 5:2–31 sung by Deborah and Barak upon the defeat of Sisera.

SHIRAT MOSHEH. Song of Moses. Exuberant hymn of triumph and gratitude, at Exodus 15:1–18, sung by Moses and the Children of Israel after crossing the Sea of Reeds and witnessing the drowning of the Egyptians.

SHOFAR. Ram's horn sounded for memorial blowing on Rosh Ha-Shanah and other occasions.

SHUL. Synagogue.

SIDDUR. Prayer book.

SIDRAH. Weekly Torah portion.

SIN'AT ḤINNAM. Baseless hatred.

SOD. Lit., "secret." Mystical interpretation.

SUKKAH. Temporary dwelling that the Torah instructs Jews to dwell in for the seven days of the Festival of Sukkot.

TAḤANUN. Supplication. Petition for grace and forgiveness recited daily after the morning and afternoon *Shemoneh Esrei*, except on the Sabbath, Festivals, days of joy, and Tish'ah be-Av, and in a house of mourning during the week of mourning. Also called *"nefilat appayim"* (falling on the face).

TALMID ḤAKHAM. Rabbinic scholar.

TALMUD. The record of discussions of scholars on the laws and teachings of the Mishnah. The Talmud consists of the Babylonian Talmud, codified in ca. 500 C.E., and the Palestinian Talmud, codified in ca. 400 C.E.

TALMUD TORAH. Learning of Torah.

TAMIM. Pure.

TANNA. Aramaic *teni*, "hand down orally." The term designates a teacher dating from the Mishnaic times. The *Tannaic* period covers five generations of rabbinic authorities, spanning from 20 to 200 C.E.

TEFAḤ, (PL.) TEFAḤIM. Lit., "a handbreadth." A measure of length equal to the width of four thumbs.

TEFILLAH. Prayer.

TEFILLIN. Phylacteries. Two cube-shaped black leather boxes containing four biblical passages written by hand on parchment. The

Glossary

boxes are worn during the morning services. One box is worn on the head and the other on the arm, with leather straps affixed to the boxes for attaching the boxes to the head and the arm.

TEFILLIN SHEL ROSH. Phylacteries worn on the head. These phylacteries are constructed with four separate compartments, one for each of the four biblical passages that are required to be placed inside the phylacteries.

TEFILLIN SHEL YAD. Phylacteries worn on the hand. These phylacteries contain one compartment in which a single piece of parchment containing four biblical passages is placed.

TEHIYYAT HA-METIM. Resurrection of the dead.

TESHUVAH. Repentance.

TIFERET. Beauty. One of the ten *Sefirot*.

TIKKUN OLAM. Lit., "repair of the world." Improving the welfare of society.

TINNOKOT SHEL BEIT RABBAN. School children.

TODAH. Thanksgiving. A type of peace-offering brought by an individual in the time of the Temple to express gratitude to Hashem.

TOHU VA-VOHU. Nothingness. Refers to the condition of the earth before Hashem created the world, as described at Genesis 1:2. In the rabbinic literature, refers to the first two millennia of history, before Abraham began to spread the message of Torah.

TORAH. Lit., "instruction." Refers to the Bible as a whole.

TORAH LE-SHEMAH. Learning Torah for the sake of learning Torah.

TOSAFOT. French commentators on the Talmud who lived during the 12th to 14th centuries.

TUMAT LEDAH. State of ritual impurity of a woman as a result of childbirth.

TZADDIK. Righteous person.

TZANUAH. Modest woman.

TZAYID BE-PIV. Lit., "trapping was in his mouth." According to the Midrash, the phrase refers to Esau's deception of Isaac through his words, such as by asking Isaac whether one is obligated to tithe salt or straw.

TZEDAKAH. Charity.

Glossary

TZELEM ELOKIM. Lit., "image of God." Refers to the idea that all people are created in the image of God and thus have tremendous potential for righteousness.

TZENIUT. Modesty.

TZIBBUR. The collective; community.

TZITZIT. Knotted ritual fringes attached to the four corners of a *tallit*, in accordance with the biblical mandate at Numbers 15:38 and Deuteronomy 22:12.

URIM VE-THUMMIM. The oracles in the breastplate of the High Priest.

YESHIVAH, (PL.) YESHIVOT. Institutes of Talmudic learning.

YIBBUM. Levirate marriage. Biblical requirement at Deuteronomy 25:5-10 that if a man died without children, his brother is obligated to marry his widow.

YIR'AT SHAMAYIM. Fear of Heaven.

YOM TOV. Generic term for a Jewish holiday; a day of festival on which certain activities are prohibited.

YOSHEV OHALIM. Abiding in tents. Biblical description of Jacob, alluding to his learning of Torah in the tents of Shem and Eber.

YOTZE. Fulfilled one's religious obligation.

YUD. Tenth letter of the Hebrew alphabet.

Bibliography

Aaron b. Jacob ha-Kohen of Lunel, R. *Orḥot Ḥayyim*.
Aaron b. Joseph ha-Levi, R. *Sefer ha-Ḥinnukh*. Edited by R. Yitzhak Yeshayah Weiss, R. David Zicherman, and R. Yitzhak Weinstein. Jerusalem: Makhon Yerushalayim, 1992.
Aaron, David. "Verification: Will It Work?" *New York Times*, October 11, 1987, A37.
Abrabanel, R. Isaac b. Judah. Commentary on the Torah.
Abudirham, R. David b. Joseph. *Sefer Abudraham*.
Abulafia, R. Meir b. Todros ha-Levi. *Yad Ramah*.
Adler, R. Shlomo. "Keri'at Shem Yissachar ba-Torah." *Ha-Ma'ayan* 7 (Hebrew) (Jerusalem, 1967): 19–20.
Adler, Stephen J. *The Jury: Trial and Error in the American Courtroom*. New York: Times Books, 1994.
Ahai Gaon, R. *She'iltot de-Rav Aḥai Gaon*.
Al-Batzravi, R. Shelomoh. *Devar Shelomoh: Perush le-Sefer Bereshit*. Tel Aviv, 1932.
Al-Hakam, R. Joseph Hayyim b. Elijah. *Rav Pe'alim*.
Alfasi, R. Isaac b. Jacob. *Rif* to *Bava Metzia*.
Alkabetz, R. Solomon b. Moses ha-Levi. *Manot ha-Levi*.
Alshekh, R. Moses. *Marot ha-Tzove'ot*. Commentary on the Early and Later Prophets.
———. *Torat Mosheh*. Commentary on the Pentateuch.
Alter, R. Yehudah Aryeh Leib. *Sefat Emet*. Commentary on the Torah.
Altschuler, R. Jehiel Hillel b. David. *Metzudat David*.
———. *Metzudat Tziyyon*.
Apple, Jr., R. W. "Confrontation in the Gulf; U.S. Says Its Troops in the Gulf Could Reach 100,000 in Months." *New York Times*, August 11, 1990, A1.
Arama, R. Isaac b. Moses. *Akedat Yitzḥak*.

Bibliography

Arrow, Kenneth J. "A Difficulty in the Concept of Social Welfare." *Journal of Political Economy* 58, no. 4 (August 1950): 328–346.

Asher b. Jehiel, R. *Rosh* to *Bava Batra; Bava Metzia; Shevuot.*

———. *Tosafot ha-Rosh. Sotah.*

Ashkenazi, R. Samuel Jaffe. *Yefeh To'ar* on *Midrash Rabbah.*

Auerbach, R. Shlomo Zalman. "*Beirurim u-Sefeikot be-Inyan Piku'ah Nefesh Doheh Shabbat.*" Moriah: Yarhon Torani le-Divrei Halakhah u-Mahshavah, *shanah* 3:3–4 (Sivan/Tamuz 5731/1971): 10–36.

Azulai, R. Hayyim Joseph David. *Kaf Ahat.*

Ba'al ha-Turim. Commentary on the Torah.

Bahya b. Asher, R. *Rabbeinu Behaye al ha-Torah.*

———. *Midrash Rabbeinu Behaye al Hamishah Humshei Torah.*

Bar-Illan, David. "What PLO Tells Faithful, Not What It Says to U.S., Shows Folly of Recognition." *Los Angeles Times*, December 22, 1988, M7.

Bass, R. Shabbetai b. Joseph. *Siftei Hakhamim* to *Rashi.*

Bazyler, Michael J. *Holocaust Justice: The Battle for Restitution in America's Courts.* New York: New York University Press, 2003.

Becker, Jillian. *The PLO: The Rise and Fall of the Palestine Liberation Organization.* New York: St. Martin's Press, 1984.

Berlin, R. Naphtali Tzvi Yehudah. *Ha'amek Davar.*

———. *Rinah shel Torah* on Song of Songs.

Berman, Mark A. "Kosher Fraud Statutes and the Establishment Clause: Are They Kosher?" *Columbia Journal of Law and Social Problems* 26, no. 1 (Autumn 1992): 1–76.

Besdin, R. Abraham R. *Reflections of the Rav: Lessons in Jewish Thought.* Jerusalem: World Zionist Organization, 1979.

Bierman, John. *Righteous Gentile: The Story of Raoul Wallenberg, Missing Hero of the Holocaust.* Harmondsworth: Penguin Books, 1982.

Bleich, R. J. David. "Religious Experience? Tefillah be-Tzibbur?" *Sh'ma: A Journal of Jewish Responsibility* (October 18, 1985): 146–150.

Bornsztain, R. Shmuel. *Shem mi-Shemuel: Al Seder Parshiyyot ha-Torah u-Mo'adei Kodesh.* 9th ed. 6 vols. Jerusalem, 1992.

Boyer, Paul. *By the Bomb's Early Light: American Thought and Culture at the Dawn of the Atomic Age.* New York: Pantheon, 1985.

Brands, H. W. "George Bush and the Gulf War of 1991." *Presidential Studies Quarterly* 34, no. 1 (March 2004): 113–131.

Brilliant, Joshua. "Glider Raid Warning Ignored; IDF Probes Lapses That Cost Six Lives." *Jerusalem Post*, December 5, 1987, 1.

Broder, Jonathan. "Egypt Demands U.S. Apology; Mubarak Seeks to Calm Angry Mood of Nation." *Chicago Tribune*, October 15, 1985, 1.

Bibliography

Brown, Dr. Josephine M. "The United Nations Today." *Women Lawyers Journal* 70, no. 3 (Spring 1984): 16–22.

Browning, Robert. "Rabbi ben Ezra."

Buder, Leonard. "15-Year-Old Boy Is Indicted as Adult in Synagogue Fire." *New York Times*, October 4, 1988, B3.

Budge, E. A. Wallis. *A History of Egypt from the End of the Neolithic Period to the Death of Cleopatra VII B.C. 30*. Vol. 7. London: Kegan Paul, 1902.

Bunim, Amos. *A Fire in His Soul*. Jerusalem: Feldheim, 1989.

Bunsen, Matthew. *Encyclopedia of the Roman Empire*. Rev. ed. New York: Facts on File, 2002.

Bush, George H. W. "Address Accepting the Presidential Nomination at the Republican National Convention in New Orleans." August 18, 1988.

———. "Address on Administration Goals before a Joint Session of Congress" (February 9, 1989), 1989-1 Pub. Papers 74.

———. Building a Better America (1989) (supplement to the President's Message to the Joint Session of Congress, February 9, 1989). Reprinted in H.R. Doc. No. 101–26, 101st Cong., 1st Sess. 101 (1989).

———. Letter to Congregation Kesher Israel (1990).

———. State of the Union Address, January 29, 1991. Reprinted in *New York Times*, January 30, 1991, A12.

Caine, Burton. Letter to the Editor. *New York Times*, February 5, 1989, E24.

Carmy, R. Shalom. "Destiny, Freedom, and the Logic of Petition." *Tradition: A Journal of Orthodox Thought* 24, no. 2 (Winter 1989): 17–37.

Caro, R. Joseph. *Avkat Rokhel*.

———. *Shulḥan Arukh*.

Chajes, R. Zevi Hirsch. *Maharatz Ḥayot*. Commentary on Talmud.

Chapman, Steve. "Overlooking Brutality; A Torturous Dilemma for Israel." *Chicago Tribune*, September 9, 1999, 21.

Clairborne, William. "New Scud Missile Attack Deepens Fears of Israelis." *Washington Post*, January 19, 1991, A1.

Cohen, R. Dovid. *Ohel David*. Vol. 2. Brooklyn, NY: Mesorah, 1987.

Collins, Nina L. *The Library in Alexandria and the Bible in Greek*. Leiden: Brill, 2000.

Colon b. Solomon Trabotto, R. Joseph. *She'elot u-Teshuvot ha-Maharik*.

Congressional Quarterly Inc. *Watergate: Chronology of a Crisis*. Edited by William B. Dickinson, Jr., 1973.

Crawford, J. Craig. "Why Doesn't U.S. Just Assassinate Saddam Hussein." *Seattle Times*, August 20, 1990, A1.

Culi, R. Jacob. *Me-Am Lo'ez*. Translated by R. Shemuel Yerushalmi. *Yalkut Me-Am Lo'ez: Sefer Bereshit*. Jerusalem: Mossad Yad Ezra, 1968.

Bibliography

———. *Me-Am Lo'ez*. Translated by R. Shemuel Yerushalmi. *Yalkut Me-Am Lo'ez: Sefer Shemot*. Jerusalem: Wagshal, 1968.

———. *Me-Am Lo'ez*. Translated by R. Shemuel Yerushalmi. *Yalkut Me-Am Lo'ez: Sefer Be-Midbar*. Jerusalem: Wagshal, 1969.

———. *Me-Am Lo'ez*. Translated by R. Shemuel Yerushalmi. *Yalkut Me-Am Lo'ez. Judges*. Jerusalem: Wagshal, 1974.

Cummins, Ken. "Declining Influence: America's Failure to Act in the U.N." *South Florida Sun-Sentinel*, November 10, 1985, 1.G.

Czerniak, R. Shalom Shachna. *Ḥayyim u-Verakhah: Arba'at Minim*.

Da'at Zekenim. Commentary on the Torah.

Danzig, R. Abraham. *Ḥokhmat Adam*.

Davies, Paul. *Superforce*. New York: Simon & Schuster, 1985.

Davis, Helen. "New Optimism on Fate of Wallenberg." *Jewish Week*, October 20, 1989, 19.

de Uçeda, R. Samuel b. Isaac. *Midrash Shemuel*, reprinted in R. Ezra Batzri, ed., *Midrash Shemuel: Otzar Perushim al Pirkei Avot*. Jerusalem: Haktav Institute, 2001.

Department of Economic Affairs, Statistical Office of the United Nations. *Demographic Yearbook, 1949–1950*. New York, 1950.

Derekh Eretz Rabbah.

Derekh Eretz Zuta.

Dessler, R. Eliyahu Eliezer. *Mikhtav me-Eliyahu*. Edited by R. Aryeh Carmell and R. Alter Halperin. 3 vols. Benei Berak: Hever Talmidav, 1964.

Diskin, R. Moses Joshua Judah Leib. *Ḥiddushei Maharil Diskin al ha-Torah*.

Dole, Stephen B. *Habitable Planets for Man*. New York: Blaisdell, 1964.

Draper, Theodore. *A Very Thin Line: The Iran-Contra Affairs*. New York: Hill & Wang, 1991.

Drummond, William J. "13 Die in Jerusalem Terrorist Bombing; 46 Hospitalized in Explosion, Fire: PLO Claims Responsibility for Attack." *Los Angeles Times*, July 5, 1979, A1.

Edels, R. Samuel Eliezer b. Judah ha-Levi. *Ḥiddushei Halakhot ve-Aggadot*.

Eider, R. Shimon D. *Halachos of Pesach*. Jerusalem: Feldheim, 1998.

Einhorn, R. Zev Wolf. *Perush Maharzu* on *Midrash Rabbah*.

Eliezer b. Samuel of Metz, R. *Sefer Yere'im*.

Elijah b. Solomon Zalman, R. *Be'ur ha-Gra* to *Shulḥan Arukh*.

———. *Kol Eliyahu*.

Emden, R. Jacob. *Haggahot ha-Ya'avetz*.

Emery, Fred. *Watergate: The Corruption of American Politics and the Fall of Richard Nixon*. New York: Touchstone, 1995.

Engel, R. Joseph. *Tziyyunim la-Torah*. Piotrków, 1904.

Enoch Zundel b. Joseph, R. *Etz Yosef* to *Midrash Rabbah*.

Bibliography

Epstein, R. Baruch ha-Levi. *Barukh She-Amar: Le-Tefillot ha-Ḥol.* Tel Aviv: Am Olam, 1965.
Epstein, R. Jehiel Michal. *Arukh ha-Shulḥan.*
Epstein, R. Kalonymus Kalman ha-Levi. *Ma'or va-Shemesh.* Brooklyn, NY: Imrei Shefer, 2008.
Epstein, R. Moses Mordecai. *She'elot u-Teshuvot Levush Mordekhai.*
Ettinger, R. Joseph ha-Levi. *Edut bi-Yosef.*
Ezekiel Feivel b. Zev Wolf, R. *Maharif.* Commentary on *Midrash Rabbah.*
Falcoff, Mark. "Head Hunting: Assassination as a Policy." *National Interest* 24 (Summer 1991): 103–105.
Falk, R. Joshua b. Alexander ha-Kohen. *Perishah* to *Tur.*
Fein, Esther B. "Angry Citizens in Many Cities Supporting Goetz." *New York Times,* January 7, 1985, B1.
Feinstein, R. Mosheh. *Derash Mosheh: Ḥiddushei Aggadah al ha-Torah.* Benei Berak, 1988.
———. *Iggerot Mosheh.*
Fisher, Louis. "Nonjudicial Safeguards for Religious Liberty." *University of Cincinnati Law Review* 70 (2001): 31–94.
Fraenkel, R. David b. Naphtali Hirsch. *Korban ha-Edah* to Palestinian Talmud.
Freedman, Lawrence and Efraim Karsh. *The Gulf Conflict 1990–1991: Diplomacy and War in the New World Order.* Princeton, NJ: Princeton University Press, 1993.
Friedman, Thomas L. "Israeli Army Assailed Over Glider Raid." *New York Times,* November 28, 1987, A3.
———. "Syria-Based Group Says It Staged Israel Raid." *New York Times,* November 27, 1987, A1.
Frimer, Aryeh A. and Dov I. Frimer. "Women's Prayer Services—Theory and Practice." *Tradition: A Journal of Orthodox Thought* 32, no. 2 (Winter 1998): 5–118.
Gerondi, R. Jonah b. Abraham. *Rabbeinu Yonah.* Commentary to Mishnah and Talmud.
Gerondi, R. Nissim b. Reuben. *Ḥiddushei ha-Ran.*
Gifter, R. Mordechai. *Pirkei Torah.* Vol. 1. Wickliffe, OH, 1992.
Ginzberg, Louis, ed. *Ginzei Schechter.* Vol. 1. New York: Beit Midrash ha-Rabbanim ba-Amerika, 1928.
Glick, Shimon M. "A Humane Alternative to National Suicide." *Jerusalem Post International Edition.* October 24, 1987, 9.
Goldberg, Carey. "Family Search for Wallenberg Turns to Soviet Prison Records." *Jewish Week,* October 27, 1989, 21.
Gombiner, R. Abraham Abele b. Hayyim ha-Levi. *Magen Avraham* to *Shulḥan Arukh.*
Goshko, John M. and David B. Ottaway. "U.S. Reassures Israel, Sets Talks with PLO; Reagan Says 'We Have Not Retreated' from Ally." *Washington Post,* December 16, 1988, A1.

Greenberg, R. Aharon Yaakov. *Iturei Torah: Likkut, Nisaḥ u-Biur*. 6 vols. Tel Aviv: Yavneh, 1967–1970.
Greenberg, Joel. "It Depends on What's 'Non-Violence.'" *Jerusalem Post*, November 27, 1987, 8.
Grieco, Joseph, G. John Ikenberry and Michael Mastanduno. *Introduction to International Relations: Enduring Questions & Contemporary Perspectives*. London: Palgrave, 2015.
Grusman, R. Aharon Yehudah. *She'elot u-Teshuvot Ve-Darashta ve-Ḥakarata*. Jerusalem, 1996.
Gwertzman, Bernard. "Reverberations; The U.S. May Pay a High Price for Its Triumph." *New York Times*, October 20, 1985, A1.
———. "Toward the Summit: Gauging the Outcome; On Road to the Summit: A Parallel to '55." *New York Times*, November 15, 1985, A12.
———. "U.S. Intercepts Jet Carrying Hijackers; Fighters Divert It to NATO Base in Italy; Gunmen Face Trial in Slaying of Hostage." *New York Times*, October 11, 1985, A1.
Haberman, Clyde. "The Iraqi Invasion; Quick Action by Turkey on Sanctions a Startler." *New York Times*, August 8, 1990, A10.
———. "Mideast Accord: The Secret Peace/A Special Report; How Oslo Helped Mold the Mideast Pact." *New York Times*, September 5, 1993, A1.
Hager, R. Hayyim Meir. *Imrei Ḥayyim: Kuntrus ha-Likkutim al ha-Torah u-Moadim*. Tel Aviv: Makhon Zekher Hayyim, 1976.
Halliday, Fred. "The Crisis of the Arab World: The False Answers of Saddam Hussein." *New Left Review* 184 (November–December 1990): 69–74.
Hanson, Christopher. "Missile Accord Has Risks: Moscow Still Leads in Conventional Arms." *Sun Sentinel*, September 19, 1987, 10A.
Haralick, Robert M., Eliyahu Rips, and Matityahu Glazerson. *Torah Codes: A Glimpse into the Infinite*. New York: Mazal & Bracha, 2005.
Hershey, Jr., Robert D. "Industrial Output Declines 1.7% in Latest Indicator of Recession." *New York Times*, December 15, 1990, 1.1.
Hezekiah b. Manoah, R. *Ḥizkuni*. Commentary on the Torah.
Hirsch, R. Samson Raphael. Commentary on the Pentateuch.
Hoffman, Bruce. *Inside Terrorism*. 2nd ed. New York: Columbia University Press, 2006.
Horowitz, R. Isaiah ha-Levi. *Shenei Luḥot ha-Berit ha-Shalem*, vol. 3 (Haifa: Yad Ramah Institute, 2006).
Ibn Attar, R. Hayyim b. Moses. *Or ha-Ḥayyim*. Commentary on the Pentateuch.
Ibn Ezra, Abraham b. Meir. Ibn Ezra. Commentary on the Torah.
Ibn Migash, R. Joseph. *Ri mi-Gash*. Commentary on Talmud.
Ibn Paquda, R. Bahya b. Joseph. *Ḥovot ha-Levavot*.
Isaac b. Joseph of Corbeil, R. *Sefer Mitzvot Katan*.
Ishbilli, R. Yom Tov. *Ḥiddushei ha-Ritva*.

Bibliography

Israel Ministry of Foreign Affairs. Statement by Prime Minister Rabin on the Removal of Hamas Activists, December 20, 1992, Israel Ministry of Foreign Affairs. Vol. 13–14, no. 44 (1992–1994).

Issachar Berman b. Naphtali ha-Kohen, R. *Mattenot Kehunnah.*

Isserles, R. Moses. *Darkhei Mosheh* to *Tur.*

———. *Rema* to *Shulḥan Arukh.*

———. *She'elot u-Teshuvot ha-Rema.*

Jacob b. Asher, R. *Tur. Perush ha-Tur al ha-Torah le-Rav Yaakov ben Ha-Rosh.* Jerusalem: Feldheim, 2006.

Jehiel Michel b. Uzziel, R. *Nezer ha-Kodesh* on *Midrash Rabbah.*

Jerusalem Post. "Mustn't Be Hesitant on Policy, Rabin Says." December 10, 1975, 1.

———. "The PLO Missiles." January 30, 1991, 4.

Jervis, Robert. "Mutual Assured Destruction." *Foreign Policy* 133 (November–December 2002): 40–42.

Jewish Telegraphic Agency. "Israeli Government Stands Firm, Refusing to Let Deportees Return." December 22, 1992.

Jones, Alex S. "Poll Finds Iranian Affair Hurt Credibility of U.S. Journalism." *New York Times,* January 16, 1987, A1.

Josephus, Flavius. *Antiquities of the Jews.*

Joyner, Christopher C. "Sanctions, Compliance and International Law: Reflections of the United Nations' Experience against Iraq." *Virginia Journal of International Law* 32, no. 1 (Fall 1991): 1–46.

Kadi, Leila S. *Basic Political Documents of the Armed Palestinian Resistance.* Beirut: Palestinian Research Center, 1969.

Kagan, R. Israel Meir ha-Kohen. *Mishnah Berurah.*

Kahane, Meir. "Emigration Is the Only Solution." *Judaism* (Fall 1977): 393–404.

Kallah Rabbati.

Kallir, R. Eleazar b. Eleazar. *Ḥavvot Yair.*

Kamenetsky, R. Yaakov. *Emet le-Yaakov: Al Arba'at Ḥelkei ha-Tur ve-ha-Shulḥan Arukh.* Edited by R. Daniel Yehudah Neustadt. Cleveland: Makhon Emet le-Yaakov, 2000.

———. *Emet le-Yaakov: Sefer Iyyunim ba-Mikra al ha-Torah.* 3rd ed. New York, 2007.

Kanievsky, R. Yaakov Yisrael. *Shiurin shel Torah.* Benei Berak, 1990.

Karelitz, R. Abraham Isaiah. *Ḥazon Ish.*

Kasher, R. Menachem Mendel. *Torah Shelemah.* Jerusalem: Beit Torah Shelemah, 1992.

Katz, R. Reuben Hoeshke b. Hoeshke. *Yalkut Re'uveni.*

Katzman, Abner. "Kuwait Leaders-in-Exile Run Vast Financial Empire." *Philadelphia Inquirer,* October 18, 1990, B9.

Kaufman, Tamar. "Berkeley Prof, Known for Civil Rights, Penalizes Jewish Students on Yom Kippur." *Jewish Advocate,* October 26, 1989, 3.

———. "Jewish Grant Piqued Interest of Dalai Lama." *Jewish Week*, October 27, 1989, 28.
Keeley, Michael C. "Deposit Insurance, Risk, and Market Power in Banking." *American Economic Review* 80, no. 5 (December 1990): 1183–1200.
Kimhi, R. David. *Radak*. Commentary on Exodus. Reprinted in *Perush Rabbi David Kimḥi (Radak) al ha-Torah*. Edited by R. Moshe Kamelhar. 3rd ed. Jerusalem: Mossad HaRav Kook, 1982.
———. Commentary on the Prophets.
Kinzer, Stephen. "War in the Gulf: Germany; Kohl Is Sending $165 Million in Humanitarian Aid to Israel." *New York Times*, January 24, 1991, A15.
Kitov, R. Eliyahu. *Sefer ha-Parshiyyot*. Jerusalem: Yad Eliyahu Kitob, 1985.
Klapholtz, R. Yisroel Yaakov. *Otzar Aggadot ha-Torah: Likkutei Aggadot she-Ne'esfu mi-Talmud Bavli vi-Yerushalmi Midrashim ve-Sifrei Rishonim*. Benei Berak: Pe'er ha-Sefer, 1981.
Klarman, Seth A. "Blundering Down Wall Street; How Trading Wisdom for '80s Greed Has Put Us in '90s Trouble." *Washington Post*, November 25, 1990, C3.
Knisbacher, Mitchell. "Aliyah of Soviet Jews: Protection of the Right of Emigration under International Law." *Harvard International Law Journal* 14, no. 1 (1973): 89–110.
Kol Bo.
Kolin, R. Samuel b. Nathan ha-Levi. *Maḥatzit ha-Shekel* to *Magen Avraham*.
Kovetz Peirushei ha-Rishonim al Bereitat Pitum ha-Ketoret. Israel, 2005.
Kramer, Doniel Z. *The Day Schools and Torah Umesorah: The Seeding of Traditional Judaism in America*. New York: Yeshiva University Press, 1984.
Lamm, R. Norman. *Faith and Doubt: Studies in Traditional Jewish Thought*. New York: Ktav, 1971.
Landau, R. Ezekiel b. Judah. *She'elot u-Teshuvot Noda Bi-Yehudah*.
Lefkovits, Etgar. "Meimad Threatens to Leave Coalition over Secular Reform." *Jerusalem Post*, January 22, 2001, 3.
Leithauser, Brad. "Kasparov Beats Deep Thought." *New York Times*, January 14, 1990, A32.
Levine, R. Aaron. *Case Studies in Jewish Business Ethics*. Hoboken, NJ: Ktav, 2000.
———. "Discussion on Milton Friedman, Capitalism and the Jews." In *Morality of the Market: Religious and Economic Perspectives*, edited by Walter Block, Geoffrey Brennan, and Kenneth Elzinga, 446-459. Vancouver, BC: Fraser Institute, 1985.
———. *Economic Morality and Jewish Law*. New York: Oxford University Press, 2012.
———. *Economics and Jewish Law*. Hoboken, NJ: Ktav, 1987.
———. *Moral Issues of the Marketplace in Jewish Law*. Brooklyn, NY: Yashar Books, 2005.

Bibliography

Levine, R. Aharon. *Ha-Derash ve-ha-Iyyun.* Vol. 2. Biłgoraj: N. Kronenberg, 1931.
———. *She'elot u-Teshuvot Avnei Ḥefetz.* Munich: Vaad ha-Hatzalah, 1948.
Lewin, Avrohom Shmuel. "Rabin Blasts Civil Rights Groups for Supporting Terrorists." *Jewish Press*, December 25, 1992, 58.
Lewis, Anthony. "Reagan and the Russians." Abroad at Home. *New York Times*, October 4, 1987, A23.
———. "There Should Be Hope." Abroad at Home. *New York Times*, November 14, 1985, A35.
Liebeskind, Michelle G. Lewis. "Back to Basics for Victims: Striking Son of Sam Laws in Favor of an Amended Restitutionary Scheme." *Annual Survey of American Law* 29 (1994): 29–78.
Linton, Ralph and Adelin Linton. *We Gather Together: The Story of Thanksgiving.* New York: Henry Schuman, 1949.
Lipschutz, R. Israel b. Gedaliah. *Tiferet Yisrael.*
Lockwood, Christopher. "Jordanian Joy at Strike on Israel." *Jerusalem Post*, January 21, 1991, 5.
Loew b. Bezalel, R. Judah. *Gur Aryeh.*
———. *Kitvei Maharal mi-Prague.* Edited by Abraham Kariv. Vol. 1. Jerusalem: Mossad HaRav Kook, 2001.
Long, William and Marjorie Miller. "20,000 Feared Dead in Colombia Eruption; Volcanic Blast Triggers Huge Mudslides." *Los Angeles Times*, November 15, 1985, 1.
Lowy, Joan. "Iraqis Have It Better than US, GI Guards Say." *Pittsburgh Post-Gazette*, February 14, 1991, A11.
Luntshits, R. Ephraim Solomon b. Aaron. *Keli Yakar.* Commentary on the Pentateuch.
Luria, R. Isaac b. Solomon. *Siddur ha-Ari.*
Luria, R. Solomon b. Jehiel. *Yam shel Shelomoh.*
Magida, Arthur J. "The Dalai Lama Listens for Jewish Secrets." *Jewish Week*, October 27, 1989, 28, 42.
Maimonides. Guide of the Perplexed 3:12–13.
———. *Mishneh Torah.*
———. *Perush ha-Mishnayot.*
———. *Sefer ha-Mitzvot.*
Majaess, Daniel J. "Concerning the Distance to the Center of the Milky Way and Its Structure." *Acta Astronomica* 60, no. 1 (March 2010): 55–74.
Marcus, Ralph. "Jewish and Greek Elements in the Septuagint." In *Louis Ginzberg Jubilee Volume: On the Occasion of His Seventieth Birthday*, edited by Alexander Marx, Saul Lieberman, Shalom Spiegel, and Solomon Zeitlin, 227–245. New York: American Academy for Jewish Research, 1945.
Masekhet Soferim.

Mauro, Paulo. "Corruption and Growth." *Quarterly Journal of Economics* 110, no. 3 (1995): 681–712.
McDonough, Frank. *Neville Chamberlain, Appeasement and the British Road to War*. Manchester: Manchester University Press, 1998.
Mecklenburg, R. Yaakov Tzvi. *Ha-Ketav ve-ha-Kabbalah*.
Megillat Ta'anit.
Meir b. Barukh of Rothenburg, R. *Haggahot Maimuniyyot* to *Mishneh Torah*.
Meir Simhah ha-Kohen of Dvinsk, R. *Meshekh Ḥokhmah*.
Meislin, Richard J. "Earthquake Rocks Mexico; Hundreds Are Feared Dead as Buildings Fall and Burn." *New York Times*, September 20, 1985, A1.
———. "President Invites Inquiry Counsel; Poll Rating Dives; 46% Approve Reagan's Work, Down 21 Points." *New York Times*, December 2, 1986, A1.
Mekhilta.
Midrash Aggadah.
Midrash Bereshit Rabbati. Edited by Hanoch Albeck. Jerusalem: Mekitzei Nirdamim, 1940.
Midrash ha-Gadol.
Midrash Rabbah.
Midrash Shoḥer Tov.
Midrash Tanḥuma.
Midrash Tanḥuma ha-Kadum ve-ha-Yashan.
Miller, Judith. "Hijackers Yield Ship in Egypt; Passenger Slain, 400 Are Safe; U.S. Assails Deal with Captors." *New York Times*, October 10, 1985, A1.
———. "Summit Finale: Western Allies Seen Encouraged; Reagan Report Pleases NATO Leaders." *New York Times*, November 22, 1985, A13.
Miller, R. Avigdor. *Career of Happiness: True Joy in the Home*. Brooklyn, NY: Yeshiva Gedolah Bais Yisroel, 2000.
———. "The Ten Commandments of Marriage 1." Thursday Night Audio Lecture No. 620.
Mishnah. *Avot; Berakhot; Ḥallah; Pesaḥim; Sanhedrin; Shevi'it; Sukkah; Uktzin*.
Mizrahi, David Toufic. "If Oil Isn't Important, Who in the Middle East Is?" *Washington Post*, November 3, 1985, C1.
Mizrahi, R. Elijah. *Sefer ha-Mizraḥi*.
Mordecai b. Hillel ha-Kohen, R. *Mordekhai*.
Moses b. Jacob of Coucy, R. *Sefer Mitzvot Gadol*.
Nahmanides. *Ramban*. Commentary on the Torah.
Nelson, Jack. "Iraqi Missiles Strike Israel; Others Reported Fired at Saudi Arabia Bases." *Los Angeles Times*, January 18, 1991, 1.
New York Jewish Week. "PLO Unit Takes Credit for Jerusalem Bombing." March 2, 1984, 18.

Bibliography

———. "Rabin: Peace Is Up to the Arabs." July 27, 1974, 16.
———. "Study Says PLO Murdered 1,131 in Last 10 Years." February 11, 1979, 3.
New York Times. "Islamic Anti-Semitism." October 18, 2003, A12.
———. "Mideast Accord; Statements by Leaders at the Signing of the Middle East Pact." September 14, 1993, A12.
———. "Professor Criticized for Exam on Yom Kippur." October 14, 1989, A26.
North, Douglass C. *Institutions, Institutional Change and Economic Performance*. Cambridge: Cambridge University Press, 1990.
Norzi, R. Jedidah Solomon Raphael b. Abraham. *Minḥat Shai*.
Oberdorfer, Don. "Summit Brings Better Ties but No Arms Breakthrough; INF Pact Activated; Delay Is Seen for Treaty on Long-Range Missiles." *Washington Post*, June 2, 1988, A1.
Oxford Dictionary of the Jewish Religion. Edited by Adele Berlin. 2nd ed. New York: Oxford University Press, 2011.
Pear, Robert. "U.S. Agrees to Talks with P.L.O., Saying Arafat Accepts Israel and Renounces All Terrorism." *New York Times*, December 15, 1988, A1.
Perlman, R. Yeruham Yehudah Leib. *Or Gadol: Teshuvot u-Ketavim*. Jerusalem, Makhon Yerushalyim, 1987.
Pertman, Adam. "INF Treaty Ratified in Time for Summit." *Boston Globe*, May 28, 1998, 1.
Pesikta de-Rav Kahana.
Pesikta de-Rav Kahana (Buber ed.).
Pirkei de-Rabbi Eliezer.
Portaleone, R. Abraham b. David II. *Shiltei ha-Gibborim*.
Preil, R. Elazar Meir. *Ha-Ma'or*.
Putka, Gary. "NATO Quandary: As Missile Pact Looms, the West Is Groping for a Defense Strategy—Old Policy Verges on Success, and That Seems to Raise More Fears than Cheers; 'We Have No Time to Lose.'" *Wall Street Journal*, June 11, 1987, 1.
Rabinowitz, R. Zadok ha-Kohen. *Peri Tzaddik*.
Radler, Melissa. "US Vetoes Condemnation of Security Fence at UN." *Jerusalem Post*, October 16, 2003, 3.
Reich, Walter. "A Tactical War of Words; Talks Will Determine Value of What Arafat Says." *Los Angeles Times*, December 24, 1988, M4.
Reischer, R. Jacob b. Joseph. *Iyyun Yaakov*.
Richardson, James D., ed. *A Compilation of the Messages and Papers of the Presidents, 1789–1897*. Vol. 1. Washington, DC, Government Printing Office, 1898.
Rotem, Michal. "Hamas: Driven by Ardor and a Global Mission." *Jerusalem Post*, December 18, 1992, 5.

Rubin, Barry. *Revolution until Victory?: The Politics and History of the PLO.* Cambridge, MA: Harvard University Press, 1996.

Rubin, Trudy. "Glasnost Has Brought a New Type of Antisemitism to the Soviet Union." *Philadelphia Inquirer,* January 26, 1990, A.19.

Saadiah Gaon, R. *Ha-Emunot ve-ha-De'ot.*

Samuel b. Meir, R. *Rashbam.* Commentary on the Torah.

Sanger, David E. "Callers Support Subway Gunman." *New York Times,* December 25, 1984, 1.1.

Sasslower, R. Jacob Koppel b. Aaron. *Naḥalat Yaakov.*

Schiff, Alvin I. *The Jewish Day School in America.* New York: Jewish Education Committee Press, 1966.

Schlesinger, George N. "The Anthropic Principle." *Tradition: A Journal of Orthodox Thought* 23, no. 3 (Spring 1988): 1–8.

Schmalz, Jeffrey. "Hurricane Left Grievous Wounds to Land and Spirit of Puerto Rico." *New York Times,* October 1, 1989.

Schmitt, Eric. "Scud Missiles; An Arsenal of Terror." *New York Times,* January 19, 1991, 15.

Schwartz, Richard A. *Encyclopedia of the Persian Gulf War.* Jefferson, NC: McFarland, 1998.

Schwartz, Yoel. *Ha-Tekufah be-Aspaklaria Toranit: Meura'ot 5750–5751 u-Milḥemet ha-Mifratz.* Jerusalem: Devar Yerushalayim, 1991.

Sciolino, Elaine. "Peres, at the U.N., Proposed to Visit Jordan for Talks." *New York Times,* October 22, 1985, A1.

Scotchmer, Paul F. "Glasnost, God and Gorbachev." *Chicago Tribune,* January 21, 1988, 19.

Scott, John and Gordon Marshall, eds. *A Dictionary of Sociology.* 3rd ed. New York: Oxford University Press, 2009.

Sefer ha-Yashar.

Segal, R. David b. Samuel ha-Levi. *Divrei David.*

Seigel, Reginald. "Arab Nations Attack Israel." *UPI NewsTrack,* May 15, 1948.

Sforno, R. Obadiah b. Jacob. *Sforno.* Commentary on the Torah.

———. *Kavvanot ha-Torah.*

Shabbetai b. Meir ha-Kohen, R. *Siftei Kohen* to *Shulḥan Arukh.*

Shapira, R. Hayyim Meir Yehiel. *Tiferet Ḥayyim.* Warsaw: Kleiman, 1920.

Shapiro, Haim. "Haredim Conflicted over Secular Candidates." *Jerusalem Post,* December 11, 2000, 3.

Shapley, Harlow. "A Determination of the Distance to the Galactic Center." *Proceedings of the National Academy of Sciences of the United States of America* 25, no. 3 (March 15, 1939): 113–118.

Shneur Zalman of Liadi, R. *Shulḥan Arukh ha-Rav.*

Shternbukh, R. Mosheh. *Teshuvot ve-Hanhagot.* Jerusalem, 1997.

Bibliography

Sifrei to Numbers and Deuteronomy.
Sofer, R. Abraham Samuel Benjamin. *Ketav Sofer*.
Sofer, R. Moses. *She'elot u-Teshuvot ha-Ḥatam Sofer*.
———. *Torat Mosheh*.
Sofer, R. Simeon. *Mikhtav Sofer*. 2 vols. Jerusalem, 1952.
Solomon b. Isaac, R. *Rashi*. Commentary on the Torah and Talmud.
Soloveichik, R. Ahron. *Logic of the Heart, Logic of the Mind: Wisdom and Reflections on Topics of Our Times*. Jerusalem: Genesis Jerusalem Press, 1991.
Soloveitchik, R. Joseph B. *Days of Deliverance: Essays on Purim and Chanukah*. New York: Toras HoRav Foundation, 2007.
———. *Ḥamesh Derashot*. Jerusalem: Makhon Tal Orot, 1974.
———. *The Lonely Man of Faith*. New York: Doubleday, 1965.
Soloveitchik, R. Yosef Dov. *Beit ha-Levi al Derush u-Milei de-Aggadata*. Jerusalem, 1985.
Stern, R. Yehiel Michel. *Kashrut Arba'at ha-Minim*. Jerusalem: Makhon Imrei David, 1992.
Strashun, R. Samuel b. Joseph. *Ḥiddushei ha-Rashash*.
Talmud (Babylonian). *Avodah Zarah; Bava Batra; Bava Kamma; Bava Metzia; Berakhot; Eruvin; Gittin; Ḥagigah; Ḥullin; Keritot; Ketubbot; Kiddushin; Megillah; Menaḥot; Nedarim; Niddah; Pesaḥim; Rosh ha-Shanah; Sanhedrin; Shabbat; Shevuot; Sotah; Sukkah; Ta'anit; Yevamot; Yoma*.
Talmud (Jerusalem). *Ḥagigah; Pesaḥim; Shabbat; Shevuot; Sotah*.
Tanna de-vei Eliyahu. Seder Eliyahu Rabba.
Targum Onkelos.
Targum Yonatan.
Taubman, Philip. "The World: Gorbachev's Groundwork for Summit No. 3." *New York Times*, October 11, 1987, A2.
Thackery, H. St. John. *The Septuagint and Jewish Worship: A Study in Origins*. London: Oxford University Press, 1921.
Tobiah b. Eliezer. *Midrash Lekaḥ Tov (Pesikta Zutarta)*.
Torat Kohanim.
Tosafot. Commentary on Talmud. *Bava Batra; Bava Kamma; Bava Metzia; Berakhot; Gittin; Kiddushin; Menahot; Sanhedrin; Shabbat; Sukkah; Ta'anit*.
Tosafot Yeshanim.
Treadwell, David. "Brisk Sale of Gas Masks in U.S." *Jerusalem Post*, January 27, 1991, 7.
Trebilcock, Michael and Jing Leng. "The Role of Formal Contract Law in Economic Development." *Virginia Law Review* 92, no. 7 (2006): 1517–1580.
Trunk, R. Israel Joshua. *Likkutei Torah*. Reprinted in R. Hayyim Elazar Wachs. *Nefesh Ḥayah al ha-Torah: Bereshit; Derashot le-khol ha-Shanah*. Brooklyn, NY: Zinger, 2001.

Tucker, Spencer C., ed. *Encyclopedia of Middle East Wars: The United States in the Persian Gulf, Afghanistan, and Iraq Conflicts*. 5 vols. Santa Barbara, CA: ABC-CLIO, 2010.

Twersky, R. Mayer. "Halakhic Values and Halakhic Decisions: Rav Soloveitchik's Pesak Regarding Women's Prayer Groups." *Tradition: A Journal of Orthodox Thought* 32, no. 3 (Spring 1998): 5–18.

U.S. Department of State. "Statement Denying Visa for Arafat." November 26, 1988. Reprinted in the *New York Times*, November 27, 1988, A5.

van der Heide, Albert. "PARDES: Methodological Reflections on the Theory of the Four Senses." *Journal of Jewish Studies* 34 (1983): 147–159.

Vital, R. Hayyim b. Joseph. *Sha'ar Ru'ah ha-Kodesh*.

Walcott, John and Gerald F. Seib. "Reagan and Gorbachev Sign Ban on Intermediate-Range Missiles; They Promise to Seek Cuts in Long-Range Arsenal as 3-Day Summit Starts." *Wall Street Journal*, December 9, 1987, 1.

Washington Post. "The Persian Gulf War; Excerpts from the President's News Conference." March 2, 1991, A12.

Weinraub, Bernard. "Iran Payment Found Diverted to Contras; Reagan Security Adviser and Aide Are Out." *New York Times*, November 26, 1986, A1.

Weiss, R. Avraham. *Women at Prayer: A Halakhic Analysis of Women's Prayer Groups*. 3rd ed. Hoboken, NJ: Ktav, 2001.

Weisser, R. Meir Loeb b. Jehiel Michel. *Malbim*. Commentary on the Torah.

Weissmandl, R. Michel Dov. Cited in *Sekhar ve-Onesh*. Vol. 3. 2001.

Wharton, Tony. "Captive Audience Treated Well; POWs Can Be Tools of War or Friends for Life." *Virginian-Pilot & Ledger Star*, March 3, 1991, C1.

Wines, Michael and Doyle McManus. "U.S. Sent Iran Arms for Hostage Releases; Weapons Were Supplied for Aid in Freeing 3 in Lebanon, Government Sources Say." *Los Angeles Times*, November 6, 1986, 1.

Witztum, Doron, Eliyahu Rips, and Yoav Rosenberg. "Equidistant Letter Sequences in the Book of Genesis." *Statistical Science* 9, no. 3 (1994): 429–438.

Wolowelsky, Joel B. "Modern Orthodoxy and Women's Changing Self-Perception." *Tradition: A Journal of Orthodox Thought* 22, no. 1 (Spring 1986): 65–81.

Woodbury, David O. "Here Is the Utopian Promise of the Peacetime Atom." *Look*, August 9, 1955, 26–31.

Yadler, R. Benzion. *Tiferet Tziyyon* on *Midrash Rabbah*.

Yalkut Shimoni.

Ze'ev Wolf of Zhitomir, R. *Or ha-Me'ir*.

Zohar.

Zuckerman, R. Hayyim Yaakov. *Otzar Hayyim*. Tel Aviv, 1966.

Name Index

Aaron, 264n12, 274, 277, 288, 290, 304, 334–335, 376–379, 381n6, 417–418, 425, 432
Aaron b. Jacob ha-Kohen of Lunel, R., 208n2
Aaron b. Joseph ha-Levi, R. (*Ra'ah*), 37n3, 87n16, 309n4, 329n4, 329n10
Aaron, David, 10n4
Abba Jose b. Kesari, 12n11, 28n4
Abbahu, R., 143n6, 360n4, 382n12
Abbaye, 390n10
Abel, 11, 24–25, 29, 40
Abiathar, 102n7, 102n11
Abigail, 343
Abimelech, 50n2, 105n10, 114, 122–125, 132
Abiram, 274
Abrabanel, R. Isaac b. Judah, 181n15, 289
Abraham, 35, 42, 45, 49–55, 57–65, 67, 69–71, 74–76, 80, 81n7, 85–90, 95–98, 103–106, 109, 113–115, 118–120, 123–124, 126, 131n3, 174, 210, 211n16, 214, 294, 322, 325n2, 342n2, 345, 397n9, 398, 412

Absalom, 100–101, 239–240
Abudirham, R. David b. Joseph, 386
Abulafia, R. Meir b. Todros ha-Levi (*Ramah*), 354n10
Adam, 34, 131n2, 267, 334, 385, 387n15
Adler, R. Shlomo, 142n2
Adler, Stephen J., 371
Adoniyahu, 100–102
Ahai Gaon, R., 81n10, 365n3
Ahitophel, 100
Akedat Yitzḥak. See Arama, R. Isaac b. Moses
al-Batzravi, R. Shelomoh, 74n5
Albeck, Hanoch, 181n11
Alfasi, R. Isaac b. Jacob (*Rif*), 36n7
Al-Hakam, R. Joseph Hayyim b. Elijah (*Ben Ish Ḥai*), 336n1
Alkabetz, R. Solomon b. Moses ha-Levi, 232n3
Alshekh, R. Moses, 19n11, 294n3
Alter, R. Yehudah Aryeh Leib (*Sefat Emet*), 89, 390

Name Index

Altschuler, R. Jehiel Hillel b. David
  Metzudat David, 256n10
  Metzudat Tziyyon, 102n10
Amalek, 138, 236–237, 332–335, 353, 407
Anah, 181–182
Andrai, Sándor, 20n17
Antoninus, 179
Apple, Jr., R. W., 296n11
Arafat, Yasser, 102, 332, 334–335, 367
Arama, R. Isaac b. Moses (*Akedat Yitzhak*), 11, 290
Ard, 205
Arizal. See Luria, R. Isaac b. Solomon
Arrow, Kenneth J., 132
Arukh ha-Shulhan. See Epstein, R. Jehiel Michal
Ashbel, 205
Asher b. Jacob, 343, 425
Asher b. Jehiel, R. (*Rosh*), 245n12, 329n2
Ashkenazi, R. Samuel Jaffe (*Yefeh To'ar*), 63n10, 65n3, 70n4
Auerbach, R. Shlomo Zalman, 165n7
Avi Sokho, 279
Avi Zanoah, 279n1
Avkat Rokhel. See Caro, R. Joseph
Awad, Mubarak, 173
Azulai, R. Hayyim Joseph David (*Hida*), 34n3

Bahya b. Asher, R. (*Rabbeinu Behaye*), 59, 70n4, 87n14, 88n1, 174n8, 189n10, 255n6, 349–350, 376n6, 378n21, 404, 424n10, 425n12, 426n17, 428nn4–5, 429nn6–8
Barak b. Abinoam, 331
Bar-Illan, David, 332n3
Barzillai, 239–240
Bass, R. Shabbetai b. Joseph (*Siftei Hakhamim*), 98n10, 118n7, 168n6, 176n2, 190n15, 278n10, 296n10, 385n4, 397n9, 428n1

Bath-sheba, 99–102, 241
Batyah, 280
Batzri, R. Ezra, 306n10
Bazyler, Michael J., 75n9
Becker, Jillian, 165n8, 334n10
Beit ha-Levi. See Soloveitchik, R. Yosef Dov
Bekher, 205
Bela, 205
Ben Evyatar, 279n1
Ben Ish Hai. See Al-Hakam, R. Joseph Hayyim b. Elijah
Benaiah b. Jehoiada, 102n12
Benjamin, 58, 59, 139, 198–199, 204–206, 215, 220–221
Berdichever Rav. See Levi Yitzhak of Berdichev, R.
Berkowitz, David, 370n3
Berlin, Adele, 336n1
Berlin, R. Naphtali Tzvi Yehudah (*Netziv*)
  Ha'amek Davar, 109n4, 125n8, 144nn7–8, 172, 203n1, 215n1, 232n5, 263, 288, 298n3, 333n4
  Rinah shel Torah, 326n7
Berman, Mark A., 66n7
Besdin, R. Abraham R., 270n2
Bezalel, 418–421
Bierman, John, 19n14
Bilhah, 144, 206n13
Bleich, R. J. David, 128n11
Block, Walter, 360n5
Bornsztain, R. Shmuel (*Shem mi-Shemuel*), 114n9, 322, 323n12, 326n6, 327n10, 426n21
Boyer, Paul, 11n9
Bradford, William, 146
Brands, H. W., 338n10
Brennan, Geoffrey, 360n5
Brilliant, Joshua, 172n2
Broder, Jonathan, 59n10

Name Index

Brown, Josephine M., 101n6
Browning, Robert, 220n8
Buder, Leonard, 38n7
Budge, E. A. Wallis, 209n7
Bunim, Amos, 73n1
Bunim, Irving M., 73
Bunsen, Matthew, 209n7
Bush, George H. W., 146, 147n8, 294n5, 385, 388, 395–396, 408

Cain, 9, 11–12, 24–25, 27–29, 40
Caine, Burton, 384
Canaan, 39
Carmy, R. Shalom, 128n14
Caro, R. Joseph
 Avkat Rokhel, 255n3
 Shulḥan Arukh, 208n3, 245n8, 266n4, 267n8, 312nn3–4, 313n5, 313nn7–8, 329n2, 360n6, 361n7, 366n8, 386nn6–7, 389n2, 397n11
Chajes, R. Zevi Hirsch (*Maharatz Ḥayot*), 131n3
Chamberlain, Neville, 169n10
Chapman, Steve, 30n10
Clairborne, William, 339n13
Cohen, R. Dovid, 311n12
Collins, Nina L., 209n6
Colon b. Solomon Trabotto, R. Joseph (*Maharik*), 146n2
Crawford, J. Craig, 296n8
Culi, R. Jacob (*Me-Am Lo'ez*), 54, 57, 67n15, 86n11, 90n6, 95, 123n4, 133n11, 181n15, 188n8, 189n9, 191n18, 220n6, 223n3, 325n4, 326n6, 342, 345, 353, 378n20, 396n2, 408n14, 412n8
Cummins, Ken, 101n6
Czerniak, R. Shalom Shachna, 313n6

Da'at Zekenim, 118n4, 141n1, 142n4, 180n4, 427n1

Dan, 342, 425
Danzig, R. Abraham, 361n7
Darkhei Mosheh to *Tur*. See Isserles, R. Moses
Dathan, 274
David, 17–20, 52, 80, 82, 87n13, 100–102, 169, 238n19, 239–241, 243, 264n12, 280n6, 343n10, 377, 381n6, 407
Davies, Paul, 15n9
Davis, Helen, 19n13
de Uçeda, R. Samuel b. Isaac, 306n10
Deborah, 328–331, 341–343
Demetrius of Phaleron, 209n7
Dessler, R. Eliyahu Eliezer (*Mikhtav me-Eliyahu*), 45, 182n20
Dickinson, Jr., William B., 273n1
Dinah, 164–165, 172–173, 251–253
Diskin, R. Moses Joshua Judah Leib (*Maharil Diskin*), 423n2
Divrei David. See Segal, R. David b. Samuel ha-Levi
Dole, Stephen B., 14n5
Draper, Theodore, 273n2
Drummond, William J., 334n9

Eber, 119, 180, 205
Edels, R. Samuel Eliezer b. Judah ha-Levi (*Maharsha*), 104n2, 211n15, 319n1
Edut bi-Yosef. See Ettinger, R. Joseph ha-Levi
Ehi, 205
Eichmann, Adolph, 19
Eider, R. Shimon D., 313n10
Einhorn, R. Zev Wolf (*Maharzu*), 70n4, 88n1, 104n4
Eleazar the High Priest, 209
Eliab, 337
Eliezer, 95–96, 99, 103–104, 106–107, 131n3
Eliezer, R., 311n12

Name Index

Eliezer b. Joel ha-Levi, R. (*Ra'avyah*), 398n12
Eliezer b. Samuel of Metz, R., 361n10
Eliezer the Great, R. *See* Eliezer, R.
Elijah, 299
Elijah b. Solomon Zalman, R. (Vilna Gaon or *Gra*), 49n1, 146n6
Elisha, 79–82
Elkanah, 128
Elzinga, Kenneth, 360n5
Emden, R. Jacob (*Ya'avetz*), 58
Emery, Fred, 273n1
Emet le-Yaakov. *See* Kamenetsky, R. Yaakov
Engel, R. Joseph, 387n13
Enoch Zundel b. Joseph, R. (*Etz Yosef*), 70n4, 220n5, 262n2, 291n8, 385n4
Ephraim, 235
Ephraim Solomon b. Aaron of Luntshits, R. (*Keli Yakar*), 51, 86n11, 87n14, 119, 121n15, 294n4, 298n5, 296n6, 424n7, 428n2
Epstein, R. Baruch ha-Levi (*Torah Temimah*), 147
Epstein, R. Jehiel Michal (*Arukh ha-Shulḥan*), 266n3, 329, 366n8, 367n9, 397n11
Epstein, R. Kalonymus Kalman ha-Levi, 147n11
Epstein, R. Moses Mordecai, 366n5
Esau, 81, 106, 109–110, 117–119, 121, 130–132, 137–139, 153, 159–160, 162, 163, 168–170, 177, 179–183, 250, 322
Ettinger, R. Joseph ha-Levi, 71n9
Etz Yosef. *See* Enoch Zundel b. Joseph, R.
Eve, 267, 334, 385
Ezekiel b. Buzi, 281n6, 408
Ezekiel Feivel b. Zev Wolf, R. (*Maharif*), 70n4
Ezra, 208, 211–213, 350

Falcoff, Mark, 296n8
Falk, R. Joshua b. Alexander ha-Kohen (*Sema*), 208n2
Farber, R. Yosef, 73
Farrakhan, Louis, 102
Fein, Esther B., 261n1
Feinstein, R. Mosheh
    Derash Mosheh, 293n1
    Iggerot Mosheh, 254n1, 366n5
Finkel, R. Nosson Tzvi (*Ha-Sabba mi-Slabodka*), 240n5
Fisher, Louis, 66n9
Fraenkel, R. David b. Naphtali Hirsch, 88n1
Freedman, Lawrence, 294n5, 338n11, 339n15
Friedman, Milton, 360n5
Friedman, Thomas L., 171n1, 172n2
Frimer, Aryeh A., 128n11
Frimer, Dov I., 128n11

Gad, 429
Gehazi, 80, 82
Gera, 205
Gerondi, R. Jonah b. Abraham (*Rabbeinu Yonah*), 50n2, 98n11
Gerondi, R. Nissim b. Reuben (*Ran*), 145
Gideon, 235, 237–238
Gifter, R. Mordechai, 279
Ginzberg, Louis, 133n11, 209n6
Glazerson, Matityahu, 306n6
Glick, Shimon M., 62
Goetz, Bernhard, 261–262
Gog, 408
Goldberg, Carey, 19n13
Goldman, S. Simcha, 66n9
Gombiner, R. Abraham Abele b. Hayyim ha-Levi (*Magen Avraham*), 127–128, 208n2, 267n9, 386n8, 403n1
Gorbachev, Mikhail S., 9n1, 10n3, 167, 291nn6–7

Name Index

Goshko, John M., 333n3
Gra. See Elijah b. Solomon Zalman, R.
Greenberg, R. Aharon Yaakov, 240n5, 432n3
Greenberg, Joel, 173n7
Grieco, Joseph, 12n13, 168n2
Gur Aryeh. See Loew b. Bezalel, R. Judah
Gwertzman, Bernard, 57nn1–2, 120n11

Ha'amek Davar. See Berlin, R. Naphtali Tzvi Yehudah
Ha-Ari. See Luria, R. Isaac b. Solomon
Habakkuk, 82
Haberman, Clyde, 29n9, 296n9
Ha-Derash ve-ha-Iyyun. See Levine, R. Aharon
Ha-Emunot ve-ha-De'ot. See Saadiah Gaon, R.
Ḥafetz Ḥayyim. *See* Kagan, R. Israel Meir ha-Kohen
Ha-Gadol mi-Minsk. See Perlman, R. Yeruham Yehudah Leib
Hagar, 50n2, 69–71
Hager, R. Hayyim Meir (*Imrei Ḥayyim*), 87n16
Haggahot Maimuniyyot. See Meir b. Barukh of Rothenburg, R.
Haggith, 100
Ha-Ḥozeh mi-Lublin. See Horowitz, R. Jacob Isaac
Ha-Ketav ve-ha-Kabbalah. See Mecklenburg, R. Yaakov Tzvi
Halliday, Fred, 338n8
Ham, 34, 39, 41
Haman, 138, 232n3
Ha-Ma'or. See Preil, R. Elazar Meir
Ḥamesh Derashot. *See* Soloveitchik, R. Joseph B.
Hamor, 172–173, 252–253
Hannah, 128, 343

Hanson, Christopher, 11n5
Haran, 124n6
Harbonah, 406, 407, 409
Haralick, Robert M., 306n6
Ha-Sabba mi-Slabodka. See Finkel, R. Nosson Tzvi
Ḥatam Sofer. *See* Sofer, R. Moses
Ḥavvot Yair. *See* Kallir, R. Eleazar b. Eleazar
Ḥazon Ish. *See* Karelitz, R. Abraham Isaiah
Hershey, Jr., Robert D., 225n1
Hever, 279n1
Hezekiah, 408
Hezekiah b. Manoah, R. (*Ḥizkuni*), 141n2, 339
Ḥida. *See* Azulai, R. Hayyim Joseph David
Ḥiddushei Halakhot ve-Aggadot. See Edels, R. Samuel Eliezer b. Judah ha-Levi
Hilkiah, 378n21
Hillel, 193n4
Hirsch, R. Samson Raphael, 8, 45, 61n5, 62n8, 96n3, 134n13, 139, 165, 172n6, 248, 263, 264n10, 290, 298, 381n9
Hiyya, 243–244
Ḥizkuni. *See* Hezekiah b. Manoah, R.
Hoffman, Bruce, 334n10
Ḥokhmat Adam. *See* Danzig, R. Abraham
Horowitz, R. Isaiah ha-Levi (*Shelah ha-Kadosh*), 294n3, 396n2
Horowitz, R. Jacob Isaac (*Ha-Ḥozeh mi-Lublin*), 147n11
Ḥovot ha-Levavot. *See* Ibn Paquda, R. Bahya b. Joseph
Huppim, 205
Hur, 334–335, 418, 420
Hussein, Saddam, 275, 295, 338, 406, 407, 409

Name Index

Ibn Attar, R. Hayyim b. Moses (*Or ha-Ḥayyim*), 44n1, 71, 88n1, 110, 144n10, 164, 220, 255n7, 289n1, 294nn3–4, 376n7, 413n9, 423

Ibn Ezra, Abraham b. Meir, 118, 134n12, 146n7, 278n10, 288n11, 376n7

Ibn Migash, R. Joseph (*Ri mi-Gash*), 398n12

Ibn Paquda, R. Bahya b. Joseph, 147n9

Ikenberry, G. John, 12n13, 168n2

Imrei Ḥayyim. See Hager, R. Hayyim Meir

Irit, 84

Isaac, 86–87, 89–90, 95–97, 103–106, 109–110, 113–115, 118, 119, 120n13, 124–125, 126, 130–134, 170, 177, 178, 180–181, 250, 294, 322, 412

Isaac b. Joseph of Corbeil, R., 361n10

Isaiah, 82, 281n6, 421

Ishbili, R. Yom Tov (*Ritva*), 329n4

Ishmael, 50n2, 89–90

Issachar, 131, 141–144, 152, 254–256, 425, 428n4

Issachar Berman b. Naphtali ha-Kohen, R. (*Mattenot Kehunnah*), 291n8

Isserles, R. Moses (*Rema*)
Darkhei Mosheh to Tur, 398n12
Rema to *Shulḥan Arukh*, 254n1, 255n3, 365n4
She'elot u-Teshuvot ha-Rema, 398n12

Iturei Torah. See Greenberg, R. Aharon Yaakov

Iyyun Yaakov. See Reischer, R. Jacob b. Joseph

Jacob, 51, 52n12, 81, 105, 106, 115, 117–121, 128n12, 130–133, 137–138, 142, 144, 149–151, 152–154, 159–162, 163, 165, 166, 168–170, 172–173, 175–176, 177–178, 179–181, 187–191, 204, 205n5, 206, 218–220, 222–223, 231, 232n4, 234–235, 237, 243, 247–248, 250–253, 254, 294, 320–321, 322, 413, 421, 429n7

Jacob b. Asher, R. (*Tur*), 147n11, 208n3, 208n5, 266n4, 267nn8–9, 361n7, 366n8, 386n6, 386n8, 389n2, 397n11, 398n12

Japheth, 34, 35

Jehiel Michel b. Uzziel, R., 70n4

Jeremiah, 212

Jervis, Robert, 12n13, 168n2

Jethro, 263, 277

Joab b. Zeruiah, 241

Jones, Alex S., 242n1

Joseph, 51, 59, 119, 125, 128n12, 137–139, 169, 187–189, 191, 192–193, 198, 203–207, 214–217, 218–221, 222–223, 226–227, 231–233, 234–235, 238, 243, 245, 247, 248, 274, 319–321, 323, 344, 345, 425–426, 429n7

Josephus, Flavius, 209n7

Joshua, 18, 236–238, 299, 350, 405n7

Joshua b. Hanina, R., 181n12

Josiah, 378

Joyner, Christopher C., 296n11

Judah, 59, 161, 187–191, 193, 198, 206, 215, 217, 219n2, 342, 418, 425, 429

Judah ha-Nasi, R., 179

Kadi, Leila S., 368n14

Kagan, R. Israel Meir ha-Kohen (*Ḥafetz Ḥayyim*), 312n4, 313n8

Kahane, Meir, 61, 215

Kallir, R. Eleazar b. Eleazar, 176n1

Kamelhar, R. Moshe, 423n5

Kamenetsky, R. Yaakov, 49n1, 127n10

Kanievsky, R. Yaakov Yisrael (*Steipler Gaon*), 313n8

Karelitz, R. Abraham Isaiah (*Ḥazon Ish*), 313n8

Name Index

Kariv, Abraham, 299n8
Karsh, Efraim, 294n5, 338n11, 339n15
Kasher, R. Menachem Mendel, 411n2
Kasparov, Gary, 269–272
Katzman, Abner, 338n9
Kaufman, Tamar, 67nn11–13
Keeley, Michael C., 226n2
Keli Yakar. See Ephraim Solomon b. Aaron of Luntshits, R.
Kesher Israel Congregation, 146
Ketav Sofer. See Sofer, R. Abraham Samuel Benjamin
Kimhi, R. David (*Radak*), 101n4, 146n7, 150n3, 206n13, 270n16, 256n10, 379n21, 423n5
Kinzer, Stephen, 340n19
Klapholtz, R. Yisroel Yaakov, 57n5
Klarman, Seth A., 226n2
Klinghoffer, Leon, 56n1
Knisbacher, Mitchell, 292n9
Kohl, Helmut, 340n19
Kol Bo, 208n2
Kolin, R. Samuel b. Nathan ha-Levi, 403n1
Korach, 378n19
Korban ha-Edah. See Fraenkel, R. David b. Naphtali Hirsch
Kotler, R. Aharon, 313
Kotzker Rebbe. See Morgensztern, R. Menahem Mendel, of Kotzk
Kramer, Doniel Z., 65n5

Laban, 119, 133–134, 149–151, 153–154, 160–161, 175, 176, 178, 180, 181
Lady Potiphar, 216, 320n3, 345
Lamm, R. Norman, 14n7
Landau, R. Ezekiel b. Judah (*Noda bi-Yehudah*), 313n8, 382n15
Lappidoth, 329
Leah, 120, 142n4, 144, 147, 149–151, 152–155, 160, 206

Lefkovits, Etgar, 299n9
Leithauser, Brad, 269
Lemekh, 29
Levi, 164, 172, 250–253, 254–256, 264, 424
Levi bar Hama, R., 281n7
Levi Yitzhak of Berdichev, R. (*Berdichever Rav*), 256
Levine, R. Aaron, 143n5, 360nn5–6, 366n6, 397n11, 398n14
Levine, R. Aharon (*Reisha Rav*)
  Avnei Hefetz, 169n7
  Ha-Derash ve-ha-Iyyun, 169n7, 376n6, 424n6
Lewin, Avrohom Shmuel, 197n2
Lewin, R. Isaac, 65n6
Lewis, Anthony, 10n2, 167n1
Liebeskind, Michelle G. Lewis, 370n3
Linton, Adelin, 146n4
Linton, Ralph, 146n4
Lipschutz, R. Israel b. Gedaliah, 313n6
Lockwood, Christopher, 339n14
Loew b. Bezalel, R. Judah (*Maharal*)
  Gur Aryeh, 50n4, 160, 205, 223n6, 249n6, 334n7, 370n2
  Kitvei Maharal mi-Prague, 299n8
Long, William, 194n5
Lot, 49, 50–52, 53–54, 57, 67, 75–76, 84, 86n9, 90, 174, 398
Lowy, Joan, 409n17
Luria, R. Isaac b. Solomon (*Arizal* or *ha-Ari*), 294n3
Luria, R. Solomon b. Jehiel (*Maharshal*), 244

Magen Avraham. See Gombiner, R. Abraham Abele b. Hayyim ha-Levi
Magida, Arthur J., 67n12
Magog, 408
Maharal. See Loew b. Bezalel, R. Judah

Name Index

Maharam me-Rotenburg. See Meir b. Barukh of Rothenburg, R.
Maharatz Ḥayot. See Chajes, R. Zevi Hirsch
Maharif. See Ezekiel Feivel b. Zev Wolf, R.
Maharik. See Colon b. Solomon Trabotto, R. Joseph
Maharil Diskin. See Diskin, R. Moses Joshua Judah Leib
Maharsha. See Edels, R. Samuel Eliezer b. Judah ha-Levi
Maharshal. See Luria, R. Solomon b. Jehiel
Maharzu. See Einhorn, R. Zev Wolf
Maḥatzit ha-Shekel. See Kolin, R. Samuel b. Nathan ha-Levi
Maimonides (*Rambam*), 388n18
  Guide of the Perplexed, 14
  Mishneh Torah, 16n10, 80n3, 127, 163–164, 172n5, 211n18, 223n8, 245nn8–9, 266n3, 285, 286n3, 312n3, 313n7, 328n1, 354n10, 361n7, 366n8, 367n9, 397n11, 381n6, 389n2, 390n5, 407n3, 423n2, 425n16
  Perush ha-Mishnayot, 50n2, 74n4, 118n3
  Shemoneh Perakim, 286n3
Majaess, Daniel J., 14n6
Malbim. See Weisser, R. Meir Loeb b. Jehiel Michel
Manasseh b. Hezekiah, 149, 154
Manasseh b. Joseph, 235
Manot ha-Levi. See Alkabetz, R. Solomon b. Moses ha-Levi
Marcus, Ralph, 209n6
Marshall, Gordon, 25n3
Marx, Alexander, 209n6
Mastanduno, Michael, 12n13, 168n2

Mattenot Kehunnah. See Issachar Berman b. Naphtali ha-Kohen, R.
McDonough, Frank, 169n10
McManus, Doyle, 244n6
Me-Am Lo'ez. See Culi, R. Jacob
Mecklenburg, R. Yaakov Tzvi (*Ha-Ketav ve-ha-Kabbalah*), 87n14
Meir, R., 382
Meir b. Barukh of Rothenburg, R. (*Maharam me-Rotenburg*), 398n12
Meir Simhah ha-Kohen of Dvinsk, R. (*Or Same'aḥ* or *Meshekh Ḥokhmah*), 275n6
Meislin, Richard J., 122n2, 194n5
Mephibosheth, 18–19
Meshekh Hokhmah. See Meir Simhah ha-Kohen of Dvinsk, R.
Metzudat David. See Altschuler, R. Jehiel Hillel b. David
Metzudat Tziyyon. See Altschuler, R. Jehiel Hillel b. David
Mikhtav me-Eliyahu. See Dessler, R. Eliyahu Eliezer
Mikhtav Sofer. See Sofer, R. Simeon
Miller, R. Avigdor, 108
Miller, Judith, 56n1, 167n1
Miller, Marjorie, 194n5
Miriam, 263n8, 264n12, 272, 321, 326
Mishnah Berurah. See Kagan, R. Israel Meir ha-Kohen
Mishneh Torah. See Maimonides
Mizrahi, David Toufic, 216n8
Mizrahi, R. Elijah (*Re'em*), 428n1
Mohamad, Mahathir, 42n7
Mordecai b. Hillel ha-Kohen, R. (*Mordekhai*), 366n5, 398n12
Mordekhai. See Mordecai b. Hillel ha-Kohen, R.
Morgensztern, R. Menahem Mendel, of Kotzk, 114n9

Name Index

Moses, 5, 44–45, 210, 212n21, 250, 251, 253, 256, 262–264, 270–271, 274–275, 276–277, 279–281, 287–288, 290, 291, 294–295, 298, 304, 319, 325, 334, 344–345, 350–351, 377, 388n18, 404–405, 410–413, 417–420, 424, 425, 426, 427, 429n8, 431–432
Moses b. Jacob of Coucy, R., 361n10
Muppim, 205

Naaman b. Benjamin, 205
Naḥalat Yaakov. See Sasslower, R. Jacob Koppel b. Aaron
Nahmanides (Ramban), 41, 51n11, 60, 70, 71n13, 72n14, 87n15, 88n1, 118, 127, 139n9, 164, 172n5, 189n11, 193, 209n9, 223n8, 226n4, 248, 251, 253, 276n2, 298n5, 305n5, 308–309, 376n7, 405n7, 411, 419, 429n14
Naphtali, 331, 342
Nathan, 100–102
Nebuchadnezzar, 208
Nehemiah, R., 12, 28n5
Nelson, Jack, 339n13
Netziv. See Berlin, R. Naphtali Tzvi Yehudah
Neustadt, R. Daniel Yehudah, 127n10
Nezer ha-Kodesh. See Jehiel Michel b. Uzziel, R.
Nimrod, 49n2, 54, 57, 64–65, 67, 75, 131n2
Nixon, Richard, 122, 273
Noah, 34, 35, 36, 39, 40–42, 44–45, 104n5
Noda bi-Yehudah. See Landau, R. Ezekiel b. Judah
Norzi, R. Jedidiah Solomon b. Abraham (Minḥat Shai), 141n1

Oberdorfer, Don, 9n1, 291n6
Oholibamah, 181

Or ha-Ḥayyim. See ibn Attar, R. Hayyim b. Moses
Or ha-Me'ir. See Ze'ev Wolf of Zhitomir, R.
Or Same'aḥ. See Meir Simhah ha-Kohen of Dvinsk, R.
Orḥot Ḥayyim. See Aaron b. Jacob ha-Kohen of Lunel, R.
Ottaway, David B., 333n3

Pear, Robert, 332n2, 367n13
Penuel, 237
Peretz, 188
Peri Tzaddik. See Rabinowitz, R. Zadok ha-Kohen
Perishah to Tur. See Falk, R. Joshua b. Alexander ha-Kohen
Perlman, R. Yeruham Yehuda Leib (Ha-Gadol mi-Minsk), 165n7
Pertman, Adam, 9n1, 291n6
Pesikta de-Rav Kahana, 28n2, 412n7
Pharaoh, 49n2, 58, 74–76, 125, 216, 219, 248, 262, 263, 264, 271–272, 274, 276, 279, 285–288, 289–291, 295, 298, 319, 321–322, 325–326, 331, 337, 408
Pirkei de-Rabbi Eliezer, 42n5, 49n2, 85n8, 103n1, 164n4, 320n6
Pirkei Torah. See Gifter, R. Mordechai
Portaleone, R. Abraham b. David II, 429n14
Potiphar, 192, 216n6
Preil, R. Elazar Meir, 366n5
Ptolemy II Philadelphus, 5, 209, 210n12
Putka, Gary, 10n5

Qualye, Dan, 385

Ra'ah. See Aaron b. Joseph ha-Levi, R.
Ra'avyah. See Eliezer b. Joel ha-Levi, R.
Rabbeinu Beḥaye. See Bahya b. Asher, R.

Name Index

Rabbeinu Yonah. See Gerondi, R. Jonah b. Abraham
Rabin, Yitzhak, 58n6, 197
Rabinowitz, R. Zadok ha-Kohen, 280n3
Rachel, 120, 139, 142, 144, 149–151, 152–155, 160, 206, 320
Radak. See Kimhi, R. David
Radler, Melissa, 30n11
Ramah. See Abulafia, R. Meir b. Todros ha-Levi
Rambam. See Maimonides
Ramban. See Nahmanides
Ran. See Gerondi, R. Nissim b. Reuben
Rashash. See Strashun, R. Samuel b. Joseph
Rashbam. See Samuel b. Meir, R.
Rashi. See Solomon b. Isaac, R.
Rav, 243–244
Rav Ḥayyim Brisker. See Soloveichik, R. Hayyim
Rava, 390
Re'em. See Mizrahi, R. Elijah
Reagan, Ronald, 9, 56n1, 122, 125, 167, 273, 291n6, 332
Rebecca, 95–97, 99–101, 103, 104n4, 106, 109, 126, 130–131, 133, 134, 138, 168, 178, 180
Reich, Walter, 332n3
Reischer, R. Jacob b. Joseph, 244
Reisha Rav. See Levine, R. Aharon
Rema. See Isserles, R. Moses
Reuben, 152–155, 161, 188, 189, 191, 219n2, 250, 342, 429n8
Ri mi-Gash. See Ibn Migash, R. Joseph
Richardson, James D., 146n5
Rif. See Alfasi, R. Isaac b. Jacob
Rinah shel Torah. See Berlin, R. Naphtali Tzvi Yehudah
Rips, Eliyahu, 306n6
Ritva. See Ishbili, R. Yom Tov

Rosenberg, Yoav, 306n6
Rosh b. Benjamin, 205
Rosh. See Asher b. Jehiel, R.
Rotem, Michal, 199n6
Rubin, Barry, 334n9
Rubin, Trudy, 227n8
Ruth, 52

Saadiah Gaon, R., 13, 14, 16n10, 285n1
Safra, R., 81, 365, 367
Samuel, 243, 377
Samuel b. Meir, R. (*Rashbam*), 125n9, 161n7, 376n7
Sanger, David E., 261n1
Sarah, 49n2, 50, 58, 69–71, 74–75, 88–90, 98, 105, 109, 113–114, 123–124, 210, 397n9
Sasslower, R. Jacob Koppel b. Aaron, 141n2
Schiff, Alvin I., 65n5
Schlesinger, George N., 15n9
Schmalz, Jeffrey, 194n5
Schmitt, Eric, 339n13
Schwartz, Richard A., 339n15
Schwartz, Yoel, 338n7
Sciolino, Elaine, 120n12
Scotchmer, Paul F., 291n7
Scott, John, 25n3
Sefat Emet. See Alter, R. Yehudah Aryeh Leib
Sefer Abudraham. See Abudirham, R. David b. Joseph
Sefer ha-Ḥinnukh. See Aaron b. Joseph ha-Levi, R.
Sefer ha-Mizraḥi. See Mizrahi, R. Elijah
Sefer ha-Parshiyyot. See Kitov, R. Eliyahu
Sefer Mitzvot Gadol. See Moses b. Jacob of Coucy, R.
Sefer Mitzvot Katan. See Isaac b. Joseph of Corbeil, R.

Name Index

Sefer Yere'im. See Eliezer b. Samuel of Metz, R.
Segal, R. David b. Samuel ha-Levi (*Turei Zahav* or *Taz*), 354n9
Seib, Gerald F., 9n1, 291n6
Seigel, Reginald, 115n12
Sema. See Falk, R. Joshua b. Alexander ha-Kohen
Sforno, R. Obadiah b. Jacob (*Sforno*), 74n5, 88n1, 126n3, 224, 280
Sforno. See Sforno, R. Obadiah b. Jacob
Shabbetai b. Meir ha-Kohen, R. (*Siftei Kohen* or *Shakh*), 254n1
Shakh. See Shabbetai b. Meir ha-Kohen, R.
Shapira, R. Hayyim Meir Yehiel, 314n13
Shapiro, Haim, 299n9
Shapiro, R. Meir, of Lublin, 396, 432n3
Shapley, Harlow, 14n6
She'elot u-Teshuvot Levush Mordekhai. See Epstein, R. Moses Mordecai
She'elot u-Teshuvot Ve-Darashta ve-Ḥakarata. See Grusman, R. Aharon Yehudah
She'iltot de-Rav Aḥai Gaon. See Ahai Gaon, R.
Shekhem, 164–166, 172–173, 251–253
Shelah ha-Kadosh. See Horowitz, R. Isaiah ha-Levi
Shem, 34–35, 119, 180, 205
Shem mi-Shemuel. See Bornsztain, R. Shmuel
Shemayah b. Netanel, 279n1
Shemoneh Perakim. See Maimonides
Shenei Luḥot ha-Berit. See Horowitz, R. Isaiah ha-Levi
Shiltei ha-Gibborim. See Portaleone, R. Abraham b. David II
Shimi b. Gera, 240

Shimon b. Gamliel, R., 364
Shimon b. Yohai, R., 170n11, 376
Shneur Zalman of Liadi, R., 360n6
Shternbukh, R. Mosheh, 407n3
Shulḥan Arukh. See Caro, R. Joseph
Shulḥan Arukh ha-Rav. See Shneur Zalman of Liadi, R.
Siftei Ḥakhamim. See Bass, R. Shabbetai b. Joseph
Siftei Kohen. See Shabbetai b. Meir ha-Kohen, R.
Simeon, 164, 172, 198, 250–253, 429n8
Simeon b. Lakish, R., 281n7
Sisera, 330–331, 341
Sofer, R. Abraham Samuel Benjamin (*Ketav Sofer*), 336n1
Sofer, R. Moses (*Ḥatam Sofer*), 142, 147
Sofer, R. Simeon (*Mikhtav Sofer*), 309n6
Solomon, 100–102, 239, 241, 280n6
Solomon b. Isaac, R. (*Rashi*)
Chronicles, 256n10
Deuteronomy, 251n3, 256n10, 355n12
Ecclesiastes, 255n6
Exodus, 98n10, 236n9, 251, 255n8, 262n3, 264n12, 271n5, 274n3, 275n4, 276nn1–2, 277n3, 277nn6–7, 278n10, 286n5, 290n4, 296n10, 299n7, 303n1, 310n10, 314n11, 321n9, 334n13–14, 340n20, 354n9, 362n13, 369n1, 376n6, 377n18, 382n12, 403n1, 404nn5–6, 408n12, 411n3, 419nn8–9, 420n11, 423n1, 424n7, 425n11, 427n1, 428n2, 429n9, 429nn11–13, 432n2
Genesis, 6n3, 11n8, 28, 29n8, 45n6, 49n2, 50n5, 54n5, 62n8, 64n1, 69n3, 70–71, 75n8, 80n7, 90n4, 96, 98n10,

Name Index

104nn4–5, 105n8, 106n11, 113, 114n6, 118n3, 118n7, 119n10, 120n14, 124, 125n9, 125n11, 126n1, 127n4, 128n12, 129n15, 131n2, 137n1, 138n5, 138n7, 144n11, 149nn1–2, 151n8, 153n3, 159n1, 161nn4–5, 168n6, 170n11, 170n13, 176n2, 177n4, 178nn6–7, 180n5, 180n8, 181, 182nn18–19, 187, 188n1, 188n7, 190n15, 190n17, 192n1, 205n2, 205nn4–5, 206n7, 206nn12–14, 211n15, 211n17, 219n2, 219n4, 221n10, 223n5, 226nn5–6, 231n1, 234n1, 235nn2–3, 251n4, 255n8, 293n2, 310n10, 320, 333n6, 385n5, 397n9, 398n16
Jeremiah, 144n10, 150n3
Job, 134n12
Joshua, 236n12
Judges, 329n7
Kings, 102nn10–12, 241n14, 379n21
Leviticus, 38n8, 310n10, 361n11, 375n3, 376n4
Mishnah, 49n2, 74n4, 252n7
Numbers, 87n12, 354n7, 382n14
Samuel, 240n7, 240n10
Song of Songs, 221n9
Psalms, 98n11, 146n7
Talmud, 97n7, 98n11, 205n5, 210n11, 210nn13–14, 211n16, 224, 236n10, 266n3, 267n8, 268n10, 297n1, 310n11, 354n10, 355n13, 361n9, 362n13, 369n1, 385n3
Soloveichik, R. Ahron, 97
Soloveichik, R. Hayyim (*Rav Ḥayyim Brisker*), 407
Soloveitchik, R. Joseph B., 61, 128, 270, 387n16, 407n3

Soloveitchik, R. Yosef Dov (*Beit ha-Levi*), 118, 119n8, 217, 267n7, 381n11
Steipler Gaon. See Kanievsky, R. Yaakov Yisrael
Stern, R. Yehiel Michel, 313n6
Strashun, R. Samuel b. Joseph (*Rashash*), 70n4

Tamar, 187–189, 193, 425, 429n7
Tanna de-vei Eliyahu, 329n6, 411n1
Tarfon, R., 143
Targum Onkelos, 118n3, 131n2, 234n1
Targum Yonatan, 28n6, 88n1, 206n15, 216n6, 235n4, 286n5, 343n10
Taubman, Philip, 10n3
Taz. See Segal, R. David b. Samuel ha-Levi
Terah, 124n6
Teshuvot ve-Hanhagot. See Shternbukh, R. Mosheh
Thackery, H. St. John, 209n6
Tiferet Ḥayyim. See Shapira, R. Hayyim Meir Yehiel
Tiferet Tziyyon. See Yadler, R. Benzion
Tiferet Yisrael. See Lipschutz, R. Israel b. Gedaliah
Tobiah b. Eliezer, R., 264n11, 286n4, 375n2
Toledano, Nissim, 197
Torah Shelemah. See Kasher, R. Menachem Mendel
Torah Temimah. See Epstein, R. Baruch ha-Levi
Tosafot, 190n16, 266n3, 312n4, 360, 378n21, 389, 390n3, 397n11
Toviah, 279n1
Treadwell, David, 339n13
Trump, Donald, 24

475

Name Index

Trunk, R. Israel Joshua, of Kutno (*Yeshuot Malko*), 64n2, 329n10
Tucker, Spencer C., 338n13, 406n1, 407n2, 409n16
Tur. See Jacob b. Asher, R.
Turei Zahav. See Segal, R. David b. Samuel ha-Levi
Twersky, R. Mayer, 128n11
Tziyyunim la-Torah. See Engel, R. Joseph

Uri, 418
Uriah, 241

van der Heide, Albert, 336n1
Vilna Gaon. See Elijah b. Solomon Zalman, R.

Wachs, R. Hayyim Elazar, 64n2
Walcott, John, 9n1, 291n6
Wallenberg, Raoul, 19–21
Washington, George, 146, 388
Weinraub, Bernard, 122n1
Weinstein, R. Yitzhak, 37n3, 309n4
Weiss, R. Avraham, 128n11
Weiss, R. Yitzhak Yeshayah, 37n3, 309n4
Weisser, R. Meir Loeb b. Jehiel Michel (*Malbim*), 37n2
Weissmandl, R. Michel Dov, 91n7
Wharton, Tony, 409n17
Wines, Michael, 244n6
Witztum, Doron, 306n6
Wolowelsky, Joel B., 265–266
Woodbury, David O., 11n9

Ya'avetz. See Emden, R. Jacob
Yad Ramah. See Abulafia, R. Meir b. Todros ha-Levi

Yadler, R. Benzion (*Tiferet Tziyyon*), 287n8
Yael, 330
Yalkut Me-Am Lo'ez. See Culi, R. Jacob
Yalkut Re'uveni. See Katz, R. Reuben Hoeshke b. Hoeshke
Yam shel Shelomoh. See Luria, R. Solomon b. Jehiel
Yefeh To'ar. See Ashkenazi, R. Samuel Jaffe
Yehoshafat, 407
Yekutiel, 279
Yered, 279n1
Yerushalmi, R. Shemuel, 54n4, 67n15, 86n11, 90n6, 95n1, 123n4, 133n11, 181n15, 188n8, 191n18, 220n6, 223n3, 325n4, 326n6, 342n5, 345n2, 353n1, 378n20, 396n2, 408n14, 412n8
Yeshuot Malko. See Trunk, R. Israel Joshua, of Kutno
Yether, 237
Yishmael, R., 362
Yohanan b. Zakkai, R., 181n12
Yoheved, 262, 263n8, 264n12
Yose, R., 108, 125, 390

Zalmunna, 237
Ze'ev Wolf of Zhitomir, R., 255n5
Zebah, 237
Zebulun, 131, 143, 152, 254, 256, 331, 342, 425, 428
Zerach, 188
Zibeon, 181–182
Zicherman, R. David, 37n3, 309n4
Zimri, 429
Zohar, 44n1, 82n12, 105n6, 133n11, 255n6, 325n2, 342n2, 379n22, 385n3
Zuckerman, R. Hayyim Yaakov, 395n5

Subject Index

Abraham, 45, 74–76, 80, 85–90, 95–98, 103–106, 113–115, 118–120, 210, 211n16, 214, 294, 322, 325n2, 342n2, 412
    Abimelech, 123–124
    Akedah, 80n7, 86
    blessing by Hashem, 35, 42, 126
    circumcision, 54, 60, 397n9, 398
    Covenant between the Parts, 50n2, 64, 118, 211, 345
    Eliezer, 104, 131n3
    Four Kings, 53–54, 57–59, 174
    Jewish identity, 67
    King of Sodom, 58, 67, 75
    Land of Israel, 60–63
    Lot, 49–52
    Nimrod, 49n2, 54, 57, 64–65, 67, 75
    Pharaoh, 74–75
    Sarah, 69–71, 74, 88–90, 109, 124n6
    Ten Trials, 49n1, 53, 96
Achille Lauro affair, 56
Afternoon Prayer, 105
Ahavat ḥinnam, 220

Aḥdut. See Jewish unity
Akedah, 80, 84–85, 133, 322
American legal system, 25, 38, 369, 371
Anavah. See Humility
Ark, 375–379, 380, 382, 385n3, 396, 419–420
Asarah Harugei Malkhut. See Ten Martyrs

Baseless hatred. See *sin'at ḥinnam*
Bath-sheba, 99–102, 241
Bein adam la-Makom, 224, 248, 433
Bein adam le-ḥavero, 178, 224, 248
Benjamin
    Joseph, 59, 139, 204, 205, 215, 220–221
    Judah, 198–199, 206
    sons of, 205
Berit milah, 54, 60, 61
Birthright, sale of, 117–121
Blessings
    to Abraham, 35, 42, 126
    by Isaac, 130–134, 160, 170, 177–178

Subject Index

Blessings (*continued*)
  by Jacob, 128n12, 166, 231–232, 250–251, 253
  on the Torah, 389, 391
Breastplate of the High Priest, 425
Bush, President George H. W., 388
  budget deficit, 395–396
  letter to Congregation Kesher Israel, 146, 147n8
  oath of office, 384
  Persian Gulf War, 294n5, 408n15

Cain, 24–25, 27–29, 40
  Abel, murder of, 11, 24
  death of, 29
  divine sign given to, 11–12, 28
Cherubim, 375–379, 382, 396, 399
Coercion in Jewish law, 423
Communism, 225–226
Converts
  made by Abraham and Sarah, 113
  treatment in Jewish law, 311, 361
Covenant between the Parts, 50n2, 61–62, 64, 118, 190, 211, 215–216, 345

Darkhei shalom, 243
Dathan and Abiram, 274
David
  Absalom, 100, 239
  Adoniyahu, 100, 102
  anointment of, 243, 377
  Barzillai, 239–240
  Bath-sheba, 100–102, 241
  Jonathan, 17–18
  Mephibosheth, 18–19
  Messiah son of, 169, 238n19
  Miriam, 264n12
  mitzvot, summary of, 80, 82
  Psalms, 80, 280n6
  royalty, 87n13, 381n6
  Ruth, 52
  Solomon, 100–101, 241
  war, 407
Deborah
  judge, 329, 341
  military leader, 329–331, 341
  Song of, 328–331, 341–343
Dinah, 164–165, 172–173, 251–253
Duda'im, 142, 152–155

Ein od mi-levaddo, 354, 377
Emunah, 98
Exodus from Egypt, 305, 308–311, 314
Ezra, 211
Jacob, 223
Erev rav, 404
Esau
  angel of, 177, 322
  deceiver, 109–110
  Isaac's blessings, 130, 250
  Jacob, reconciliation with, 159–160, 162, 168–170
  Joseph, 137–139
  kibbud av of, 179–183
  Rebecca, 106, 131
  sale of birthright, 81, 117–119, 121, 130–132, 153
Evening Prayer, 105, 110n7, 390
Evil Inclination, 22–23, 37–39, 89, 90, 114, 280–281, 312
Exodus from Egypt, 295, 298, 310, 314, 329, 344
Ezra's ordinances, 211–213, 350–351

Falsehood, 243–244, 364–368
Fear of Heaven, 106–107, 223, 237, 298, 314–315
Four Cups, 297–299
Four Sons, 303
Free will, 16, 190, 285–288, 326

Subject Index

Generation of the Flood, 33, 37, 45, 334
Ge'ullah. See Redemption
Gog and Magog, 408
Good Inclination, 22–23, 37–38, 90, 280–281
Gratitude. See *Hakkarat ha-tov*

Hakkarat ha-tov, 147, 181, 276–278, 355
Ḥamas, 33–34, 37–38
Hamas, 197, 199
High Priest, 102, 209, 375–378, 383, 424–425, 427
Holocaust, 7, 42, 51, 169, 191, 305, 331, 420–421
   Kristallnacht, 101
   reparations, 75
   Wallenberg, 19–21
Holy of Holies, 375–379
Honor of the Torah, 16, 143, 420–421

Imitatio Dei, 7, 15
INF Treaty, 9, 291, 367
Intermarriage, 252
Iran-Contra Affair, 122, 273
Isaac, 103–106, 113–115, 294, 412
   Abimelech, 124–125
   Akedah, 86–87, 322
   birth of, 89
   blessing from Hashem, 120n13
   blessing of sons, 118–119, 130–134, 170, 177, 178, 250
   Esau, 110, 180–181
   Ishmael, 90
   prayer, 105, 126
   Rebecca, 95–97, 103, 109–110
   wells of Abraham, 114
Israeli Defense Forces, 171
Israelite bondsman, 359–361
Issachar, 131, 141–144, 152, 254–256, 425, 428n4

Issachar–Zebulun partnership, 131, 254–256

Jackson–Vanik Amendment, 291
Jacob
   angel of Esau, 159, 177–178, 322
   blessing
      from Hashem, 51, 232n4
      by Isaac, 130–133
      of Joseph, 128n12, 231
      of sons, 231, 250–253
   burial of, 247
   dream of, 52n12, 234
   Esau, reconciliation with, 137–138, 159–162, 168–170, 179–181
   Joseph
      reunion with, 218–220, 222–223
      sale of, 187–191
      sons of, 235
   Laban, 175–176
   Leah, 144, 149–151, 152–154
   ma'aseh avot siman le-banim, 115
   name of Israel, 413
   purchase of birthright, 106, 117–121, 130–133
   Rachel, 144, 149–151, 152–154
   Shekhem, 163, 165, 172–173
   truth, 81
Jewish destiny, 15, 87, 101, 115, 187–191, 192–194, 214, 216–217, 274–275, 377–379
Jewish education, 21, 65, 252, 299, 303, 314–315, 396–399, 423, 433
Jewish identity, 49–52, 54–55, 61, 252
Jewish leadership, 87, 276, 281, 430
Jewish sovereignty, 61, 99–102
Jewish unity, 166, 433
Joseph
   blessing by Jacob, 128n12, 231–233

Subject Index

Joseph (*continued*)
  with brothers in Egypt, 59, 198, 203–207, 215, 243
  burial of, 344–345
  dreams of, 214–215, 321
  economic policy in Egypt, 215–216, 226–227, 248
  Esau, contrast with, 137–139
  iron casket of, 245
  Messiah, 169, 191, 238
  reunion with Benjamin, 220–221
  reunion with Jacob, 219–220, 222–223
  sale into slavery, 187–189, 192–193
  sons of, 235
  Splitting of Sea of Reeds, 319–321, 323
  stone of, 426
  title of, 125
  vow to Jacob, 51
Joshua, 18, 236–238, 299, 350, 405n7
Justice, 7, 82n14, 120, 244, 261–264, 273–274, 293, 324–327, 364, 367–368, 410, 412
  Divine Attribute, 87n14, 192–194
  Egypt, 263, 274
  Holocaust, 75
  Judah, 161, 193–194
  Sea of Reeds, 325
  terrorism, 56
Juvenile crime, 38

Kahane movement, 61, 215
Kedushah prayer, 14–16
Ketoret, 353, 383, 426, 428–430
Kibbud av ve-em, 119, 138, 179–183, 355
Kiddush ha-Shem, 331, 426
Kol ha-mosif gore'a, 384–387
Korban pesaḥ. See Paschal offering
Kristallnacht, 101

Laban, 119, 133–134, 149–151, 153–154, 160–161, 175, 176, 178, 180, 181

Land of Israel, 51, 278, 298, 326, 334, 413
  Isaac, 105
  Joseph, 245
  Joshua, 18, 236, 299, 305
  settlement, 60–63, 299
Leah, 120, 142n4, 144, 147, 149–151, 152–155, 160, 206
Lifnim mi-shurat ha-din, 361, 365
Love your fellow as yourself, 240

Ma'ariv. See Evening Prayer
Ma'aseh avot siman le-banim, 64, 72, 75, 105–106, 113–115, 132, 139, 182
MAD. See Mutual Assured Destruction
Manna, 236, 353, 376, 378–379
Marriage
  Abraham, 69–71, 109
  Isaac, 95–98, 109
  Jacob, 149–151, 154
  levirate, 189n11
  silence in, 108–110
  Splitting of the Sea of Reeds, 323
Mattan Torah. See Revelation at Sinai
Menorah, 329, 380–382, 426, 433
Messiah, 52, 91, 162, 169, 187–191, 194, 227, 238, 294, 340, 408
Middah ke-negged middah, 119, 133, 193, 286–288
Midwives in Egypt, 263–264, 274
Minḥah. See Afternoon Prayer
Miracles
  birth of Isaac, 71
  Exodus from Egypt, 298, 412
  Gideon, 237
  Joseph, survival of, 219
  Joshua, 238, 299
  necessity of, 209, 308
  Oil of Anointment, 377
  Revelation at Sinai, 299
  Septuagint, 209

Splitting of the Sea of Reeds, 319, 322, 326–327
Staff of Aaron, 288
Tabernacle, construction of, 396, 433
Ten Plagues, 285–288, 294–296, 298–299, 325, 337, 353
Mirmah, 62, 117–121, 132, 133
Mitkabbed be-kalon shel ḥavero, 142–144
Mitzvot
  between man and God, 224, 248, 433
  between man and his fellow, 178, 224, 248
  effect on character, 433
  hukkim, 306, 309
  invisible misconduct, 310
  mishpatim, 306
  time-bound mitzvot, 386
Moral climate of society, 7, 28, 124, 151, 193, 241, 304–305, 366, 399, 410
Morning Prayer, 105, 390–391, 408
Moses, 5, 212n21, 304, 388n18
  Aaron, 425
  Amalek, 334
  Batyah, 262
  blessings of Tribes, 250–251, 253, 256
  hakkarat ha-tov, 277
  Joseph, 344–345
  justice, 263–264
  leadership, 274–275, 276–277, 270–271
  names of, 279–281
  Oil of Anointment, 377
  Plagues, 287–288, 291, 295, 298
  prayer, 44–45, 404–405, 410–413
  Sea of Reeds, 319, 325
  Septuagint, 210
  Tabernacle, 417–420, 424, 426, 427, 431–432
  Torah, 350–351
Mutual Assured Destruction (MAD), 12, 167–168, 170

Noah
  blessing from Hashem, 34, 42
  Ham, 39
  personality, 40–42
  planting of a vine, 41–42
  prayer, 44–45
Noahide Laws, 163–164, 172n5, 223n8

Oil of Anointment, 376–379, 426
Oslo Accords, 29n9

Palestine Liberation Organization, 29n9, 165n8, 199, 332–335, 339–340, 368
Pardes, 336–340
Paschal offering, 133n8, 309, 314
Persian Gulf War, 339, 406–409
PLO. *See* Palestine Liberation Organization
Prayer, 45, 127
  afternoon (*Minḥah*), 105
  Elleh Ezkerah, 189n10
  evening (*Ma'ariv*), 105, 390–391
  Hannah, 128, 343
  Isaac and Rebecca, 126
  Jacob, 159
  Kedushah, 14–16
  morning (*Shaḥarit*), 105, 390–391
  Moses, 44, 404
  Neilah, 322n10
  Noah, 44–45
  Shemoneh Esrei, 291n8
  women, 127–129
Preemptive war, 163–166
Priesthood, Jewish, 87, 161, 264, 378n19, 380–382
Prophecy
  Aaron, 274, 277
  Deborah, 328
  Ezra, 211

Subject Index

Prophecy (*continued*)
  Isaiah, 421
  Joseph, 203–204, 321
  Moses, 279, 280
  Nathan, 100, 102
  Rachel, 320

Rachel, 120, 139, 142, 144, 149–151, 152–155, 160, 206, 320
Reagan presidency
  Achille Lauro affair, 56n1
  disarmament talks, 9, 167, 291n6
  Iran-Contra affair, 122, 125, 273
  Middle East, 332
Rebecca, 99–101, 103
  Isaac, 95–97, 109, 126
  Eliezer, 99, 104n4
  Esau, 106, 138, 180
  Jacob, 130–131, 133, 168, 178
  Laban, 134
Redemption
  from Egypt, 192, 224, 271, 275, 290, 294, 297–299, 308, 314
  future, 115, 192, 144, 190–191, 294–295, 297–299, 323
Religious freedom, 64–68, 146–147, 291
Reproof, 25, 37, 110, 175–176, 217, 286, 378n21
Resurrection of the dead. See *Tehiyyat ha-metim*
Reuben, 152–155, 161, 188, 189, 191, 219n2, 250, 342, 429n8
Revelation at Sinai, 60, 118, 210, 299, 349–350, 353
Ribbit, 310
Royalty, Jewish, 87, 99, 102, 264, 380–382

Sabbath
  candles, 266–267, 386–387
  delight, mitzvah of, 120n13
  in Egypt, 291
  Ezra's ordinances, 350–351
  Showbread, 390
  Tabernacle, 420
  workplace accommodation of, 66
Sanhedrin, 102, 211n18, 240, 255, 362n12, 371
Sarah, 105, 113–114, 397n9
  Abimelech, 50n2, 123–124
  Abraham, 69–71, 109
  burial of, 98
  Hagar, 69–71
  laughter, 88–90, 210
  Pharaoh, 49n2, 50, 58, 74–75
Separation of church and state, 387, 398
Septuagint, 208–209
Servitude in Egypt, 51, 286
  avodat perakh, 270
  Covenant between the Parts, 61, 118–119, 190, 211, 216
  Joseph, 189, 204, 214, 216, 321
  Moses, 264, 270, 345
Shabbat Shirah, 336
Shaharit. See Morning Prayer
Shehitah, 65
Shekhem, 163–166, 172–173, 251–253, 322
Shem and Eber, 119, 180, 205
Shema, 223, 365, 390–391
Shirah, 408, 409
  Deborah, 328–331, 341–343
  Sea of Reeds, 272, 321–323, 326, 337–338
Shirat Devorah. See Song of Deborah
Shunammite Woman, 79–82, 404
Sin of the Golden Calf, 208, 403, 417, 423, 431–432
  Hur, 334
  Moses' prayer, 44, 410–412, 431
  punishment, 251, 405n7, 410–411
Sin'at hinnam, 194, 220

Subject Index

Sodom, 45n1, 50, 84–86, 90, 397n9, 398–399
Solomon, 100–102, 239, 241, 280n6
Son of Sam Laws, 370
Song of Deborah, 328–331, 341–343
Soviet Jewry, 290–292
Soviet Union
  INF Treaty, 9, 291, 367
  Jewry, 290–292
  Wallenberg, 20
Splitting of the Sea of Reeds, 272, 319, 323, 326–327, 328, 330, 342, 353
Staff of Aaron, 288, 376, 378–379
State of Israel
  Jewish character of, 61
  Palestinian charter, 199
  settlement of the land, 61
  sign of divine favor, 331, 333
  terrorism, 58, 171
Symbolism
  bigdei ḥamudot, 133
  Cherubim, 396
  coronation of Solomon, 102
  Gideon, 237
  ḥagigah, 133
  Isaac and Rebecca, 97
  ketoret, 383
  lentils, 119
  manna, 376
  Menorah, 381
  neck, 221
  oil, 381n10
  pesaḥ, 133
  Sabbath lights, 267
  salt, 84–87
  Staff of Aaron, 378
  Staves of the Ark, 375
  stones of the Breastplate, 424–426

Tabernacle, 220, 329, 385n3, 397
  appurtenances of, 375, 377, 380, 396
  construction of, 395–397, 417–420, 422–424, 426, 427, 431–433
  destruction of, 221
Talmud Torah, 389–391
Tefillah. See Prayer
Tefillin, 67, 309, 314–315
Teḥiyyat ha-metim, 121, 139, 343
Temple, 51, 96, 149–150, 206, 208, 211, 221, 251, 376, 378, 421
Ten Commandments, 96, 354
Ten Martyrs, 189, 362
Ten Plagues, 291, 285–288, 294–296, 298–299, 321, 325, 337, 353
Terrorism, 29, 30, 43, 56–59, 164, 171–174, 197, 199, 330, 332, 334–335, 338, 367
Thanksgiving, 145–148
Three Cardinal Sins, 74, 90
Tohu va-vohu, 57–58, 96, 113–114
Torah le-shemah, 256, 381–382
Tzeniut, 150–151, 341
Tzitzit, 67, 310

United Nations, 101n6, 115n12, 294n5, 295n6, 332, 338n12

Wise Son, 303–307, 308–310
Women, Jewish
  prayer, 127–129, 343
  Sabbath, 265–268, 385–386
  time-bound mitzvot, 386–387

Yetzer ha-ra. See Evil Inclination
Yetzer tov. See Good Inclination
Yir'at Shamayim. See Fear of Heaven

The fonts used in this book are from the Arno family

Other Works by Rabbi Dr. Aaron Levine

Free Enterprise and Jewish Law: Aspects of Jewish Business Ethics (1980)

Economics and Jewish Law (1987)

Economic Public Policy and Jewish Law (1993)

Case Studies in Jewish Business Ethics (2000)

Moral Issues of the Marketplace in Jewish Law (2005)

The Oxford Handbook of Judaism and Economics (Editor) (2010)

Economic Morality and Jewish Law (2012)

Seasons of Nobility: Sermons on the Festivals (2019)

Maggid Books
The best of contemporary Jewish thought from
Koren Publishers Jerusalem Ltd.